YEATS'S
INTERACTIONS WITH
TRADITION

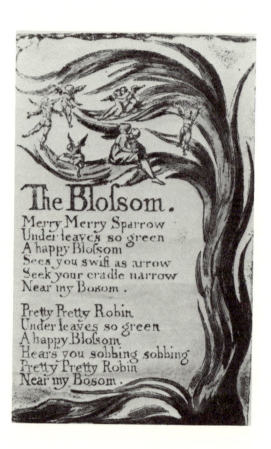

The Blossom.

Merry Merry Sparrow
Under leaves so green
A happy Blossom
Sees you swift as arrow
Seek your cradle narrow
Near my Bosom.

Pretty Pretty Robin
Under leaves so green
A happy Blossom
Hears you sobbing sobbing
Pretty Pretty Robin
Near my Bosom.

YEATS'S
INTERACTIONS WITH
TRADITION

PATRICK J. KEANE

University of Missouri Press • Columbia, 1987

Copyright © 1987 by
The Curators of the University of Missouri
University of Missouri Press, Columbia, Missouri 65211
Printed and bound in the United States of America

Library of Congress Cataloging-in-Publication Data

Keane, Patrick J.
   Yeats's Interactions with Tradition

   Bibliography: p.
   Includes index.
   1. Yeats, W. B. (William Butler), 1865–1939—
Criticism and interpretation. 2. Influence (Literary,
artistic, etc.) I. Title.
PR5908.I52K43 1987   821'.8   86–30883
ISBN 0–8262–0645–X (alk. paper)

∞™ This paper meets the minimum requirements of
the American National Standard for Permanence of Paper
for Printed Library Materials, Z39.48, 1984.

Frontispiece illustration used by permission of the
Harry Elkins Widener Memorial Collection, Harvard
University.

TO MARGARET KEANE

ACKNOWLEDGMENTS

Prior to its submission to the University of Missouri Press, no one had read this book in its entirety. Thus its faults are all mine and its subsequent improvements largely attributable to the judicious readings given it by George Mills Harper and Richard Finneran. (I am also grateful to Mary FitzGerald for sending me a draft of the "Irish Airman" poem and to Jay Rogoff for suggesting Whitman's influence on "Fragments.")

These are not my only debts. Though it is a good deal less than the abundant recompense they deserve, this book would not have been possible without the initial guidance and eventual friendship of these eight:

John Unterecker, whose *Reader's Guide* first enabled me to see Yeats's *Collected Poems* as an integrated whole;

M. L. Rosenthal, whose critical example, an intrinsic repossession of texts, has kept me from straying altogether from poems to the interactions among them;

David V. Erdman, whose year-long seminar (NYU, 1969) on the French Revolution and its impact on Blake, Wordsworth, and Coleridge demonstrated the full potential of historical scholarship;

Robert Boyers, whose interest in my work stimulated me to live up to his expectations and to at least emulate his own remarkable industry;

George Mills Harper, whose uncranky mastery of everything to do with Yeats and the occult first revealed to me the depth of this poet's immersion in mysterious wisdom;

Jon Stallworthy, whose voluntary reading of a long typescript I was submitting to Oxford University Press combined generosity and encouragement;

Harold Bloom, whose studies in poetic influence, command of Romanticism, and uncanny detection of Yeats's winding path through that great tradition led me into my own version of the labyrinth; and

Helen Vendler, whose brilliant close readings continue to serve all of us as models of what poems can yield to lucidity and love.

There have been supportive colleagues and friends both at Skidmore (in addition to Bob and Peggy Boyers, they include Ralph Ciancio, Bud Foulke, Tom Lewis, Don and Judy McCormack, and Phil West) and at Le Moyne (Susan Bordo, Barron Boyd, Randy Fertel, Roger Lund, Jonathan Schonsheck, Bruce Shefrin, and Bill Shaw). I am also grateful to Le Moyne's capable Faculty secretaries, Maryann DeMichele and Joan Mattes;

to various Faculty Research and Development committees at Le Moyne; and, for three grants, to the National Endowment for the Humanities. What clarity the book has owes much to Barbara Poole, who typed the whole of a sprawling manuscript.

There are others to whom my bonds are less scholarly than personal. They include relatives (Maureen, Stephen, and Keeley Hanratty) and my ex-wife, Ann Knickerbocker, and her parents, Bob and Audrey. Two of my friends have read much of my work, Bob Moynihan and Jim Sanford. And I want to mention five other friends: John Robson, who was always there; Jim Cerasoli, the only one of my boyhood friends who reads my stuff and one of the few figures in the Bronx Democratic organization who has kept his hands clean; Elizabeth Costello, who has had much to do with the spirit in which I finished this book, a book she has very capably proofread; and two Fordham friends: Mike Carew, who always suspected I would inflict books on people; and Bill Baumert, whose friendship has been as constant as his generosity, which includes the annual lending of an Atlantic Ocean cabana in which much of this book was written.

I would like to thank A. P. Watt Ltd. on behalf of Anne Yeats and Michael Yeats, and Macmillan Publishing Company, Inc., New York, for permission to quote from the following works: *The Variorum Edition of the Poems of W. B. Yeats,* edited by Peter Allt and Russell K. Alspach, © 1957; *Autobiographies,* © 1963, renewed by Bertha Georgie Yeats; *Essays and Intro- ductions,* © 1961 by Mrs. W. B. Yeats; *Explorations,* © 1962 by Mrs. W. B. Yeats; *The Letters of W. B. Yeats,* edited by Allan Wade, © 1954 by Anne Butler Yeats; *Mythologies,* © Mrs. W. B. Yeats; *A Vision,* © renewed 1965 by Bertha Georgie Yeats and Anne Butler Yeats. Grateful acknowledgment is also made to Yeats's authorized biographer, Roy Foster, and to A. P. Watt Ltd. for permission to quote unpublished material from the Yeats Archives, Center for Contemporary Arts and Letters, State University of New York, Stony Brook.

Earlier versions of chapters 3, 4, and 9 appeared in *Salmagundi* 68–69 (1985–1986), the *Bulletin of Research in the Humanities* 82 (1979), and the *Yeats Eliot Review* 8 (1986), respectively.

Finally, this study of Yeats is dedicated to Margaret Keane, my mother; any negative criticisms of it should be addressed to her. She will respond, I assure you.

P.J.K.
Syracuse, N.Y.
1 May 1987

CONTENTS

I. INTRODUCTION

II. OUT OF MORE THAN *SPIRITUS MUNDI*: THE STRANGE BIRTHS OF SPINNING JENNY AND ROUGH BEAST

III. SINGING IN CHAINS

ABBREVIATIONS

References to Yeats's work are abbreviated and included parenthetically in the text. Except in the case of longer poems, I have generally not included page citations when the work cited or alluded to is identified by title. Though I cite the Variorum edition, there is much to recommend *W. B. Yeats: The Poems* (1983), in which the editor, Richard J. Finneran, rightly reorders the posthumous poems in accordance with Yeats's intentions.

Au	*Autobiographies*. London: Macmillan, 1955.
E&I	*Essays and Introductions*. London & New York: Macmillan, 1961.
Ex	*Explorations*. London: Macmillan, 1962; New York: Macmillan, 1963.
L	*The Letters of W. B. Yeats*, ed. Allan Wade. London: Rupert Hart-Davis, 1954; New York: Macmillan, 1955.
LDW	*Letters on Poetry from W. B. Yeats to Dorothy Wellesley*, intro. Kathleen Raine. London & New York: Oxford University Press, 1964.
LTSM	*W. B. Yeats and T. Sturge Moore: Their Correspondence, 1901–1937*, ed. Ursula Bridge. London: Routledge & Kegan Paul, 1953; New York: Oxford University Press, 1963.
LTWBY	*Letters to W. B. Yeats*, ed. Richard J. Finneran, George Mills Harper, and William M. Murphy. 2 vols. London: Macmillan, 1977; New York: Columbia University Press, 1977.
Mem	*Memoirs*, ed. Denis Donoghue. London: Macmillan, 1972; New York: Macmillan, 1973.
Myth	*Mythologies*. London & New York, 1959.
UP1	*Uncollected Prose by W. B. Yeats*, vol. 1, ed. John P. Frayne. London: Macmillan, 1970; New York: Columbia University Press, 1970.
UP2	*Uncollected Prose by W. B. Yeats*, vol. 2, ed. John P. Frayne and Colton Johnson. London: Macmillan, 1975; New York: Columbia University Press, 1976.
V-A	*A Critical Edition of Yeats's A Vision* (1925), ed. George Mills Harper and Walter Kelly Hood. London: Macmillan, 1978.
V-B	*A Vision*. London: Macmillan, 1962.
VP	*The Variorum Edition of the Poems of W. B. Yeats*, ed. Peter Allt and Russell K. Alspach. New York: Macmillan, 1957.
VPl	*The Variorum Edition of the Plays of W. B. Yeats*, ed. Russell K. Alspach. London & New York: Macmillan, 1966.

Labour is blossoming or dancing where
The body is not bruised to pleasure soul,
Nor beauty born out of its own despair,
Nor blear-eyed wisdom out of midnight oil.
O chestnut-tree, great-rooted blossomer,
Are you the leaf, the blossom or the bole?
O body swayed to music, O brightening glance,
How can we know the dancer from the dance?
   —Yeats, "Among School Children"

A common error is, to form a judgment of a drama from a single part in it; and to look upon this part itself in an isolated point of view, not in its connection with the whole. . . . It is a trunk with boughs, leaves, buds, blossoms and fruit. Are they not all one, and thereby means of one another?
   —Goethe, on Hamlet in *Wilhelm Meisters Lehrjahre*

The ordinary mind . . . sees only contradiction in . . . variety. The bud disappears when the blossom breaks through, and we might say that the former is refuted by the latter; in the same way when the fruit comes, the blossom may be explained to be a false form of the plant's existence, for the fruit appears as its true nature in place of the blossom. These stages are not merely differentiated; they supplant one another as being incompatible with one another. But the ceaseless activity of their own inherent nature makes them at the same time moments of an organic unity, where they not merely do not contradict one another, but where one is as necessary as the other; and this equal necessity of all moments constitutes the life of the whole.
   —Hegel, Preface to *The Phenomenology of Mind*

The contentment of the tree in its roots, the happiness of knowing that one is not wholly accidental and arbitrary but grown out of a past as its heir, flower and fruit, and that one's existence is thus . . . justified—it is this which is today usually designated as the real sense of history. . . . [But] when the study of history serves the life of the past in such a way that it undermines continuing and especially higher life, when the historical sense no longer conserves life but mummifies it, then the tree gradually dies unnaturally from the top downwards to the roots—and in the end the roots themselves usually perish too. Antiquarian history itself degenerates from the moment it is no longer animated and inspired by the fresh life of the present.
   —Nietzsche, *On the Uses and Disadvantages of History for Life*

The lyric poet's . . . poetry is no rootless flower.
   —Yeats, "Friends of My Youth"

PREFACE

I

The frontispiece, Blake's design for his Song of Innocence "The Blossom," bears a Romantic family-resemblance to the chestnut tree in the final stanza of "Among School Children." Yeats's "great-rooted blossomer" may even be thought of as "completing" the Blakean blossom in much the same sense in which—as Yeats put it in asserting the most crucial "interaction" in his creative life—"Nietzsche completes Blake and has the same roots" (L 379). Whatever their differences, blossom and great-rooted blossomer are both dynamic images of exuberant efflorescence, of that energy Blake called eternal delight. With its tensile, sinewy, even phallic force, anticipating Van Gogh's cypress trees, Blake's flame-flower expresses controlled generative power erupting in the creative joy suggested by the tiny winged figures cavorting in its crest.

My argument in the present volume is that Yeats's strength, particularly in the later works, stems from his roots in tradition—roots he bends to his own purposes to "complete" his presumably truncated precursors. While Yeats's alterations, even transformations, of his legacy are often audacious, his creative freedom is the fruit of his submission to

> that stern colour and that delicate line
> That are our secret discipline
> Wherein the gazing heart doubles her might.
> (VP 326)

Yeatsian creativity, in short, is precisely what he called it in the opening word of that rhapsodic final stanza of "Among School Children": "Labour," a labor "rooted" in discipline and "blossoming or dancing" in an ecstasy transcending yet inseparable from those roots. The chestnut tree itself can blossom into the heavens only because its roots are planted deep in the earth. Yeats's Romantic icon is organic, its integrated unity of leaf, blossom, and bole recalling Goethe and Hegel, its rootedness similar to that of the "Tree on the Mountainside" in Nietzsche's *Zarathustra*:

> It is with man as it is with the tree. The more he aspires to the height and light, the more strongly do his roots strive earthward, downward, into the dark, the deep.
> (*Thus Spoke Zarathustra* 1.8)

xiii

One of my two central emphases is on Yeats as a gravitational poet whose "art theories depend upon" the "rooting of mythology in the earth," a delving "down, as it were, into some fibrous darkness, into some matrix out of which everything has come" (LTSM 114, E&I 429). Contrasting his *antithetical* path to the *primary* way of Eastern mysticism, Yeats referred to it as "a dynamic and substantializing force as distinguished from the eastern quiescent and supersensualizing state of the soul—a movement downwards upon life, not upwards out of life" (L 469). His orientation was that of Nietzschean Homer—"Homer is my example and his unchristened heart"— and of Sophocles' chthonic Oedipus, who "sank down body and soul into the earth," an earth "riven by love," in contrast to Christ who, "crucified standing up, went into the abstract sky soul and body" (VP 503, V-B 27-28).

My second and even more pervasive emphasis, on Yeats's roots in tradition, involves the labyrinthine complexity of his interaction with his poetic and philosophic precursors. Not only the best but also "the most original parts" of a poet's work may be those, said Eliot in "Tradition and the Individual Talent," in which "the dead poets, his ancestors, assert their immortality most vigorously." For Yeats, who agreed with his mentor Blake that "the thankful receiver bears a plentiful harvest," "works of art are always begotten by previous works of art" and "supreme art is a traditional statement of heroic and religious truths passed on from age to age, modified by individual genius, but never abandoned" (E&I 352, Au 490). "Talk to me of originality and I will turn on you with rage," Yeats raged in the essay he intended as "A General Introduction for My Work" (E&I 522). He would have been delighted rather than surprised by a recent critic's discovery, a wonderful illustration of the paradox of "originality," that "Milton's pledge to pursue 'Things unattempted yet in prose or rhyme' is itself a quotation from the *Orlando Furioso*."[1]

But rootedness in tradition means nothing without the blossoming of the individual talent; the Modernist imperative—in the words of Ezra Pound— is "Make it new!" What is required is an artistic equivalent of the organic interdependence of "root, shoot, blossom" (VP 600), of Goethe's "boughs, leaves, blossoms and fruit . . . all one, and thereby means of one another." Though Yeats misconstrues the famous passage from *The Phenomenology of Mind* ("I had . . . never thought with Hegel . . . that the spring vegetables were refuted when over," V-B 72–73), Hegel does *not* argue that the supplanted "bud" is "refuted by" the "blossom," and the blossom in turn refuted by the "fruit." We "*might* say that," except that—in keeping with Hegelian dialectic, in which thesis and antithesis are synthesized into a

---

1. Milton, *Paradise Lost* 1.16. David Quint, *Origin and Originality in Renaissance Literature: Versions of the Source*, 216. See also the opening chapter, "The Originality Paradox," in Thomas McFarland, *Originality and Imagination*. Blake's axiom ("The thankful receiver bears a plentiful harvest") occurs in *The Marriage of Heaven and Hell* (hereafter cited as MHH), plate 20. Blake's work is quoted throughout from *The Complete Poetry and Prose of William Blake*, ed. David V. Erdman, commentary by Harold Bloom.

higher form—the successive stages of bud, blossom, and fruit are simultaneously "moments of an organic unity, where they do not merely not contradict one another, but where one is as necessary as the other; and this equal necessity of all moments constitutes . . . the life of the whole."

What is necessary in the literary equivalent of this organic "life of the whole" is a simultaneity of tradition and innovation, an interactive re-creation of the past in which one's inheritance, to quote Nietzsche, continues to inspire and be inspired by the "fresh life of the present," in which unwithered "roots" continue to nourish the "flower and fruit." The challenge is to maintain a fruitful tension between continuity and discontinuity; to preserve and reanimate the life of the past while avoiding the antiquarian mummification ridiculed by Nietzsche.

Though Nietzsche's final emphasis in this passage is on liberation from the mummifying potential of the past, he is adamant throughout his work in opposing the naive assumption that human nature is best expressed in unrestrained freedom. In the "arts just as in ethics . . . all there is or has been on earth of freedom" and "masterly sureness" has developed only because of sustained "obedience" to what the undisciplined resent as "the tyranny . . . of capricious laws." But there is nothing unnatural in submission to such laws; indeed, it is "precisely" this disciplined obedience that constitutes "nature." The "most natural" state of the artist, "giving form in the moment of inspiration," is "far from any letting himself go"; "strictly and subtly" the artist "obeys thousandfold laws precisely then." In short, " 'nature' teaches hatred of the *laisser aller*, of any all-too-great freedom, . . . as a condition of life and growth" (*Beyond Good and Evil* §188). While the "weak," lacking "power over themselves," hate "the constraint of style," interpreting themselves as "*free* nature" (which actually means being "arbitrary" and "disorderly") the "strong and domineering natures enjoy their finest gaiety in such constraint and perfection under a law of their own" (*The Gay Science* §290). Thus Nietzsche can describe himself, in a poem, as "in most loving constraint, free," and repeatedly advocate "dancing in chains" as an ethical and artistic ideal.[2]

This paradoxical fusion of autonomy and obedience, of gaiety under self-imposed constraint, is shared by Yeats, who eschews "free verse" in favor of those "traditional metres . . . I compel myself to accept" and without which "I would lose myself, become joyless" (E&I 522). The "bonds that they gladly accept" mean more to the "skilful handed," he insists, than "the freedom" that amounts to a "right to choose those bonds" that have always reduced triflers and bunglers to "faithful servants of the law."[3] This is to

---

2. Nietzsche refers to "dancing in chains" in *The Wanderer and His Shadow* 140; but to "dance in chains" is a repeated Nietzschean metaphor. See *Werke und Briefe: Historisch-Kritische Gesamtausgabe*, ed. under the supervision of the "Stiftung Nietzsche-Archiv," 1:202–3, 3:310–11. The Nietzsche poem appears in the *Gay Science* section of *Ecce Homo*, trans. Walter Kaufmann (New York: Vintage Press, 1967).

3. Yeats, *Is the Order of R.R. & A.C. to remain a Magical Order?*

"stoop to a mechanical / Or servile shape, at others' beck and call" (VP 417).

Yeats's distinction, crucial to the thought and symbolism of German and English Romanticism, is that between slave and master, the mechanical and the organic, between edicts imposed from without and internal development under a law of one's own, "a power within powers, as one sees ring within ring in the stem of an old tree" (E&I 158). One such tree, Yeats's "great-rooted blossomer," is an image fusing labor with a creative bursting out, a genetically rooted blossoming that—like Blake's phallic flame, "the generative principle breaking from its crest in the form of tiny winged and happy figures"[4]—seems a befitting emblem of Yeats's interactions with tradition.

II

"The force that through the green fuse drives the flower" drove him as well, says Dylan Thomas, a poet who, "green and dying, . . . sang in my chains." Nietzsche danced in his chains; Yeats danced *and* sang in *his*. The chains are those of time, necessity, discipline, tradition: inherited forms in which—fettered—creative spirits paradoxically find their freedom, their power enhanced by constraint. Since what Yeats repeatedly called the "roots" shape a poet's subsequent blossoming, the "Essential Tension"—to borrow the title of Thomas Kuhn's lecture adumbrating his landmark study *The Structure of Scientific Revolutions*—is between "Tradition and Innovation," what Eliot called "Tradition and the Individual Talent," or M. H. Abrams "Tradition and Revolution."

The full subtitle of Abrams's *Natural Supernaturalism* is *Tradition and Revolution in Romantic Literature*, a literature of which Yeats's work is a vital part, a story of continuity and transformation. In much of what follows, I will be examining selected Yeats poems as texts and pretexts, cutting into them to expose exemplary cross sections revealing Yeats's interactions with tradition, especially the Romantic tradition. By Romanticism I mean what Yeats meant: an anti-mechanist, anti-Enlightenment movement encompassing the six major English Romantic poets, extending forward to Nietzsche,

---

4. Commenting on the "phallic symbol" in the poem (the sparrow "swift as arrow" seeking satisfaction in the blossom of the maiden's bosom), Sir Geoffrey Keynes adds:

The cryptic symbolism carries the meaning of the poem with the utmost delicacy, and it is equalled by the beauty of the design. This illustrates the organ of generation both flaccid and erect, with the generative principle breaking from its crest in the form of tiny winged and happy figures. One has found its goal in the maiden's bosom; she sits contentedly among the flying joys, distinguished by her green dress and large angel's wings, since she, with her prospective motherhood, is an ideal figure to the male during the act of generation.

Facsimile edition of *Songs of Innocence and of Experience*, with an introduction and commentary by Sir Geoffrey Keynes, commentary on plate 11.

who "completes Blake and has the same roots," and backward (beyond Hermeticism and Renaissance vitalism) to Plato and Plotinus, especially to the Neoplatonic paradigm of primal unity, emanation into multiplicity and fragmentation, and a restoration to unity.

But in Yeats, for whose Crazy Jane "Nothing can be sole or whole / That has not been rent," thematic and tonal emphasis is at least as much on what Blake called the "fall into Division" as on the "Resurrection to Unity." In short, Yeatsian Romanticism, especially as reinforced by Nietzsche, becomes increasingly "*antithetical*," a life-affirming vitalism opposed, in Yeats's dialectical quarrel with himself, to "*primary*" religious transcendence.[5] "I mock Plotinus' thought / And cry in Plato's teeth." "Homer is my example and his unchristened heart." As these defiant, even fierce, declarations affirm, Yeats's subject, for all his obsession with the supernatural, is *this* world, envisioned as somehow both darkened and irradiated by its interaction with the other.

The pages that follow trace literary, philosophic, and spiritual interactions in order to suggest how certain Yeats poems came to be, thematically and verbally. Though all the chapters but one focus on specific poems, the approach moves beyond *explication de texte* since I am concerned both with "how Yeats did it" (to quote Ezra Pound) and, in the vernacular, with where Yeats is "coming from." This inevitably involves genetic speculation and, doubtless, some creative reading, some participation in the contemporary self-reflexive critical process. At the same time, though much influenced by that master deconstructionist Nietzsche, I do not treat texts as utterly indeterminate and subject to interpretive freeplay. Like John Livingston Lowes in *The Road to Xanadu*, Giorgio Melchiori in *The Whole Mystery of Art*, Abrams in *Natural Supernaturalism*, and Leonard Unger in *Eliot's Compound Ghost*, I try to distinguish among sources, influences, echoes, associations, and analogues as well as between connections made in Yeats's mind and those made in my own. I therefore have recourse to open or covert allusion as a clue to interaction, or what Julia Kristeva calls "intertextuality"; in short, my theory of "influence," though indebted to Harold

---

5. Yeats's great quarrel with himself, though he sees it as the antagonism at the heart of the world as well, is between the "*primary*" and the "*antithetical*." The *primary* or "objective" is "democratic," "that which serves," is directed "towards God" and "the soul's disappearance in God"; it is associated by Yeats with the self-denying Christian era, "levelling, unifying, feminine, humane, peace its means and end." The *antithetical* or "subjective" is "aristocratic," directed "towards Nature" and "the soul's ultimate, particular freedom"; it is associated by Yeats with the "polytheistic" pagan world of heroes and poets, when power, pride, passion, and conflict were "good," not "evil." "Hierarchical, masculine, harsh, surgical," this world is to be reborn in an "*antithetical* dispensation" which "must reverse our era." Yeats's gyre-reversing annunciations are thematically incarnated in "Leda and the Swan," "The Mother of God," and "The Second Coming." In the scheme of *A Vision*, from which these definitions are taken (V-B 85, 104, 52, 262–63), lunar phases 23 through 7 are predominantly *primary*, 9 through 21 predominantly *antithetical*, 8 and 22 being equal mixtures, while no human life is possible at 1 and 15, the dark and full moon respectively.

Bloom, remains enchanted by what Bloom's colleague John Hollander has recently referred to as "the Figure of Echo."[6]

The most obvious level of interaction in Yeats is—Yeatsian. As is well known, his poems, tactically deployed in deliberately constructed individual volumes, are strategically configured so as to form a total oeuvre, a sacred book of the arts. "I must leave my myths and images," he said in 1901, "to explain themselves as the years go by and one poem lights up another" (VP 847). It is one source of Yeats's "poetic strength" (in Balachandra Rajan's reflection of the critical consensus) that the "whole truth" of his work is "best approached, not by a single poem, but by a procession of poems" moving along "a curve of possibilities." Each "individual poem is not only vividly itself but also has behind it, holding it in position, the context of a considerably larger presence; and the apparent extremism of many poems is held in check by their correction elsewhere in the constellation of intention."[7]

It is appropriate that Yeats should have spoken of his poems' cumulative wholeness and mutual illumination in the first year after the close of the nineteenth century. For beyond the context provided by the procession and interaction of the poems in his own canon, the *full* meaning of those poems is found only in the context of a still larger presence: their "roots" in, and allusive interaction with, a variety of traditions, the most important being Yeats's legacy from the end of the eighteenth and beginning of the nineteenth centuries.

In addition to his Romantic heritage ("We were the last romantics"), Yeats, "steeped in the supernatural" (Au 116), was also a participant in the occult tradition, the "perennial philosophy" of Plato, Plotinus, and their heirs (though even Plato had Pythagoras, Parmenides, and Heraclitus along with Socrates as precursors), and including an occult ragbag packed with Hermeticists and Kabbalists, Indian monks and Soho mediums.

Yeats's third tradition, though he laid intellectual claim to it belatedly, was the Anglo-Irish. Its principal ornaments were that "God-appointed" confounder of the empiricists, Bishop Berkeley; the fountainhead of organic conservatism and anti-Jacobinism, Edmund Burke; and, above all, Jonathan Swift—whose presence haunted Yeats and through whose "dark grove he passed, and there / Plucked bitter wisdom that enriched his blood," a rite of passage honorifically attributed to Parnell as one of Yeats's lonely ("his master solitude") Anglo-Irish heroes (VP 481, 543). Together, they provided sufficient intellectual vigor and authority, buttressing the earlier example of Blake, to mount a concerted attack on scientific rationalism,

---

6. The volumes referred to are Hollander's *The Figure of Echo: A Mode of Allusion in Milton and After*; Lowes's famous 1927 study of Coleridge, *The Road to Xanadu: A Study in the Ways of the Imagination*; Melchiori's study of Yeats, *The Whole Mystery of Art: Patterns in the Work of W. B. Yeats*; and Ungar's of Eliot, *Eliot's Compound Ghost: Influence and Confluence*.

7. Rajan, *W. B. Yeats: A Critical Introduction*, 189.

mechanistic materialism, the whole detested but dominant world view of the Anglo-French Enlightenment.

The impact on Yeats of his excited reading of Nietzsche, for whom (like Gide) he was "waiting before he met him," almost constitutes a tradition in itself. A confirming and liberating influence, "that strong enchanter" completed Blake, reinforced Yeats's developing vision of an aristocratic heroic ideal ("a table of values; heroic joy always"), and provided an authoritative counterweight antithetical to the *primary* lure of the supernatural (L 379, E&I viii). It was Nietzsche above all who "rooted" Yeats in the earth.

These, then, are the "interactions" with which I am primarily concerned; taken together, they are the binding and yet liberating chains in which Yeats chose, or was chosen, to sing. This theme of interaction, of grateful reception and creative alteration and transformation, provides the connective tissue unifying the chapters that follow. It is also an Ariadne's thread through the labyrinth, for the specific subject matter of those chapters may seem arbitrary. Given the canonical integrity of Yeats's work, other poems might have served as well—or I might have dealt with many poems (as I do in Chapter 5) in all of the chapters. But after (among other volumes) Ellmann's *Identity*, Unterecker's *Reader's Guide*, Rajan's *Critical Introduction*, and the collection entitled *An Honoured Guest*, there seems little need for another Baedeker through Yeats Country.[8] For a variety of motives, not all of them clear even to me, these particular texts suggested themselves.

While I would like to believe that I have succeeded in unfolding some of the latent processes of Yeats's thought, there is no pretense to anything like the "whole truth" to which Rajan refers. Not only have I concentrated on the poetry and thought of Yeats's last—though greatest—twenty years to the virtual exclusion of his plays and of almost all of his earlier work, but I have also chosen to press particular (largely *antithetical*) positions rather hard in order to make a point.

Another caveat is more sweeping. The stories I tell are meant, in part at least, to self-destruct; they provide contexts that, once they have served their purposes, should be relegated to "background." In a recent study, Helen Vendler offers "four simple recommendations for a neophyte deciphering [Wallace] Stevens." The third involves contextual reading. "If each poem is a new experiment, the ground on which it experiments is the past, both the past of the genre and the past of the *oeuvre*." Consequently, we are to "look for the context of the poem, both in Stevens' whole canon and in his poetic predecessors." But this recommendation, like her other three, is "pedagogical and provisional"—to be followed by a fifth and final recommendation, to "*undo* all you have done, and read the poem afresh. . . . In short, you must repossess the poem as it exists on the page in all its origi-

---

8. The volumes mentioned are Richard Ellmann's *The Identity of Yeats*; John Unterecker's *A Reader's Guide to William Butler Yeats*; Rajan's *W. B. Yeats*; and *An Honoured Guest: New Essays on W. B. Yeats*, ed. Denis Donoghue and J. R. Mulryne.

nality and strangeness."[9] Everything I say about genesis, canonical context, assimilation and alteration, is meant to illuminate Yeats's creative process; when the individual poems I focus on are repossessed, retrieved from the dark matrix of their origins, they will stand forth, I hope, "more truly and more strange."

Why delve down into the "fibrous darkness" in the first place? Because what Vendler says of Stevens's later poems is true of Yeats's as well: their language is "dense with past usage, both his own and that of other poets" (*Wallace Stevens*, 78), and the intertextual repercussions can fascinate. The interactions I trace tend to reveal Yeats's poems as palimpsests in which earlier poems are still visible, frequently in distorted form. The same is true, if less intensely, of interactions between poems and ideas, "poetic" or otherwise. I realize that not all the interactions I trace, including connections between *poesis* and the history of ideas, will engage the passionate attention of every reader. But "at least," as Northrop Frye once said of the connection between his study of Blake and his *Anatomy of Criticism*, "the question is interesting to me, and so provides the only genuine motive yet discovered for undertaking any research."[10]

9. Helen Vendler, *Wallace Stevens: Words Chosen Out of Desire*, 4, 44. The phrase at the end of my paragraph is from Stevens—the conclusion of "Tea at the Palaz of Hoon."
10. Frye, "The Road of Excess," 119–20.

I

INTRODUCTION

CRITICAL PROLEGOMENON

Influence is clearly distinguishable from imitation . . . what a man does either repeats or rejects what someone else has done—repeats it in another tone, refines or amplifies or simplifies it, loads or overloads it with meaning, or else rebuts, overturns, destroys and denies it, but thereby assumes it and has invisibly used it.

—Paul Valéry, *Collected Works*, 8.241

All there is or has been on earth of freedom, subtlety, boldness, dance, and masterly sureness, . . . in the arts just as in ethics, has developed only owing to the "tyranny of . . . capricious laws"; and in all seriousness, the probability is by no means small that precisely this is "nature" and "natural"—and *not* that *laisser aller*.

Every artist knows how far from any feeling of letting himself go his "most natural" state is—the free ordering, placing, disposing, giving form in the moment of "inspiration"—and how strictly and subtly he obeys thousandfold laws precisely then. . . .

What is essential "in heaven and on earth" seems to be, to say it once more, that there should be *obedience* over a long period of time and in a *single* direction: given that, something always develops, and has developed, for whose sake it is worthwhile to live on earth; for example, virtue, art, music, dance, reason, spirituality.

—Nietzsche, *Beyond Good and Evil*, 188

How but in custom and in ceremony
Are innocence and beauty born?
—Yeats, "A Prayer for My Daughter"

I

The herculean labors of contemporary Yeats scholarship inspire awe, gratitude—and occasional bemusement, for the shark-toothed cogs of the Industry *can* grind exceeding small. We now descend on "that noble quarry" (Richard Ellmann's description of the poet) toting such scholarly equipment as computer-prepared concordances to the poetry and plays, for which there are variorum editions, commentaries, and "prolegomena." More recent ammunition includes a new edition of the poetry (*W. B. Yeats: The*

Poems, edited by Richard J. Finneran), a scholarly edition of the first version of *A Vision* (edited by George Mills Harper and Walter K. Hood), and much else newly arrived or looming on the horizon.[1] Though we were first armed with clues cunningly provided by the poet himself, even Yeats's sight might now be troubled by the image of a legion of scholars editing and annotating, coughing up the ink-flood recorded in the monumental *Classified Bibliography* of Yeatsian criticism, a project ongoing in one of two Yeats annuals.[2]

By the time of the semicentennial of the poet's death (1989), the authorized biography, delayed first by crossed signals between Michael Yeats and Denis Donoghue and then by tragedy, may finally be among us: that task, interrupted by the untimely death of F. S. L. Lyons, has been assigned to his

1. Those struggling to keep abreast can find judicious guidance in Richard Finneran's bibliographical essays on Yeats in the two volumes on research in Anglo-Irish literature edited by Finneran for the Modern Language Association. Yearly accounts appear in the *Yeats Annual*, prepared by K. P. S. Jochum, whose *W. B. Yeats: A Classified Bibliography of Criticism* superseded all previous bibliographical work on Yeats. For a brief guide to those from whom we have learned most about Yeats, see the bibliography in *William Butler Yeats: A Collection of Criticism*, ed. Patrick J. Keane. Two recent volumes having only excellence in common are Douglas Archibald's *Yeats* and James Olney's *The Rhizome and the Flower: The Perennial Philosophy—Yeats and Jung*. The latter reminds us that, in addition to the myriad examinations of the poems and plays, including drafts, there are all those "conjunctive" studies: Yeats and the occult, and Eastern thought, and the Japanese Noh, and the English Renaissance, and Anglo-Ireland, and Romanticism, and Symbolism, and Modernism, and so forth, as well as studies, several of book length, of more specific relationships: Yeats and Plato, and Plotinus, and Dante, and Shakespeare, and Ben Jonson, and Castiglione, and Swift, and Burke, and Blake, and Shelley, and Keats, and Balzac, and Pater, and Morris, and Wilde, and Nietzsche, and Synge, and Joyce, and Graves, and Beckett, and Auden. Yeats's relationship with Eliot and Pound, earlier discussed by Richard Ellmann and others, has recently been extended in Terence Diggory's demonstration of Yeats's subsequent, and surprisingly pervasive, influence on modern and contemporary American poets: *Yeats and American Poetry: The Tradition of the Self*.

2. Yeats's clues are scattered among well-wrought installments of autobiography, diaries, critical essays, prose passages intended to gloss certain poems, working drafts of many of the poems themselves—some doubtless tossed away by a carefully careless poet confident they would be retrieved by his wife. "The intellect of man is forced to choose / Perfection of the life or of the work" (VP 495). Perhaps. But as parts of one "completed symbol" (V-B 187), everything, the life included, was to serve the work. "I have no sympathy," said Yeats in the unpublished lecture "Friends of My Youth," with the thought "that a poet's life concerns nobody but himself. . . . Above all it is necessary that the lyric poet's life should be known that we should understand that his poetry is no rootless flower but the speech of a man." The life was, however, to have the same deliberate shape as the work. That too took some hammering. To a friend who had published some of his letters to her, Yeats wrote that if she was planning to publish more he would like to see them first: "I might even, in defiance of all right conduct, improve them" (L 586). A violation, he admitted with a sense of both humor and decorum; but as a maker he reserved to himself the same right and will to power asserted by his Cuchulain: "I make the truth!" (VPl 1056).

Searchers for "the truth" Yeats said he "must embody . . . in the completion of my life" (L 922) have grown increasingly intimate. His annotations and underlinings are published in Edward O'Shea's *A Descriptive Catalog of W. B. Yeats's Library*. The autobiographical papers marked "Private . . . containing much that is not for publication now if ever" (Mem 19) are wholly given up to unfamiliar affections; probing has even turned up the name of the surgeon (one Norman Haire) who performed Yeats's Steinach "rejuvenation" operation in 1934. Yeats may have started it all; he may have embarked on what Ian Fletcher has called a "quest for self-transparency," but he is also said to have remarked to his wife, "I don't want them to know all about everything."

fellow historian Roy Foster. Already the first volumes in a triad of multi-volume projects have appeared: the fourteen-volume *Collected Edition* of Yeats's canon is being edited for Macmillan by Richard Finneran and George Mills Harper; the *Collected Letters*, in about a dozen volumes, is being published by Oxford under the general editorship of John Kelly; and, dwarfing even these enterprises, the Cornell series of Yeats manuscripts is projected at no less than thirty to thirty-five meticulously edited (and expensively priced) volumes of poetry, plays, and selected prose, including family papers. Even Yeats's annotations and markings in the books now kept at the home of his daughter, the painter Anne Yeats, have been cataloged (by Edward O'Shea), as have most of the holdings in the Yeats Archive at the State University of New York in Stony Brook. In time, presumably, it will all be available, down to the last recorded syllable and the final doodle.

All this, on top of the interpretive books and articles that continue to be churned out, gives added resonance to the question of one of Yeats's late personae: "What is there left to say?" In much of what follows I have not said what intrinsic critics tell us needs most to be said. Shortly after the poet's death, Allen Tate prophetically warned that in a period of growing interest in so massive an achievement, "Yeats's special qualities will instigate special studies of great ingenuity, but the more direct and more difficult problem of the poetry itself will probably be delayed." A decade and a half later, Hugh Kenner could claim that there was "still room for a book on Yeats which examines what he had to say." For years now, M. L. Rosenthal has argued, most compellingly in *Sailing into the Unknown* (1978) and *The Modern Poetic Sequence* (1983), that Yeats's achievement was being buried rather than clarified by much of the scholarship, that what was needed was retrieval and repossession by a criticism focused on the poems themselves.[3] Agreeing, I have nevertheless found it impossible to restrict myself to purely intrinsic criticism in writing about Yeats's poems. It went against the grain; not mine, I've come to accept, but Yeats's.

As early as 1939, one of the principal practitioners of the New Criticism, Cleanth Brooks, explicated Yeats's poems in connection with *A Vision*. Ten years later, Donald Stauffer insisted that an understanding of the individual Yeats lyric required "knowledge of at least the main body of his poems." In a 1952 article, "Yeats and 'The New Criticism,'" G. S. Fraser flatly declared purely intrinsic criticism inadequate when applied to Yeats. In "The Sacred Book of the Arts" (1955), Hugh Kenner brilliantly illustrated the unifying architecture of *Collected Poems*. These critical approaches, deployed by Ellmann in *The Identity of Yeats* (1954), also informed John Unterecker's *A Reader's Guide to William Butler Yeats* (1959), which stressed Yeats's organization of poems into books and books into a total canon (while still manag-

---

3. Tate, "Yeats's Romanticism: Notes and Suggestions." Kenner, "Unpurged Images." Rosenthal's *Sailing into the Unknown* examined the work of Yeats, Pound, and Eliot; *The Modern Poetic Sequence: The Genius of Modern Poetry* was co-authored with Sally M. Gall.

ing to give the more significant individual lyrics their intrinsic due). These developments were part of a general movement away from the New Critical orthodoxy. First myth and archetype criticism, then phenomenology, structuralism, new forms of influence-study, reception theory, and finally and most radically deconstruction—all assaulted the conception of a literary work as autonomous. Northrop Frye and Harold Bloom, for example, went beyond "Tradition and the Individual Talent" in arguing that a work could not be understood by itself but only in relation to other works of literature. The Belgian phenomenologist Georges Poulet read individual works as part of an author's overall "spiritual project"; this approach was developed in terms of Yeats's career and canon by Poulet's then-disciple J. Hillis Miller in a chapter of his *Poets of Reality* (1965).[4]

When, fifteen years ago and just out of graduate school, I was asked to assemble a collection of critical essays on Yeats, I tried to impose on the book a concentrically expanding hermeneutic circle,

a focal scheme in keeping with Yeats's own widening gyre of commitments: to the individual poem; to the particular volume of which it is a part; to the canon in which that volume takes its place; to the literary tradition—"We were the last romantics"— within which and against which Yeats worked; and finally, to the world of paradigm and archetype which lured him, supplied him with images, and often repelled him.

Of the major critics I chose, one, Northrop Frye, had been criticized elsewhere by two of the others. Despite their admiration of his *Anatomy of Criticism*, they noted his failure, or refusal, to convey "the personal presence" of any of the thousands of works discussed (Frank Kermode), thus leaving us "somewhat short of the poetry. Structure is fine, but what about texture?" (Denis Donoghue). Of course, Kermode and Donoghue dealt with myth and genre; they too charted crucial Yeatsian symbols. But whereas Frye's concern is with a set of repetitive variations on the same themes, with the schematization of the multitudinous ways in which the recurrent is embodied, theirs is with the particular poetic embodiments themselves. If we would be faithful to Yeats (I said then), our concern must be "like his, with both."[5] Along with others represented in that anthology (Rosenthal, Rajan, T. R. Whitaker, Ellmann), I remain concerned with the

---

4. Brooks's essay, which first appeared in *Southern Review* 4 (1938), may be found in his *Modern Poetry and the Tradition*. Stauffer, "The Reading of a Lyric Poem," *Kenyon Review* 11 (1949); reprinted in his *The Golden Nightingale: Essays on Some Principles of Poetry in the Lyrics of William Butler Yeats*. Fraser's article is reprinted in his *Vision and Rhetoric: Studies in Modern Poetry*; Kenner's in his *Gnomon*. The position of Frye and Bloom is anticipated by Eliot in "Tradition and the Individual Talent" (1919) and in "The Function of Criticism" (1923), in which literature is conceived of as "systems in relation to which, and only in relation to which, individual works of literary art, and the work of individual artists, have their significance." *Selected Prose of T. S. Eliot*, ed. Frank Kermode, 68. Miller's study of Yeats is in *Poets of Reality: Six Twentieth-Century Writers*.

5. Keane, *William Butler Yeats: A Collection of Critical Essays*, 4, 7.

linguistic texture of Yeats's poems; at the same time—like Frye, Poulet, Miller, and Bloom (in their very different ways)—I am concerned with the underlying consciousness, imagination, vision. While, compared to Frye or to Geoffrey Hartman, I am positively fettered to a poem's words, I admire from a middle distance the audacious Yeatsian "unless" (VP 407) in Hartman's preface to *Beyond Formalism* (1970): "An emphasis on words is discriminatory as well as discriminating *unless* it guides us to larger structures of the imagination."

The present study tries to engage those larger structures of the imagination by focusing on Yeats's allusive interactions with the various traditions—literary, philosophic, occult—in which he was rooted and in the context of which he intended his work to be read. His themes, symbols, and poetic devices are sanctioned by history, authenticated by precedent, and yet peculiarly, indelibly, his own. He sings bound and wound in the chains of tradition and necessity, but the voice is unmistakably his. Though Yeats was adamant about his traditionalism, his poetry demonstrates the truism that the genuine innovator plays by preestablished rules in order to discover what Eliot called the "really new." At the same time, the true genius is master of the rules he has earned the privilege of breaking. The paradox familiar to readers of Eliot and Pound—explicit in such titles as "Tradition and the Individual Talent," "The Modern Tradition," "The Tradition of the New"—is implicit in Pound's Modernist imperative, which acknowledges that there is an "it" to "make new." In the words of one of Yeats's chief precursors, Blake, it is "the thankful receiver" who "bears a plentiful harvest."[6]

My main interest here, similar to that in an earlier study of interactions in the poetry and thought of Robert Graves (*A Wild Civility*, 1980), is the fruitful tension between tradition—where all's accustomed, ceremonious—and Yeats's individual talent, his legacy as it is made new in the particular poems under consideration. A combination of genetic and intrinsic criticism, I'm persuaded, reveals the characteristic Yeats poem as a sort of palimpsest, with the difference that the still partly visible precursor-texts have been assimilated and altered rather than imperfectly erased. Though—as in the case of "The Second Coming," "A Dialogue of Self and Soul," and "From 'The Antigone'"—I sometimes trace a poem's development through working drafts, my ultimate concern is not with process but with the finished poem.

Nothing is got for nothing. In addition to sacrificing space that could be devoted to, say, Yeats's metrical and sonic effects, there are clear and present dangers in a critical approach stressing interactions with "precursor-texts." One is obvious: the danger of putting things into the poem rather

---

6. One of Blake's Proverbs of Hell (MHH, Plate 9). The other titles, in addition to that of Eliot's famous essay, are of books: the important compendium, *The Modern Tradition*, ed. Richard Ellmann and Charles Feidelson, and Harold Rosenberg's *The Tradition of the New*.

than getting them out. I've tried, not always successfully I'm sure, to avoid irrelevancy and a tendentious offloading of allusions and analogues by striving for that admixture of flexibility, tact, and instinctive sense of pitch that keeps a commentary pertinent. What makes the tracing of sources and interactions pertinent is, in part, the degree to which the search illuminates the specific work under consideration: "how the detailed knowledge of the sources might affect our assessment of the finished lyric." That is a question raised in Richard Finneran's assessment of my own work,[7] to which I'd add a comment made in a review of my book on Graves. There is "considerable point in bringing out relationships between poems," wrote Philip Hobsbaum, "if this is done in such a way as to illuminate the individuality of the poets concerned." Not just the poems but also the *poets*, with all that that entails.

Since my critical methodology is both genetic and canonical, something needs to be said about each, in the course of which it may be useful to resound a few familiar tocsins.

II

The tiles in the vast mosaic of Yeats's *Collected Poems* are inevitably of varying value. But Yeats, who obeyed the injunction to "hammer your thoughts into unity" (Ex 263), sometimes seems no less demanding of us than he was of himself; and he was unsatisfied with less than "all"—an attitude, and a favorite word, he shares with his mentor Blake. To fully comprehend the work of a man whose "myths and symbols were intended to explain themselves as the years go by and one poem lights up another" (VP 847), it *is* necessary to know, if not all, at least much of the total canon. "Casual visitors to the *oeuvre* have seldom left substantial tracks," we are told in the first of Finneran's bibliographical essays on Yeats.[8]

Admirers of the poet should, perhaps, be more concerned about this state of affairs, a source of potential weakness as well as of strength. The "potential achievement" of Yeats's method "lies in its capacity to create a whole which is greater than the sum of its parts and which gives every part its valid place in a universe. Its potential weakness is the danger that the parts may suffer in their individual life, that they may become not experience but assertions, fitted into the curve instead of spontaneously proclaiming it."[9]

The author of that balanced statement has no doubt that the weight falls overwhelmingly on the side of achievement rather than of weakness. Despite the extreme skepticism of Yvor Winters and F. R. Leavis, and the more complex canon-adjustments of Harold Bloom and Denis Donoghue, Yeats certainly wrote a more than respectable number of poems that are

7. Finneran, *Recent Research on Anglo-Irish Writers*, 138. Hobsbaum, review of *A Wild Civility: Interactions in the Poetry and Thought of Robert Graves* in *Yearbook of English Studies* (1982).
8. *Anglo-Irish Literature: A Review of Research*, 217.
9. Rajan, *W. B. Yeats: A Critical Introduction*, 189.

both majestic and, as the term is usually understood, "autonomous." Others, lesser achievements, are at times more signature than substance, vehicles of a forced bravado or some other recognizably Yeatsian gesture, stylistic or attitudinal. These would include the obviously minor work (not much), poems overly dependent on the "System," and such near self-parodies as "The Gyres" and "Under Ben Bulben," poems that have an obvious, perhaps indispensable, function in the canon but that are, in themselves, something less than fully successful. As a number of critics have insisted, it is no service to Yeats to make every one of his later poems the subject of indiscriminate critical idolatry (Au 151).

The canonical or contextual question is intimately bound up with the debate about intentionalism and poetic genesis. A decade and a half after his famous pronouncement, in "Tradition and the Individual Talent," that "the more perfect the artist, the more completely separate in him will be the man who suffers and the mind which creates," Eliot advanced the argument another step, stressing the autonomy of the public poem. In *The Use of Poetry and the Use of Criticism* he said, "I prefer not to define, or to test, poetry by means of speculations about its origins: you cannot find a sure test for poetry, a test by which you may distinguish between poetry and mere good verse, by reference to its putative antecedents in the mind of the poet."[10]

In the midforties, W. K. Wimsatt and Monroe Beardsley published their two celebrated articles on "Intention" and "The Intentional Fallacy," the purpose of which, Wimsatt said a quarter-century later, was "to rescue poems from the morass of their origins." In resuming the genetic debate, Wimsatt summed up what seemed to him the "antithetically opposed sides":

An art work is something which emerges from the private, individual, dynamic, and intentionalistic realm of its maker's mind and personality; it is in a sense (and this is especially true of the verbal work of art) made of intentions or intentionalistic material. But at the same time, in the moment it emerges, it enters a public and in a certain clear sense an objective realm; it claims and gets attention from an audience; it invites and receives discussion, about its meaning and value. . . . If the art work has emerged at all from the artist's private world, it has emerged into some kind of universal world. The artist was not merely *trying* to do something worthy of notice in that world. He has done it. Artistic activity has produced a valued result. Some critics will wish to talk about just that result. Other critics, however, will not. These will be the critics who entertain an antithetic drive toward viewing the art work as

10. *The Use of Poetry and the Use of Criticism*, 140. In "Tradition and the Individual Talent," Eliot extolled "impersonality." In his 1940 Memorial Lecture on Yeats, he distinguished "two forms of personality," connecting Yeats with the second and greater form: that of the poet who, "out of intense and personal experience, is able to express a general truth; retaining all the particularity of his experience, to make of it a general symbol." Eliot here echoes Yeats's own comment in *Autobiographies* that he wove "an always personal emotion . . . into a general pattern of myth and symbol."

mainly a token of its source, a manifestation of something behind it, that is, the consciousness or personality of the artist. . . . These critics, wishing to throb in unison with the mind of the artist, will wish to know all about that individual artist and as much as possible about his historic context. At the very least, they will wish to know not only the poem in question, but also all his other poems, his essays, letters, and diaries, his thoughts and feelings, and not only those which occurred before the poem and might in any sense have caused it, but (in the more recent idiom) all those which came after it at any time and are thus a part of the whole personality of which the poem is an expression, the system of contexts of which it is a part.

The enemy is any critical approach that treats the author's mind outside the poem as a key to his meaning inside the poem, particularly those approaches in which the author's life and canon or some parts of them "are urged as a surrounding and controlling context for the poem or some details of it," what Wimsatt calls canonical historicism and "Vista-Vision intentional-ism." Such procedures—biographical, canonical, associative—can, of course, produce illumination; but a critic "habitually concerned with this sort of evidence . . . will in the long run produce a far different sort of comment from that of a critic who is mainly concerned with the public linguistic and cultural elements of the poem."[11]

True enough; but, partly for polemical reasons, Wimsatt draws the battle lines too rigidly. One can be concerned (not necessarily "habitually" or "mainly") with the genesis of a poem without reductively viewing it as "*mainly* a *token* of its source." We can even, practicing genetic or phe-nomenological criticism, "wish to throb in unison with the mind of the artist" without having to feel perverse. Indeed, undeterred by the inten-tionalistic "fallacy," readers shaped rather than shrunk by what Geoffrey Hartman calls the "New Critical Reduction" (an intermediate stage be-tween the old "Arnoldian Concordat" and the deconstructionists' "Revi-sionist Reversal") frequently went on to imagine that the "apex of critical insight and aesthetic experience" was precisely this "realization of the au-thor's intention, [the reader's] penetration into the author's self-conscious-ness in the very act of creation."[12] Of course, in such acts of penetration,

---

11. Wimsatt, "Genesis: An Argument Resumed" (1968) in his *The Day of the Leopards: Essays in Defense of Poems*, 11–39. I quote from pp. 11–12, 37, 34, 24, 26, 30. The Wimsatt-Beardsley articles—which appeared first in *A Dictionary of World Literature* (1944) and *Sewanee Review* (1945)—were subsequently reprinted in Wimsatt's *The Verbal Icon* (1958). A surprisingly simi-lar position is taken by Roland Barthes in two polemical essays published in 1963 and reprinted the following year in his *Essais critiques*. Despite the great difference between Anglo-American New Criticism and *la nouvelle critique*, Barthes and Wimsatt would agree that an "immanent" analysis of the dynamic structure of a work yields very different results than approaches that seek causal explanations outside the work—including explaining the work as the product of the author's psyche.

12. Hartman's terms are taken from his *Criticism in the Wilderness: The Study of Literature Today*. The "apex" remark is Kenneth Johnson's, from a review-essay of Hartman's book in *College English* 43 (1981):473–74.

deconstructionists and other re-cognizers now claim to see what the author did *not*, what he or she repressed or distorted or was historically, linguistically, or psychologically incapable of seeing.

The demarcations separating authorial intention, the verbal icon, and "strong" reading have grown ghostlier in the post-structural world of affectivist, revisionary, and deconstructionist criticism; but some of the orthodox arguments still carry weight in the case of Yeats. Referring specifically to Yeats—who, more than most poets, invites or compels canonical and genetic approaches—Hugh Kenner, Richard Ellmann, and Denis Donoghue, though all aware of Yeats as a canonical architect, have also warned against persistent diversions from the particular texts under discussion.[13]

Instead of addressing themselves to the poems, Kenner complained in 1956,

a brief generation of critics assaulted the doors of that Gothic fortress, *A Vision*, or scrutinizing its interior by periscope reported that it was full of bats. Worse followed: an immense limbo, consisting of the poet's diaries, notebooks, drafts and unpublished mss., was opened to certified explorers after his death, and the heady possibility that the clues to what Yeats had been making lay in his lumber room, or in the chips from his workbench, overwhelmed everyone who has so far reported. It is doubtful if what a major writer actually published has ever been so little trusted.

Kenner, writing thirty years ago, was certainly wrong in thinking this the labor of a *brief* generation of critics, but there is something sobering even today about his contention that there is still room for a book on Yeats that examines what is actually happening in his poems. In tracing Yeatsian interactions, I have chased sources, scrutinized chips from the workman's bench, straddled the lines between poetic intention and achievement, critical annotation and explication. At the same time, individual poems addressed have been subjected to intrinsic analysis; one can be interested in intention and process without ignoring the result: what Yeats "had to say."

Ellmann, one of the earliest and the least dispensable of the "certified explorers" alluded to by Kenner, came, in a sense, to agree with him that the poems themselves were becoming lost in a tangle of comparative and genetic scholarship. In a 1964 essay entitled "Yeats without Analogue," Ellmann argued persuasively that the search for "Yeats's sources and analogues" had become "disproportionate" and wondered what, finally, they all "prove." He answered his own question with another: "what is the use of trying to isolate creative motivation?" To this he responded: "The only effect is to minimize the role of the poet in shaping his impressions." Insisting that "Yeats is in some present peril everywhere of being swal-

13. For the comments cited in the next three paragraphs, see Kenner, "Unpurged Images," 615, 617; Ellmann's 1964 *Kenyon Review* essay "Yeats without Analogue," reprinted as the preface to the 2d ed. of his *Identity of Yeats*, v-xxii (vi-ix); and Donoghue's "The Hard Case of Yeats," 6, 4, 3.

lowed up by the great whale of literary history," Ellmann asked a final rhetorical question: "Even if connections can be made . . . is it not time to emphasize disconnections instead?" In pursuing intention and motivation, particularly in discussing analogues and in charting interactions with sources, one can profit from such warnings. Tactful reading will stress the disconnections between Yeats and his sources at least as much as the connections and, far from "minimizing" the poet's role in "shaping his impressions," will emphasize, as Ellmann himself does in *The Identity of Yeats*, the shaping imagination that creatively hammered so many disparate, sometimes seemingly intractable, materials into unity.

Donoghue, having abandoned the authorized biography, and writing with notably diminished confidence in Yeats's poems and plays as an "achieved . . . body of work separable from its origins," argued in "The Hard Case of Yeats" (1977) that the ideal critical study would deal with virtually everything, but "never take his [Yeats's] word for anything, or mistake the intention for the achievement." Glossing, admittedly a dodge of some tone-deaf Yeatsians, was taken to task as illustrative of a larger problem. While arguments about other major poets are conducted in the open,

the argument about Yeats has not really been conducted at all. Or it has been enforced in Yeats's favor by silence, vested interest, and the partiality of academic scholarship. Some parts of Yeats's work are difficult. Scholars are attracted to the most difficult task among tasks not impossible. One example: Yeats's poem "The Statues" is difficult. To make sense of it you have to provide a fairly elaborate gloss upon several passages. The materials for this elucidation are available in Yeats's prose. The act of elucidation is satisfying, it gives the critic a feeling of having achieved something. Energy spent on the elucidation seems to verify the poem. The fact that the argument of the poem is as unconvincing after the elucidation as before, if reasonably tough criteria of sense are applied, is easily dispelled by the unbroken circuit of interest between poem and elucidation. So commentaries proceed. They are not good enough.

"The word 'Yeats,'" Donoghue noted, "invokes a loosely formed but extraordinarily potent mythology in which we are discouraged from making the strict discriminations we would normally make between poems, plays, anecdotes, photographs, images, senate speeches, séances, ideas, love affairs, friendships, and visions." A "hard case" indeed for the intrinsic critic.

Nevertheless, two items on Donoghue's own rather indiscriminate list, "images" and "visions," seem intimately enough connected with the poetry. So—though challenged by much Modernist criticism—is a third: "ideas." Yeats's, like most significant poetry, *is* a poetry of ideas. Discussing verse we rightly concentrate on such technical details as genre, form, diction, syntax, image, symbol, sound, cadence, tone, and the like, but none of this refutes the fact that thought is usually—in Yeats's case always—being conveyed, ideas embodied. The greatness of a work, Yeats agreed with Pater, "depends upon subject matter" (E&I 522). Even if the proper question is *how* rather than *what* a poem means, it *does* mean.

The ideas in themselves are important, though finally less crucial than the aesthetic use the poet makes of them. Yeats sought "a system of thought that would leave my imagination free" (V-A xi). Blake "used" his idea of the enslaving "system" of "Bacon, Newton, Locke" to free him to create his own (*Jerusalem* 10:20, 93:21). Wordsworth, in the Immortality Ode, "made the best use" he could, "as a Poet," of Platonism or, rather, Neo-platonism. The same, as Yeats realized (Ex 353), is true of Joyce's symbolic "use" of Vico's cycles in *Finnegans Wake*. A similar pattern of use and abuse obtains in Yeats's employment of the ideas and images of Locke, the Neo-platonists, Vico, and a host of others from Heraclitus to Whitehead, from Homer to the English Romantics. Where does it all end? The cadences and imagery at the famous conclusion of Joyce's early masterpiece "The Dead" echo both the *Iliad* and, of all things, a Bret Harte short story; who knows what might be discovered from a study of the detective novels and cowboy stories that, in Yeats's later years, absorbed almost as much time as his pondering of English Romanticism, German and Italian philosophy, Indian mysticism, and Anglo-Irish magnanimity. We can rejoice that the books preserved at Anne Yeats's home do *not* include the poet's bedside pulps; otherwise . . .

Yeatsians have more than enough serious interactions and encounters to keep them busy. According to Eliot, the work of the genuine new poet is at its best and most original precisely when "the dead poets, his ancestors, assert their immortality most vigorously." "Talk to me of originality and I will turn on you with rage," asserted traditionalist Yeats. "I have before me an ideal expression in which all that I have, clay and spirit alike, assists; it is as though I most approximate that expression when I carry with me the greatest possible amount of hereditary thought and feeling" (E&I 522; Ex 293).

This is to sing in chains forged by a variety of ancestors. Though the heritage is not restricted to *poetic* utterance, Yeats, both eclectic and selective in finding and carrying with him what served his purposes, always responded to "hereditary thought *and* feeling," not only to the content but also to the form and tone of whatever he read, whether in verse or prose. Yeats's own prose was Paterian, and so was Pater's, as Yeats felt obliged to remind the master in the margin of his copy of *Plato and Platonism*. Establishing his approach as one of detached historical criticism, Pater had declared that the scholar,

in reading Plato, is not to take his side in a controversy, to adopt or refute Plato's opinions, to modify, or make apology for, what may seem erratic or impossible in him; still less, to furnish himself with arguments on behalf of some theory or conviction of his own. His duty is rather to follow intelligently, but with strict indifference, the mental process there, as he might witness a game of skill.

Yeats was buying none of this "strict indifference" as either a "duty" or an ideal of the scholarly reader and writer. Rather, he noted in the margin, "it is part of his duty to love or hate what he reads; form is all important to this. Pater's own solemn strain cannot be heard with indifference."[14]

It was out of this kind of passionate response—an example of "strong" or "Nietzschean reading"—that much of Yeats's own creative work derives. "We do not seek truth in argument or in books," he wrote in his 1930 diary, "but clarification of what we already believe" (Ex 310). "Ultimately," wrote Nietzsche in *Ecce Homo* ("Why I Write Such Good Books" 1), "nobody can get more out of things, including books, than he already knows" from personal experience; he added that anyone who claimed to understand his own work "had made up something out of me after his own image." Nietzsche gaily admitted to being such a reader himself: *inevitably*, his heirs—contemporary deconstructionist and revisionary readers—would declare. "Really strong poets can read only themselves," claims Bloom in explaining the ways of misprision. "For them to be judicious is to be weak." Discussing Yeats's annotations on Nietzsche, Erich Heller claims that many of Yeats's glosses "ride rough-shod over Nietzsche's meanings. . . . It is certainly not the mind of the *poet* but rather the mind of the thinker that tends to vanish as soon as Yeats becomes entangled, in the margin, with Nietzsche's ideas." It is hard to resist the considerable truth, and the light charm, of Heller's image for creative misprision: "He who has bees in his bonnet reads not so much for the love of what he reads as for the honey to be made from it; and not since Blake has there been, in the history of great English poetry, a bonnet like Yeats's, buzzing with so many agile bees."

In annotating Nietzsche, Yeats was certainly seeking for clarification of what he already believed *and* for the "honey" of poetic generation. But closer study of those annotations reveals a genuine engagement with Nietzsche's ideas. This mixture of insight and creative appropriation is typical of Yeats's response to the work—the ideas, the form, the individual *tone*—of those who mattered to him most. Fortunately, it is possible, as Douglas Archibald has recently said,

approximately to define and assess Yeats's encounters, what happens when his imagination meets the words or work, consciousness or presence, of another human being. Those encounters lie at the heart of his poetry. He may have been more gifted and fortunate in devouring and converting influences than any other modern artist save Picasso. To understand him we must take into account his extraordinarily

14. O'Shea, *A Descriptive Catalog*, item 1538.

athletic intellect and capacious imagination, his eclecticism, and his ability to transform everything to poetic use.[15]

To elucidate this creative transforming of sources requires an awareness that, in however diminished a way, reflects that of Yeats himself, a poet who constantly judged himself against his predecessors, defining his own winding path as following or diverging from the main track of his philosophic and literary precursors—particularly the Neoplatonists and the poets in the Romantic tradition. Yeats believed, "Supreme art is a traditional statement of heroic and religious truths passed on from age to age, modified by individual genius, but never abandoned," and "Works of art are always begotten by previous works of art" (Mem 73, Au 490, E&I 352). Yeatsian interactions and encounters sometimes take the form of what Bloom calls *clinamen* or *tessera*: the creative swerving from, or "completion" of, a precursor. More simply—on most occasions, and like most artists—Yeats varies, alters, modifies, bends the inherited materials to his own aesthetic purposes. It is a matter less of exploitative irresponsibility than of the thankful receiver bearing a plentiful harvest. In terms of Yeats's great Irish contemporaries, it might be said that what Synge does with the ancient myth of Deirdre, or Joyce with Homer and Vico, Yeats does with the Metaphysicals and the Romantics, among many others. As Auden says, appropriately enough in his elegy on Yeats, the words of dead men are "modified in the guts of the living."

Yeats's modifications are the work of the mind as well as the guts. Since, for us no less than for Yeats, the poetry is the sine qua non, the present study may be seen as extending Giorgio Melchiori's dual aim in exploring "the mental pattern upon which Yeats's poetry is built": "to trace, as far as this is possible, the mental process by which Yeats's poems have come into being" and to identify, at least tentatively, some of the principles by which Yeats "succeeded in ordering . . . various experiences . . . into the single structure of a poem."[16]

While Melchiori and John Livingston Lowes before him brilliantly pursued associational roads to Byzantium and Xanadu, I am intrigued by the poem less as a "coalescence" of sources than as a palimpsest or pentimento at once revealing and altering those sources. Some admirably balanced accounts of poetic assimilation and supersession are given in M. H. Abrams's seminal study of tradition and Romantic innovation, *Natural Supernaturalism* (1971). Abrams is perhaps our preeminent literary historian; not all, especially those devoted to *Quellenforschung*, have his subtlety and tact in

---

15. Archibald, *Yeats*, xii. Heller's remarks (in the preceding paragraph) first appeared in a 1968 *Encounter* article on Yeats's annotations on Nietzsche; later reprinted in the expanded edition of Heller's *The Disinherited Mind: Essays in Modern German Literature and Thought*, 329–47.

16. Melchiori, *The Whole Mystery of Art*, 1, 2.

discriminating analogue from influence and in showing precisely *how* a poet's heritage is transmuted. Fearing Yeats's disappearance into the whale's belly, Ellmann suggested paying less attention to motivating sources and more to the subtle ways in which Yeats deviated from them. That emphasis tallies in a modest way with the theory of influence promulgated by Harold Bloom. According to his notion of misprision, an ephebe deliberately misreads his masters; thus he negotiates a creative swerve freeing his imagination (or so he thinks) from the mighty ancestors who both nurture and threaten his art. This Oedipal struggle for imaginative *Lebensraum*, later elaborated in Bloom's theoretical tetralogy, was first advanced in *Yeats* (1970), largely a study of the poet's deliberate distortion of his chief precursors, Blake and Shelley. In his complementary study, *Transformations of Romanticism* (1976), George Bornstein refers, in the chapter on Yeats, to "that distortion which, more than sources and influences, comprises literary history." The Bloomian term "transformative influence" is applied by J. B. Foster, in *Heirs to Dionysus* (1981), to the creative alteration of Nietzsche performed by Lawrence, Malraux, Mann, and, to a lesser extent, Gide and Yeats.[17]

My own general orientation is indebted to all these precursors, as well as to the primarily intrinsic emphasis of such mentors as M. L. Rosenthal and Helen Vendler. My approach in much of what follows may be clarified by the long-winded title of Chapter 5. Even there, however, emphasis falls on the specific ways in which these "variations" play out. Despite the tracing of interactions, I try to attend as well to matters at the local level, especially tonal variations, within individual poems. It is not necessary for mere literary scholars and critics to put it as grandly as Blake—"To Generalize is to be an Idiot To Particularize is the Alone Distinction of Merit"—in order to agree that the only critical path to valid and significant generalization is through intense study of specific works, immersion in what Blake called the "minute particulars."[18]

III

This study of Yeatsian interactions begins and ends with literally minute particulars—short poems. In Chapter 2, "What Then?" and "An Acre of Grass" (1936), matched poems of old age, provide a preliminary test of the method employed in the remainder of the book—a method placed in context in the preceding survey of the state of Yeats scholarship and of contemporary critical trends. Yeats's 1927–1928 "translation" of the Eros Chorus from Sophocles' *Antigone* serves as a coda. The main body of the book also

---

17. Abrams, *Natural Supernaturalism: Tradition and Revolution in Romantic Literature*. Bornstein, *Transformations of Romanticism in Yeats, Eliot, and Stevens*, 30–31. An earlier book by Bornstein, *Yeats and Shelley*, also complements Bloom's *Yeats*. As for Bloom himself, his theory of influence and its distortive "revisionary" strategies has shaped all his work since the book on Yeats. Foster, *Heirs to Dionysus: A Nietzschean Current in Literary Modernism*.

18. Blake, annotations on Reynolds, *Works* (in Blake's *Poetry and Prose*, 630); the term *minute particulars* appears frequently in *Jerusalem*.

begins and ends with short poems: "Fragments," examined in Chapter 3, appeared, as separate fragments, in the prefaces to two Yeats plays: part I in the introduction to *The Words upon the Window-pane*, part II in the introduction to *The Resurrection*. In both cases the fragments serve as gnomic, concrete crystallizations following more or less generalized discussions of intellectual history—not only a characteristic maneuver in Yeats's prose but also a clue to the way his epigrammatic poems are to be read. When "Fragments" first appeared in the canon, in the 1933 *Collected Poems*, Yeats backplaced it in the 1928 volume *The Tower*, carefully inserting this poem about the "birth" of the spinning jenny immediately after the equally epigrammatic "Two Songs from a Play" and before "Wisdom" (with its strange account of the begetting of Jesus) and that history-telescoping dramatization of another mythological begetting, the sonnet "Leda and the Swan."

On the other hand, "An Irish Airman Foresees His Death," examined in Chapter 8, never appeared separately; it was from the first a pendant to "In Memory of Major Robert Gregory" and part of what is here called the "Gregory cluster" in the 1919 edition of *The Wild Swans at Coole*. Thus, while it seems as self-sufficient ("autonomous," "autotelic") a poem as Yeats ever wrote, it too falls under the canonical dispensation in which his myths and images are left "to explain themselves as the years go by and one poem lights up another."

"Fragments" is in part lit up by "The Second Coming," the subject of Chapter 4. Both poems offer visionary glimpses of strange, and strangely related, births out of more than *Spiritus Mundi*. In ten lines, "Fragments" brings to bear all three of Yeats's traditions—Romantic, occult, and Anglo-Irish—as well as his recently acquired "feminist" sensibility, in order to turn the tables on the hated mechanists and empiricists: a feminist table-turning projected on a more apocalyptic scale in "From 'The Antigone.'" Responding to the Bolshevik Terror of 1918 as a "second birth" of the "French Revolutionary crimes" of the 1790s (see Chapter 4), Yeats produced, in "The Second Coming," an apocalyptic epic in twenty-two lines. Along with much else (including Blake, Shelley, Nietzsche, and the occult), it fuses an elegiac Burke with a trepidatious but prophetic Wordsworth, roots that are well beneath the surface but decisive to the growth of the finished poem.

The poems dealt with in Chapter 5 are discussed in terms of their interaction with and *antithetical* deviation from their precursor-texts—not because they are not "self-sufficient," but because appreciation of their full resonance requires that they be located, or relocated, in the context from which they derive their genetic impulse, the inspiration and the irritation that produced the pearl of *antithetical* response in the first place.

If, as "Fragments" (II) reveals, the occult was an ally in Yeats's assault on positivism and materialism, it also presented a danger. T. S. Eliot's career-culminating poem, "Little Gidding," endorses "A condition of complete simplicity / Costing not less than everything." Appropriately, since the dramatic crux of that poem is Eliot's respectful but chastising encounter with the ghost of pagan Yeats, he is here fusing the Yeatsian "condition of fire" (Myth 356) with Baron von Hügel's "the costingness of regeneration" (from *The Mystical Element of Religion*). In "Little Gidding" Eliot also echoes "Vacillation," the very poem in which Yeats rejects both the condition of fire ("Struck dumb in the simplicity of fire!") and the Catholic theologian with whom Eliot found himself in accord: "So get you gone, Von Hügel, though with blessings on your head."[19]

Yeats's resistance to the *primary* or "religious" condition of complete simplicity, its allure more Neoplatonic than Christian though with elements of both, is the task of his *antithetical* side in the quarrel with himself. The *antithetical* is the impulse of the subjective, Homeric self "turned from spirit" to seek and affirm "life." That was Yeats's formulation—under "Day" and "Homer" in opposition to "Night" and "Socrates/Christ"—in a crucial diagram he sketched in 1902 in the margins of a volume of Nietzsche,[20] and it was Nietzsche more than anyone else who armed Yeats in this Homeric contest with that life-denying asceticism here designated the "religious." As Yeats announces in the concluding section of "Vacillation": "Homer is my example and his unchristened heart." Yet he continues to vacillate, even so emphatic a declaration as this being checked in other poems by provisional simplifications of experience. Alteration rather than outright, sustained rejection is more characteristic of antinomial Yeats. In Chapter 5, I track this typical handling of "religious" materials in individual poems, instances of Yeats's alteration of ghostly paradigms, whether Platonic, Neoplatonic, or Christian.

Chapter 6, focusing more exclusively on the relationship with Nietzsche, addresses one paradox among several inherent in the *antithetical*; in this case, the *antithetical* self's suspension between chance and choice, the assertion of its "ultimate, particular freedom" in a world Yeats increasingly saw as determined, with both the individual life and the larger movements of history shaped by the inexorable circuits of sun and moon delineated in *A Vision*. How does the self, having rejected one machine (the Newtonian clockwork universe of dead matter in motion), find freedom and even exultation in a universe roughly calculable by wheels and interlocking gyres? Yeats's paradoxical solution—defining freedom as the recognition of necessity, asserting that creative man is at once "predestinate and free"—goes beyond stoic and Spinozistic fatalism to the astringent tragic joy of Nietzsche's

---

19. VP 502, 503. Both the drafts and the final version of part II of "Little Gidding" confirm the preeminent part played by Yeats in Eliot's "familiar compound ghost," an identification made by Eliot in his correspondence with John Hayward, Maurice Johnson, and Kristian Smidt. For details, see Helen Gardner, *The Composition of "Four Quartets,"* 64–67, and Diggory, *Yeats and American Poetry*, 115–17, 239.

20. Yeats's annotations are in an anthology of Nietzsche lent to him in 1902 by John Quinn. It was returned and is now in the Special Collections Department of Northwestern University: *Nietzsche as Critic, Philosopher, Poet and Prophet*, comp. Thomas Common (1901). This diagram was sketched in the margin of p. 122.

similar recognition, culminating in *Amor Fati* and the embrace, whether fierce or serene, of Eternal Recurrence. For obvious reasons, the central poetic text for both these chapters—on the altering or varying of received religious doctrine, and on the paradox of joyful freedom within constraint—is "A Dialogue of Self and Soul," Yeats's own "choice" of the myth of Eternal Recurrence rather than the "religious" myth of escape from the cycle of life.

The focus in Chapter 6 on the "Nietzschean" paradox of exultant freedom within constraint reflects my conviction not only that this attempt to simultaneously accept and surmount determinism is the dangerous but finally fruitful antagonism at the heart of much of Nietzsche's and Yeats's thought and work, but also that the tension and its possible resolution in "tragic joy" is chief among Nietzsche's many gifts to Yeats.

Questions of fate and destiny, of individual freedom and joy, are embodied in heroes who exultantly "choose" their "fate." Yeats's Irish Airman begins his monologue, "I know that I shall meet my fate," yet he insists that what "drove" him to that fate was his own "lonely impulse of delight." To establish part of the context in which that and other difficulties presented by the Airman poem are to be grappled with, I read the elegy immediately preceding it, cocking a mischievous eye. My subversive argument in Chapter 7 is that Yeats partially undermined his elegiac tribute, not only by its own excesses and by caveat, but also by interaction with its covert sources. The result is a poem less about Robert Gregory than about his elegist, the true heir of that "secret discipline" practiced by the visionary company in whose ranks Yeats only seems to enlist the slain hero.

The Airman monologue (Chapter 8) also raises the question of membership in the visionary company—in this instance, the band of solitary and self-destructive questers among whom Yeats found his boyhood idols. After reading "An Irish Airman Foresees His Death" intrinsically, as the self-contained poem it seems to be, I place it in the context that shaped it: a heroic tradition including both the classical heroic code and the "band" Browning's chief quester refers to as consisting of "all the lost adventurers, my peers"—in Browning's case, as in Yeats's, his own precursors in the Romantic tradition, especially Shelley's Visionary-Poet in *Alastor*. I conclude, after speculating on the possible spiritual connotations of the Airman's adjective, "lonely," by reaffirming the Airman's autonomy, another vindication of *antithetical* swordsman versus *primary* saint (L 798), as in that central poem to which I keep returning, "A Dialogue of Self and Soul."

The Coda, dealing with a short lyric that is itself a coda, explores the interaction with Sophocles in a minor poem occupying a surprisingly strategic position in Yeats's canon: "From 'The Antigone.'"

I've dipped into detail in sketching the Gregory chapters because I suspect that it is there above all that my arguments and attendant source-hunting may seem tendentious, if not perverse. But those chapters are meant to reveal, not so much some obscure animus toward Robert Gregory, as the

complex undertow even in poems of apparently straightforward glorification. If the reader of the chapter on the elegy, no matter how resistant to the
extremities among which I run my course, is finally persuaded that Yeats
partially deconstructs his own elaborately constructed mold of elegiac courtesy, I will have made the point my tracing of allusions was meant to
support. The Airman poem was chosen because, while it lights and is lit up
by the elegy, it challenges my critical emphasis on context and interaction. I
try to show that while it is, in the words of Rajan quoted in part II of my
Preface, "vividly itself," it also "has behind it, holding it in position, the
context of a considerably larger presence"—something more obviously
true, from the title on, of "From 'The Antigone.'" To read the Airman
monologue in *that* context is to read not quite the same poem. It would not
of course be true to say, of elegy or monologue or "translation," that they
have been, as a result of my positioning of them, changed utterly. But, like
all the poems discussed in the book, they may (in Shelley's most urbane
understatement) be "somewhat changed."

The transformations may at times seem more mine than Yeats's. In the
chapter that follows, for example, I bring in much material in what amounts
to an extended gloss on "What Then?" I am not pronouncing all such
"interactions"—whether definite, probable, plausible, or merely possible—
necessary to an understanding of so simple a poem as "What Then?," nor
even claiming that they are required to place "What Then?" and its companion, "An Acre of Grass," in a reasonable context, whether Yeatsian or
involving larger literary, philosophic, and spiritual traditions. But if we can
know too much about a given poem's "background," we can never know
enough about the creative process itself. I must also confess that the connections and themes touched on seem to me intimately relevant to "What
Then?" and "An Acre of Grass," both in their ideational and verbal genesis
and as completed artifacts.

In conclusion, then, my interest is in both product and process, blossom
and root, the finished poem and its genesis: how it came to be the precise
configuration on the page. That is seldom if ever a thing-in-itself. The
meaning of Yeats's poems tends to take place in their canonical interaction
and in the broader interaction between those poems and their "sources"—
philosophic, occult, historical, and, of course, literary. But the time has
come to put these generalizations to the test through an examination of
minute particulars. I've chosen to begin with two short, essentially autobiographical poems written by an old man on the themes of old age and
creativity: themes that preoccupied Yeats from as early as *The Wanderings of
Oisin* (1889) but that necessarily struck closer to home for a man past
seventy.

2

"WHAT THEN?" AND "AN ACRE OF GRASS": THE "ECHOING GREEN" AT RIVERSDALE

The intellect of man is forced to choose
Perfection of the life, or of the work,
And if it take the second must refuse
A heavenly mansion, raging in the dark.
  —Yeats, "The Choice"

My wife said the other night, "AE was the nearest to a Saint you or I will ever meet.
You are a better poet but no saint. I suppose one has to choose."
  —Yeats, 1935 letter to Dorothy Wellesley

Once when continually ill, in 1937, he rang his bell for me in the night to ask me to
stay with him for a while and said, "When I am ill I feel I am becoming a Christian
and I hate that."
  —Mrs. Yeats, 1952 letter to Peter Allt

An aged man is but a paltry thing,
A tattered coat upon a stick, unless
Soul clap its hands and sing, and louder sing
For every tatter in its mortal dress.
  —Yeats, "Sailing to Byzantium"

It is precisely such "contradictions" that seduce one to existence.
  —Nietzsche, *The Genealogy of Morals*[1]

Two years before his death, W. B. Yeats received a telephone call request-
ing a representative poem to be printed in *The Erasmian*, the magazine of his
old Dublin high school, Erasmus Smith. Not well enough to write a new
poem for the occasion, he told the editor he would choose an "unpublished
poem among his recent writings which would be suitable for a school

---

1. Nietzsche, *The Genealogy of Morals* 3.3. For Yeats's letter to Dorothy Wellesley, written
shortly after the death of AE (George Russell), see L 838. Peter Allt quotes the letter to him
from Mrs. Yeats in "Yeats, Religion, and History," 648.

magazine." The editor, A. Norman Jeffares, subsequently called at Riversdale—the "small old house" of "An Acre of Grass" and "What Then?"— and picked up a copy of the poem Yeats had chosen. "What Then?" appeared in *The Erasmian* in April 1937:

His chosen comrades thought at school
He must grow a famous man;
He thought the same and lived by rule,
All his twenties crammed with toil;
"What then?" sang Plato's ghost. "What then?"

Everything he wrote was read,
After certain years he won
Sufficient money for his need,
Friends that have been friends indeed;
"What then?" sang Plato's ghost. "What then?"

All his happier dreams came true—
A small old house, wife, daughter, son,
Grounds where plum and cabbage grew,
Poets and Wits about him drew;
"What then?" sang Plato's ghost. "What then?"

"The work is done," grown old he thought,
"According to my boyish plan;
Let the fools rage, I swerved in naught,
Something to perfection brought";
But louder sang that ghost, "What then?"[2]

How well does the poem satisfy its primary criterion, suitability for a school magazine? Certainly it is transparently simple in its "story," structure, metrics, and diction. The latter, in one sense, is as cliché-ridden as a stilted freshman report: Chosen comrades . . . lived by rule . . . friends indeed . . . dreams came true . . . according to plan. . . . But not *all* is according to "his," as opposed to Yeats's, "plan." As the stock language suggests, the reader is being "set up" all along, as is the hero, whose charted progress is punctuated by an alien singing coming on the heels of the couplet in each *a b a a b* stanza until, suddenly "louder," it climactically resonates with a cosmic irony worthy of Hardy.

"What Then?," in short, presented its initial audience with a signal lesson in sophisticated handling of refrain and incremental repetition, the "what then?" modulating from a jaunty, narrative-expediting "what happened

2. VP 576–77. There were minor punctuational differences in the *Erasmian* printing, and a few slight variants are not recorded in VP; see Robin Skelton, "The First Printing of W. B. Yeats's 'What Then?'" The poem subsequently appeared in the Cuala Press *New Poems* (1938) and, posthumously, in *Last Poems and Plays* (1940). Jeffares's account is in his *W. B. Yeats, Man and Poet*, 2d ed., 302, n. 5.

next?" to that final spiritual challenge and apparent dismissal. Not that the body of the poem is free of irony. The third stanza in particular is tonally complex—bald reportage in the form of a catalog that is at once self-satisfied, poignant, and comic. House, wife, daughter, son, plum, cabbage, poets, wits: they seem to be on the same level of importance, and what is important is that all "about *him* drew." "He" is the magnetic center of his universe, the object and subject of the poem's thrice-repeated verb, "thought." The one thing that has not been given sufficient "thought" is the simple fact of mortality itself. The refrain therefore functions as the return of the repressed; without it, the poem would amount to little more than a third-person report of an old man's self-congratulatory litany of accomplishment, a tale of self-discipline and toil rewarded. The "what then?," especially in that final intensification, sardonically punctures the balloon, emptying a fullness "crammed" with achievement as well as toil.

Of the conflicting "messages" being transmitted, which would the students at Erasmus Smith High School have been likeliest to receive? Out of its thesis and antithesis the poem generates, I believe, a characteristically Yeatsian synthesis; but surely few of those students would have seen beyond the manifest "contradiction." For, while "he" is being presented to the class as a notable example of what can be attained by hard work, simultaneously the poet is figuratively scraping his fingernails on the blackboard by imparting a seemingly disillusioned and disillusioning lesson on the futility of human effort, perhaps even of human life.

The life of accomplishment being challenged is "his." Whose? Even the dullest student would have been aware, despite the distancing "he," that the poem was autobiographical and that William Butler Yeats—distinguished alumnus, husband and father, former senator of the Irish Free State, and winner of the Nobel Prize for Literature—had indeed grown "a famous man." Yet here he was, patting himself on the back with his right hand while undercutting it all with his left in the form of that sinister refrain: a bemused and finally terrifying assertion that the best-laid plans, even if they *don't* go astray, open to the void. No wonder Yeats referred to the lyric as "a melancholy biographical poem . . . with the burden 'Sang Plato's ghost "What then?"'" (L 895). The deflationary technique of that "burden" resembles that of Byron, a notable pricker of his own idealistic balloons, who allied himself with "Plato . . . Who knew this life was not worth a potato," and with "Solomon," the purported author of Ecclesiastes, whose dialectic of aspiration and disillusioned reaction so profoundly influenced the sudden shifts in Byron himself. ("He raises our hopes," Hazlitt complained, "only to dash them to earth again, and break them to pieces the more effectively from the height they have fallen.")[3]

---

3. Hazlitt makes this complaint in *The Spirit of the Age.* Byron lumps the Preacher of Ecclesiastes ("Solomon") with Plato and others in response to the accusation that he (Byron) underrates "human power and virtue, and all that." His point in *Don Juan* 7.3 is that he is not alone in his skepticism.

Even before he had "grown old," Yeats's "boyish plan" would have been colored by Ecclesiastes, which, along with Revelation, was his favorite biblical text as a boy (Au 24), as it was Byron's. But its sad wisdom no more caused him to abandon plans and dreams than the taunting and literally haunting song of Plato's ghost obliterates the litany of achievement given in the body of this poem. Yet, if the proud recital of accomplishment intensifies, so does the climactically amplified refrain: *"But louder sang that ghost, 'What then?'"* If "he" gets the bulk of the poem, Plato's ghost gets the refrain and the last, unanswerable question: an apportionment, dramatic reversal, and apparent spiritual triumph similar to that executed with *quiet* power in Herbert's "The Collar," a poem earlier altered by Yeats in "Father and Child."[4]

"What Then?" would seem to be a self-consuming artifact, a text that deconstructs itself on a level simple enough to be perceived even among schoolchildren. Those students familiar with Yeats's poetry, detecting yet another of those self-contesting internal dialogues at the heart of his work, might have noticed that "What Then?" interacts with such poems as "A Dialogue of Self and Soul" and "The Choice." The latter begins, "The intellect of man is forced to choose / Perfection of the life, or of the work"; "What Then?" specifies that the "something to perfection brought" was "the work." Must, therefore, the extremist consequence posed in "The Choice" now be faced: "and if it take the second must refuse / A heavenly mansion, raging in the dark"? Though it is not "he" but the "fools" who do the raging in the later poem, the spiritual question remains: "what then?"

"The Choice" is verbally and thematically echoed, but the Yeatsian poem with which "What Then?" most fully interacts was written (at least in its first version) nearly half a century earlier. "The Man Who Dreamed of Faeryland" is a catalog of might-have-beens. The tenderness of love, freedom from "money cares," the maintenance of "a fine angry mood" leading to "vengeance" upon mockers, and, finally, "unhaunted sleep" in the grave: all have been lost, spoiled by a repeated, cruel "singing" whose theme is a golden and silver Otherworld of immutable beauty. Yeats's delicate lyricism (in part derived from Blake's *Book of Thel*) emphasizes first the pathos, then the bitter frustration, of a dreamer who succumbs to the lure of the unattainable, dying without ever having lived and finding "no comfort," even in the grave.

Responding almost point by point in "What Then?," Yeats presents us with an old man who has entered fully into the world of human experience, indeed a man who seems (so the refrain suggests) to have followed the principal teaching of Nietzsche's Zarathustra: "Remain faithful to the earth, and do not believe those who speak to you of supernatural hopes." No tantalizing dreams of Faeryland have thwarted *this* man in his long-calcu-

---

4. See below, Chapter 5. In "The Collar," of course, the "triumph" is shared by the Childe and his heavenly Father.

lated pursuit, and attainment, of fame, "sufficient money for his need," love, comfort, and, above all, the "perfection" of an art so accomplished that from its pinnacle the artist can dismiss, with a disdain even finer than anger, "fools" whose mockery stemmed from malice, jealousy, creative impotence, or sheer stupidity. Let them rage; he swerved in naught, and this is the result. Living and writing well, the poem claims and demonstrates, is the best vengeance against mocking voices, whether human or superhuman. But of course all this alternates with the most mocking of mocking voices. If the paralyzed dreamer of the Faeryland poem is a worldly "failure," and the old man of "What Then?" a worldly "success," that success, however real, is recognized as less than all: the voice of the Otherworld sings on.

The effect of the refrain in "What Then?" is not only to challenge and threaten "he" (and us) with the ghostly singing of an ambassador from the spiritual world but also to warn against the complacency of a serene old age. It is a point quietly made, through allusion, in the body of the poem as well. "His" expression of accomplishment mounts to a crescendo in the final stanza, but the very lines in which it is announced—"'The work is done,' grown old he thought, / 'According to my boyish plan'"—echo the assertion made by Wordsworth on behalf of his "happy warrior," who,

Among the *tasks* of real life, hath wrought
Upon the *plan* that pleased his *boyish thought*.

The echo is, as usual in Yeats, subtle and thematically functional. He would have no objection to yet another formulation of the Wordsworthian credo that the child is father to the man. To the extent that the happy warrior has "singleness of aim," leans to "homefelt pleasures" (despite a "faculty" for "turbulence"), and "finds comfort in himself and in his cause," Wordsworth's idealized hero resembles the old man of "What Then?" with all his "happier dreams" of domestic pleasures. But—and here is the crucial difference, and the point of the allusion—it can hardly be said of the Yeatsian old man that he "makes his moral being his prime care" or, still less, that he,

While the mortal mist is gathering, draws
His breath in confidence of Heaven's applause.[5]

That is precisely the confidence *lacking* in "What Then?," whose otherwise supremely confident old man is presumably shaken out of his ease by the "louder" singing from the world beyond. What *he* hears is *not* heavenly

5. "Character of the Happy Warrior," lines 3–5, 40, 58–59, 81–83. Though reflecting aspects of Wordsworth's brother John and of Lord Nelson, Wordsworth's happy warrior is an idealized hero—like Yeats's "Fisherman," a "man who does not exist."

approval but a threat, reminding him that he has not made his moral being his prime care, that the perfection he achieved was aesthetic not spiritual, of the work, not of the life.

Not that Wordsworthian complacency, to say nothing of the vulgarity of spiritual "applause," is itself to be applauded, let alone emulated. That is a point reinforced by another Wordsworth-related verbal echo in "What Then?," in which the "small old house" with "grounds where plum and cabbage grew" deliberately recalls a prose passage in which Yeats imagines "a poet, when he is growing old," buying "some small old house where, like Ariosto, he can dig his garden," deluding himself that he will "never awake out of vision"—until he remembers "Wordsworth withering into eighty years, honoured and empty-witted" (Myth 342). In thus depicting Wordsworth, Yeats is in accord with Shelley, who employed as epigraph to his *Alastor* Wordsworth's lines about the good dying first while those whose "hearts are dry as summer dust, / Burn to the socket"—a bitter Shelleyan irony since, poetically, Wordsworth even then was well on his way to the latter fate (see also Chapter 8).

It was a fate Yeats began to fear for himself at the very time he wrote the passage in *Per Amica Silentia Lunae* describing the Wordsworthian "withering." That same year (1917) and the next, in the poems I refer to later as the "Gregory cluster," Yeats depicted himself as an aging malingerer, shuffling along on dry autumnal paths or slowly burning damp faggots in sorry contrast to the young horseman and pilot consumed in the swift flames of heroic action. His model for a heroic old age appears in the same passage of *Per Amica*: "Landor, who lived loving and hating, ridiculous and unconquered, into extreme old age, all lost but the favour of his Muses . . . 'The Mother of the Muses, we are taught, / Is Memory; she has left me; they remain, / And shake my shoulder, urging me to sing'" (Myth 342). But the passage—and the "Anima Hominis" section of *Per Amica* as a whole—ends with the image of Wordsworth, once a "great poet" (Ex 334), withering into bodily and imaginative decrepitude, honored but long since deserted by his Muses.

That was a consummation devoutly to be avoided. The Yeatsian "Prayer for Old Age" (1934) is that he be guarded "From all that makes a wise old man / That can be praised of all." He wants intellectual power, but only "those thoughts which have been conceived not in the brain but in the whole body"—a Donne-like "thinking of the body," because "He that sings a lasting song / Thinks in a marrowbone" (VP 553, E&I 235). In *Last Poems*, Yeats resolutely, programmatically, resists the Wordsworthian fate. As the "mortal mist" gathers about *him*, Yeats, with a passionate intensity both sexual and intellectual, refuses to act the part of the dignified laureate withering into an honored, uncreative old age. Scandalously ("loving and hating, ridiculous and unconquered"), he plays instead the indecorously randy role of "wild old wicked man," spurred (again in language borrowed from

Donne) "into song" by "lust and rage."[6] If his personae include that of the "fool," it is a calculated performance, "for the song's sake." Far from empty-witted, he cries out to be granted "an old man's eagle mind" and the creative energy to "remake" himself. Despite his accomplishments, he is the opposite of complacent. To the question with which Shelley's doppelgänger challenged him in the days preceding his death ("How long do you mean to be content?"), Yeats declares, in the 1938 "Are You Content?," "I am *not* content" (VP 587, 591, 553, 576, 604).

Yeats's reckless, wanton old man recalls those earlier personae, fools and beggars who mock the long-range planning of those who, like the old man of "What Then?," settle down. "An aimless joy is a pure joy," according to a 1918 poem celebrating "zig-zag wantonness" and ridiculing all who have "marked a distant object down":

If little planned is little sinned
But little need the grave distress.
What's dying but a second wind?
    (VP 337–38)

That nonchalance is a far cry from the fear instilled by Plato's ghost in the lifelong planner of "What Then?" In another beggarman poem (VP 299–300), the speaker betrays his own wasteful virtues. By getting "a comfortable wife and house," he plans to "grow respected at my ease," only to "hear amid the garden's nightly peace . . . The wind-blown clamour of the barnacle-geese"—a natural clamor that, nevertheless, seems almost as alien and threatening to respected old men as the singing of Plato's ghost.

Despite his disdain for, and dread of, the dotage of Wordsworth, Yeats may have envied the happy warrior his "confidence of heaven's applause." Yet he cannot have the old man of "What Then?" confident of *that* when it is precisely the "heavenly mansion" that seems forsworn in choosing perfection of the work. Such perfection is a good, and the defiant old man is justly proud of this ripened fruit of his toil. But what does it profit a man to gain the whole world and lose his immortal soul?—or as Yeats himself put it in the late thirties, Easternizing and altering the Christian question: "according to the Indians a man may do much good yet lose his own soul" (Ex 415).

As we might expect, considering Yeats's immersion in Eastern thought in the thirties, Indian mysticism helps illuminate "What Then?" But if the progress of "he" in the poem parallels the first two *āśramas* (stages of life) in Hindu doctrine (*brahmacarya*, the period of discipline and education, and *garhasthya*, the life of the active worker and family man), he certainly does not

---

6. "The Spur" is a seeming fusion of Donne's "to rage, to lust" and the "wings and spurres" of "desire and sense" ("Loves Deity" and "Song: Sweetest love, I do not goe").

pass through *vānaprasthya* (the gradual loosening of social bonds) to the fourth and final stage of *sānnyasa*, that of the contemplative, ascetic, world-renouncing hermit.

This was all abundantly familiar to Yeats from his study of Indian mysticism, including two books to which he wrote introductions in the early and mid-thirties: Hamsa's *The Holy Mountain* and *An Indian Monk* by Shri Purohit Swami, with whom he collaborated in the winter of 1935 on a translation of the *Upanishads*. Yeats's fellow-student of Hinduism, Dermott MacManus, reports that the poet and his wife even gave up their communications with the spirits of *A Vision* because they came to consider them "incompatible with the . . . teaching of Hinduism."[7] Yet Western minds, if they follow the Eastern way, become "unfit for the work forced upon them by Western life" (Au 482; cf. L 896). According to Yeats's 1934 sonnet "Meru," which takes off from an image in the 1909 paragraph just cited, "Civilization" is "manifold illusion," and man's life of thought a

Ravening, raging, and uprooting that he may come
Into the desolation of reality:
Egypt and Greece, good-bye, and good-bye, Rome!

From this perspective, with its breakthrough from desolation to gay dismissal, the old house, wife, children, friends, plums, cabbages, poets, wits, even the perfected work itself, of "What Then?" seem small indeed. The perspective is, of course, Indian, as the sestet of the sonnet confirms:

Hermits upon Mount Meru or Everest,
Caverned in night under the drifted snow,
Or where that snow and winter's dreadful blast
Beat down upon their naked bodies, know
That day brings round the night, that before dawn
His [man's] glory and his monuments are gone.
    (VP 563)

In "Sailing to Byzantium," artworks were "Monuments of unageing intellect," enduring reflections of the soul's "own magnificence"; here man's monuments and magnificence alike are swept clean away. Only the desolation of spiritual "reality" remains, the "what then?" of Plato's ghost. In the passage of "Il Penseroso" that most haunted Yeats, the lyric speaker, his midnight lamp gleaming in his "high lonely tower," would

---

7. MacManus was interviewed by Kathleen Raine, who reports this information in "Hades Wrapped in Cloud," in *Yeats and the Occult*, ed. George Mills Harper, 105. For the introductions to the two books mentioned, as well as an introduction to the Mandukya Upanishad, see E&I 426–37, 448–87. The same volume contains Yeats's 1912 introduction to the English translation of Tagore's *Gitangali* (E&I 387–95). His introduction to Patanjali's *Aphorisms of Yoga* appeared in 1938.

unsphere
The spirit of Plato to unfold
What worlds, or what vast regions hold
The immortal mind that hath forsook
Her mansion in this fleshy nook.

    (85–92)

The ghost "Milton's Platonist" (VP 373) would magically bring back to
earth from the eternal sphere is the spirit-form of that Plato who, even in
the flesh (in Yeats's most celebrated performance among schoolchildren),
"thought nature but a spume that plays / Upon a ghostly paradigm of
things" (VP 445); that Plato whom Yeats identified in the thirties with his
"symbolic Asia" and who was, therefore, as Richard Ellmann says (*Identity*,
203), "a fitting spokesman to cast doubt upon the European world of ap-
pearances and events, of brilliant achievements and successes." But when he
wrote "What Then?," Yeats's symbolic Asia meant specifically Indian mystical thought. It is almost as if he put in the breathless mouth of Plato's
ghost the *tatah kim* ("what then?") of the famous Indian hermit-poet Bhartrihari. His *Satakas*, consisting of three cycles of poems, conclude with a
group dealing with renunciation of "all worldly desires and ends." As a
philosopher, says Bhartrihari, "I sit on a hard stone in a cave on the mountainside, and time and again I laugh when I think of my former life."[8] A few
pages further on, he says:

You may have gained glory, and all your desires may have been accomplished: what
further? Your feet may have been placed on the necks of your enemies: what further?
You may by your good fortune have gathered friends about you: what further? . . .
You may have had innumerable horses, elephants, and attendants: what then? You
may have enjoyed good food: what then? Or you may have eaten wretched food
toward the end of day: [*tatah kim*] what then?

    (*Vairagyasatakas* 71, 72)

This is strikingly close to the tone and development of "What Then?," with
the same litany of accomplishments undercut by the same deflating question
from the spiritual perspective.

    Yeats may or may not have read this translation of Bhartrihari. It is
interesting to note, however, that it was published in 1913, the year Yeats
wrote the hermit-poems collected in *Responsibilities*,[9] and under the imprint
of T. Werner Laurie, the London publisher of several of Yeats's books,
including the first edition of his own philosophic work, *A Vision*. Further-

---

  8. *The Satakas or Wise Sayings of Bhartrihari*, trans. J. M. Kennedy, Vairagyasataka §47.
  9. In one of these, "The Three Hermits," the titular characters take the air by a "cold and
desolate sea." While the first mutters a prayer and the second rummages for a flea, "On a
windy stone, the third, / Giddy with his hundredth year, / Sang unnoticed like a bird"—rather
like the Bhartrihari of Vairagyasataka §47.

more, by an intriguing coincidence, Bhartrihari's translator was J. M. Kennedy, who also translated a work that had, according to Yeats's wife, a direct influence on "What Then?" and its companion poem, "An Acre of Grass." The passage to which George Yeats directed A. Norman Jeffares was aphorism 542 of *The Dawn of Day*, the title of both Kennedy's and Johanna Volz's translation of Nietzsche's *Die Morgenröte*; the passage is marked by a check, presumably by Yeats himself, in the index of his copy of the book. Checked by Yeats or not, the aphorism was read by Yeats, serving him as a warning against two dangers: the temptation of accomplished old men to complacently rest (as Poet Laureate Wordsworth literally had) on their laurels, and the danger, as in the case of the man who dreamed of Faeryland, of being, in Nietzsche's penultimate phrase in *The Dawn*, "wrecked on the infinite."

Jeffares himself rightly seizes on the question with which *The Dawn* ends: will people say of "we aeronauts of the intellect" that it was our fate "to be wrecked on the infinite? Or, my brethren? or—?" But Jeffares's comment that "the 'or' is recaptured in the final crescendo of the refrain in Yeats's poem" misses the point, making the whole connection of "What Then?" with Nietzsche seem tenuous.[10] In fact, the Nietzschean "or" opens up the possibility of an eagle-like soaring of intellectual aeronauts who will not be wrecked on the infinite; this is precisely the opposite of the threat implicit in the louder singing of Plato's ghost.

George Yeats was right to specify aphorism 542, in which Nietzsche describes the old as weary and seeking enjoyment. While such an "old thinker" appears to raise himself "above his life's work," actually he "spoils it by infusing into it a certain amount of fantasy, sweetness, flavour, poetic mists, and mystic lights. This is how Plato ended." Becoming "soft and sweet like autumn fruit," reposing "in the luminous adulation of a woman," losing his desire for "real disciples" (that is, "true opponents"), the old thinker "surrounds himself with objects of veneration, companionship, tenderness, and love." He wishes to become an institution, but, by "canonizing himself," he has "drawn up his own death-warrant; from now on his mind cannot develop further. His race is run; the hour-hand stops . . . he has passed the climax of his powers, and is very tired, very near the setting of his sun." He has become, Yeats would say, "Wordsworthian."

It is on this situation that "What Then?" and "An Acre of Grass" play their variations. In the latter, only picture and book remain, along with an acre of green grass for air and exercise,

Now strength of body goes;
Midnight, an old house
Where nothing stirs but a mouse.

10. "Jeffares . . . tries, on perhaps very tenuous grounds, to relate the refrain" to the Nietzsche passage. George Brandon Saul, *Prolegomena to the Study of Yeats's Poems*, 163. For Jeffares's comments, see *W. B. Yeats, Man and Poet*, 295, 337, n. 66, and his *Commentary on the Collected Poems of W. B. Yeats*, 458–60.

My temptation is quiet.
Here at life's end . . .

But, recovering, Yeats (no Eliotic Gerontian) takes to heart both Nietzsche's warning against the weariness of old age in *The Dawn* and his advocacy of "frenzy" in the *Twilight of the Idols*:

Grant me an old man's frenzy,
Myself must I remake
Till I am Timon and Lear
Or that William Blake
Who beat upon the wall
Till Truth obeyed his call . . .

Yeats believed that "Nietzsche completes Blake and has the same roots" and that Nietzsche's "thought flows always, though with an even more violent current, in the bed Blake's thought has worn" (L 379, E&I 130). Whatever their differences, Blake would agree with Nietzsche on the dangers of reposing in the "luminous adulation of a woman" (for Blake, the moony "married land" of Beulah, a drowsy refuge from the "fury of Poetic Inspiration")[11] and of losing the desire for "real disciples" who are "true opponents" (*The Dawn* §542). "Opposition is true Friendship," we are told in *The Marriage of Heaven and Hell*, a work in which we also encounter "Eagle-like men" of genius who create, in an "infinite" that is "inside," an interior imaginative expansion inverting Newtonian "space" (MHH, plates 20, 15). In *The Dawn*, "Nietzsche completes Blake" by employing similar imagery. The "minds" of men of genius are "like winged beings" that "rise far above them" (§347): an image that dominates the book's final vision of "daring birds," aeronauts of "the intellect" whose minds "will fly farther" and, rising "far above our own heads and our failures," will see "hundreds of birds more powerful than we are, striving whither we ourselves have also striven" (§575). But Nietzsche's "space" is as internal and "mental" as Blake's: these birdlike geniuses are *Übermenschen* who will *not* be "wrecked on the infinite." It is this kind of winged mind that Yeats, fusing Blake and Nietzsche, cries out to be granted in the final stanza of "An Acre of Grass":

A mind Michael Angelo knew
That can pierce the clouds,
Or inspired by frenzy
Shake the dead in their shrouds;
Forgotten else by mankind,
An old man's eagle mind.

---

11. Blake, *Milton*, plate 30:19. For a discussion of the role of Blake and Beulah in Joyce's *Ulysses*, see my "Time's Ruins and the Mansions of Eternity."

Timon and Lear, Blake and Michelangelo, are named; but the "Nietzschean" character of that mind is indicated both by its inspiring frenzy and by yet another echo—this time of Lionel Johnson's "The Church of a Dream," cited by Yeats in the year he wrote "An Acre of Grass" as the poem by his friend he recalled "most vividly" (E&I 493). "Although the world autumnal be, and pale," in Johnson's poem,

Still in their golden vesture the old Saints prevail;
Alone with Christ, desolate else, left by mankind.

In Yeats's transmutation, characteristic of his *antithetical* alterations of the "religious" position, it is not the "old Saints" but the cloud-piercing eagle mind of an old poet that prevails, and *not* "Alone with Christ, desolate else," but in the visionary company of great artists and impassioned heroes, "Forgotten else by mankind."

It is a mind "inspired by frenzy," for only such frenzy "can make the truth known" by enabling one to "remake" the "self" ("An Acre of Grass," lines 20, 21, 14). The hero, Yeats wrote in *A Vision*, is "wrought to a *frenzy* of desire for *truth* of *self*" (V-B 127, italics added). Yeats's sole example is Nietzsche; appropriately, since here—as in "An Acre of Grass," in "The Spur," perhaps even in his 1934 decision to literally "remake" himself so as to "embody truth" (L 922) by undergoing the Steinach sexual "rejuvenation" operation—Yeats is in accord with the Nietzschean doctrine of "frenzy":

Toward a psychology of the artist. If there is to be art, if there is to be any aesthetic doing and seeing, one physiological condition is indispensable: frenzy [*Rauch*]. . . . All kinds of frenzy . . . above all, the frenzy of sexual excitement, this most ancient and original form of frenzy. . . . What is essential in such frenzy is the feeling of increased strength and fullness. . . . A man in this state transforms things until they mirror his power—until they are reflections of his perfection. This *having to* transform into perfection is—art.[12]

Such are the Dionysian origins, beyond Apollonian craft and form, of that "something *to perfection* brought" in "What Then?"

The old man of that poem—also tempted by the "quiet" of a small old house and garden, surrounding himself with companionship, tenderness, and love—retains some frenzy: "Let the fools rage," he rages. But he *is* guilty, in the language of *The Dawn*, of "canonizing himself"—not as saint but as artist. "You are a . . . poet but no saint," Yeats's wife once told him. "I suppose one has to choose" (L 838). "The work is done," says the old man of "What Then?," pronouncing the canon complete, raising himself "above his life's work."

12. Nietzsche, *Twilight of the Idols*, "Skirmishes of an Untimely Man" 8, 9.

That poetic self-canonization is shaken by its necessary contrary in the Yeatsian dialectic, the admonishing challenge of the Saint, here dramatized as the ghost of the principal singing-master of the soul. For late Yeats resists but does not dismiss that challenge. Indeed, he both defied and celebrated that singing, believing

An aged man is but a paltry thing,
A tattered coat upon a stick, unless
Soul clap its hands and sing, and louder sing
For every tatter in its mortal dress. . . .
   (VP 407)

The soul that must "sing, and louder sing" returns austerely in "What Then?" as Plato's ghost, who "sang" and "louder sang." Being dead, part of his own "ghostly paradigm," Plato is no longer (as he was in "Among School Children") one of Yeats's examples of the price of growing "a famous man." "It means," Yeats wrote of the great stanza on Plato, Aristotle, and Pythagoras, "that even the greatest men are owls, scarecrows, by the time their fame has come." Plato and his fellow philosophers are "old clothes upon old sticks to scare a bird"—or "old *coats*," as the line appeared in the glossing letter to Olivia Shakespear (L 719), even closer to the "tattered coat upon a stick" of "Sailing to Byzantium."

In "What Then?" the owl has become a nightingale, the scarecrow a ghost, but the singing is no longer (as it was in "Sailing to Byzantium") allied with but has become antipodal to man's aesthetic and intellectual "monuments." In the later poem, the melancholy burden of the spiritual song mocks man's enterprise, a mockery that Yeats both fiercely resisted and—as an anti-materialist—endorsed. In part, he agreed with Nietzsche's contention in *The Birth of Tragedy* that Plato and Socrates together typify "the abstractly perfect man, good, wise, just, a dialectician—in a word, the scarecrow." He might even "mock Plotinus' thought / And cry in Plato's teeth" (VP 415), perhaps remembering that Nietzsche's Zarathustra invited men to "laugh at their gloomy sages and at whoever had at any time sat on the tree of life like a black scarecrow."[13] But while Yeats might, like Nietzsche, caricature Plato as a scarecrow, he remained drawn to what Nietzsche denigrated in *The Dawn* §542 as the "mystic lights" of Plato. In annotating selections from the *Genealogy of Morals*, Yeats agreed with Nietzsche that the "Night" of the Soul (associated with Socrates, Plato, and Christ) had to be antithetically opposed by the life-affirming "Day" of the Self (associated with Homer). He could even, in "Vacillation," make the Nietzschean

13. The first of these two Nietzsche passages is from the Haussmann translation of *Die Geburt der Tragödie* (the text in Yeats's library). The passage is cited by F. A. C. Wilson, *Yeats's Iconography*, 178. The second is from *Thus Spoke Zarathustra* 3.12 ("On Old and New Tablets"). Yeats's copy of *Zarathustra*, included in a catalog of his books compiled in the 1920s, is now missing. My quotations are from the Walter Kaufmann translation.

choice his own ("Homer is my example and his unchristened heart") and, in "A Dialogue of Self and Soul," oppose to "the breathless starlit air" of pure spirit his silk-wound sword of life: "all these I set / For emblems of the day against the tower / Emblematical of the night." "But why," he asked, resisting Nietzschean atheism in the margin of one of the *Genealogy* excerpts, "does Nietzsche think that the night has *no* stars?"[14]

Though, as he admitted, he always wrote "coldly" of God (Ex 305), Yeats was reluctant to acknowledge that it was only "weariness," as Nietzsche's Zarathustra claimed, that "created all gods and afterworlds," a case of the body despairing of the earth, touching the "ultimate walls with the fingers of a deluded spirit," and wanting to "crash through these ultimate walls . . . over there to 'that world,'" that "dehumanized inhuman world which is a heavenly nothing." Yeats believed there was something on the other side of those ultimate walls; he even has his Blake "beat upon the wall." But Yeats, for all his table-rapping sessions, was as unwilling as Zarathustra to "fly away from earthly things"[15]—a flight whose "sincerest advocate" Nietzsche specified in the *Genealogy of Morals* (3.25), "Plato versus Homer: that is the complete, the genuine antagonism—there the sincerest advocate of the 'Beyond,' the greatest slanderer of life;[16] here the instinctive deifier, the *golden* nature. To place himself in the service of the ascetic ideal is therefore the most distinctive *corruption* of an artist that is at all possible."

Thus the singing of Plato's formidable ghost—compounded of mockery, threat, and transcendental siren-song—is to be strenuously resisted. Such otherworldly singing crushed the man who dreamed of Faeryland and would, in Nietzsche's ironic twist, *corrupt* the artist, who must suffer and celebrate life, delighting in it and even deifying it rather than slandering it in the name of some world "Beyond." "Do not believe those who speak to you of supernatural hopes!" "Yet the 'supernatural life,'" Yeats scribbled in the margin alongside this passage of *Thus Spoke Zarathustra*, "may be but the soul of the earth, out of which man leaps again, when the circle is complete."[17] Perhaps; but with that naturalizing of the supernatural the prophet of Eternal Recurrence would have no argument.

In the light of such a marginal note, the singing of Plato's ghost seems less metaphysical than dramatic, part of that lifelong Yeatsian agon in which

---

14. VP 403, 477–78. Anthology annotations, pp. 122, 124.

15. *Thus Spoke Zarathustra* 1.3 ("On the Afterworldly") and 1.22 ("On the Gift-Giving Virtue").

16. In one of the notes collected in *The Will to Power*, Nietzsche speaks of "Platonic slander of the senses, preparation of the soil for Christianity" (§427). Of course, Nietzsche liked to slander Plato himself. Every group, he observed in another note in *The Will to Power*, tends to reduce its opponents to caricatures: "Among immoralists it is the moralist: Plato, for example, becomes a caricature in my hands" (§374). We find a similar tendency in Yeats's body-soul debates. Plato's ghost in "What Then?" is in fact a far more formidable opponent than Soul or Crazy Jane's Bishop.

17. Yeats's final annotation in the Thomas Common anthology, p. 193; from *Zarathustra* preface 3.

"the swordsman throughout repudiates the saint, but not without vacillation. Is that perhaps the sole theme?" (L 798). It is, provided Yeats can
either dehumanize and distance the spiritual or, conversely, draw the circle
large enough to encompass—which is to say, *reinterpret*—the spiritual. The
genuine tension in "What Then?" results from the sustained "vacillation"
between two apparently contradictory states of consciousness, the dialectical "conflict" of which "all things are made" (L 918). Though Cleanth
Brooks simplifies Yeats's religious position, specifically his attitude toward
Christianity, he is of course right to note that in Yeats's work, the later
work particularly, "there is rarely a simple rejection of any thesis; there is
rather a kind of poetic dialectic in which the antithesis is played hard over
against the thesis in order to develop a dramatic comment in which the
opposites shall both remain alive and valid in a higher synthesis"—*aufgehoben*, in Hegel's influential term.[18]

Thus, in "What Then?," Yeats can proudly summarize his career (the
industry of youth, the successes and hard-earned happiness of middle age,
and the achieved greatness of old age); comment upon all, both from a
mortal perspective (through a self-mocking parody, based in large part on
Nietzsche, of a "Wordsworthian" old age) and *sub specie aeternitatis* (by
putting in Plato's breathless mouth the "what then?" of a Bhartrihari); and
still maintain a balanced tension between recital and challenge, between
"this" world and "that," between the conflicting claims of Self and Soul. In
dramatically deploying these forces, Yeats was performing as a Hegelian—
still more a Blakean or Nietzschean—dialectician for whom there is no
progression "without Contraries" (MHH, plate 3). Just that dialectical
point, progressing to an affirmation of human life, is made in the *Genealogy
of Morals*, in a passage (3.3) in which Nietzsche celebrates those "well-
constituted, joyful mortals who are far from regarding their unstable equilibrium between 'animal and angel' as necessarily an argument against existence—the subtlest and brightest among them have even found in it, like
Goethe and Hafiz, one more stimulus to life. It is precisely such 'contradictions' that seduce one to existence" (compare *Ecce Homo* 1.2).

We feel the truth of this in reading, say, the Byzantium poems or "A
Dialogue of Self and Soul" or the Crazy Jane sequence or "Supernatural
Songs." The same seduction to existence may be operative even in "What
Then?," a lesser poem set far from the starlit dome that disdains all that man
is, far from the lonely tower where Self and Soul debate. Jane can pit Love's
own "mansion" against the Bishop's "heavenly mansion." In "What Then?,"
the heavenly mansion seems forsworn and love's modest residence is "a
small old house" occupied by an aged artist and his family: a precarious stay
against the ghostly paradigm of Plato himself. But, since artistic accom-

---

18. Brooks, *The Hidden God*, 51. In Hegel, oppositions are *aufgehoben*, that is, simultaneous-
ly annulled, preserved, and raised to a higher level. Abrams refers to the term as "that triple
German equivoque" that Hegel "made into one of the most influential of metaphysical ideas"
(*Natural Supernaturalism*, 177).

plishment transcends materialistic success and since the refrain is no substitute for the poem as a whole, the ghost's question functions not only as a
spume-disdaining Platonic taunt and Indian *tatah kim* but also as a challenge
in the Nietzschean sense: as "one *more* stimulus to life"—and to "art,"
defined by Nietzsche as "this *having to* transform into perfection." Let the
fools rage, let the ghost sing; Yeats's claim endures: "I . . . / Something to
perfection brought."

*   *   *

In his 1930 diary, Yeats conceded of the claims of Self and Soul, of the
antithetical impulse toward self-realization and individual freedom as opposed to the primary "surrender to God of all that I am," that one was "as
much a part of truth as the other" (Ex 304). In poetically dramatizing the
dispute between Self and Soul, however, he usually "enlisted under one
banner and—for the time being—served it zealously," though "with misgivings, knowing the cost of severance."[19]

The poet who at once affirms and mocks his own human and artistic
accomplishment by dramatizing the cost of severance in the question posed
by Plato's ghost is the same man who always remembered with pleasure a
remark made in conversation by Lionel Johnson: "I wish those people who
deny the eternity of punishment could realize their unspeakable vulgarity"
(Au 223). Blakean Yeats was not relishing the threat of hellfire, that eternal
torment of others that provides, according to Tertullian and Aquinas, one
of the chief blisses of the saved and that seemed to Nietzsche the ultimate
example of plebeian *ressentiment*.[20] Yeats's pleasure was instead patrician.
He shared with austere, hieratic Johnson a contempt for crass materialists,
those vulgar modern descendants of the Anglo-French Enlightenment. In
the poem next to be explored and extrapolated from, Yeats finds his truth,
not in the singing of a Platonic ghost or more explicit eternal threat, but in a
litany quite different from that given in "What Then?" The occult litany of
"sources" in "Fragments" is meant to mock the materialists and to validate
a counter-Enlightenment wisdom that comes "Out of a medium's mouth"
and "Out of dark night."

19. Denis Donoghue, in *William Butler Yeats*, ed. Keane, 114.
20. *Genealogy of Morals* 1.15.

II

OUT OF MORE THAN *SPIRITUS MUNDI*:
THE STRANGE BIRTHS OF SPINNING JENNY AND ROUGH BEAST

3

AS IN A GLASS DARKLY: YEATS'S COUNTER-ENLIGHTENMENT AS CRYSTALLIZED IN "FRAGMENTS"

The mischief began at the end of the seventeenth century when man became passive before a mechanized nature. That lasted to our own day with the exception of a brief period between Smart's *Song of David* and the death of Byron, wherein imprisoned man beat upon the door. . . . Soul must become its own betrayer, its own deliverer, the one activity, the mirror turn lamp.

—Yeats, Introduction to the *Oxford Book of Modern Verse*

Where got I that truth?
Out of a medium's mouth. . . .
—Yeats, "Fragments" (II)

When I saw at Mrs. Crandon's objects moved and words spoken from some aerial centre, where there was nothing human, I rejected England and France and accepted Europe. Europe belongs to Dante and the witches' sabbath, not to Newton.
—Yeats, 1933 letter to Olivia Shakespear

"Or, to simplify the tale" (Ex 359). With that optional infinitive Yeats introduced the opening section of the two-part poem I will be temporarily recomplicating. To simplify is, sometimes, to clarify, more frequently to distort. But we often *have* to simplify, and we increasingly if reluctantly recognize something anticipated by such sixteenth-century skeptics as Montaigne but anathema to the Enlightenment, with its faith in objectivity, the constancy of human nature, and the universality of human goals: namely, we recognize the inevitability of perspectivism, that, as Blake said and Yeats repeated, "the eye altering alters all." Further, as that master perspectivist Nietzsche remarks in his "Fragment of a Critique of Schopenhauer," also echoed by Yeats, "the errors of great men are venerable because they are more fruitful than the truths of little men."[1]

---

1. Blake, "The Mental Traveller." The line is cited by Yeats in "The Symbolism of Poetry" (E&I 159). Nietzsche, *Musarionausgabe* 1.393, in *The Portable Nietzsche*, 30. Cf. Yeats: "Schopenhauer can do no wrong in my eyes: I no more quarrel with his errors than I do with a mountain

I have chosen another brief and purportedly "fragmentary" work offering a perspective on the Enlightenment and its seventeenth-century background: a perspective that reveals, if not all, at least much of the essential
Yeats. This epigrammatic poem, written between 1931 and 1933 and actually entitled "Fragments," is an example of what the poet praised as his own
true mask, "simplification through intensity" (V-B 140). It is also a meeting
place for Yeats's three central traditions: the Romantic, the occult, and the
Anglo-Irish, as well as an oblique example of the deeper wisdom he seems
to have attained by submitting himself to the female perspective of Crazy
Jane and a Woman Young and Old. Here is the poem:

I

Locke sank into a swoon;
The Garden died;
God took the spinning-jenny
Out of his side.

II

Where got I that truth?
Out of a medium's mouth,
Out of nothing it came,
Out of the forest loam,
Out of dark night where lay
The crowns of Nineveh.

Is it anti-intellectual obscurantism? sentimental archaism? a fruitful error
more venerable than the truths of little men? or the imaginative "truth" it
proclaims itself to be—"profound and salutary, . . . magnificent as a work
of imagination," despite certain excesses, as Yeats remarked of Spengler's
Decline of the West? (LTSM 150). An attempt at an answer might begin with
an epigram upon which Yeats plays in his own epigram. If we think of
modern history in terms of rondure, of a curve from the pre-Enlightenment
scientific revolution to the scientific revolution of our own century, we may
be reminded not only of Pope's "Epitaph, Intended for Sir Isaac Newton in
Westminster Abbey"—"Nature and Nature's laws lay hid in night, / God
said, *Let Newton be!* and all was light"—but also of J. C. Squire's modern
squelch—"It did not last: the Devil, howling *Ho! / Let Einstein be!* restored
the status quo."

The restoration—paradoxically, through a second scientific revolution—
of an ancient status quo re-flooding the universe with pre-Newtonian darkness in part parallels the revaluation of "Fragments," with its restoration of

---

cataract. Error is but the abyss into which he precipitates his truth" (LTSM 117–18). Nietzsche's "necessary fictions" are discussed in the final chapter of Hans Vaihinger's *The Philosophy
of "As If,"* 2d ed., and in my own "On Truth and Lie in Nietzsche."

a pre- (and post-) Newtonian darkness. Three kinds of darkness should be distinguished. The first is the nightmare to which Yeats, following Blake, reduced the Enlightenment itself—by which they meant the eighteenth century and its immediate precursors, particularly Blake's unholy trinity of "Bacon, Newton, Locke." The second is the "dark night" or deeper wisdom of the irrational or the more-than-rational: a darkness suppressed by the Enlightenment but that Yeats, immersed in the occult as well as in the Romantics, found both "luminous" and "fruitful" (E&I 332). The third, Yeats having just created two poetic sequences spoken by women, is the mystery of the feminine, the fecund darkness of woman and of Nature, which the mechanistic rationalists and Enlightenment *lumières* either wooed in order to conquer and demystify or turned from and fled.

I The Background: Locke, Newton, Mechanism; Berkeley, the Romantics, Whitehead

"Locke sank into a swoon." Why Locke in particular? Usually, he is one of a triad, though always coupled with a partially misunderstood Newton. Misunderstood because, like the Romantics before him, Yeats responds less to Newton—a repressor of his own youthful Hermeticism, but still a theist as repelled as the Cambridge Platonists were by Godless mechanism—than to the Newtonian "system," the mathematicophysical theory of "celestial mechanics" that, gradually cut loose during the course of the eighteenth century from the divine hand that kept the planets in motion, "lost its religious and metaphysical sublimity and became a self-sufficient material mechanism."[2] In the process, Pope's light-bringer was himself transformed, changing through changing perspectives. For Coleridge, at the age of twenty-three in his *Religious Musings*, "Adoring Newton his serener eye / Raises to heaven," only to become, by the time Coleridge is thirty, "a mere materialist." Wordsworth vacillated, but, in the majestic lines added to *The Prelude* after 1830, the statue of Newton at Cambridge suggested "The marble index of a mind for ever / Voyaging through strange seas of Thought, alone." Blake, of course, passionately maintained his understandable if unfair hostility: another simplification through intensity.

Yeats was echoing Blake when he declared: "Descartes, Locke, and Newton took away the world and gave us its excrement instead" (Ex 325). In an

2. Douglas Bush, *Science and English Poetry: A Historical Sketch, 1590–1950*, 83: "Blake, Coleridge, and Wordsworth, in rebelling against a mechanistic universe and upholding an animistic one, were much closer to Newton himself than they realized." Hans Eichner has recently noted not only that "Newton could never quite rid himself of the notion that God must exist to keep the planets in motion" but also that "even that arch-materialist the Baron d'Holbach, as late as 1770, ascribes to dead matter an innate 'nisus,' or striving, which, rather than gravitation, accounts for the fall of bodies" ("The Rise of Modern Science and the Genesis of Romanticism," 9). In his note to this sentence, Eichner adds a remark relevant to the present chapter: "In the rest of this paper, so as not to obscure the main issues, I ignore the residual vitalism evident in many seventeenth- and eighteenth-century scientists." Certainly, the Romantic philosophers and poets tended to ignore that residue.

earlier draft of this statement, Yeats pitted the appropriate Anglo-Irish champion against the chief villain: "Locke took away the living world and gave instead its excrement; Berkeley gave back the living world but the newspapers talk as if it were still an excrement."[3] In his 1931 essay on Berkeley, discussing the utilitarianism of what he ironically refers to as the much-lauded "English empirical genius," Yeats contrasts "truth," which is "moth-like and fluttering and yet can terrify," to the "abstractions" to which men give "belief, service, devotion." In a passage reflecting his reading, five years earlier, of Whitehead's *Science and the Modern World*, Yeats observes that of all these "serviceable" abstractions,

the most comprehensive, the most useful, was invented by Locke when he separated the primary and secondary qualities; and from that day to this the conception of a physical world without colour, taste, sound, tangibility, though indicted by Berkeley as Burke was to indict Warren Hastings fifty years later, and proved mere abstract extension, a mere category of the mind, has remained the assumption of science, the groundwork of every text-book. It worked, and the mechanical inventions of the next age, its symbols that seemed its confirmation, worked even better, and it worked best of all in England where Edmund Spenser's inscription over the gates of his magic city seemed to end "Do not believe too much": elsewhere it is the grosser half of that dialectical materialism the Socialist Prince Mirsky calls "the firm foundation-rock of European Socialism," and works all the mischief Berkeley foretold.

   (E&I 400–401)

Yeats began this essay by lamenting the decline of "imagination," which "sank after the death of Shakespeare." Intensity had "passed to another faculty," that of the philosophic intellect, and Yeats expressed his "delight" in Irish Berkeley, who defined "the philosophy of a 'neighboring nation,'" . . . the philosophy of Newton and Locke, in three sentences, [and] wrote after each that Irishmen thought otherwise" (E&I 396). The argument can (and has) been made that, far from refuting Locke, Berkeley misunderstood his position, particularly on the distinction between primary and secondary qualities. It can also be argued that, despite the inconsistencies and confusion with which it is presented, Locke's distinction (anticipated by Descartes, Galileo, and Newton, among others) is valid, in the sense that it "works." No matter; what did matter to Yeats was that, as that hater of abstractions Berkeley had said, "We Irishmen think otherwise" (E&I 333–34).

There was reason to think otherwise. At the commencement of the Enlightenment, "shortly after the schools of Newton and Locke had completed their work," Berkeley had, notes Whitehead, "made all the right

    3. Typescript of Yeats's introduction to *Fighting the Waves* in National Library MS. 8774(2); quoted by Donald Torchiana, *W. B. Yeats and Georgian Ireland*, 249, n. 89.

criticisms, at least in principle," had "laid his finger exactly on the weak spots which they had left."[4] In Matthew Arnold's "Memorial Verses," Goethe, reading each "human wound" and "weakness," "struck his finger on the place, / And said: *Thou ailest here, and here!*" Whitehead's diagnostic image would be an appropriate echo of "Memorial Verses" since the occasion of that poem was the death of one of the principal heroes of *Science and the Modern World*, Wordsworth, and the most plangent note was Arnold's cry in the wilderness now that "few or none" were left to hear nature's "voice right": "where will Europe's latter hour / Again find Wordsworth's *healing* power?"

That power was most profoundly gauged by Coleridge. What had to be "healed," as Berkeley had insisted from the outset, was the wound inflicted by Lockean sensationalism and mechanistic philosophy; and the man chosen to be physician to the post-revolutionary iron age of dereliction and dismay was, Coleridge believed, Wordsworth—who of course concurred in his friend's judgment. In *Biographia Literaria*, attacking the division produced by Locke and the mechanists, Coleridge asked rhetorically, "What is harmony but a mode of relation, the very *esse* of which is *percipi*?" He borrowed Berkeley's Latin axiom to make the same point in his distinction, in *The Friend*, between the "intuition of things which arises when we possess ourselves, as one with the whole," and the alienated state in which "we think of ourselves as separated beings, and place nature in antithesis to the mind, as object to subject, thing to thought, death to life." The dissociating demons are Descartes and Locke, named by Coleridge in the important letter of May 1815 in which, having just read the disappointing *Excursion* and the great "Prospectus" to *The Recluse*, he reminded Wordsworth of their plan for *The Recluse* as a whole:

I supposed you first . . . to have laid a solid and immoveable foundation for the Edifice by removing the sandy Sophisms of Locke, and the Mechanic Dogmatists . . . Next, I understood that you would take the Human Race in the concrete . . . to have affirmed a Fall in some sense . . . attested to by Experience & Conscience . . . to point out however a manifest Scheme of Redemption from this Slavery, of Reconciliation from this Enmity with Nature . . . in short, the necessity of a general revolution in the modes of developing and disciplining the human mind by the substitution of Life, and Intelligence . . . for the philosophy of mechanism which in every thing that is most worthy of the human Intellect strikes *Death*.[5]

The same enslaving epistemology and philosophy of mechanism; the same Fall and Death; the same need for the reintegration of fragmented

---

4. Whitehead, *Science and the Modern World*, 66–67.
5. *Collected Letters of Samuel Taylor Coleridge*, ed. Earl Leslie Griggs, 4:574–75. For the Coleridge passages quoted earlier in this paragraph, see *Biographia Literaria* 1.117-18, and *The Friend* 1.520 (texts cited from *The Collected Works of Samuel Taylor Coleridge*, gen. ed. Kathleen Coburn).

Man, divided from himself and from Nature (Wordsworth's "goodly universe" to which "the discerning intellect" should be "wedded . . . / In love and holy passion"): all recur in Locke's swoon, the Garden's death, and the lifeless, asexual birth of the spinning jenny, with Yeats substituting Life for Death by way of the bizarre yet fecund "sources" given in part II of the poem. Wordsworth and Coleridge would doubtless find Yeats's proposed cure almost as dangerous as the illness; but "Fragments" remains Romantic and retains its power, diagnostic if not quite "healing," because redemption, reconciliation, and mental-emotional revolution, the three Rs called for in Coleridge's letter and projected in Wordsworth's "Prospectus," have yet to be accomplished.

By the turn into the second quarter of our century (when Whitehead published and Yeats read the immensely influential *Science and the Modern World*), Western man, devastated by the horrors of the Great War and more firmly than ever in the grip of positivism and materialism, certainly needed redeeming. What was required at the very least was a wider conception of reality, a conception standing, in Whitehead's Coleridgean phrase, "nearer to the complete concreteness of our intuitive experience." As Yeats must have been delighted to discover, the "difficult and profound" Whitehead (L 712) recognized as kindred spirits both the Romantics and Berkeley.[6]

Not, of course, that Whitehead accepted the bishop's theological idealism. Berkeley's "immaterialist hypothesis" is that inert, mindless, material substance is an impossibility. For Berkeley as for Blake (to whom "Mental Things are alone Real"), *esse est percipi*; to be is to be perceived, or to be the active perceiver, that is, God. Yeats agreed—with a crucial Blakean proviso. "The essential sentence" in Berkeley, Yeats wrote his friend Sturge Moore, "is of course 'things only exist in being perceived,' and I can only call that perception God's when I add Blake's 'God only acts or is in existing beings or men'" (LTSM 80, slightly misquoting MHH, plate 16).

Berkeley, Yeats noted, refuted Locke's troublesome distinction. Nothing, Berkeley argued, having so-called primary qualities (solidity, extension, figure, mobility) can exist without having the secondary qualities (those producing the various sensations: color, odor, sound, warmth, and so forth);

---

6. The *differences* are, of course, obvious—not only between Whitehead and Berkeley but also between Berkeley and the Romantics. Nevertheless, Whitehead and Yeats were right to ally themselves with Berkeley and Berkeley with the Romantic poets. The point is worth reaffirming since precisely the opposite position is argued by Donald Davie in "Yeats, Berkeley, and Romanticism," a 1955 *Irish Writing* article reprinted in *English Literature and British Philosophy*, ed. S. P. Rosenbaum. Focusing on Berkeley as philosopher of common sense rather than as subjective idealist, Davie, in order "to buttress" his "case for an anti-Romantic Yeats," argues that "later Yeats . . . rejects Romanticism," partly in the name of Berkeley. His own bias against Romanticism allows Davie, normally a scrupulous reader, to quote Yeats as having declared "The romantic movement seems related . . . to Locke's mechanical philosophy" (279, 282, 283). The ellipsis, of course, reverses Yeats's whole position. This sentence in his essay on Berkeley actually begins: "The romantic movement seems related to the idealist philosophy; the naturalistic movement, Stendhal's mirror dawdling down a lane, to Locke's mechanical philosophy" (E&I 404).

since the latter cannot exist "without the mind," neither can the former. Therefore no distinction between the two is possible.

In Yeats's estimation, Berkeley restored the living world for all of us, even, during his *annus mirabilis*, for "abstract" Coleridge:

Berkeley thought that by showing that certain abstractions—the "primary qualities"—did not exist he could create a philosophy so concrete that the common people could understand it. . . . During the year and a half in which Coleridge wrote almost all his good poetry, the first part of *Christabel*, *The Ancient Mariner*, *Kubla Khan*, he was influenced by Berkeley. . . . Berkeley's insistence on the particular and his hatred of abstraction possibly delivered Coleridge . . . though but for a time. (Ex 304)

The later Berkeleyan position that it is "through the particular we approach the Divine Ideas" also appealed to Yeats; but *his* man was essentially "the Berkeley of the *Commonplace Book*," who valued concrete particulars for themselves (Ex 299, 304).

It is no more necessary for us than it was for Whitehead or Yeats to follow Berkeley all the way to extreme perceptual idealism in order to appreciate his "realist" critique of the limitations of scientific materialism or to grasp, as Whitehead and Yeats did, his connection with the Romantic poets. "The nature poetry of the romantic revival," wrote Whitehead of Wordsworth, Coleridge, and Shelley,

was a protest on behalf of the organic view of nature, and also a protest against the exclusion of value from the essence of matter of fact. In this aspect of it, the romantic movement may be conceived as a revival of Berkeley's protest which had been launched a hundred years earlier. The romantic reaction was a protest on behalf of value. (*Science*, 94)

The strictly quantitative, objective world indifferent to human values, the inhuman world of Locke's primary qualities: this alone was Nature to the mechanists. Sensations projected by the mind "clothe" bodies in external nature; but we must be under no illusions. These bodies, in Whitehead's memorable replication of seventeenth-century scientific philosophy,

are perceived as with qualities which in reality do not belong to them, qualities which in fact are purely the offspring of the mind. Thus nature gets credit which should in truth be reserved for ourselves: the rose for its scent: the nightingale for his song: and the sun for his radiance. The poets are entirely mistaken. They should address their lyrics to themselves, and should turn them into odes of self-congratulation on the excellency of the human mind. Nature is a dull affair, soundless, scentless, colourless; merely the hurrying of material, endlessly, meaninglessly. (*Science*, 54)

It was to this sardonic description of "the mechanical theory" that Yeats directed Sturge Moore in the March 1926 letter in which he announced, "I have just got Whitehead's *Science and the Modern World*," a book "I think I shall be in fair agreement with." A few days later he had "read the greater part of it and so far it seems to me my own point of view. He proves, as I think, that the mechanical theory is untrue (though it works, like other untrue things) and substitutes a theory of organism." Whitehead's "whole doctrine of organism," Yeats added, implies the presence of "mind," for "organism without mind—'choice'—in some sense would be mechanism" (LTSM 87,89). Yeats was of course accurate in his implicit assumption that it was against this mechanistic conception of nature that the Romantics protested, though their rebellion took a reciprocal form more epistemologically complex than Whitehead's ironic contrast suggests: that of what Wordsworth called an "ennobling interchange" between mind and nature, the latter conceived as "what we half-create and what perceive" (*Prelude* 13.375; "Tintern Abbey").

In any case, the soundless, scentless, colorless, meaningless world that was the "practical outcome of the characteristic scientific philosophy which closed the seventeenth century" was a conception—Whitehead continued in a passage remembered by Yeats in his Berkeley essay—notable for "its astounding efficiency."

It has held its own as the guiding principle of scientific studies ever since. It is still reigning. Every university in the world organizes itself in accordance with it. No alternative system of organizing the pursuit of scientific truth has been suggested. It is not only reigning, but it is without a rival.

And yet—it is quite unbelievable. This conception of the universe is surely framed in terms of high abstractions, and the paradox only arises because we have mistaken our abstractions for concrete realities.[7]

The mistake was what Whitehead called the Fallacy of Misplaced Concreteness: the confusion of scientific abstractions with the living world we actually experience through perceptions and sensations no less real and valuable for having been stigmatized as merely "secondary" and "subjective." Sharing Berkeley's and Whitehead's anti-abstractionist emphasis on human values and on the universe as a concrete, organic unity, Yeats used the bishop's own language in his 1930 diary: "Berkeley restored the world, . . . the world that only exists because it shines and sounds." (Which does not make Yeats a simple materialist: "True art is expressive and symbolic, and makes . . . every sound, every colour, . . . a signature of some unanalysable imaginative essence.")[8]

7. *Science and the Modern World*, 54–55. For other remarks of Whitehead close to Yeats's in the Berkeley essay, see 66, 67, 75, 86, 88, and 94.
8. Ex 325, E&I 140.

From the 1920s on, the attack on "Locke's mechanical philosophy" (E&I 404–5) could be pressed from either side of the Anglo-Irish position represented by Berkeley. One could either adopt, as both Whitehead and Yeats did, his commonsense realism or celebrate, as Yeats does in "Blood and the Moon,"

God-appointed Berkeley that proved all things a dream,
That this pragmatical, preposterous pig of a world, its
      farrow that so solid seem,
Must vanish on the instant if the mind but change its
      theme.

In the early days, however, Yeats's armory against Lockean mechanism and mental passivity consisted of Blake (another Irishman, according to the fanciful genealogy of Yeats and his Blake co-editor Edwin Ellis), Shelley, and the occult, particularly varieties of Platonic and Neoplatonic tradition. He was in accord with Thomas Taylor's vigorous contrast in his *Commentaries of Proclus* (1788–1789): "According to Mr. Locke, the soul is a mere rasa tabula, an empty recipient, a mechanical blank. According to Plato she is an ever-written tablet, a plenitude of forms, a vital intellectual energy."

But the crucial figure, early and late, was Blake; Yeats borrowed his perspective, his prejudice, and his principal villain. When, in the important introduction to his play about Swift, *The Words upon the Window-pane*, Yeats declares, "I can see in a sort of nightmare vision the 'primary qualities' torn from the side of Locke, . . . some obscure person somewhere inventing the spinning jenny" (Ex 358–59), his nightmare parallels Blake's horrified vision of the "Loom of Locke" (*Jerusalem* 15:15) spinning us back to chaos as the inevitable consequence of the bifurcation of object and subject, primary and secondary qualities. "Deduct from a rose its redness," wrote Berkeleyan Blake, "from a lilly its whiteness, from a diamond its hardness, from a sponge its softness, from an oak its heighth, from a daisy its lowness, & rectify every thing in Nature as the Philosophers do, & then we shall return to Chaos, & God will be compelld to be Excentric if he Creates."[9] Thus, in Blake's myth, the Fall from Eden is manifested as the creation of Lockean matter, a chaotic Ulro of dead objects passively perceived by minds reduced to so many *tabulae rasae*.

II. The Nightmare:
Spinning Jenny versus Living Eve

Yeats is never closer to Blake than in "Fragments" (I), where he emulates not only his mentor's attack on Locke but also his genius for epigram and

---

9. Blake, Marginalia on p. 532 of Lavater's *Aphorisms on Man* (1789), in the Erdman edition of Blake, *Poetry and Prose*, 584–85.

crystallization, Blake being, as Northrop Frye has said, "perhaps the finest gnomic artist in English literature."[10] In Yeats's gnomic vision, which Douglas Bush has called "certainly the shortest and perhaps not the least comprehensive history of modern civilization,"[11] the Enlightenment is revealed as a nightmare for the imagination; and the monster that rides this spirit-sealing sleep of reason is the mechanistic conception of matter, symbolized by the invention epitomizing the Industrial Revolution:

> Locke sank into a swoon;
> The Garden died;
> God took the spinning-jenny
> Out of his side.

This parody of Genesis 2 makes God an "Excentric" creator indeed. It replaces the divinely anesthetized flesh of Adam with Locke's imaginatively inert body (sunk in that fall into division Blake called "Single vision & Newton's sleep") and substitutes for Eve, the beautiful embodiment of Adam's dream, a mechanical contraption, a cog in the dark Satanic mills of which it is proleptic.[12]

The replacement of Eve by spinning jenny recalls the anti-industrialist myth of Henry Adams (familiar to Yeats), in which a nurturing, paradoxically sexual Virgin is replaced by the Dynamo, emblematic of the death of the female principle, the mechanization of organic nature, and the withering both of sexual vitality and of the religious impulse. In his similarly "feminist" emphasis, discussed below, Yeats swerves from Blake. Nevertheless, Yeats's Locke, Garden, machine, and delivering deity are all Blakean. Blake's God of the fallen world, Urizen, presides over an Enlightenment world-machine perceived as the "Loom of Locke" washed by the "Waterwheels of Newton":

> cruel Works
> Of many Wheels I view, wheel without wheel, with cogs tyrannic
> Moving by compulsion each other.[13]

The Urizenic God whose stony law governs this celestial machine as well as the "intricate wheels invented, wheel without wheel, / . . . to bind to labours in Albion" workers in "sorrowful drudgery to obtain a scanty pittance of bread" (*Jerusalem* 65:26) is the God who takes objectified matter, in the confirming symbolic form of the spinning jenny, from the side of Locke. That machine is a far cry from the "beating heart" torn from the

---

10. Frye, *Fearful Symmetry: A Study of William Blake*, 5.
11. Bush, *Science and English Poetry*, 158.
12. For the allusions, see Blake's 1802 letter to Butts (Erdman 693) and the lyric "And did those feet?"
13. *Jerusalem* 15:15, 17–19.

"side" of "holy Dionysus" in the poem preceding "Fragments" in Yeats's *Collected Poems*—unless we recall that for Harvey, the seventeenth-century discoverer of its function, the heart, too, was a "piece of machinery in which one wheel gives motion to another," a hydraulic pump consisting of Blakean "Water-wheels."[14] In any case, the grotesque birth of the spinning jenny is the direct consequence (for Heraclitean Yeats, all things live each other's death, die each other's life) of the Garden having "died," a death caused by Locke's swoon. Yeats's Garden, as the parody of Genesis confirms, is Edenic; but it is also Blakean and anti-Blakean.

In his assault on the fundamental denial with which Locke opens the *Essay Concerning Human Understanding*, Blake insists that "Innate Ideas are in Every Man, Born with him," and that, since he "Brings All that he has or Can have Into the World" with him, "Man is Born *Like a Garden* ready Planted & Sown."[15] Despite the organic imagery, however, Blake is merely employing a simile for the innate wisdom of man, who is not passive material shaped by the external world but its active maker. That material world itself—the fallen "vegetable" world of Nature he calls "Generation"—Blake always dismisses with contempt as an alien hindrance to vision, the female delusion "Vala." Indeed, the Satanic trio of "Bacon, Newton & Locke," constituting "the feminine Tabernacle" in "the temple of Natural Religion," worships "the Goddess Nature, / Mystery, Babylon the Great" (*Jerusalem* 66:14, 93:21–24). Yeats's Garden, on the other hand—though, like Blake's, primarily an image of ready-planted innate wisdom and of prelapsarian unified consciousness—is organic and feminine. That identification—confirmed by the "medium's mouth" and "forest loam" of part II—is clear in part I, where the Garden dies to give birth to a mechanical substitute for Eve.

While Adam delved, Eve spun; so did that industrial spin-off of the Deists' clockwork universe, James Hargreaves's mechanical "jenny." Seizing on the emblematic non-coincidence that the machine has a woman's name, Yeats offers what would seem an un-Blakean equation: the suppression of the "living world" taken away by Locke with estrangement from and suppression of the vital female principle. Indeed, the biblical text parodied in "Fragments" (I) began that unhappy story.

Though canonically relegated to the second chapter of Genesis, the Yahwistic version of woman's creation—in which God causes deep sleep to fall upon Adam, from whose side he removes the unneeded rib he makes into Eve (Gen. 2:21–22)—predates the Priestly version (Gen. 1:26–27), in which God says let "us" make *adam* (a human being, derived from *adamah*, soil) in "our" image, after "our" likeness, the resultant creation being "male and

---

14. Harvey is quoted by Herbert Butterfield, *The Origins of Modern Science, 1300–1800*, 62.

15. Blake, Reynolds Marginalia (in Erdman, *Poetry and Prose*, 637, 645–46; my italics). Blake notes in the Reynolds Marginalia that he read Locke's *Essay* with "Contempt & Abhorrence" (650).

female" together—in one tradition, Adam and unsubservient Lilith. More than a different tradition, the patriarchal Yahwistic version, in which a dependent helpmeet is belatedly created out of her precedent lord, both demotes woman and, in effect, usurps her creative function.[16] "The specific consciousness we call scientific," notes James Hillman, "is the long-sharpened tool of the masculine mind that has discarded parts of its own substance, calling it 'Eve,' 'female,' and 'inferior.'"[17] Blake, despite his dread of the unredeemed "Female Will," would agree: his apocalyptic myth calls for the reintegration of the divided self through reunion with the discarded female "Emanation."

In "Fragments" (I), Eve falls victim to mechanization, a mechanization including that of the birth process itself. As in Genesis 2, the delivery is from a male "parent," but, perverting even that vision, the offspring is a machine. The role of both creator and midwife is performed by a masculine God; needless to say, there is no sexual contact. The "swoon" in the poem, neither sexual nor female, is simply the imaginative oblivion of the empiricist, the actual place of delivery his "side"—a dry, "clean, well-lighted place" far removed from what Yeats's Woman Young, identifying her womb with earth's female flesh, calls her "dark declivities."[18]

As recent creator of both the Woman Young and Old and Crazy Jane sequences, Yeats would have been particularly sensitive to the gynophobic aspects of mechanistic rationalism, that "masculinization of thought" and "flight" from "woman's fertile body" at the heart of Cartesian rationalism and British empiricism.[19] "Fragments" (I) accurately telescopes this slice of Western intellectual (and emotional and political) history. The masculinization begun in Genesis 2 and confirmed by orthodox Christianity was completed with a vengeance by the mechanical philosophers of the seventeenth and eighteenth centuries. Expanding on the doctrine that God the Father created the cosmos with no feminine assistance and made Eve out of Adam, they diminished woman's role even in human procreation. According to one of several bizarre "containment" theories—the animalculist version of *emboîtement*—microcosmic prototypes of the whole human race were said to have been formed in the Adamic semen by the Creator, *ab origine mundi*; in the words of the Leibnizian G. F. Meier, "Adam carried all men in his seed." Whether in this animalculist or in less extreme versions, preforma-

16. Alternatively, one *could* argue that woman is the culminating creation, coming at the end of an ascending order of creation and made from human tissue rather than from clay.

17. Hillman, "On Psychological Femininity," in *The Myth of Analysis*, 250.

18. VP 535–36. The drafts of this poem, "Parting," reveal that its marvelous concluding noun first entered the poem as an adjective, "declivitous," describing mountain slopes. Hemingway's phrase, the title of his short story, was perceptively applied to "Fragments" by Robert Bly in *News of the Universe*.

19. A much-discussed subject. See, for example, Karl Stern, *The Flight from Woman*; Simone de Beauvoir, *The Second Sex*; Carolyn Merchant, *The Death of Nature*; Brian Easlea, *Witch-Hunting: Magic and the New Philosophy*; and Susan Bordo, *The Flight to Objectivity: Essays on Cartesianism and Culture*.

tionist theory posited total creation at a single stroke by a Father God, a theory the eighteenth-century French naturalist Charles Bonnet pronounced "one of the most beautiful victories of pure reason over the senses."[20]

What, for the mechanist *lumières*, enhanced the "beauty" and "purity" of this Cartesian triumph was that it minimized or, at its extreme, utterly obliterated the "impure," sensuous, and darkly mysterious function of woman in procreation. For Descartes and his fellow mechanists, the world is remade so that all generativity and creativity falls to the "father" rather than the female "flesh" of the world. "The specifics of mechanistic reproductive theory are a microcosmic recapitulation of the mechanistic vision itself."[21] From the mechanists' perspective, matter, no longer *Mater*, was objectified, perceived as barren, Descartes's inert *res extensa*, and sharply demarcated from the knower—an epistemological separation that can only lead to emotional alienation and estrangement, what Coleridge called "Enmity," Nature being utterly "other," in fact, dead. The Western mechanical philosophers, having chosen to cut themselves "adrift from 'mother earth,'" left themselves with "no alternative but to appropriate the physical world . . . mechanically and asexually" (Easlea, *Witch-Hunting*, 245).

That appropriation and exploitation took the form of the ongoing bourgeois Industrial Revolution to which the scientific revolution had given birth: the very "tale" simplified through intensity in the first of Yeats's "Fragments." The simplification takes the form of a nightmare vision in which Nature is dead, the flow of sexual energy stemmed, and the womb itself superfluous—all victims of a distanced, detached masculinization and mechanization. Along with the Garden of Eden and of innate ideas, what has "died" in "Fragments" (I) is the feminine principle—whether we think of it in terms of the organic world view, of the biological birth process, or of the industrial replacement of the womblike cottage and woman spinner by the regimented, rectangular factory with its foreman and many-spindled machines. As Yeats once put it in a wry understatement, "Machinery had not separated from handicraft wholly for the world's good" (Au 192).

In his imaginative contrast of a mechanistic Enlightenment with vital Romanticism, Yeats is one-sided, but his compelling synopsis of the pre-Enlightenment and his parody of the Yahwistic myth in Genesis seem "salutary and profound." In his copy of *Science and the Modern World*, a text emphasizing the dynamic organicism he also encountered in the mechanical-organic distinction Coleridge lifted from A. W. Schlegel, Yeats synopsized Whitehead's chapter "The Romantic Reaction" with another variation on the Genesis 2 creation-metaphor: "The dry rib (Pope) becomes Eve (Nature) with Wordsworth."[22]

Yeats's marginal shorthand also synopsizes the Romantic project. The

---

20. Both Meier and Bonnet are cited by Easlea, *Witch-Hunting*, 148–49.
21. Bordo, *The Flight to Objectivity*, 110.
22. O'Shea, *A Descriptive Catalog*, item 2258.

rationalists and empiricists, with their sapless abstraction, had dried the marrow from the bone. Through imagination, emotion, intuition, and an inner sympathetic consciousness of the creative flow underlying and pervading the universe, the Romantics had reanimated everything the rationalists, perennially blind to these deeper modes of awareness, had mechanized and masculinized, desiccated and deadened. Romanticism had restored the world of creative vitality: *natura naturans*, personified since the Middle Ages as a goddess (in a place "so sote and grene," said Chaucer, "upon an hil of floures, / Was set this noble Goddesse of Nature") and by Wordsworth as "the mysterious mother of humanity, brooding in omnipresence."[23] For Yeats, suspended between Blake and Wordsworth, Nature was to be demechanized less by being humanized than by being transformed into living symbol. His equation of Enlightenment Pope, "whom I dislike" (L 773), with the dry rib and of Romantic Wordsworth with the living Eve is therefore a symbolic simplification through intensity. What he wants is the sharpest possible contrast between sterility and vitality. While later Wordsworth saw the rationalist light, Yeats, like Blake, permanently accepted the view that the turn toward mechanism and materialism—for him, the immediate legacy of seventeenth-century analytic thought—epitomized the whole of the Anglo-French eighteenth century. We might protest the blackening of Descartes and Newton, Locke and Pope, with a brush perhaps more appropriately applied to Holbach or, to follow the logic of Yeats's metaphor of the birth of the spinning jenny, to La Mettrie with his scandalous "Man a Machine." But here, as elsewhere, Yeats sees the whole scientific age and subsequent Enlightenment as in a Blakean glass, darkly—though the Yeatsian countervision, unlike Blake's, is another, and female, form of mysterious darkness.

Another kind of "glass" is implicit in the scene presented in "Fragments" (I). When Yeats's Locke swoons, he succumbs to antivisionary passivity. The Edenic Garden that "died" is populated not only by the noble Goddess of Nature but also by innate ideas. It is that Blakean Garden allied to "the Grove of Academia, where Plato's heirs maintained the existence of a more active perception," and the Garden of Platonic forms itself, "Henry More's Anima Mundi" (Myth 346), that, as Yeats knew, "Spenser could still celebrate as the Gardens of Adonis."[24] The chief of "Plato's heirs," the emanationist philosopher who replaced Plato's reflective metaphor of the mind (as opposed to the active Platonic soul) with the projective metaphor of an overflowing fountain of light, was Plotinus, as indispensable an ancestor for Yeats as for Coleridge:

I may not hope from outward forms to win

23. Chaucer, *The Parliament of Fowles*, lines 296, 302–3. Alfred Cobban's accurate description of Wordsworthian nature occurs in his *Edmund Burke and the Revolt against the Eighteenth Century*.

24. Whitaker, *Swan and Shadow: Yeats's Dialogue with History*, 100.

The passion and the life, whose fountains are within.

O Lady! we receive but what we give,
And in our life alone does Nature live:
Ours is her wedding garment, ours her shroud![25]

Here, in the Dejection ode, adapting the luminous fountain image of
Plotinus and emotionalizing Kant, Coleridge, like Berkeley and Blake,
breaks down Cartesian and Lockean separations by asserting that *res cogitans*
and *res extensa* are *not* mutually exclusive, that there *is* no objective "primary" world, that Nature exists and moves us only as it is conditioned by
our subjective states. "Nature in herself," said Yeats, "has no power except
to die and to forget" (E&I 171). According to the ode (originally, and
significantly, Coleridge's verse-epistle to the woman he loved), Nature is
either alive, "wed" to us by our own inner spirit and power, or dead, an
"inanimate cold world"; it all depends on what *we* bring to the experience of
perception. In his synopsis of the offending doctrine of the mind as *tabula
rasa*, Coleridge, examining the "necessary consequences of the Hartleian
theory" of associationism, spoke of the passive role to which we are reduced, "the mere quicksilver plating behind a looking-glass; and in this
alone consists the poor worthless I!" Yeats inserted in his copy of *Biographia
Literaria* at this page in chapter 7 (the same chapter from which he borrowed
his image of the contemplative-creative mind as "a long-legged fly upon the
stream") a small piece of paper on which he wrote, "plating behind a
looking glass."[26] In his correspondence with Sturge Moore, he deplored the
turning of the "mind . . . into the quicksilver at the back of the mirror," and
he declared in the Berkeley essay: "Something compels me to reject whatever—to borrow a metaphor of Coleridge's—drives mind into the quicksilver" (LTSM 67, E&I 407).

Coleridge found active freedom in a creative fusion of Plotinus, Berkeley,
and Kant.[27] So did Yeats, or at least later Yeats. At age twenty-five he had
equated "freedom of the spirit and imagination" with "romanticism" (UP
1:183), and to his early Romantic allies Blake and Shelley he had later added
Berkeley, Kant, and Coleridge. But the passive mirror remained, and the

25. Coleridge, "Dejection: An Ode," lines 45–49.
26. Inserted at p. 57 of Yeats's edition (1876); see O'Shea, *A Descriptive Catalog*, item 401. A
few pages later, Coleridge describes a "small water-insect on the surface of rivulets" and how
"the little animal wins its way up against the stream, by alternate pulses of active and passive
motion, now resisting the current, and now yielding to it in order to gather strength and a
momentary *fulcrum* for a further propulsion. This is no unapt emblem of the mind's self-
experience in the act of thinking. There are evidently two powers at work, which relatively to
each other are active and passive," with an "intermediate faculty": the imagination. According
to Yeats's "Long-legged Fly," the "mind moves upon silence . . . Like a long-legged fly upon
the stream."
27. A fusion that can be traced in *Biographia Literaria*. For an excellent discussion of Coleridge's "Romantic Vision," see the two Coleridge essays in M. H. Abrams's *The Correspondent
Breeze: Essays on English Romanticism*.

effect of such passivity was literary as well as psychological. The "Three Essentials" on which Yeats said in his 1930 diary he would found literature as well as life were Kant's Freedom, God, and Immortality. "The fading of these three before 'Bacon, Newton, Locke' has made literature decadent. Because freedom is gone we have Stendhal's 'mirror dawdling down a lane'"—Stendhal's definition of the novel as *un miroir promene per grands chemins* supplied Yeats with the perfect metaphor for the mimetic "mechanical philosophy of the French eighteenth century" (Ex 332–33, VPl 568).

But the most prominent mechanist apostle of mind's passivity remained the climactic figure in Blake's British trinity. While a strong case can be made for anticipation of the Romantic Imagination in Lockean psychology (the secondary sense-qualities adumbrate Kant and the Romantics in constituting the mind's addition to perception),[28] Romantics from Blake to Yeats identify Locke above all others with the image of the mind-in-perception as a passive receiver of external impressions, a *tabula rasa* on which sensations inscribe themselves. The related metaphor is that of a mirror; it was this mimetic metaphor that had to be transformed, to be replaced by something active, unifying, autonomous, a projective "light" having nothing to do with the "Enlightenment." "From the soul itself must issue forth / A light," Coleridge declared in the Dejection ode. "Soul," said Yeats in his introduction to the *Oxford Book of Modern Verse*, "must become its own betrayer, its own deliverer, the one activity, the mirror turn lamp." Our creativity restored through the power of imagination, we shall awaken from the Lockean "swoon" that withered the Garden, taking away the "living world" and the living Eve and leaving only waste matter, the world's "excrement."

III. The Tables Turned

But the mind's reduction to a passive role *revealed in a vision* of Locke's swoon, the Garden's death, and the grotesque, lifeless birth of an industrial machine out of the side of the inert empiricist and rationalist: where got Yeats *that* "truth"? Not, if we are to believe the second fragment, from Blake; and certainly not from reading Locke, or a standard text on the genesis of the Industrial Revolution. Yeats answers his own question:

Where got I that truth?
Out of a medium's mouth,
Out of nothing it came
Out of the forest loam,

---

28. In a perceptive analysis of Locke's *Essay*, R. S. Crane has noted that the Romantic indignation at Locke's model of the mind as a "passive recipient" of external impressions or "at most a mechanical manipulator of the simple ideas it has derived from these" ignores Locke's "complementary emphasis on the activity of the mind" ("Notes on the Organization of Locke's *Essay*," 1:288-301).

Out of dark night where lay
The crowns of Nineveh.

Beneath the positivist-baiting ironic humor, this is receptive creation as a fertile countertruth to mechanical birth "out of" the side of Locke. The anaphora is Whitmanian—"Out of the cradle endlessly rocking, / Out of the mocking bird's throat, the musical shuttle, / Out of the Ninth-month midnight"—with Yeats's "forest loam" and "dark night" suggesting the cycle of fertility and birth in contrast to the sterile "birth" of the spinning jenny, just as the fecundity of Whitman's "cradle" and "Ninth-month midnight" contrast with the "sterile sands" of the next line of the proem to "Out of the Cradle Endlessly Rocking."

As presented here, Yeats's counter-Enlightenment is at once part of the collective unconscious and individualistic: "Where got I that truth?" It is also—and here Yeats's Continental precursors include Schelling and Bergson as well as one aspect of Nietzsche—vitalistic, dynamic, organic, intuitionist, irrationalist. "Neither loose imagination, / Nor the mill of the mind / Consuming its rag and bone, / Can make the truth known," but if it is properly disciplined rather than loose, "the imagination has some way of lighting on the truth that reason has not" (VP 575, E&I 65). "It is nothing to me," Yeats told Sturge Moore in 1926, "that my special experience is not yet shared by the majority of teachers in universities (which is what is meant by 'proved'). What matters to me is that it is my experience . . . , an expression of faith" that "arises from a special experience, just as . . . Nietzsche's does when he says 'Am I a barrel of memories that I should give you my reasons?'" (LTSM 99, 103).

Up to a point, "Fragments" gives us what Blake offered as the definition of the most sublime poetry: "Allegory addressed to the Intellectual powers" and "altogether hidden from the Corporeal Understanding," that merely bodily knowledge consisting of sense perception and ideas derived from sensory data. Yeats agreed with Blake that man is more than the *tabula rasa* inscribed by such light as enters through the sensory openings ("Five windows light the cavern'd Man") to which the passive self is limited by Lockean epistemology. At the same time, Blake would be appalled by Yeats's "answers," whether occult or earthy, to the question "Where got I that truth?"—even though the question itself recalls Oothoon's rebellious response to being "told . . . that I had five senses to inclose me up." "With what sense is it that the chicken shuns the ravenous hawk?" she asks in Blake's *Visions of the Daughters of Albion*; "With what sense does the bee form cells?" The answer can only be: with one of what Blake calls the "enlarged & numerous senses" (MHH, plate 11), some instinct beyond the five windows enumerated by empiricism, the philosophy of the five senses given by a weeping Urizen "into the hands of Newton & Locke."

But "out of" a "medium's mouth," out of "forest loam," out of "dark night"! Precisely what a horrified Blake finds at the root of fallen "natural"

perception—a secret, sexualized, occult darkness—Yeats celebrates as the
hidden matrix of vision, with the "Goddess Nature, Mystery, and Babylon
the Great," all condemned by Blake, affirmed by his prodigal son in the
form of fecund forest loam and the mysterious dark night where lay the
crowns of Nineveh, repository of Assyro-Babylonian mythology. Indeed,
Eve, replaced by a machine in the withered Garden of part I of "Fragments," is restored in the form of the mysterious city of part II, since, as
Yeats seems to have known, the Assyrians named their capital city after
Nin-Eveh: "Holy Lady Eve," the Mother-Womb or Goddess of the Tree of
Life in their mythology. Whether patriarchally demoted, as in Genesis 2, or
mechanistically obliterated, as in "Fragments" (I), the repressed "Eve"
proves irrepressible. As Erich Neumann observes in *The Great Mother*:

Unless the male spirit is able—as in mathematics—to construct a purely abstract
world, it must make use of the nature symbols originating in the unconscious. But
this brings it into contradiction with the natural character of the symbols, which it
distorts and perverts. Unnatural symbols and hostility to the nature symbol—e.g.
Eve taken out of Adam—are characteristic of the patriarchal spirit. But even this
attempt at revaluation usually fails, as an analysis of this symbolism might show,
because the matriarchal character of the nature symbol asserts itself again and
again.[29]

So, in "Fragments" (II), overcoming the mechanistic perversion of what
was already scripturally distorted, matriarchal Eve returns, the "unconscious" and the "nature symbol" reasserted in earthy forest loam and in the
ancient city named for her as well as in the feminine mystery of the "medium's mouth."

If this sounds like Yeats as his most occult, archaistic, and obscurantist, it
is also Yeats at his subtlest and wittiest. He always hankered after the vatic
authority conferred by access to ancient mysterious wisdom, but here there
is sophistication as well. In a nice paradox, his oracular chant directs table-
turning irony against the very century that prided itself on the perfection of
the ironic mode. This litany of "sources" offering inspired access to truth,
and therefore the sources of his art, is not *merely* occult mumbo jumbo
intended to befuddle and enrage what Blake called the "Idiot Reasoner" or
"Idiot Questioner." The details are chosen with care, reflecting the fact that
Yeats's no less than Pope's is a poetry of allusion. To illustrate: according to
the Popean synopsis of the Enlightenment's verdict, "Nature and Nature's
laws *lay hid in night*, / God said: 'let Newton be,' and *all was light*"; but
Yeats's countertruth comes defiantly: "Out of *dark night* where *lay* . . . ."

---

29. Neumann, *The Great Mother: An Analysis of the Archetype*, 50. For the Blake references in
the preceding paragraph, see Blake's letter to Butts, 16 July 1803; *Europe: A Prophecy*, introductory plate (iii.1); *Visions of the Daughters of Albion* 2:31, 3:2–4; *The Song of Los* 4:16–17; *Jerusalem*
93:23–24. The "idiot Reasoner" referred to in the paragraph following "laughs at the Man of
Imagination" (*Milton* 32:6).

Where lay what? Precisely that ancient wisdom dismissed as occult mummery by the hyperrational Enlightenment; and the crowns of ancient Nineveh "lay," just as in Pope's use of the verb, only temporarily hidden, waiting to be re-revealed. Again, the eighteenth-century physical theory of knowledge, already implicit in Aristotle but derived preeminently from Newton and Locke, was based on the maxim *nihil est in intellectu quod non antea fuerit in sensu* (nothing is in the intellect that was not first in sense). But, and this is admittedly to flirt with epistemological nihilism, it is precisely *ex nihilo*, "Out of *nothing*," that the truth emerges for Yeats—who was not the first to notice that the famous *nihil est* maxim was, ironically, a general principle unverifiable by scientific induction, an *a priori* Trojan horse within the walls of the Empiricist city.

It is a nonempirical magic city that Yeats evokes, here as in "Vacillation." "The crowns of Nineveh": the oracular phrase conjures up monuments of unaging intellect, all those things Yeats specifically connected with "Nineveh's crown" in the introduction to his 1926 play *The Cat and the Moon*: "belief," "imagination," "the wisdom of the ages," that "early phase of every civilization . . . buried under dream and myth." Or, once again, though less successfully, to "simplify":

Decline of day
A leaf drifts down;
O dark leaf clay
On Nineveh's crown!
  (Ex 400–401)

The quatrain described, said Yeats, "Vico's circle and mine" (Ex 401), Vichian cyclicism providing, like Nietzschean recurrence, an antidote to what Yeats dismissed as the most vulgar innovation of the Enlightenment, the linear "idea" of "progress"; this, the "sole religious myth of modern man, is only two hundred years old" (Ex 355). "'Progress' is merely a modern idea," sneered Nietzsche, "that is, a false idea" (*Antichrist* §4). The gyring passage of history through cyclical phases, for "Vico saw civilization rise and sink" (Ex 354), is synopsized in this mini-poem in images—quarried "out of" Vico, Shelley, Spengler, and Arthur O'Shaughnessy—of autumnal death, decay, preservation, and renewal of what "lay" hidden: the "buried" past thrust "back in the human mind again," as Yeats says in "Under Ben Bulben." The fecund humus, "dark leaf clay," anticipates the Dionysian "forest loam" and "dark night" of "Fragments" (II). In both cases, we have what Yeats called a delving "down, as it were, into some fibrous darkness, into some matrix out of which everything has come" (E&I 429).

The genetic matrix—the "rich, dark nothing" from which artists committed to the gyres "disinter" ancient wisdom (VP 565)—is emphatically organic, earthy; it is the antithesis of the Garden's death and the sterile mechanical birth of "Fragments" (I). It is also a cumulative organicism Yeats associated with "instinct" and "emotion"—and with O'Shaughnessy's "Ode," as truncated in Palgrave's *Golden Treasury*. "A little lyric evokes an emotion," Yeats wrote in "The Symbolism of Poetry"; and as it "grows more powerful, it flows out, with all it has gathered, among the blind instincts of daily life, where it moves a power within powers, as one sees ring within ring in the stem of an old tree. This may be what Arthur O'Shaughnessy meant when he had his poets say they had built Nineveh with their sighing" (E&I 157–58).

These Amphionic dreamers "wandering by lone sea-breakers, / And sitting by desolate streams" experience, in Yeats's gloss, "the emotions that have come to solitary men in moments of poetical contemplation," creators who "make and unmake mankind, and even the world itself" (E&I 158, 159). Through "dream," says O'Shaughnessy, they go forth to "conquer a crown"—not a worldly but an imaginative, mental crown, making "the crowns of Nineveh" in "Fragments" roughly equivalent to "thought's crowned powers" (in the phrase from Shelley's *Prometheus Unbound* quoted by Yeats in "Blood and the Moon").

O'Shaughnessy's final stanza provided the author of "Fragments" (I) with a death and a birth. In addition, the chant with which the dead yet vital poets make their claim resonates, as in "Fragments" (II), from the ancestral earth:

> We, in the ages lying
>   In the buried past of the earth,
> Built Nineveh with our sighing,
>   And Babel itself with our mirth;
> And o'erthrew them with prophesying
>   To the old of the new world's worth;
> For each age is a dream that is dying
>   Or one that is coming to birth.

All Yeats's references to the "Ode" center on Nineveh: the city built by the sighing of poets, an aesthetic projection of emotion. "Only an aching heart / Conceives a changeless work of art," said Yeats of the ancestral sword given him by Junzo Sato. "In Sato's house, / Curved like new moon, moon-luminous, / It *lay* five hundred years" (VP 421)—just as the crowns of Nineveh "lay," ancient and mysterious, waiting to become another Yeatsian symbol. That description of Sato's sword is from a *Tower* poem; and when, in the 1933 *Collected Poems*, Yeats inserted "Fragments" in *The Tower*, he placed it immediately after an equally epigrammatic work. "Two Songs from a Play" begins with a goddess (not "God") taking a "beating heart" (not a spinning jenny) "out of" the "side" not of Locke but of Dionysus, and it ends with one of Yeats's most memorable images of human emotion as all-creative: "Whatever flames upon the night / Man's own resinous heart has fed."

When, in "Fragments," the golden crowns of Nineveh flame up "Out of dark night," what is evoked is more O'Shaughnessy's city of the poetic imagination than Ashurbanipal's capital. For Yeats looked, not merely back to old Nineveh rather than ahead to O'Shaugnessy's progress-minded "new world's worth," but *cyclically* ahead, to the resuscitation of the ancient—a past buried, dark, chthonic, Dionysian. The Vichian or Heraclitean cycle takes the form of a return to the fecund Garden prematurely declared dead by the Enlightenment, that worth*less* new age now itself declared a stillborn machine-birth following upon an imagination-deadening "swoon." Empiricism, mechanism, rationalism, industrialism: *this* is the anti-poetic "dream" that is—or should be—"dying," overthrown by ancestral voices prophesying war against the Enlightenment, voices evoked from the buried past of the earth. It is, as Yeats says, a past not dead but sleeping, "buried under dream and myth," and for that very reason more profound than any empirical knowledge. The anti-positivist "truth" behind the luminous facade of the Enlightenment is thus revealed as a return of the repressed, of the imaginative mythopoeic energy overthrown and held down by the spiritless, oppressive deadness of mechanistic philosophy. Like Nietzsche's Dionysus and Yeats's own rough beast of "The Second Coming," the occult revelation of "Fragments" is a genuine vision of something on its way back to the surface, a cyclical eruption again "coming to birth."

Like many European Romantics before him, and some myth-centered primordialists after him, Yeats tended to adopt a conservative, aristocratic, even reactionary form of irrationalism, looking back with nostalgia toward some golden, organic, prescientific age of faith or myth, to a dark backward and abysm of time when dryads haunted the forest boughs, before new philosophy called all in doubt, before thought was mechanized by the *philosophes* and life itself mechanized by industrialism, before Newton analytically unraveled the beauty of the rainbow, before Locke dissociated sensibility and fractured concrete reality by severing primary from secondary sense-qualities. On the psychological level, this backward gaze implies that man is governed, not by the newly "enlightened" intellect, but by dark, archaic instincts that can themselves grow luminous. Yeats could not, he declared, "break from . . . tradition," from that "'deposit' certain philosophers speak of," without "breaking from some part of my own nature, and sometimes it has come to me in supernormal experience; I have met with ancient myths in my dreams, brightly lit; and I think it allied to the wisdom or instinct that guides a migratory bird" (E&I viii)—or that guides Oothoon's birds and cell-forming bee. Paralleling Jung and anticipating recent thinking about both the bicameral brain and the reemergence of the culturally repressed mythic and feminine perspectives, Yeats celebrates what he repeatedly called "deeps of the mind" (V-A 212), the instinctual

"dark" half that transcends, is proof against, and provides an epistemologically legitimate alternative to, discursive reasoning, whatever divisive form
it takes, whether Cartesian dualism, Lockean empirical psychology, the
bifurcation of nature and split between fact and value discussed by Whitehead, Eliot's "dissociation of sensibility," or the cutting of the lines of
communication "between the conscious and unconscious zones of the human psyche" in consequence of which "we have been split in two."[30]

Aware that his position was an imperiled one in the modern world, Yeats
chose to defend it by going on the offensive. Ellmann, in his study of
Yeats's relationship to Wilde, Eliot, Pound, and Auden, imagines a dialogue in which the latter accurately accuses Yeats of belonging to the Ro-
mantic-Symbolist "school": "You think of yourself as a god who creates
the subjective universe out of nothing." Ellmann's Yeats responds by turning back upon Auden—who found Yeats's supernatural interests "embarrassing"—that allusion ("Out of nothing") to "Fragments": "You belong to
the school of Locke; you split the world into fragments."[31] In the waste land
of the fragmented modern world, Yeats might have said of his little poem,
"these 'Fragments' I have shored against my ruin, and if you positivists find
the shoring weird, so much the better." For what, in Pope's phrase, "*lay* hid
in *night*" was, precisely, the hidden, the occult. The crowns of Nineveh "*lay*
in dark *night*," out of which Yeats draws up a wisdom antithetical to that of
Blake's "Bacon, Newton, Locke."

In "Fragments," Yeats is twisting the tails of the British empiricists; at the
same time, of course, his table-turning joke—Joyce would call it "joco-
serious"—is nothing less than the structural ligament joining his two "fragments." For he derives his visionary "truth" about the death of the Garden
from that Garden, "out of" that fecund darkness or fruitful void of *Anima
Mundi* destroyed, according to the first fragment, by the fatal impact of
analytic method, the masculinization of thought, the denial of innate ideas,
the scientific restriction of inquiry to the knowable material world—everything Yeats sums up as the Lockean-Newtonian "machine-shop." But
rumors of the death of the Garden have been grossly exaggerated. That is
the Yeatsian "truth" blown back to blind the mocker's eye in "Fragments,"
a poem reminiscent (as is section V of Yeats's "Nineteen Hundred and
Nineteen") of Blake's refutation of materialism in "Mock On, Mock On,
Voltaire, Rousseau":

30. The final formulation is Joseph Campbell's, *The Hero with a Thousand Faces*, 2d ed., 388.
Eliot's famous "dissociation of sensibility" was anticipated by Yeats; both locate the problem
in the later seventeenth century. Among the poems alluded to in this long paragraph are
Keats's "Ode to Psyche," Poe's "To Science," Donne's *Anniversaries*, and Schiller's "Die
Götter Giechenlands." For Schiller, Helios and his golden chariot have been replaced by a
soulless revolving fireball, and the earth, unaware of the joys it gives, bereft of its gods,
slavishly serves the laws of gravity like a lifeless pendulum clock. The unemployed deities have
returned to their only home, the world of poetry.
31. Ellmann, *Eminent Domain: Yeats among Wilde, Joyce, Pound, Eliot, and Auden*, 123.

The atoms of Democritus
And Newton's particles of light
Are sands upon the Red Sea shore
Where Israel's tents do shine so bright.

So much for an "Enlightenment" whose very light consists of corpuscles of subtle matter in motion, a light that fades in the splendor of spiritual vision. (Blake's is a variant on a traditional figure: Donne in *Biathanatos* and Dryden in the opening of *Religio Laici* use the image of reason as a dim light that, like the moon, fades before the sun of supernatural revelation.) Though occult, feminist, and chthonic rather than biblical, Yeats's refutation is part of the same Romantic reaction against the mind-set from which industrialism springs, an atomistic materialism as fragmenting as Cartesian dualism or the Lockean cleavage of unified reality.

As a poem, Yeats's holistic and self-healing "Fragments" is no more fragmentary than the most famous of Romantic poems termed by its author "A Fragment." In fact, Yeats's and Coleridge's "fragments" both feature a city of the poetic imagination, a paradisiacal garden or "fertile ground," and a deep matrix in the forest loam. "Kubla Khan" is an odal hymn in which the poet, could he "revive within" him the music made by the visionary "damsel with a dulcimer," would attain "deep delight" and so "would *build* that dome in air." (Coleridge's building of a Xanadu of the imagination, like Blake's vow not to cease from "Mental Fight" till we have "*built* Jerusalem / In Englands green & pleasant Land," anticipates the love-labor of Keats, who would, for the neglected goddess Psyche, "*build* a fane / In some untrodden region of my mind," a rosy sanctuary dressed with "the wreathed trellis of a working brain." Poets "*built* Ninevah," too, according to O'Shaughnessy; Yeats's defense, in "Lapis Lazuli," of "poets who are always gay," even—or, especially—in the midst of tragedy, is that "All things fall and are *built* again, / And those that *build* them again are gay.") Like "Fragments" and the "Ode to Psyche," where "dark cluster'd trees / Fledge the wild-ridged mountains steep by steep," "Kubla Khan" also locates its dark truth in the womb of sylvan nature. The sublimated visions of dulcimer-playing "damsel" and airy dome are rooted in a forest's "deep romantic chasm which slanted / Down the green hill athwart a cedarn cover": a dark declivity and "savage place"

as holy and enchanted
As e'er beneath a waning moon was haunted
By woman wailing for her demon-lover!

This situates us at the meridian point or daemonic "trysting place," as Yeats called it, between poetry and religion, natural and supernatural—between "forest loam" and the "medium's mouth" of "Fragments" (II).

IV. "Out of a Mediums Mouth"

As the litany of "Fragments" (II) reveals, Yeats is engaged in a more-than-witty, more-than-Blakean, critique of what he takes to be the fatal fruit of Lockean epistemology. For Yeats swerves from Blake, going beyond the humanistic Imagination and (despite his allusion to Genesis) beyond the Hebrew Bible to seek (as Saul did) other, occult authority. But why does Yeats deliberately give priority to the most suspect, the most "vulgar" form of occult communication: truth "out of a medium's mouth"? The answer involves Yeats's attempt to occultify Jonathan Swift; it involves, again, his emphasis on the return of the repressed under female auspices; and it involves his own ("Where got *I* that truth?") "supernormal experience," ranging from the occult experiment that in part generated "The Second Coming," to séances, to the experiences behind the writing of *A Vision*.

Yeats's general appeal to the occult is, of course, one gauge of the intensity of his need to refute the materialists, to expedite what he called "the revolt of the soul against the intellect" (L 211). It was in part that need that had drawn him to Blake, had convinced him that Blake himself must have been even more steeped in mystical than in literary tradition. Yeats's occultification of Blakean Romanticism was paralleled years later by his forging of an alliance between Romanticism and the Anglo-Irish eighteenth century, an alliance opposed to the Enlightenment tradition dominated by the post-Cartesian world view of Newton and Locke. "Materialism was hamstrung by Berkeley, and ancient wisdom brought back," Yeats insisted, reinforcing Blake and Neoplatonism with Anglo-Ireland (Ex 297-98). But, as we have seen, the lesson did not take; the vulgar continued to talk as if the world had never been revitalized, as if it were still a Lockean excrement. In his introduction to *The Oxford Book of Modern Verse* (1936), Yeats conceded the dominance of mechanistic materialism: "The mischief began at the end of the seventeenth century when man became passive before a mechanized nature; that lasted to our own day with the exception of a brief period between Smart's *Song of David* and the death of Byron, wherein imprisoned man beat upon the door" (OBMV xxvi–xxvii).

This span, 1763–1824, encompasses both the birth of the Industrial Revolution (the spinning jenny itself was invented in the mid–1760s, by, inevitably, an Englishman) and the heroic but doomed Romantic counterthrust against a mechanized world and a mind made passive and drained of vitalizing mythic consciousness by Locke and the other mischief-makers of the later seventeenth century. The compelling metaphor of imprisoned man beating on the door was echoed in that Nietzschean poem examined earlier, "An Acre of Grass," written in the same year as the Oxford anthology introduction.

But along with the Romantics, especially "that William Blake / Who beat upon the wall / Till Truth obeyed his call," Yeats had in mind other vital spirits inspired by "sibylline frenzy" (VP 481). One crucial model for the "old man's frenzy" invoked by Yeats in "An Acre of Grass" was that spirit who, Yeats said, "haunts me" (Ex 345), and who figures, appropriately, as a ghostly voice in *The Words upon the Window-pane* (entitled, in its original scenario, simply *Jonathan Swift*).[32] Since "Fragments," written shortly afterward, is cited and glossed in Yeats's lengthy and impassioned introduction to the play, we rightly assume that the anti-Lockean, anti-mechanist nightmare-vision in "Fragments" has something to do with that spirit who, in the play, beats on the door, like Blake, and, unlike Blake, actually speaks "out of a medium's mouth"—a *female* medium.

What comes out of the mouth of Mrs. Henderson in *The Words upon the Window-pane* is the tragic and authoritative voice of Jonathan Swift—a cryptic utterance from, and poignant epitaph on, that Anglo-Irish Camelot overwhelmed by the Anglo-French chaos of the so-called Enlightenment. Swift's final Jobean cry in the play—"Perish the day on which I was born!"— is, like his dread of impending historical decay and his related dread of begetting children doomed to live in such a world, the ultimate consequence of his vision of the triumph of the philosophy he (and Yeats) hated. Yeats, who in the Berkeley essay notes Swift's "disbelief in Newton's system and every sort of machine" (E&I 402), reinforces the Swiftian connection with "Fragments" (part I of which he quotes in this introduction) by referring as well to Swift's tragic "half-mad" recognition "that the mechanicians mocked in *Gulliver* would prevail," that the Anglo-Irish "moment of freedom could not last." Indeed, Yeats adds, hard upon the death of Swift came Rousseau, that begetter of "the *sans-culottes* of Marat" (Ex 363). As John Corbet, the pivotal character in the play, puts it, Swift "foresaw the ruin to come, Democracy, Rousseau, the French Revolution" (VPl 942). Corbet's summation is repeated in the introduction to the play (Ex 350), a telescoping defined by Yeats in his 1930 diary as "the thought of Swift, enlarged and enriched by Burke" (Ex 297).

This declension from bad to worse to worst not so surprisingly synopsizes Yeats's own view of the French Revolution as an anarchic flood loosed by the mechanistic materialism and democratic utopianism allegedly preached by the *philosophes* of the Enlightenment; opposed valiantly but in vain by Edmund Burke, the Anglo-Irish successor of Swift and Berkeley; and traced back, fairly or unfairly, to the chief precursors of the Enlightenment. Of course, the whole notion of "precursors" has validity only from the perspective of the future, and Yeats is doubly unhistorical in dragging Locke and Newton into the new century to present them with their deformed progeny, the *philosophes* and *sans-culottes*. Yet this glimpse of a partial truth seems (partially) validated by its own passionate intensity.

32. For the genesis of the play, written rapidly in September-October 1930, see Mary FitzGerald, "Out of a Medium's Mouth: The Writing of *The Words upon the Window-pane*." The Swift-Yeats relationship has been brilliantly explored by both Donald Torchiana and Douglas Archibald.

Yeats's earlier response to the revolutionary consequences of the Lockean "swoon" was a related but still more compelling visionary glimpse: of twenty centuries of "stony sleep" vexed to "nightmare." Suppressed energy awakens in the form of an animated Sphinx rising up in the desert of a desiccated civilization. The "rough beast" of "The Second Coming," like the nightmare "truth" presented in "Fragments" (I), comes "out of" a deep source, "*Spiritus Mundi.*" Slouching toward Bethlehem to be born (another perversion of the birth process), it is not only a nightmare more formidable than that of the birth of the spinning jenny but another direct response to the Industrial and French revolutions, which Yeats, with the help of Burke and Wordsworth, saw as having come to "second birth" in the deformed infant of Marxist-Leninist materialism.

That is the tale, simplified through intensity, traceable in the first drafts of "The Second Coming," written in January 1919. The poem's immediate genesis was the Russian Revolution and the Bolshevik Terror of 1918, which, in the working manuscripts, Yeats associates with the murderous excesses of the French Revolution. A reference in the poem's initial draft to "Marie Antoinette" signals Yeats's equation of the mob's assault on the French queen at Versailles (immortalized by chivalrous Burke, a counter-revolutionary champion celebrated by name in this same first draft) with the "more brutal" slaughter of the Tzarina Alexandra and the rest of the Russian royal family by the Bolsheviks' Cheka execution squad in 1918. But this immediate genesis of "The Second Coming" is another story, one continued in the next chapter.

The *deep* genesis of the poem also had a "female" element. Marie Antoinette was assaulted; the poet of the "clairvoyant" section of "The Second Coming," overwhelmed by vision, resembles a woman physically over-powered—correlating with the brutally "mastered" Leda and the terrified Virgin Mary of this poem's two cyclical companions, "Leda and the Swan" and "The Mother of God." The nature of the "rough beast" (the phrase, revealingly, is borrowed from the description of Tarquin in Shakespeare's *The Rape of Lucrece*)[33] is clearly sexual. "Moving its slow thighs," the sinis-ter shape rises up "somewhere in sands of the desert," its phallic energy possibly reflecting Yeats's own sexual awakening. That occurred when, at the age of fifteen, he partially buried his body in sand while at the beach; "the weight of the sand began to affect the organ of sex," causing an erection and an utterly unexpected orgasm (Mem 71).

The sexuality of the poem's genesis is labyrinthine. In an 1890 symbolic card experiment with MacGregor Mathers, the head of his occult order, the Golden Dawn, Yeats suddenly saw "a gigantic Negro [a "desert and a Black Titan" in the published version] raising up his head and shoulders among great stones" (Mem 27; Au 186): the prefiguration of the libidinal, Diony-sian upsurge envisioned in "The Second Coming." This visionary capacity

---

33. See A. M. Gibbs, "The 'Rough Beasts' of Yeats and Shakespeare."

was sporadic in Yeats; but there were members of the Order of the Golden Dawn who seemed abundantly gifted with such powers. A number of Golden Dawn male adepti grumbled that the Order clairvoyants were virtually all women, one of the men going on to brand them, "with one or two exceptions, mere astral tramps—psychic nymphomaniacs." Though he admired the women, Yeats too envied them their visionary capacity to think in pictures, to form vivid mental images.[34] Even the prophetic "frenzy" attributed to Swift in "Blood and the Moon" must cross sexual lines to be honorifically designated "sibylline," and in the sibylline relish with which Yeats himself refutes the rationalists' masculinization and deadening of nature in "Fragments" we may detect a reversal of the old Freudian bugaboo, penis envy. In his description of the experiments with Mathers, Yeats admits that *his* "mental image" lacked the marvelous power of the "crowning moment" attained by Florence Farr. When it was his turn, "sight came slowly, there was not that sudden miracle as if the darkness had been cut with a knife, for that miracle is mostly a woman's privilege" (Au 185). This simile reappears in the drafts of the clairvoyant section of "The Second Coming." Groping for figurative language with which to introduce the mysterious moment just prior to the vision of the vast image rising up out of *Spiritus Mundi*, Yeats first wrote: "Before the dark was cut as with a knife."[35]

By then, January 1919, Yeats had for over a year been experiencing directly the sort of psychic powers that were "mostly a woman's privilege." In his reference to a medium's mouth in "Fragments" he may be thinking above all of his wife. Yeats's tribute to her, and to the feminine "voice" he was soon to experiment with in the Crazy Jane and Woman Young and Old sequences, comes toward the end of "The Gift of Harun Al-Rashid" (1924):

The voice has drawn
A quality of wisdom from her love's
Particular quality. The signs and shapes;
All those abstractions that you fancied were
From the Great Treatise of Parmenides;
All, all those gyres and cubes and midnight things
Are but a new expression of her body
Drunk with the bitter sweetness of her youth.
And now my utmost mystery is out.

(VP 469)

34. The disgruntled occultist was Israel Regardie; of his several books on the order, the major work is *The Golden Dawn*. O'Shea (*A Descriptive Catalog*, item 514) reports that the page corners are turned back at p. 56 of a book Yeats had on the Delphic Oracle; the page deals with "women as mediums and oracles."

35. Yeats Archives, Stony Brook; also transcribed by Jon Stallworthy in *Between the Lines: Yeats's Poetry in the Making*, 22.

Writing of the genesis of the occult revelation that purportedly came through his young wife's loving mediumship—significantly, as a concrete embodiment of abstractions—and that he described in *A Vision*, Yeats concludes: "Unexpectedly . . . came a symbolical system" (Ex 394). As illustration, he immediately cites the recently written "Fragments" (II), which repeats the verb "came" ("Out of a medium's mouth, / Out of nothing it came") and in turn recalls Yeats's surprised reaction to his wife's automatic writing—"What *came* was so exciting, so profound"—as well as Mrs. Henderson's distinction in *The Words upon the Window-pane*: "We do not call up spirits," she explains to the skeptical Corbet, "we make the right conditions and they *come*" (V–B 8, VPl 946).

It is out of this female medium's mouth that the words of Swift (along with those of Stella and Vanessa) come in *The Words upon the Window-pane*; and it is out of a medium's mouth that Yeats claimed to receive "that truth" about the connection between mechanistic philosophy and industrialism in the form of an image. The birth of the spinning jenny from the side of passed-out Locke is in fact a striking example of thinking in pictures, of that visual "power," as Ruskin put it in *Modern Painters*, "of seeing anything we describe as if it were real."[36] Readers of "Fragments" (I) can have little doubt about the power of Yeats's visual imagination. We may, however, still hesitate at the medianic threshold of "Fragments" (II). Clearing away the rubbish from the mouth of the sibyl's cave is one thing (even Locke and Blake could agree on the need to do that); finding our truth in what comes out of the sibyl's mouth is quite another. A year or so after beginning "Fragments," Yeats, a lifelong participant in séances, attended several "convincing" sessions conducted by the Boston medium Mrs. Crandon. They are referred to in two 1933 letters (L 803–4, 807) to his most intimate correspondent, Olivia Shakespear. The second, written in March, reveals the darkest aspect of that supernormal "dark night" identified in "Fragments" (II) as an inspiring source of his countertruth to the vision of the Enlightenment.

In the final sentences of that letter, Yeats refers to Swedenborg's description of "two spirits meeting, and as they touch they become a single conflagration"—a sexualized spiritual vision embodied in such late poems as "A Last Confession," whose lyric speaker is a woman, and "Ribh at the Tomb of Baile and Aillinn," in which the speaker, a heterodox monk, reads his "holy book" in the light provided by the copulating spirits of the titular lovers. Yeats concludes his letter by asserting that Swedenborg's "vision may be true, Newton's cannot be. When I saw at Mrs. Crandon's objects moved and words spoken from some aerial centre, where there was nothing human, I rejected England and France and accepted Europe. Europe belongs to Dante and the witches' sabbath, not to Newton" (L 807).

We can appreciate the final dramatic flourish as the sort of "overstatement

---

36. Ruskin, *Works, Library Edition*, 4:226n.

. . . yet with its measure of truth" Yeats ascribes to a different sort of enthusiasm on the part of Corbet in the Swift play (VPl 959). At the same time, we may wish that the tempering skepticism regarding Swedenborg's vision (which "*may* be true") was also permitted to qualify the final, casual, anti-intellectual consignment of Europe (in 1933!) to the *selva oscura* and traffic with the demonic. In fact, the Europe Yeats "accepts" in this letter "belongs to" *both* scientist and black sabbath—and to the witch-*hunters*, whose murderous craze not so paradoxically coincided with the rise of the misogynist scientific revolution. Lilith, long since identified as queen of the demons, had still to be suppressed—at the stake.

In spite of such rhetorical gestures, Yeats's was a modern mind, aware of the distinction between poetic myth and its *primary* contraries: "empiricism" and "religion," themselves opposites. "Some will ask," he noted in the introduction to the 1937 edition of *A Vision*, "whether I believe in the actual existence of my circuits of sun and moon." While some of them were "plainly symbolical," Yeats was unsure about others, those dividing "actual history" into "periods of equal length."

To such a question I can but answer that if sometimes, overwhelmed by miracle as all men must be when in the midst of it, I have taken such periods literally, my reason has soon recovered; and now that the system stands out clearly in my imagination I regard them as stylistic arrangements of experience comparable to the cubes in the drawing of Wyndham Lewis and to the ovoids in the sculpture of Brancusi.

Following this gesture (partially in deference to Ezra Pound) toward an urbane modernism, Yeats concludes by returning to the language of Heraclitus, with his mystical concept of "justice" (*Dike*). These circuits of sun and moon, wrote Yeats, "have helped me to hold in a single thought reality and justice" (V-B 24–25).

Thus poised, Yeats is at his most appealing and powerful: at once skeptical and open, urbane yet hungry for miracle. In the correspondence with Sturge Moore, Yeats based his philosophic case for mystical reality on such dubious evidence as Frank Harris's anecdote of Ruskin's phantom cat and the scientifically inexplicable floral aroma of St. Teresa's exhumed body (LTSM 122), a phenomenon that also enters "Vacillation" (VIII): "The body of St. Teresa lies undecayed in tomb, / Bathed in miraculous oil, sweet odours from it come." Nevertheless, as Moore's friend and editor Ursula Bridge records:

Sturge Moore believed that Yeats was essentially scientific in spirit, with a desire to be convinced intellectually of the truth of mysticism that was never fulfilled, so that although he was always stirred in his imagination by the paraphernalia of mysticism, and strongly attracted by the attendant thrill of conspiracy, yet he remained at heart a sceptic.

(LTSM xvii–xviii)

As she also notes, Yeats, though often disarmingly anecdotal about his "evidence," sometimes "fell into the temptation of seeking to establish his beliefs by the science he wished to discredit" (LTSM xvii). "I accept all the miracles," Yeats wrote, both in a letter (L 790) and in "Vacillation" (VIII). Yet in the presence of the supernormal he also claimed, though in positivistic language parodying scientific (Cartesian, Gulliverian, Urizenic) objectivity, to have "made the usual measurements, plummet-line, spirit-level and . . . taken the temperature by pure mathematic" (L 921); and we know that he once had blood said to be miraculously dripping from a religious icon surreptitiously sent off to the laboratory for scientific analysis (Maud Gonne's response had been to drop devoutly to her knees).[37] But the burden of proof was on reason, and there were times when, Yeats felt, the rationalists, having no answers, simply fell back on a perverse and arid skepticism. Better to be open-minded, to accept "whatever has been believed in all countries and periods, and only reject any part of it after much evidence, instead of starting all over afresh and only believing what one could prove" (Au 78). So much for the Cartesian method.

While Yeats maintained a skeptical intelligence, he was convinced that there were genuine mysteries, spiritual and imaginative truths not subject to the mill of the analytic mind, consuming its rag and bone. In the introduction to the Swift play, he tells of a Polish psychologist who managed to substitute for a mischievous mediumistic "control" a more compliant spook who "left a photograph of its hand and arm upon an unopened coil of film in a sealed bottle." In mediumship, Yeats concludes, because it is "dramatisation," "almost always truth and lies are mixed together. But what shall we say of their [certain controls'] knowledge of events, their assumption of forms and names beyond the medium's knowledge? What of the arm photographed in the bottle?" (Ex 365–66).

These, at least, are questions, not—though Yeats instantly goes on to "those witches described by [Joseph] Glanvil"[38]—a reckless abandonment of hard-won reason to the occult seductions of the Witches' Sabbath. If the Anglo-French *lumières* were hubristic in apotheosizing Descartes's "clear and distinct ideas," if, as Pascal warned, "too much clarity darkens," what of the consequence of too much *darkness*? There is obvious danger in either excess—submission to the mechanistic, "masculine" light of pure reason or to the organic, "feminine" darkness, at least when it becomes associated with the occult, with superstition, with the Witches' Sabbath, and, in murderous and paradoxical reaction, with the witch-*hunt*. Conceptually—and

---

37. For the story of Yeats's examination of the bleeding icon, see George Mills Harper, "'A Subject for Study': Miracle at Mirebeau." Maud Gonne's reactions are described in Nancy Cardozo, *Lucky Eyes and a High Heart: The Life of Maud Gonne*, 292.

38. Yeats is referring to Glanvil's notorious *Sadducismus Triumphatus*, which attacked rationalizing skeptics and proto-atheists who denied the existence of such spiritual entities as ghosts and witches. A bookmark is inserted at the section on witchcraft in Yeats's edition (O'Shea, *A Descriptive Catalog*, item 750).

this in part accounts for the title—Yeats's "Fragments," separately, are no more satisfactory than this stereotypical masculine-feminine dichotomy. We prefer fusion: the lighting up of the darkness, the mingling of male and female in spiritual vision, as adumbrated in a famous sentence, out-Patering Pater, in Yeats's *Per Amica Silentia Lunae*: "I shall find the dark grow luminous, the void fruitful, when I understand that I have nothing, that the ringers in the tower have appointed for the hymen of the soul a passing bell" (Myth 332).

Even in *this* life, however, before the passing bell, we can be surrounded by a numinous vitality unexplainable by the rationalists and materialists: a spiritual world that, like Yeats's mythology as a whole, is "rooted in the earth" (LTSM 114), forest loam no longer barren, earth made holy once again. "All about us," Yeats concludes his introduction to *The Words upon the Window-pane*, "there seems to start up a precise inexplicable teeming life, and the earth becomes once more, not in rhetorical metaphor, but in reality, sacred" (Ex 369). By its own Vichian "poetic logic," "Fragments" demonstrates, as does the ode Keats sings into the "soft-conched ear" of the neglected goddess, that it is *not* "too late for antique vows," for an imaginative return to "the fond believing lyre, / When holy were the haunted forest boughs, / Holy the air, the water, and the fire." But there is an ominous difference. It was still possible for visionary Keats to claim, "even in these days so far retired / From happy pieties . . . , / I see, and sing, by my own eyes inspired" ("Ode to Psyche," lines 36–41). It seems both a falling off, and a measure of mounting anti-scientific desperation in the face of the positivists' dominance, that Yeats, in reasserting the sacredness of the earth, must claim to find his chthonic truth and his inspiration, not in a Keatsian or Blakean or Wordsworthian autonomy, but in a medium's mouth. Clearly, the later poet required not only a Muse but also a Sibyl, however vulgarized, to assist his Anglo-Irish and Romantic precursors in dismantling the machine-shop of Newton and Locke.

*   *   *

That Enlightenment construct, with cogs tyrannic, was to be replaced by a paradisiacal vision both pastoral—a restored Garden, an earth once more become sacred—and urban: a city of the imagination; call it Jerusalem, Xanadu, Byzantium, or Nineveh. Whether Garden or holy city, organic or an artifice of eternity, Yeats's paradisiacal vision is mythic, a myth deployed against, and antithetical to, the positivistic myths of the Enlightenment: the epistemological bifurcation of the concrete world of experience and the pseudo-religions of Science and Progress.

Garden and city are utopian, a mixture of myth and spilt religion. But so violent was Yeats's antipathy to the dominant scientific mind-set that it took the form of a rearguard antimyth no less violent, one willing to traffic with witches and charlatans but with unadulterated contempt for the prophets of *scientific* utopianism, especially for that heir of mechanistic materialism who dismissed "religion" as *das opium des Volkes*:

Should H. G. Wells afflict you
Put whitewash in a pail;
Paint: "Science—opium of the suburbs"
On some waste wall.
    (Ex 377)

The "waste wall" is that of a lavatory in the world reduced (by Descartes, Newton, Locke, and company) to a waste land of "excrement." This graffito standing Marx on his head (as Marx and Engels had turned Hegel on *his*) is proposed in Yeats's 1934 introduction to *Fighting the Waves* (the prose version of his most beautiful play, *The Only Jealousy of Emer*). In this same introduction, after quoting a "famous old athlete" who dismissed "the communion of saints" in favor of "the communion of the *Tuatha de Danaan*" (the suppressed pagan divinities of ancient Ireland), Yeats noted, "Science has driven out the legends, stories, superstitions that protected the immature and the ignorant with symbol." Now that Sir William Crookes, not only a psychical researcher but also a distinguished chemist, had reported seeing "a flower carried in broad daylight slowly across the room by what seemed an invisible hand" (Ex 374–76), a "new science" must, says Yeats, take the place of the lost legends. The program is Whitehead's, the search for an "alternative system of organizing the pursuit of scientific truth" (SMW 54), though Whitehead would hardly endorse the Yeatsian *Scienza nuova*. Surely some revelation is at hand, however, and Yeats, as the attacking general, has chosen his primary targets and an appropriate marching song:

Move upon Newton's town,
The town of Hobbes and of Locke,
Pine, spruce come down
Cliff, ravine, rock:
What can disturb the corn?
What makes it shudder and bend?
The rose brings her thorn,
The Absolute walks behind.
    (Ex 377)

This vengeful advance, a more mysterious Birnam Wood come to the mechanists' Dunsinane, takes the interrogatory form of the awe-inspiring Sublime, a terrible beauty allying the organic (tree, grain, formidable flower) with the spiritual (the Platonic-Plotinian Absolute). The "raft" of modern science, "roped together at the end of the seventeenth century," may, if it "so much as glance at [Crookes's] slow-moving flower, part and abandon

us to the storm." Certainly, Yeats continues, "the science that shapes opinion," while applauding Crookes's chemical research, "has ignored his other
research that seems to those who study it the slow preparation for the
greatest, perhaps the most dangerous, revolution in thought Europe has
seen since the Renaissance, a revolution that may, perhaps, establish the
scientific complement of certain philosophies that in all ancient countries
sustained heroic art" (Ex 374).

This "revolution in thought" recalls Coleridge's projected "revolution in
developing and disciplining the human mind" by substituting vital intelligence for mechanism, which "strikes *Death*." Yeats anticipates not the "old
simple celebration of life tuned to the highest pitch" but something more
deliberate, self-conscious, systematized, "as must be at a second coming"
(Ex 374). He specifies an ordered hierarchy, a modern equivalent of "Plato's
Republic," but the Yeatsian *parousia* had been projected a decade and a half
earlier, in "The Second Coming," as a *violent* advent initiating, or rather
reestablishing, such an order. "For years," he wrote in the introduction to
The Resurrection,

I have been preoccupied with a certain myth that was itself a reply to a myth. I do
not mean a fiction, but one of those statements our nature is compelled to make and
employ as a truth though there cannot be sufficient evidence. When I was a boy
everybody talked about progress, and rebellion against my elders took the form of
aversion to that myth. I took satisfaction in certain public disasters, felt a sort of
ecstasy at the contemplation of ruin. . . . Had I begun *On Baile's Strand* or not when I
began to imagine, as always at my left side just out of the range of the sight, a brazen
winged beast that I associated with laughing, ecstatic destruction?

Yeats goes on in this paragraph (Ex 392–93) to cite his 1902 play *Where
There Is Nothing*—which features a Nietzschean beast with the literally hi-
larious name of "Laughter, the mightiest of the enemies of God"—and a
footnote designates the brazen winged beast he "began to imagine" around
1902 as "afterwards described in my poem 'The Second Coming'" (Ex
393n). The paragraph ends with Yeats's citation of "Fragments" (II) as
illustrating a "systematized" revelation: the "symbolical system" that came
to him unexpectedly through the mediumship of his wife.

The "truth" revealed in "Fragments" came "out of" a variety of inexplicable sources—occult and chthonic. But the sources, as we have seen, were
also Anglo-Irish and Romantic. In "The Second Coming," Yeats's most
frequently cited poem, the vast image of a rough beast comes "out of"
Spiritus Mundi, a "birth" more formidable than, and counter to, that of the
spinning jenny. To demonstrate how intimately related these counterbirths
and counter-Enlightenment visions are requires exploration of another genesis: the Anglo-Irish and Romantic birth-process of "The Second Coming"
itself.

4

REVOLUTIONS FRENCH AND RUSSIAN:
BURKE, WORDSWORTH, AND THE GENESIS OF YEATS'S "THE
SECOND COMING"

Works of nature and art one does not get to know as they are finished; one must, to some extent, catch them in their genesis.
  —Goethe

As my unwieldy title suggests, this chapter covers what would seem to be perilous terrain. First, my argument is based largely on the drafts of a poem rather than on its public text; while my ultimate concern is with the published poem, I may be thought to have confused achievement with intention, the perfected artifact with the chips from the workman's bench. Second, I make use of markings and marginalia, also unpublished. While one poet's annotations on another can be fascinating, mere underlinings are less so, and the significance of both varies from scribbler to scribbler. Third, not only am I engaged in the marshy and much-debated areas of influence and source study, I am arguing for the positive influence of the one major Romantic poet whose work Yeats is thought to have generally disregarded, if not despised. Fourth and finally, despite my effort to sketch in other contexts, I will seem to place disproportionate emphasis on the political aspects of a poem of obvious psychological, mythological, and archetypal density. These objections, I think, will be accommodated in the course of what follows.

I. Nightmare Visions:
The Contemporary Political Context and Yeats's Reading of Burke and Wordsworth

Of Yeats's three great "traditions," the first two, Romanticism and the occult, were early and pervasive influences. The third, the Anglo-Irish heritage of Berkeley, Swift, and Burke, Yeats began to lay claim to only in his fifties. The convergence of these three traditions is nowhere clearer than in "The Second Coming," a poem central to Yeats's work in every conceivable way:

Turning and turning in the widening gyre
The falcon cannot hear the falconer;
Things fall apart; the centre cannot hold;
Mere anarchy is loosed upon the world,
The blood-dimmed tide is loosed, and everywhere
The ceremony of innocence is drowned;
The best lack all conviction, while the worst
Are full of passionate intensity.

Surely some revelation is at hand;
Surely the Second Coming is at hand;
The Second Coming! Hardly are those words out
When a vast image out of *Spiritus Mundi*
Troubles my sight: somewhere in sands of the desert
A shape with lion body and the head of a man,
A gaze blank and pitiless as the sun,
Is moving its slow thighs, while all about it
Reel shadows of the indignant desert birds.
The darkness drops again; but now I know
That twenty centuries of stony sleep
Were vexed to nightmare by a rocking cradle,
And what rough beast, its hour come round at last,
Slouches towards Bethlehem to be born?

Yeats's major precursors, Shelley and Blake, are overtly and covertly present—verbally echoed, apocalyptically registered, and creatively swerved away from in a Bloomian *clinamen*. The occult and spiritualistic tradition is certainly represented in the clairvoyant and Egyptological second part of the poem. The vast image or animated Sphinx out of *Spiritus Mundi* has been properly traced back to the gigantic Negro or Black Titan rising up from the desert: the most dramatic of the mental images induced in Yeats during that 1890 symbolic card experiment with MacGregor Mathers, the dominant figure in the Order of the Golden Dawn. The rough beast itself seems to be a fusion of the dragons of Revelation and comparative mythology with Blake's Urizen, his Tyger, and his bestial Nebuchadnezzar, slouching on all fours at the conclusion of *The Marriage of Heaven and Hell*. Other components are drawn from Shelley's stony pharaoh Ozymandias and his Demogorgon, for Yeats a nightmare denizen, along with the beast of "The Second Coming," of the mysterious Thirteenth Cone of *A Vision*. There is also a resemblance, its lineage going back to the beast of Yeats's uncanonical play *Where There Is Nothing*, to the eternally recurrent "savage cruel beast" of Yeats's "strong enchanter," Nietzsche—a Dionysian, libidinal, eruptive force incapable of being "mortified" by what Nietzsche condescendingly called in *Beyond Good and Evil* these "more humane ages."[1]

The key to the power of "The Second Coming"—the notoriously conflicted tone of the speaker, his mingled anguish, terror, and exultation—can be discussed in purely intrinsic terms. It is there, for example, in the masterly "at last" at the end of the penultimate line. But few would deny that the poem's mysterious subterranean power is tapped by attunement to its Romantic and occult reverberations. And what of the third "tradition," the most explicitly political? That "The Second Coming" has something to do with "politics" no reader is likely to deny; but to demonstrate that its immediate genesis was political requires us to pursue the beast into Yeats's working manuscripts.

"The Second Coming" is not unique in its political origins. Students of the genesis of any Yeats text should turn to the poem in which the poet himself, looking back on more than a half century of creativity, traced the genetic history of his themes and images. And since the working manuscripts of that poem—"The Circus Animals' Desertion"—display Yeats's usual pruning of personal material, it makes sense to examine the drafts. Such an examination reveals that "the foul rag-and-bone shop of the heart," that fecund matrix of Yeats's "masterful images," is filled with some truly minute particulars. The familiar catalog seems particular enough:

A mound of refuse or the sweepings of a street,
Old kettles, old bottles, and a broken can,
Old iron, old bones, old rags, that raving slut
Who keeps the till.

But in the drafts we find "old orange peel, dirt, the sweepings of the street / Old bits [of] newspaper. . . ."

The items in the final catalog are not random selections, and neither is this farrago. As a young man, Yeats thought accommodation to democratic vulgarity a necessary "baptism of the gutter" and practical politics "the dirty piece of orange peel in the corner of the stairs as one climbs up to some newspaper office."[2] Yeats's collocation of old orange peel, dirt, street, and old newspapers implies, therefore, an embittered acknowledgment that while his themes and masterful images may have been completed in pure

---

1. For Yeatsians steeped in the poet's Romantic and occult interests, the symbolic shorthand of this paragraph will be largely superfluous; for most others, annoyingly cryptic. Help can be found most rapidly by checking what is said about "The Second Coming" in: Hazard Adams, *Blake and Yeats: The Contrary Vision*; Harold Bloom, *Yeats*; and George Bornstein, *Yeats and Shelley* and *Transformations of Romanticism in Yeats, Eliot, and Stevens*. For the experiment with Mathers, see Yeats's first (long unpublished) account (Mem 27). Yeats's fin-de-siècle play *Where There Is Nothing* features a beast derived in part from his recent discovery, Nietzsche; for whose "savage cruel beast," see *Beyond Good and Evil* §229. See also George Mills Harper's "The Creator as Destroyer: Nietzschean Morality in Yeats's *Where There Is Nothing*."

2. See L 339 and Au 225. For other contemptuous remarks on the newspapers and politicians, see "The Old Stone Cross" (VP 598) and LTSM 154.

mind, they often had their roots in his passionate response to contemporary political events, both local ones and those he followed in the newspapers. Some work has been done in this area, particularly by Donald Torchiana, Conor Cruise O'Brien, and Elizabeth Cullingford, and the authorized biography of Yeats will be the work of two distinguished historians, F. S. L. Lyons and Roy Foster. But with that biography and completion of the multivolume *Collected Letters* still years away, we need someone to study the newspapers and periodicals Yeats read and then trace their influence on his thought and work. In short, we need someone to do for Yeats what has been done for Blake and Coleridge by David V. Erdman and Carl Woodring. In the meantime, we know from its drafts that the poem with which we are concerned definitely had its roots in Yeats's troubled response to the political situation in Europe in 1917–1919.

The evidence of the manuscripts is buttressed by the testimony of Mrs. Yeats. "The Second Coming," she said in the 1960s, took off from Yeats's "apprehensions about the socialist revolutions in Germany, Russia, and Italy during and after World War I."[3] Accurate in substance, the list is slightly misleading. Yeats's dread of Marxism was essentially focused on Leninist Communism and its revolutionary challenge to a European social order left reeling after the unprecedented catastrophe of the Great War. The First Communist International Congress met within weeks of Yeats's completion of "The Second Coming" in January 1919. Both the First and the Second Comintern, held in the summer of 1920, were dominated by Lenin, despised by Yeats as a Cromwell *redivivus*.[4] At about this time, we find Yeats scribbling on an envelope "What has Ireland to do with Internationalism?" and decrying, in an unpublished fragment beginning with that question, the rebirth of "an eighteenth century fanaticism, born when philosophy was lost," which "would to-day (all the greater problems visible but unsolved) change the design of the world"—and change it mechanically rather than organically, like an artist "who imposes upon his work a symmetry, not born out of his subject, or his own mind, but anonymous and superficial, because he has not patience in discovery, nor the courage to look confusion in the face without flinching."[5]

---

3. As reported by Donald T. Torchiana, *W. B. Yeats and Georgian Ireland*, 214, n. 152.

4. Yeats's repetitive association of Lenin with Cromwell causes him to link the Puritan with the French and Russian revolutions. The effect on "The Second Coming" may have been to provide the falcon-falconer image with which the poem begins. Yeats read Marvell's "Horatian Ode upon the Return of Cromwell from Ireland" (in which Cromwell is depicted as a falcon obedient to falconer Parliament) as a tribute to the noble Charles rather than to Cromwell—whose crimes included regicide and the butchery at Drogheda and Wexford. Thus both Lenin and Cromwell, "the Lenin of his day," were guilty of the destruction of an aristocratic order and of murder, including regicide. See "The Curse of Cromwell" (VP 580–81) and, for Yeats's comment on the poem and his description of Cromwell as "the Lenin of his day," LDW 119, E&I 255, 375–76.

5. Yeats Archives, Stony Brook. The question is asked on the flap of a Manila envelope (dated November 1920) containing proofs of the Cuala Press edition of *Michael Robartes and the Dancer*, the volume in which "The Second Coming" appeared. See also L 920–21.

The reborn fanaticism took, in its most fearful "symmetry," the spectral shape of the Bolshevik Revolution in Russia, which Yeats saw as a second loosing of the leveling, anarchic, murderous forces that, "when the movement was in its sunrise," Edmund Burke had temporarily held back by his opposition "in speeches and essays."[6] Yeats made these remarks in a 1924 interview; their relevance to "The Second Coming," written five years earlier, and to "Leda and the Swan," written at about this time, is clarified by Yeats's central statement in the interview: "Everything seems to show that the centrifugal movement which began with the Encyclopaedists and produced the French Revolution and the democratic views of men like Mill, has worked itself out to the end. Now we are at the beginning of a new centripetal movement." Yeats was obviously looking back to the "widening gyre" with which "The Second Coming" begins and to the centripetal movement initiated, however ominously, by the rough beast—a creature that, like Blake's draconic Antichrist, Rahab, is the manifestation of the worst, worked out to the end, before things reverse.[7] Yeats was also looking ahead to the explanatory footnote he appended, later in 1924, to the cyclical companion of "The Second Coming." In his note in *The Dial*, Yeats tells us that he wrote "Leda and the Swan" because "the editor of a political review [AE, editor of *The Irish Statesman*] asked me for a poem."

I thought, "After the individualist, demagogic movement, founded by Hobbes and popularized by the Encyclopaedists and the French Revolution, we have a soil so exhausted that it cannot grow that crop again for centuries." Then I thought "Nothing is now possible but some movement, or birth from above, preceded by some violent annunciation."[8]

The birth from below, the movement "Burke opposed . . . in speeches and essays," was of course Jacobinism. And Burke had opposed it before it had even emerged—long before the Terror, even before the September Massacres. The most famous of Burke's essays, *Reflections on the Revolution in France*, Yeats read at Oxford in 1918. He read it under the immediate impact of contemporary revolution, and, as the drafts of "The Second Coming" show, he, like most readers, remembered the passage Burke seems to have intended as the imaginative and moral centerpiece of the work: the chivalric apostrophe to Marie Antoinette. Burke's set piece is too

---

6. "From Democracy to Authority," *Irish Times* (16 February 1924), in UP 2:433–37.

7. Blake's Rahab appears in dragon form at the crisis of Blake's vision, both in *The Four Zoas* (at the end of Night VIII) and in the parallel moment in *Jerusalem* (at the end of chap. 3). Her dual function as the nadir before apocalypse is synopsized in Northrop Frye's Joycean pun: Rahab is the "Last Strumpet," the "Great Whorn" (*Fearful Symmetry*, 299).

8. VP 828. See also the long note on "Parnell's Funeral" (VP 833) for Yeats's sense of the influence of the French Revolution on Ireland: it awoke the peasantry from their sleep but "prepared for a century disastrous to the national intellect," a horrible decline from the Anglo-Ireland of Swift, Berkeley, and Burke.

familiar to require synopsis; but here is the way "The Second Coming" began:

Ever more wide sweeps the gyre
Ever further hawk flies outward
from the falconer's hand. Scarcely
is armed tyranny fallen when
when [an] this mob bred anarchy
takes its place. For this
Marie Antoinette has
more brutally died & no
Burke [has shook his] has an[swered]
with his voice. No Pit[t]
arraigns revolution. Surely the second
birth comes near—

Following these dozen lines of prose or free verse, Yeats began to write in recognizable iambic pentameter:

The [*gyres grow wider & more wide*] intellectual gyre is thesis to
The [*hawk can no more hear*] falcon cannot hear the falconer
[*The Germans*] [*to Russia*] [*to the place*]
The Germany of Marx has led to Russian [*into*] Com[munism]
There every day [*new*] some innocent has died
The cour[teous] [*mob*] to face that Recalls the mob from murder[9]

Despite the occasional conjectures Yeats's maddeningly difficult handwriting necessitates, most of the specifics and the gist of what he means are clear. The reborn eighteenth-century fanaticism that would impose its mechanical symmetry on life is identified with the introduction of Marxism into Russia. The midwife in this monstrous birth is Germany. Yeats is thinking of Marx's native country, of the German advance into Russia in 1917, and, more specifically, of the events that, in March and April 1917, led the Kaiser, hoping to get Russia out of the war or at least improve the military situation by compounding confusion, to arrange for the return to Russia of the revolutionary exiles in Switzerland. The most determined of

9. Yeats Archives, Stony Brook, 30.1.112. These drafts were first transcribed by Jon Stallworthy, *Between the Lines: Yeats's Poetry in the Making*, 16–25. Donald Torchiana offered a fuller decipherment of the first twelve lines in 1966 (*Yeats and Georgian Ireland*, 214). Stallworthy returned to the manuscripts in 1972, in *Agenda* 10 (1971–1972):24–33. The transcription reproduced in this chapter is my own, though checked against those of Stallworthy and Torchiana. Despite minor differences, all three of us agree as to Yeats's reference to "Marie Antoinette" and "Burke." (The brackets generally indicate canceled words or phrases, though in the obvious instances—Pitt, courteous, Communism—they mark my completion of scribbled words.)

the exiles conveyed in the famous sealed train across Germany to the Finland Station was of course Lenin: the plague bacillus (to use Churchill's image) that proved fatal both to the Russian monarchy and to the members of the royal family themselves.

Yeats links the upheaval in Russia with events of the French Revolution. In fact, his response to contemporary events is imaginatively shaped by his immersion in the *Zeitgeist* and literature of the Romantic period. The most obvious source is the Marie Antoinette passage of the *Reflections*. In Russia "every day some innocent has died" and the members of the Russian royal family—the Tsarina Alexandra ("this Marie Antoinette" who "has more brutally died"), her husband, and her children—have been slaughtered with no Pitt to arraign revolution, no Burke to champion the cause, either of monarchy or of simple humanity.

The drafts suggest that what Yeats responded to most intensely in Burke's chivalric paean was the brilliantly prepared-for confrontation between opposed sets of values; between the savage brutality of the anarchic mob that assaulted Versailles in October 1789 and the beauty, civilized grace, courtesy, and ethereal innocence epitomized by the queen. However hyperbolic Burke's imagery, Yeats, the great poet of antithetical conjunctions, could hardly fail to respond to the overwhelming of graceful and fragile beauty by mindless, monstrous brutality. Indeed, it was to become his most poignant, and markedly aristocratic, variation on the *ubi sunt* theme: "Many ingenious lovely things are gone / That seemed sheer miracle to the multitude" ("Nineteen Hundred and Nineteen"). Even more relevant here is that theme's appearance in a 1938 poem expressing Yeats's long-smoldering indignation regarding the failure of the vacillating "best"—now specified as George V, who did nothing to prevent the murder of the family of his look-alike cousin, "dear Nicky." Crazy Jane, resurrected for the occasion, has found "something worse" than the Bishop "to meditate on":

A King had some beautiful cousins,
But where are they gone?
Battered to death in a cellar,
And he stuck to his throne.[10]

Here, twenty years after the event, the buried thematic seed of "The Second Coming"—the absence of a Burke to champion the cause of monarchy and the family bond in the confrontation between ceremonious innocence and revolutionary brutality—finally emerges from the manuscripts. Whatever we may think of Yeats's political priorities in 1938, he was certainly right to depict the Romanovs—shot and battered to death by the Cheka execution squad in the basement of the "House of Special Purpose"

10. "Crazy Jane on the Mountain" (VP 628). On its first appearance, the poem was accompanied by an angry, but fair, attack on George V for his failure to aid his cousins—despite the fact (which Yeats did not know) that the offer of asylum was initiated by the Russian Provisional Government. See Yeats, *On the Boiler*, 30–31; reprinted, without the poem, Ex 442–43.

at Ekaterinburg—as having "more brutally died" than Marie Antoinette. His elegy (in subsequent drafts of "The Second Coming") for "innocence most foully put to death," for "the gracious and the innocent" who have been murdered while "the mobs fawn upon the murderer" and "the good are wavering & uncertain," is understandable in the light of the fate of the Romanovs, the approval (tacit or otherwise) of the Bolsheviks' action in radical circles, and the failure of conservatives and vacillating monarchs to act to prevent it. For conservative Yeats, it was a clear-cut pattern of what he later referred to as "the stimulation and condonation of revolutionary massacre" (Ex 436).

It is easy enough to see Yeats as Blake saw Burke: an embodiment of "negative pity as a reactionary social force."[11] Seizing on the tear-stained apostrophe to Marie Antoinette, Tom Paine had argued that Burke, the quixotic trumpeter of chivalric nonsense, "pities the plumage, but forgets the dying bird." William Blake was not about to sell his revolutionary birthright for a mess of plumage; where Burke had rhapsodized of the queen, "surely never lighted on this orb, which she hardly seemed to touch, a more delightful vision," Blake had responded two years later: "The Queen of France just touchd this Globe / And the Pestilence darted from her robe."[12] Like Blake, Yeats seems to echo Burke's very words and "surely . . . hardly" syntactical construction in both the drafts and the final version of "The Second Coming."[13] But the modern poet was attracted to aristocratic plumage, and the pestilence he detected in 1919 took the form (as he said in an essay written at this time) of "Utopian vapours" that had to be dispersed by men of full vision and genuine *feeling*.[14] He was also aristocratic courtier enough to empathize with Burke's exclamations: "Oh! what a revolution! and what a heart must I have, to contemplate without emotion that elevation and that fall!"[15]

The genuine feeling in the opening movement of "The Second Coming" is, indeed, Burkean, although specific details have been removed in the process of revision. "Burke" and "Marie Antoinette" disappear in a universalized tide of anarchy, victims of revision by a writer of the twentieth century with new floods and vast images, also left unspecified, to trouble his sight. But while the limiting, localized details dropped away, the characteristic Yeatsian rooting of mythology in the specific contributed substantially to the extraordinary power of the finished poem. Indeed, reading and

11. "Burke is never far from Blake's mind when he thinks of negative pity as a reactionary social force." David V. Erdman, *Blake: Prophet Against Empire*, 3d ed., 184.

12. This untitled poem—known as "Fayette" or "Let the Brothels of Paris Be Opened"— was written in late 1792 or 1793, about the same time as "The Tyger" (*Poetry and Prose*, ed. Erdman, 490–91, 779–80).

13. There is no room here to discuss the interesting syntactical parallel. The striking difference between Burke's "delightful vision" and Yeats's troubled vision may reflect, among other things, his recollection of Blake's reversal of Burke.

14. Yeats "If I Were Four-and-Twenty," Ex 262–80 (269). We will be returning to this 1919 essay.

15. This, and the citations from Burke at the end of the next paragraph, are from the "Marie Antoinette" passage in the *Reflections*.

rereading the section of "The Second Coming" that evolved out of the "Marie Antoinette-Burke" manuscripts—

Things fall apart; the centre cannot hold;
Mere anarchy is loosed upon the world,
The blood-dimmed tide is loosed, and everywhere
The ceremony of innocence is drowned;
The best lack all conviction, while the worst
Are full of passionate intensity—

one feels that, however transformed in the alembic of Yeats's own imagination, the spirit, and the politics, of Burke have survived virtually intact. Yeats has recaptured the horror and perhaps the details of Burke's gory account of the attack on the palace at Versailles that forced the king and queen to abandon that splendid sanctuary, "which they left swimming in blood . . . in this great history-piece of the massacre of innocents." More importantly, he has caught the Burkean elegiac note of "elevation" and "fall," the sense of the "unbought grace of life" and "the glory of Europe . . . extinguished forever," of "all . . . to be changed."

Shortly after Yeats's death, long before the manuscripts of "The Second Coming" came to light, one of Ireland's finest poets intuitively touched on the truth, detecting what Yeats himself called "Burke's great melody" (VP 487). "Yeats regarded his work as the close of an epoch," Austin Clarke wrote in 1939, "and the least of his later lyrics brings the sense of a great occasion. English critics have tried to claim him for their tradition but, heard closely, his later music has that tremulous lyrical undertone which can be found in the Anglo-Irish eighteenth century. So might we listen to Edmund Burke telling of his first glimpse of Marie Antoinette."[16] With the drafts of "The Second Coming" before us, registering the line that re-creates Burke's apostrophe to the French queen in six words, "The ceremony of innocence is drowned," we might say, with Blake, "what was once only imagined is now proved."

If Clarke's ear is faultless, he nevertheless overstates the case; the claim of the British Romantic "tradition" can hardly be denied. We can, however, use Anglo-Ireland as our pivot—directing us, not to Blake and Shelley, whose impact on Yeats and "The Second Coming" has been much discussed, but rather to Wordsworth and the virtually undiscussed effect on Yeats of *The Prelude*.[17]

* * *

16. Austin Clarke, "Poet and Artist," 9.
17. The best critics on the subject of Yeats in relation to Blake and Shelley are Hazard Adams, George Bornstein, and, above all and in a number of places, Harold Bloom (*Yeats*). I first tracked Yeats's rough beast back to *The Prelude* in a 1979 article; in an article published in that same year Walter Evans also argued for *The Prelude* 10.78–93 as a source. "From Wordsworth's *The Prelude* to Yeats's 'The Second Coming.'"

The specifically Anglo-Irish element in "The Second Coming" is significant for reasons more than musical. Yeats's anti-Communism reflects in
part his perception of events in 1917–1919 as a second loosing of that
anarchic tide whose darkness and confusion had overwhelmed the Anglo-
Irish eighteenth century that Yeats was just beginning to claim as his ancestral spot of time.[18] Now he feared the spread of a new Jacobinism
through Europe—even to Ireland, where, to his trepidation and Maud
Gonne's delight, Sinn Fein had triumphed in the December 1918 elections.
An important letter written to George Russell (AE) some three months after
the composition of "The Second Coming" reveals Yeats's fears for Ireland
and his awareness that the number of innocents murdered in Russia extended far beyond the ceremonious few.

Russell had told Maud Gonne's daughter, Iseult, that the Bolsheviks had
executed some four hundred people in Russia. Yeats sent his friend docu-
mentation estimating the figure at thirteen thousand, and then, in this April
1919 letter, cited to him a sentence from John Henry Thomas's March 1919
speech in the House of Commons:

"Every responsible representative of English Labour is convinced, owing to information come into its possession, that the present Russian government is worse than
that of the Autocracy."

What I want is that Ireland be kept from giving itself (under the influence of its
lunatic faculty of going against everything which it believes England to affirm) to
Marxian revolution or Marxian definitions of value in any form. I consider the
Marxian criterion of values as in this age the spearhead of materialism and leading to
inevitable murder. From that criterion follows the well-known phrase "Can the
bourgeois be innocent?"

(L 655–56)

Yeats's perspective on the Russian revolutionaries is precisely that of
Burke on the French revolutionaries. To quote a passage immediately following the portrait of Marie Antoinette: "The murder of a king, or a queen,
or a bishop, or a father, are only common homicide; and if the people are by
any chance or in any way gainers by it, a sort of homicide much the most
pardonable, and into which we ought not to make too severe a scrutiny. . . .
In the groves of their academy, at the end of every vista, you see nothing
but the gallows." It is at precisely this point—the vision of the gallows at
the end of every vista of the barbarous *philosophes*' revolutionary academy—
that, as we shall see, Burke and Wordsworth meet.

---

18. For Yeats's description of the Anglo-Irish eighteenth century as "that one Irish century
that escaped from darkness and confusion," see *Wheels and Butterflies* (Ex 345). For information
on Yeats's revaluation of his Anglo-Irish heritage, see, in addition to Torchiana's full-scale
study, T. R. Henn's chapter "The Background" in *The Lonely Tower: Studies in the Poetry of W.
B. Yeats*, 2d ed., and the chapter "Poet of Anglo-Ireland" in T. R. Whitaker's perceptive *Swan
and Shadow: Yeats's Dialogue with History*.

I have been arguing, following the clues in the drafts of "The Second Coming," that Yeats, influenced by Burke, locates in the French Revolution the pivotal confrontation between ceremonious, civilized order and anarchic chaos. As a poet very consciously in the tradition of the great Romantics, Yeats doubtless had to confront what Shelley called in a letter "the master theme of the epoch in which we live—the French Revolution."[19] But in his response to that event, Yeats, experiencing its second birth in 1917–1919, was far from the poets who most shaped his thought and work: Shelley and Blake. He distanced himself from Shelley, who seemed to him politically naive and lacking the "vision of evil," and positioned himself a "globe" away from Blake, at least in response to the plight of fallen queens. Yeats's politics and vision did not permit him to join in their radical embrace of the glad day of freedom's dawn in France. He did, however, appropriate their revolutionary imagery and displace their revolutionary energy—applying it to his own "unflinching" confrontation of the beast and to his exultant anticipation of an antithetical reversal of (among other things) their egalitarian values.

For the eye altering alters all. Depending on perspective, we have egalitarianism or leveling, nobility or tyranny. The drafts of "The Second Coming" suggest that Yeats was under no illusions about the "armed tyranny" of the Tsarist regime, but he dreaded even more the "mob bred anarchy" and "levelling" he had been reading about in Burke. The French Revolution, pledged to replace tyranny with equality, was, for Blake as for Wordsworth and Coleridge in the 1790s, rather like that "morning-star, full of life and splendour and joy" that Burke identified with Marie Antoinette as glittering Dauphiness: the symbol he contrasted to everything the Romantic poets exuberantly welcomed as the rising orb of freedom's light. In *The Prelude*, Wordsworth thrilled to "a People risen up / Fresh as the morning Star: elate we look'd / Upon their virtues." "Bliss was it in that dawn to be alive, / But to be young was very heaven."[20] But in order for France to stand, as Wordsworth said, "on the top of golden hours" (6.340), the wheel of revolution required that someone fall to the bottom. Where Burke lamented the fall of his exquisite morning star, the French queen, Wordsworth saw the oppressed become oppressors in their turn: the cyclic wheel of revolution leading—as Burke, however blindly prejudiced, had yet foreseen—to the gallows; or, to be precise, to that more efficient instrument, the guillotine.

Unlike Burke, Wordsworth, though humanly sympathetic to the plight of Louis XVI and his family, was too austere a Republican to succumb to plumage pity. At a time when Blake and Paine were responding directly to Burke's chivalric ode to Marie Antoinette, Wordsworth was filling such

---

19. *The Letters of Percy Bysshe Shelley*, ed. F. L. Jones, 1:504.
20. *The Prelude* 9.391–93, 10.692–93, in the 1805 version; 9.383–85, 11.108–9, in the 1850 version. Henceforth all citations from *The Prelude* will be from the 1850 version, which is the one Yeats read.

early poems as "Descriptive Sketches" and "An Evening Walk" with vignettes, set in France, of suffering *impoverished* women—his notice, during the great debate over the *Reflections*, that some remembered the dying bird. In addition to these early works, and to the original version of "Guilt and Sorrow" ("The Female Vagrant") and the moving story of Margaret ("The Ruined Cottage"), one recalls the dramatic moment in the Revolutionary books of *The Prelude* when the Girondin officer, Michel Beaupuy, points to the hunger-bitten French girl and movingly declares: "'Tis against *that* / That we are fighting" (9.517–18).

Though his tales of social suffering could on occasion be as sentimental as Burke's tales of monarchical suffering, Wordsworth's Republican, almost puritan, austerity largely immunized him to the glitter "of royal courts, and that voluptuous life / Unfeeling. . . ."

A light, a cruel, and vain world cut off
From the natural inlets of just sentiment,
From lowly sympathy and chastening truth;
Where good and evil interchange their names,
And thirst for bloody spoils abroad is paired
With vice at home.
　　(*Prelude* 9.345–54)

Even in the 1805 version, Wordsworth admits that there was an element here of reverse snobbery; but I suspect the passage was intended as a direct rebuttal of Burke's apostrophe to Marie Antoinette. It denies those "natural feelings" claimed for royalty and aristocracy by Burke and attempts to puncture the afflatus of his concluding sentence (in which "vice itself lost half its evil by losing all its grossness"). It may be more than coincidence that, thirty lines later, Wordsworth takes the symbol bestowed upon Marie Antoinette by Burke and returns it to the *people* uprisen fresh as the morning star.[21]

It was when those uprisen people themselves committed crimes abroad

21. In the lines quoted two paragraphs back. There is, of course, direct evidence of Wordsworth's position on the fate of the French king and queen. In his unpublished and unsent *Letter to the Bishop of Llandaff*, Wordsworth deplored "the idle cry of modish lamentation which has resounded from the court to the cottage" at the news of the execution of Louis XVI. In a letter written the following year (1794), he described himself as an opponent of monarchical and aristocratical governments and so no admirer of the British Constitution. But at Racedown in 1797 he read Burke, and it is clear even in the 1805 version of *The Prelude* that a great deal of Burke has been absorbed (the famous passage on Burke in book 7.512–43 was added after 1820). Nevertheless, as late as 1816, Wordsworth could still speak without Burke's overwrought emotion of the execution of the French king. His fate may have been "undeserved" but should serve as a warning to future monarchs (letter to Benjamin R. Haydon, 5 October 1816). And in an undated sonnet written at about this time, Wordsworth argues that modern "Emperors and Kings," remembering that they owe their thrones to the "nerve of popular reason," would do well to forswear "the oppressor's creed." For the *Letter to the Bishop of Llandaff* and this sonnet, see *The Poetical Works of William Wordsworth*, 5 vols. (1940–1949), 1:227, 3:151.

and at home in the name of liberty that Wordsworth experienced the kind of visionary "nightmares" that rode upon Yeats's sleep in "The Second Coming" and "Nineteen Hundred and Nineteen." Wordsworth's nightmare visions were, like Yeats's, of unjust tribunals, systematic murder, and monsters coming to second birth. And Yeats had encountered them not long before he wrote "The Second Coming."

Yeats's reading of Burke is referred to frequently, both by Yeats and by his critics.[22] But in exploring his response to the French Revolutionary books of *The Prelude*, and its part in the genesis of "The Second Coming," we enter unfamiliar territory. Indeed, the whole subject of Yeats's relationship to Wordsworth is sufficiently unexplored that a brief prolegomenon is required before plunging into details.

II. All Things Have Second Birth:
The Impact of Yeats's Study of the French Revolutionary Books of *The Prelude*

The major scholars of Yeats's Romanticism have declared that there is "no direct influence whatsoever of . . . Wordsworth on Yeats," that Yeats "with only rare exceptions persistently denigrated Wordsworth."[23] There is of course nothing comparable to the impact of Blake and Shelley. But Yeats did grapple with Wordsworth, his response over the years amounting to a mixture of respect and antipathy. Yeats's early Aestheticism biased him against Wordsworth, but he was not fool enough to dismiss a poet whose genius he acknowledged. Wordsworth became a haunting presence for Yeats: a giant of the imagination who diluted his gift, and whose decline after early middle age cast a warning shadow over the later Yeats, a shadow discernible, as we have seen, in such poems as "An Acre of Grass" and "What Then?"[24] More to the point here is the evidence of Yeats's reading of Wordsworth and my claim that it influenced "The Second Coming." To make a case for this assertion, it has to be demonstrated that Yeats was by January 1919 particularly well equipped to make use of Wordsworth in a

22. For a full survey, see Torchiana, *Yeats and Georgian Ireland*, 168–221, esp. 215, where one of Burke's images of the French Republic—"nothing short of the hieroglyphic monsters of Egypt, dog in head and man in body" (*Letters on a Regicide Peace*)—is suggested as a parallel to Yeats's rough beast. Yeats's study of Burke continued in the twenties. After winning the Nobel Prize in 1923, he purchased a full set of Burke with part of what he called "the Bounty of Sweden."

23. The first statement is Bloom's from *Yeats*; the second Bornstein's (*Transformations of Romanticism*, 45). Both have pointed out allusions to Wordsworth (Bloom, 356; Bornstein, 73). In addition, Bloom notes that Yeats is aligned with Wordsworth rather than Blake, as a poet less concerned with the *content* of the poetic vision than with his *relation* as a poet to his own vision (457), an observation echoed by Bornstein (48), who also notes that "Yeats and Wordsworth had more in common" than Yeats "liked to admit: chiefly, they are the greatest poets of autobiographical self-confrontation in their centuries" (46).

24. See above, Chapter 2. Yeats's image of Wordsworth "withering into eighty years, honoured and empty-witted" (Myth 342) is implicitly expanded in these matched poems, which set a defiant Blakean-Nietzschean old man against Wordsworthian dotage and complacency.

way relevant to the imagery and attitude of "The Second Coming." As a prelude to this task we can turn to Wordsworth's own *Prelude*, the work to which Yeats turned as a sort of companion and control to Burke's *Reflections*.

The change in Yeats from pre-Raphaelite denizen of the Celtic twilight to the more substantial poet who began to develop after the turn of the century and emerged almost fully formed in *Responsibilities* (1914) is, in part, sketched in his 1913 essay "Art and Ideas." Twenty years earlier, Yeats had approvingly noted Arthur Hallam's tracing of the origins of the Aesthetic movement to "Keats and Shelley, who, unlike Wordsworth, made beauty the beginning and end of all things in art."[25] By 1913, however, Yeats was questioning his conception of his own art and wondering if he ought not to "praise what I once derided." When he began to write, he admits, "I avowed for my principles those of Arthur Hallam in his essay upon Tennyson," the early Tennyson of "the school of Keats and Shelley," who, "unlike Wordsworth, intermixed into their poetry no elements from the general thought, but wrote out of the impression made by the world upon their delicate senses." Wordsworth, in Yeats's version of Hallam,

condescended to moral maxims, or some received philosophy, a multitude of things that even common sense could understand. Wordsworth had not less genius than the others—even Hallam allowed his genius; we are not told that Mary of Galilee was more beautiful than the more popular Mary; but certainly we might consider Wordsworth a little disreputable.

(E&I 347-48)

As the tone and genuine wit of this passage suggest, Yeats had begun to find his rejection of "ideas" in poetry unsatisfactory. But he set aside his doubts "while the roads were beset with geese," for Aestheticism "set us free from politics, theology, science," everything Yeats, applying Hallam, associated with Wordsworth and the sonorous later Victorians. Above all, Yeats sympathized with Dante Gabriel Rossetti, who "more than any other was in reaction against the period of philanthropy and reform that created the pedantic composure of Wordsworth." Gradually Yeats came to distrust this distrust of ideas and to acknowledge that aesthetic delight in sheer sense-impression was only one, and a minor, factor in the creation of genuine art. For one thing, "works of art are always begotten by previous works of art" (an anticipation of the enterprises of Frye and Bloom, and a justification of such genetic studies as the present volume, though we need *not* expel all history other than literary history). And Yeats had by now concluded that the Aesthetes' separation of ideas and sensory perceptions was based on a misunderstanding: "Why should a man cease to be a schol-

---

25. "A Bundle of Poets," *Speaker* 8 (22 July 1893); rpt. UP 1:277, though Frayne mistakenly prints "like" rather than "unlike Wordsworth."

ar" because he is an artist, "or why if he have a strong head should he put away any means of power?" In "our poems," he now thought, "an absorption in fragmentary sensuous beauty or detachable ideas had deprived us of the power to mould vast material into a single image. What modern poem equals the old poems in architectural unity, in symbolic importance?"

Yeats is very close to the central problems of modern poetry; but we can in the present context merely note the importance of power and unity (both symbolic and structural) in his conception of what the highest art must possess. Though he includes *The Excursion* in his list of Romantic and Victorian long poems that, for all their greatness, lack architectural unity,[26] Yeats ends his essay by calling for the remarriage of what the Aesthetes had sundered: a "reintegration of the mind" in modern poetry and art (E&I 349, 351–55).

All this would seem to apply admirably to Wordsworth, whose "best and favourite aspiration" mounted

With yearning toward some philosophic song
Of Truth that cherishes our daily life;
With meditations passionate from deep
Recesses in man's heart, immortal verse
Thoughtfully fitted to the Orphean lyre.
  (*Prelude* 1.228–34)

Coleridge may have been convinced that Wordsworth's was "an Orphic song indeed, / A song divine of high and passionate thoughts,"[27] but Yeats apparently resisted Wordsworth's achievement of that to which he aspired: a Miltonic fusion of philosophy and song, Truth and Beauty, meditation and passion, head and heart, thought and lyricism. What for Wordsworth and Coleridge was Orphean ecstasy ordered by a disciplined intellect was for Yeats a kind of mechanistic yoking of response and analysis, evidence of poetic power undercut by reflection, description, "mere" intellect. In this judgment, Yeats may have been influenced by Blake, who read Wordsworth with care but saw in him "the Natural Man rising up against the Spiritual Man Continually & then he is No Poet but a Heathen Philosopher at Enmity against all true Poetry or Inspiration." Where Wordsworth wrote (in the "Essay, Supplementary to the Preface" to his *Poems* of 1815): "The powers requisite for the production of poetry are, first, those of observation and description, . . . whether the things depicted be actually present to the senses, or have a place only in the memory. . . . 2ndly, Sensibility," Blake

---

26. His list included Shelley's *The Revolt of Islam*, Landor's *Gebir*, Tennyson's *The Idylls of the King*, and Browning's *The Ring and the Book*. The most notable omission is *The Prelude*, which Yeats had evidently not yet read (E&I 355).

27. From "To William Wordsworth," written by Coleridge after Wordsworth had read *The Prelude* to him in 1807.

declared impatiently in the margin: "One Power alone makes a Poet—Imagination The Divine Vision."[28]

Influenced by Blake or not, Yeats continued to think of Wordsworth as an impure artist. But something was nagging at him. Within two years of writing "Art and Ideas," he set himself the formidable, even Herculean, task of reading all of Wordsworth in the seven-volume set edited by his father's friend Edward Dowden. His letter of January 1915 to his father reveals an admixture of admiration, criticism (his own, mingled with that of Hallam and Blake), insight, and, above all, a determination to plow through the entire canon. As Ezra Pound, with him at Stone Cottage at the time, later put it, Yeats read Wordsworth as a duty to posterity.[29] "I have just started to read through the whole seven vols of Wordsworth in Dowden's edition," Yeats wrote.

I have finished *The Excursion* and begun *The Prelude*. I want to get through all the heavy part that I may properly understand the famous things. At the same time I am not finding the long poems really heavy. Have you any impressions of him? He strikes me as always destroying his poetic experience, which was of course of incomparable value, by his reflective power. His intellect was commonplace, and unfortunately he has been taught to respect nothing else. He thinks of his poetical experience not as incomparable in itself but as an engine that may be yoked to his intellect. He is full of a sort of utilitarianism and that is perhaps the reason why in later life he is continually looking back upon a lost vision, a lost happiness.[30]

If he managed to get through *The Excursion*, Yeats may very well have adhered to his intention to read Wordsworth in toto. What is certain is that Wordsworth was a significant presence in Yeats's thought during and immediately following the First World War. The reading of Wordsworth begun in 1915 is reflected in the remark about him "withering into eighty years" in *Per Amica Silentia Lunae* (1917) and in the allusion to "Tintern Abbey's" world of eye and ear, "both what they half create, / And what perceive," in the line in the prefatory poem to *Per Amica* ("Ego Dominus Tuus"): "We are but critics, or but half create." Both these references are negative; the second, in fact, anticipates and supports Harold Bloom's insight that "Tintern Abbey's" famous sublime passage contains a "deep

28. *Poetry and Prose*, ed. Erdman, 654–56.
29. Yeats's interest in the long poem was certainly stimulated by this relationship; but the assault on Wordsworth was certainly not Pound's idea; he thought Wordsworth "a dull sheep," though "one might learn a little about descriptions of nature from his endless maunderings" (*The Letters of Ezra Pound 1907–1941*, ed. D. D. Paige, 90). In Canto 83, Pound describes Yeats "at Stone Cottage in Sussex / . . . hearing nearly all of Wordsworth / for the sake of his conscience but / preferring Ennemoser on Witches."
30. L 590. In a letter of 1915, Yeats's father declared, "The intellectual awakening of the French Revolution has not yet really borne any poetical fruit," not even in "Wordsworth and Shelley." He said nothing about the transformation of energies and images stimulated directly by the Revolution (*J. B. Yeats: Letters to His Son W. B. Yeats and Others, 1869–1922*, ed. Joseph Hone, 206).

reservation," even an admission of "limitation" by Wordsworth.[31] In 1918, on the occasion of his tribute to Robert Gregory (who had been killed in action in January), Yeats cited, as an example of "great lyric poetry," Wordsworth's "Resolution and Independence" (UP 2:430). The year 1919 began with Yeats's composition, some two months after the Armistice, of "The Second Coming." Later in the year, he alluded to the French Revolutionary books of *The Prelude*—an allusion to which we shall return in a moment.

Yeats read the Revolutionary books of *The Prelude* (his text was the 1850 version) with particular care. They are marked, underlined, and in one instance annotated. Just as he was primarily drawn to Burke for Burke's response to the French Revolution and began to read him in 1918 for ammunition against Bolshevism, so Yeats seems most interested in Wordsworth for *his* response to the French Revolution. His interest from that angle would naturally have been highest during the period of the Bolshevik seizure of power in late 1917, the execution of the royal family in July 1918, and the continuing mass executions that so troubled Yeats and led him in early 1919 to equate Marxist values with "inevitable murder," justified by the rhetorical question: "Can the bourgeois be innocent?" While we cannot be sure *precisely* when he read books 10 and 11 of *The Prelude*, Yeats's focus on what he himself called (in an annotation on book 11) "French revolutionary crimes" strongly suggests that he read Wordsworth, as he read Burke, for insight into the second birth of such revolutionary crimes: the Bolshevik Terror in Russia in 1918–1919. It would therefore not be surprising if sections of Wordsworth's *Prelude* dealing with French revolutionary crimes played a part in "The Second Coming," a poem of January 1919 that originally began with negative references to that Revolution and its contemporary rebirth in Russia.

We may begin our examination by glancing at the essay "If I Were Four-and-Twenty," in which Yeats alludes to the Revolutionary books of *The Prelude*. In this essay—completed in July 1919 and much concerned with vision and politics—Yeats accuses most modern writers of lacking the "dramatic sense," the vision of "evil," and thus the "strength and weight" of the great writers of the past. Significantly, Balzac is excepted from this charge, while Shelley is singled out for special abuse. Balzac, praised as having dispersed the "Utopian vapours" of political optimists, was of course one of Yeats's favorite authors, and an annotation in the poet's copy of Balzac's novel *The Jealousies of a Country Town* reveals both the source of those vapors in the French Revolution and Yeats's enthusiastic linking of Balzac

---

31. Of these lines, Bloom says: "Having invoked directly his eye and ear, he makes, even more surprisingly, a deep reservation about his own perpetual powers, or rather an admission of limitation. The mighty world of eye and ear is not a balance of creation and perception, but of half-creation and full-perception. . . . What is being repressed here is Wordsworth's extraordinary pride in the strength of his own imaginings, his preternatural self-reliance" (*Poetry and Repression: Revisionism from Blake to Stevens*, 75). Yeats, I suspect, would agree.

and Nietzsche. The novelist wrote of his Shelleyan character Athanase Granson: "a lad at that age will sacrifice everything for such [Republican] ideas if he is smitten by the word Liberty, that so vague, so little comprehended word which is like a standard of revolt for those at the bottom of the wheel for whom revolt means revenge." Yeats, his stout Nietzschean stick under his arm, underlined the word "revenge" and on the front flyleaf made his sole annotation in the book: "page 89—'revenge' is equated with revolt exactly as in Nietzsche." Yeats was exactly right, and such a comment demonstrates his assimilation and implicit acceptance of Nietzsche's contention that "*ressentiment*" is the "dynamite" of the "slave revolt" in morals and politics.[32] More importantly for us, it suggests the role Nietzsche played, especially when later joined by Burke, in Yeats's crucial rejection of the values of the French Revolution. "With the French Revolution," Nietzsche declared in an aphorism in the *Genealogy of Morals* marked by Yeats, the "last political *noblesse* in Europe . . . collapsed beneath the popular instincts of *ressentiment*."[33] We are now ready for Yeats's allusion in this essay to Wordsworth.

Probably recalling Matthew Arnold's charge that Wordsworth achieved his "sweet calm" only by averting his eyes "from half of human fate," Yeats accuses of "blotting out one half of life" those who, ignoring the obvious "obstacles," believe "man finds his happiness here on earth or not at all."[34] No source is cited, but in his attack on the optimistic notion of material progress, Yeats is of course closely paraphrasing Wordsworth's most ardent praise of the French Revolution, in the early stages of which men

Were called upon to exercise their skill,
Not in Utopia,—subterranean fields,—
Or some secreted island, Heaven knows where!
But in the very world, which is the world
Of all of us,—the place where, in the end,
We find our happiness, or not at all!

(*Prelude* 11.139–44)

32. O'Shea, *A Descriptive Catalog*, item 91. This novel, the first part of which was printed as *La Vieille fille* (1836), was later incorporated with other material in the *Comédie humaine* under the collective title *Les Rivalités*. Discussing Balzac's "romanticization of power" in 1924, Yeats remarked, "All Nietzsche is in Balzac." See Michael Holroyd, ed., *The Best of Hugh Kingsmill*, 173–76. The Nietzsche quotation is from *The Antichrist*, a volume Yeats read with pencil in hand.

33. *On the Genealogy of Morals* 1.16. This was marked by Yeats, not in his own copy of the book but in the Nietzsche anthology lent him around 1902 by John Quinn and now deposited in the Rare Book Collection of the Northwestern University Library.

34. Yeats, "If I Were Four-and-Twenty" (Ex 276, 275). Arnold, "Stanzas in Memory of the Author of 'Obermann,'" lines 53–54. Arnold's appreciation of Wordsworth requires no comment; but one of his criticisms is relevant to Yeats's position. Arnold once accused Wordsworth of occasionally using "poetry as a channel for thinking aloud" (*Unpublished Letters of Matthew Arnold*, 17).

Yeats had marked these lines with a rough vertical stroke in his copy of
Wordsworth. He also marked and annotated the passage, a few pages further on, in which Wordsworth, after having glanced back to this, the height
of his hopes, reaches the nadir, his "last and lowest ebb." In that famous
passage, the moral and intellectual crisis of *The Prelude*, Wordsworth,
"dragging all precepts, judgments, maxims, creeds, / Like culprits to the
bar," found himself "endlessly perplexed," until

> demanding formal *proof*,
> And seeking it in everything, I lost
> All feeling of conviction, and, in fine,
> Sick, wearied out with contrarieties,
> Yielded up moral questions in despair.
> (11.288–305)

Yeats marked these five lines with a vertical stroke, underlined "demanding
formal *proof*" and "all feeling of conviction," and commented in the margin,
"The cause of his change. He does not seem to have been made afraid as is
generally said by French revolutionary crimes or Napoleon but by a subjective process!"[35] While, as we shall see, other passages of Wordsworth (and
of Shelley) were factors, surely these underlined words helped to shape
Yeats's most-quoted lines: "The best lack [originally 'lose'] all conviction,
while the worst / Are full of passionate intensity." We shall return to this
point. But I would like to speculate for a moment on more general reasons
for Yeats's singling out of these lines and on the thinking behind his marginal note.

As we have seen, Yeats thought of Wordsworth as a man who encum-
bered a poetic experience of "incomparable value" by yoking it to a "commonplace" intellect. But his image of Wordsworth as a poet who superim-
posed thought and "utilitarian" or "moral" ideas upon spontaneous response did not completely blind Yeats to Wordsworth's occasionally subtle
handlings of this very problem. Yeats saw, for example, the connection
between "Anecdote for Fathers" and "We Are Seven," two seriocomic
debates in which the speaker forces children to justify themselves rationally,
a dissection of vitality by demonstrative, adult categories of thought. Yeats
found "Anecdote for Fathers" (annotated in his copy of Wordsworth,
1:190) "as charming as 'We Are Seven' is abominable." He probably detested the singsong meter of the latter, perhaps had Max Beerbohm's famous cartoon ("Mr. Wordsworth at Cross-Purposes in the Lake Country")
in mind, and was doubtless annoyed by the palpable design of Wordsworth's moral maxim. "Anecdote for Fathers," which I suspect influenced
Yeats's own poem "Father and Child," is a subtler experiment; and the

---

35. Annotation in Yeats's Wordsworth: the Dowden edition, *Works* 7:215. O'Shea, *A Descriptive Catalog*, item 2292. Where I read "process," O'Shea reads "concern."

Piaget-like speaker's repeated insistence that his son justify a spontaneous choice—"Why, Edward, tell me why?"—would have reminded Yeats of his favorite among the sayings of Nietzsche's Zarathustra, "Am I a barrel of memories that I can give you my reasons?"[36] Zarathustra's rhetorical question might also have come to mind when Yeats encountered the passage he annotated in book 11 of *The Prelude*, the crisis in which Wordsworth dragged everything before the bar of analytic reason, "demanding formal *proof,* / And seeking it in every thing" until he fell into hopeless perplexity and despair. That was a Wordsworth who had not yet learned that the child is father to the man, had not yet mastered the "lore" his heart received from the boy of "Anecdote for Fathers."

The annotation on 11.301–5 quoted above is intriguing and raises "whys" of our own. Is Yeats anxious to attribute Wordsworth's crisis and his change in attitude toward the Revolution less to the course of the Revolution itself than to his inner flaw, a reliance on the analytic intellect? Or is he being sympathetic, even approving: noting that even though it brings him to despair, Wordsworth is here less outer- than inner-directed, a Yeatsian "subjective" man? Or is he scolding Wordsworth for not having been *more* repelled by "revolutionary crimes"—or for despairing after the collapse of hopes that were Utopian to begin with? The Yeatsian hero is the man who stands, "nor by vain hope nor by despair unmanned," an early version of lines written at about the same time as "The Second Coming" and "If I Were Four-and-Twenty":

He who can read the signs nor sink unmanned
Into the half-deceit of some intoxicant
From shallow wits—

The poem, "Nineteen Hundred and Nineteen," was originally entitled "The Things That Come Again," then "Thoughts upon the Present State of the World." Both the lines quoted—embodying, I suspect, an implicit contrast between Wordsworth and unflinching Yeats—and the earlier titles suggest the influence of the Revolutionary books of *The Prelude*.[37]

This is speculation. What is certain is that Yeats knew from passages he had just read in book 11 that Wordsworth was driven to "speculative schemes / That promised to abstract the hopes of Man / Out of his feelings" (a phrase underlined by Yeats) as a direct result of political events: Britain's declaration of war (February 1793), followed by French aggression

36. Yeats quotes, or slightly misquotes, this saying of Zarathustra on several occasions; see L 650; LTSM 103.

37. "Nineteen Hundred and Nineteen" (VP 429). For the draft version of the "unmanned" line and the earlier projected titles, see Curtis Bradford, *Yeats at Work*, 66, 67. The references to being "unmanned" by hope or despair and being intoxicated as a result of "shallow wits" both point to Wordsworth—described by Yeats as deluded by Utopian vapours, of "commonplace" intellect (actually "empty-witted" as an old man), and as a poet in whose work we find a "feminine element" (L 590, 710; Myth 342).

in Spain, Italy, Holland, and Germany (1794–1795), and the emergence after 1795 of Bonaparte. These events ended the blissful hope of a practical "exercise" of skill in "the very world" of "all of us," and Wordsworth, deprived of this actual embodiment of Liberty's "tenets," turned to abstract analysis of societal and individual conduct.[38]

Nevertheless, Yeats is accurate in his marginal comment. The spectacle of the French having "become oppressors in their turn," changing from a war of self-defense to "one of conquest,"[39] angered and disappointed Wordsworth but did not, as Yeats notes, produce the "change" that brought him to his "last and lowest ebb." Wordsworth read "France's doom," he tells us, "with anger vexed, with disappointment sore, / But not dismayed." Indeed, he "adhered / More firmly to old tenets" and in a desperate attempt to *prove* their validity turned to the Jacobinical rationalism he found in Godwin and other radical literature: that schematic, desiccated reason that produced the monster, Theoretical Man, so at odds with the Romantic Man of integrated mind, emotions, and spirit. It was precisely the gap between Theoretical Man and genuine thinking and feeling human beings that produced the crisis in Wordsworth and Coleridge and that led them to realize that on this question of human psychology they were not at all with the Jacobins, French or English, but with, of all people, the chief opponent of the Revolution, Edmund Burke.[40]

Whatever his hopes and fears about the French Revolution and its inexorable movement away from liberty toward oppression and that "last opprobrium," the coronation of Napoleon as emperor ("the dog / Returning to his vomit," the betrayal of the revolutionary "sun / That rose in splendour" only to "set like an Opera phantom"), Wordsworth *did* "change" as a result of what Yeats called a "subjective process." From this crisis, as everyone knows, he was saved by Nature, Coleridge, and, perhaps most of all, Dorothy. For it was she who maintained for him "a saving intercourse" with his "true self," William Wordsworth, "Poet" (a phrase possibly echoed by Yeats in his reference to "my poems, my true self"), and who led him back "to those sweet counsels between head and heart"; to, in short, what Yeats called in 1913 "the reintegration of the mind" into a unity of being in which blood, imagination, and intellect run together.[41]

---

38. *The Prelude* 11.224–26, 139–44.

39. Ibid., 11.206–16. Lenin makes the same point, going on to note that the French national wars, having become "imperialist wars, . . . in their turn engendered wars for national liberation against Napoleon's imperialism" (*Collected Works*, 19:213). Wordsworth and Coleridge would date the transformation earlier, with the French invasion of Switzerland (1798), the act of aggression they could not forgive.

40. *The Prelude* 11.211 ff. The formulation of Russell Kirk would be endorsed by many Romantics, from Wordsworth to Yeats: "Burke, rather than being an old-fashioned apologist for dying superstitions, struck through the mask of the Age of Reason to the dark complexities of human existence. . . . The Romantics followed Burke in this" (*The Conservative Mind*, 3d ed., 43).

41. *The Prelude* 11.321–69. For Yeats's reference to "my poems, my true self," see "Pages from a Diary in 1930" (Ex 308).

In context, then, Yeats's accurate analysis of the crisis in Wordsworth as subjective does not dismiss the significant impact on him of "French revolutionary crimes or Napoleon." French revolutionary crimes tormented Wordsworth to nightmare and drove him to the crisis just described—as Yeats very well knew from his reading of this and the previous book of *The Prelude*.

The care with which Yeats read book 10 can be partially gauged by his frequent markings and underlinings. The crucial point is that Yeats's fundamental concern was with Wordsworth's reactions to revolutionary crimes. For example, he checked Wordsworth's vivid description of the Reign of Terror (September 1793-July 1794), and the details of that re-creation may have lodged in the later poet's memory. Wordsworth speaks of "domestic carnage," with old men, maidens, and warriors, even "the mother from the cradle of her babe," perishing under the guillotine: "a toy that mimics with revolving wings / The motion of a wind-mill," a plaything the Jacobins worked as an eager child might ("if light desires of innocent little ones / May with such heinous appetites be compared") that it "may whirl the faster" (10.356–74). Wordsworth's figure of the mother torn from the cradle of her babe may have contributed something to the atrocity of "the mother, murdered at her door" and left "to crawl in her own blood" in "Nineteen Hundred and Nineteen,"[42] while the cradle, the innocent little ones, and even the gyre-like, wing-like whirling of the guillotine may have stirred in Yeats's memory as he began "The Second Coming," a poem whose opening draft is concerned with a bird whirling in a widening gyre and the murder of innocents by revolutionaries.

Wordsworth goes on to note the execution of a woman—not Marie Antoinette, but Madame Roland, alluding to her famous last words ("O Liberty, what crimes are committed in thy name!"). Yeats also marked the next passage, in which Wordsworth concludes his account of the Terror, describing his nightmares of mass executions and of "unjust tribunals," terrors that he felt even "in the last place of refuge—my own soul" (10.381–83, 398–415). His day-thoughts were "melancholy":

> my nights were miserable;
> Through months, through years, long after the last beat
> Of those atrocities, the hour of sleep
> To me came rarely charged with natural gifts,
> Such ghastly visions had I of despair
> And tyranny, and implements of death;
> And innocent victims . . .
>
> (10.398–404)

---

42. VP 429. For Black and Tan atrocities at Gort, including the murder of Mrs. Ellen Quinn, see *Lady Gregory's Journals, 1916–1930*, ed. Lennox Robinson, 129ff.

Yeats marked these lines with a vertical double stroke and underlined Wordsworth's phrase about the "different ritual"[43] and "countenance" required under these agonizing circumstances to "promote this second love," that is, love of man, his first love being that of "nature" (10.429–30, 417).

These nightmares are strikingly similar to those we encounter in the drafts of "The Second Coming," drafts in which "anarchy" follows "tyranny," in which we have unjust "judges," where "everyday some innocent has died," and there is "murderer to follow murderer." It hardly needs to be added that the whole idea of nightmare is crucial to the final version of "The Second Coming," in which twenty centuries of Urizenic "stony sleep" are "vexed to nightmare by a rocking cradle," and to such related poems as "Nineteen Hundred and Nineteen" and "The Gyres," in which blood-stained nightmares continue to ride upon sleep.[44]

Wordsworth's nightmares about the innocent victims of the Reign of Terror of 1793–1794 represent the bloody fulfillment of his earlier premonitions of a "second birth" of the murder unleashed in the September Massacres of 1792, that foretaste of the Terror to come. The crucial lines for us come early in book 10. This is the passage that, I believe, provided Yeats with an alternate source, in addition to Burke's *Reflections*, for his thoughts about the French royal family and the murder of innocents; most significantly, it supplied the precise image of the "second birth" of a predatory beast.

Wordsworth had returned to Paris in October. Two months earlier the king and queen had been deposed and imprisoned. The allied forces, which had invaded France in mid-August, had been decisively turned back at Valmy. The Republic was proclaimed the following day, September 21. Wordsworth's optimism was high:

> Lamentable crimes,
> 'Tis true, had gone before this hour, dire work
> Of massacre, in which the senseless sword
> Was prayed to as a judge; but these were past,
> Earth free from them for ever, as was thought,—
> Ephemeral monsters, to be seen but once!
> Things that could only show themselves and die.
>   (10.41–47)

---

43. Wordsworth is probably alluding to the creation, by the leaders of the French Revolution, of fetes and ceremonial rituals that they hoped would embody the abstract ideas of liberty, equality, and fraternity. This phenomenon, and its aesthetic and literary implications, is impressively studied in Gerald McNiece's chapter "Revolutionary Ritual and Revolutionary Lyrics," in his *Shelley and the Revolutionary Idea*.

44. Yeats Archives, Stony Brook (these manuscripts have also been transcribed by Stallworthy in *Between the Lines*). "The Gyres" (VP 564) mingles hysteria with indifference: "What matter though numb nightmare ride on top, / And blood and mire the sensitive body stain? / What matter?"

"As was *thought*": we cannot fail to note how close these lines are in self-mocking tone and even imagery to Yeats's "Nineteen Hundred and Nineteen":

O what fine thought we had because we thought
That the worst rogues and rascals had died out.
All teeth were drawn, all ancient tricks unlearned
. . .
Now days are dragon-ridden, the nightmare
Rides upon sleep . . .
. . .
The night can sweat with terror as before
We pieced our thoughts into philosophy
And planned to bring the world under a rule . . .

The "lamentable crimes" of which Wordsworth speaks involved the butchery of almost eleven hundred victims suspected of Royalist plotting. Among those dragged from prison in early September, sentenced to death by tribunals, and killed instantly by small squads of executioners was the Princess de Lamballe, maid of honor to the queen. Her body was sexually mutilated and paraded before the windows of the prison that held the royal family. This was the best documented of the atrocities that accomplished the final discredit of the Revolution among moderates in most of Europe and America. But not among genuine radicals, whose societies in England actually flourished between 1792 and 1795; and not, we notice along with Yeats, in the eyes of Wordsworth—at least not yet.[45]

What is explicit in Yeats—rejection of "Utopian" hope and "thought"—is, at this point, only implicit in Wordsworth. Back in Paris on his way to London, he was "cheered . . . with hope." He passed "the prison where the unhappy monarch lay, / Associate with his children and his wife / In bondage," and the square where many of those who had stormed the palace in August were killed. Wordsworth became perplexed, like a man who "questions the mute leaves with pain." But that night, he tells us, he "felt most deeply in what world I was"; for that night, in his "high" and "lonely" room, Wordsworth fell into a visionary trance:

              the fear gone by
Pressed on me almost like a fear to come.
I thought of those September massacres,
Divided from me by one little month,

---

45. On the September Massacres, see Gerard Walter, *Les Massacres de septembre*. An alphabetical list of 1,086 victims is given in Maton de la Varenne, *Histoire particulière des événements . . . de juin, de juillet, d'août et septembre 1792*. As E. P. Thompson and David Erdman have shown, the September Massacres did not turn radical "retreat" into "rout," as Mark Schorer once said (*William Blake: The Politics of Vision*, 164).

Saw them and touched; the rest was conjured up
From tragic fictions or true history,
Remembrances and dim admonishments.
The horse is taught his manage, and no star
Of wildest course but treads back his own steps;
For the spent hurricane the air provides
As fierce a successor; the tide retreats
But to return out of its hiding-place
In the great deep; all things have second birth;
The earthquake is not satisfied at once;
And in this way I wrought upon myself,
Until I seemed to hear a voice that cried,
To the whole city, "Sleep no more." The trance
Fled with the voice to which it had given birth;
But vainly comments of a calmer mind
Promised soft peace and sweet forgetfulness.
The place, all hushed and silent as it was,
Appeared unfit for the repose of night,
Defenceless as a wood where tigers roam.
     (10.71–93)

So much for "ephemeral monsters, to be seen," according to the optimists in whose ranks Wordsworth struggled to remain, "but once." "Conjured up" from his reading (including *Macbeth* and Blake's "The Tyger," a
copy of which may be found in Wordsworth's commonplace book) and
from his experience of nature (animal, star, sea, and that recurrent emblem
of the French Revolution, earthquake), and from the psychic equivalent of
that "hiding-place / In the great deep" that is the source of the retreating
and returning "tide," comes a deeper, more terrifying visionary intuition:
the tigers will doubtless roam again, for "all things have second birth."
     There were few qualities Yeats admired more than "unwilling belief,"
that is, the capacity to acknowledge the limitations of rationalistic optimism
and to accept the tragic facts of "evil" and suffering. "How much of the
strength and weight of Dante and Balzac comes from unwilling belief," he
asked rhetorically in "If I Were Four-and-Twenty," "from the lack of it
how much of the rhetoric and vagueness of all Shelley that does not arise
from personal feeling?" (Ex 277) Though he nowhere praises Wordsworth
as he praises Dante and Balzac, Yeats would certainly have found "unwilling belief" in this section of *The Prelude*. And he would have found something even more exciting from his point of view. For Wordsworth's reluctant surrender of his optimistic liberalism was based on genuine visionary
intuition, prophetic dreams in his high and lonely tower of a monstrous
"second birth." That Yeats remembered this passage is strongly suggested
by his original title for "Nineteen Hundred and Nineteen" ("The Things
That Come Again") and by a crucial verbal and thematic echo in the drafts

of "The Second Coming." For in the manuscripts of the poem in which a blood-dimmed tide returns and "a vast image out of *Spiritus Mundi* / Troubles [his] sight," Yeats originally referred not to a "second *coming*," but to a "second *birth*":

> Surely the second
> birth comes near—
> Surely the hour of the second birth is here . . .
> The second birth!

This phrase is far more accurate a description of the central action of Yeats's poem than is *second coming*. Yeats wanted the reverberation of the New Testament and the shock value of fusing the prophecy of the *parousia* of Christ with that of the advent of the bestial Antichrist—a beast even more terrifying than that of the Book of Revelation, for there is no Christ in the picture to subdue it. Whatever the reason for his alteration, and whatever we may feel it adds to or detracts from the poem, I suspect that one motive behind Yeats's changing of "birth" to "coming" was to cover his tracks—tracks that led back, through his reading of Burke and the Romantic poets on the French Revolution, to books 10 and 11 of *The Prelude*.[46]

III. Romanticism Revised:
The Poem's Alteration and Transcendence of Its Political and Literary Sources

In the early years of the century, Yeats had found in Balzac, Castiglione, and Nietzsche (his most exciting "counteractive to . . . democratic vulgarity")[47] the aristocratic support he needed in reappraising his role in the tradition of apocalyptic Romanticism. Later, under the immediate stimulus of the Bolshevik Revolution, Burke was enlisted as a counterrevolutionary champion. But as a poet and one of "the last romantics" (VP 491), Yeats sought support from the *poetic* tradition in which he had been nurtured. The passionate intensity with which he studied not only Burke but also Wordsworth during and immediately after World War I testifies to his hostility to Russian Communism, for him French Jacobinism reborn in an even more monstrous form, *and* to his realization that he could hardly hope to find political allies in his true precursors, Blake and Shelley.

In the drafts of "The Second Coming," Yeats couples the French and

---

46. Yeats Archives, Stony Brook (also in Stallworthy, *Between the Lines*). Bloom has argued that the poem, even in its final form, "does not justify this portentous association" with "Christ's prophecy of his Second Coming and with Revelation's account of the Antichrist" (*Yeats*, 318). Though most readers would probably disagree, the "second *birth*" remains a more accurate description of what this poem is really about. As for Yeats "covering his tracks," my study of Yeats's reading of Nietzsche has encountered many examples of just that.

47. In 1906 Yeats described Nietzsche to H. J. C. Grierson as "a counteractive to the spread of democratic vulgarity" (see Grierson's preface to V. K. Narayana Menon, *The Development of W. B. Yeats*, x).

Russian Revolutions as related anarchic phenomena—the latter (to borrow Wordsworth's image) the "fierce . . . successor" to the "hurricane" of the 1790s. Those manuscripts show him lamenting the absence in 1919 of the two chief opponents of the French Revolution—both in his initial jottings and in a second draft, where "there's no Burke to cry aloud, no Pitt."[48] Wordsworth and Coleridge (though they could never stomach Pitt) eventually came not only to admire but also largely to agree with Burke. But when he cried out for a new Burke and Pitt, Yeats revealed the full extent of his rejection of the political position of Blake and Shelley. Their demons of reaction are precisely his counterrevolutionary champions of ceremonious innocence—the "radical innocence" of "A Prayer for My Daughter," which is, in political terms, anything but radical.

The influence of Wordsworth and Coleridge is, incidentally, palpable in the "Prayer," written several weeks after "The Second Coming" and so intimately connected to it that Yeats had them printed next to each other in both *Michael Robartes and the Dancer* and the *Collected Poems*. The Wordsworthian "hurricane" blows through "A Prayer for My Daughter" in the form of a "haystack- and roof-levelling wind" and "an old bellows full of angry wind"; in the drafts we find: "What is some *demagogue's* song / *To level all things*, what is bellows-blast."[49] Furthermore, Yeats's prayer for his daughter reflects both the aristocratic conservatism of Burke and the prayers of Wordsworth and Coleridge in "Tintern Abbey" and *its* parent-poem, "Frost at Midnight."[50]

The echoes are not accidental. For at this stage of his own life and of European history, Yeats, despite his mixed, even generally negative, attitude toward Wordsworth, was emotionally and ideologically much closer to him (and to Coleridge, who assumed increasing importance for Yeats in the twenties and thirties) than to either Blake or Shelley. There is, however, interaction among these poets in the genesis of "The Second Coming."

Wordsworth described revolutionary Paris a month after the September Massacres as a fearful place "unfit for the repose of night, / Defenceless as a wood where tigers roam." Writing at the same time, Sir Samuel Romilly declared in his *Memoirs*: "One might as well think of establishing a republic of tigers in some forest of Africa." In the concluding passage of *Europe: A Prophecy*, Blake, describing the situation in early 1793, has Los call "all his sons to the strife of blood"; but it is Orc who dominates the imagery. Earlier in the poem, that "horrent Demon rose, surrounded with red stars of fire, / Whirling about in furious circles." In the finale, the light of the

---

48. Yeats Archives, Stony Brook (also in Stallworthy, *Between the Lines*).
49. Ibid. (italics added).
50. The situation in "A Prayer for My Daughter"—an anxious father near the cradle of his child—is closest to Coleridge's poem; but the details of Wordsworth's prayer for his sister in "Tintern Abbey" anticipate the details of Yeats's for his daughter; compare lines 121–34 of Wordsworth's poem with lines 33–72 of Yeats's. Further, the mixture of vulnerability and secluded protection marking Yeats's daughter—"half-hid" in her cradle and imagined becoming "a flourishing *hidden tree*"—recalls Wordsworth's secluded yet vulnerable Lucy: "A *violet* by a mossy stone / *Half-hidden* from the eye."

fury of "terrible Orc" appears "in the vineyards of red France." The sun glows fiery red, terrors fly round, chariot wheels drip blood, and "the Lions lash their wrathful tails! / The Tigers couch upon the prey & suck the ruddy tide."[51]

One suspects that Yeats, sending his rough beast into the world, has appropriated the tigers of Wordsworth and Blake (representing, as Romilly's metaphor makes explicit, revolutionary radicalism); reversed perhaps half of their political stripes (Yeats's beast representing both the end product of the vision of the Left and the first stirrings of an antithetical vision of the Right); and then somehow split his poem between attitudes of Wordsworthian trepidation and Blakean prophetic fury—though in the case of these lines from *Europe* the fury is tempered by Blake's concern about the course of events not only in England but in France itself. The speculation seems less farfetched when one considers the possibility of a fusion of these beasts of prey and Blake's "ruddy tide" in Yeats's concern that modern revolutionists are murdering the innocent with impunity, that "the blood-dimmed tide is loosed and everywhere / The ceremony of innocence is drowned," while, at the same time, an ambiguous "rough beast" is moving in the desert.

Coleridge is more analogue than source, but the "nightmare" of *The Ancient Mariner* so closely parallels the real surprise in "The Second Coming" as to suggest something more than coincidence. To the extent that the rough beast seems about to be welcomed by the conflicted speaker of "The Second Coming," it is anticipated as a violent annunciation that does not embody but, rather, precedes the reversal of gyres and the return of a hierarchical civilization, for which Yeats's most compelling model was his idealized Anglo-Irish eighteenth century. His own note to "The Second Coming" is only partially distanced by being placed in the mouth of his persona Michael Robartes: "When the revelation comes it will not come to the poor but to the great and learned and establish again for two thousand years prince & vizier. Why should we resist?" (VP 825) This is mere whistling in the dark, a manifestation of Yeats's own prejudices, dreams, Utopian "thought." Transformed in the alembic of his very human and poetic imagination, however, reckless and desperate hope is shattered as soon as it is indulged:

Surely some revelation is at hand;
Surely the Second Coming is at hand.
The Second Coming! Hardly are those words out
When . . .

When, of course, that "shape" that "troubles" Yeats's "sight" looms into view. Confronted by that shape, the Yeatsian speaker resembles Coleridge's

---

51. Wordsworth, *The Prelude* 10.92–93; Romilly, *Memoirs*, 2:5; Blake, *Europe*, plates 4 and 15.

Mariner, crying out in momentary hope (having loosed the blood-dimmed tide of his own veins) as the speck on the horizon takes "a certain shape," only to be recognized—"That strange shape drove suddenly / Betwixt us and the Sun!"—as the spectre-ship bearing Death and "the Nightmare Life-in-Death." "A flash of joy," as Coleridge puts it in the gloss, "and horror follows." The same horror follows in "The Second Coming" when the troubled gaze of the not "unmanned" but not quite "unflinching" speaker meets the gaze of the beast, "blank and pitiless as the sun." For the real surprise is not the obvious bourgeois-baiting irony that the *parousia* hoped for by the orthodox will take the bestial form of the Antichrist. The genuine shock is that Yeats's dream will be shattered—that the age to come is likely to take the form, not of any aristocracy of blood and intellect, but of the chaos its brutal engendering prefigures. If Yeats's *theories* are more naive than Blake's or Shelley's, his deepest feelings are accurate, and honest. What we are left with is the genuine uncertainty suggested by Yeats's final question mark rather than his vatic momentum and syntax. He was even more honest when, in the drafts of the poem, he explicitly acknowledged that whatever gnosis was involved was not his, but the beast's: "And now at last *knowing its* hour come round / *It* has set out for Bethlehem to be born."[52]

It is necessary to understand that "The Second Coming" ends in a genuine question; that the two "gazes" in the poem, however much they may seem to converge, retain their distinction, and that it is the beast whose gaze is blank and pitiless while the speaker's sight is troubled. Despite all his chiliastic theorizing and Nietzschean tragic joy, Yeats is not a glitteringly cold-eyed oracle who recklessly worships the cyclical birth or rebirth of energy, however monstrous its form. What we must trust, finally, is our sense of that opening Burkean music and our response to the most-quoted lines of the poem. We end with those, for here Shelley interacts with Wordsworth, and the deeper influence, I would insist, is that of Wordsworth.

The lines in question have frequently been glossed by the speech of the last Fury in *Prometheus Unbound*:

The good want power, but to weep barren tears.
The powerful goodness want: worse need for them.
The wise want love; and those who love want wisdom;
And all best things are thus confused to ill.
     (1.625–28)

These lines—the third of which is echoed in Yeats's "After Long Silence"— probably *were* in the later poet's mind. It is true, too, as Harold Bloom

---

52. *The Rime of the Ancient Mariner*, part 3. My point about the final lines of "The Second Coming" may be cryptic. The published poem implies knowledge of *two* phenomena: (1) that twenty centuries of stony sleep were vexed to nightmare by a rocking cradle, and (2) what rough beast, its hour come round at last, is slouching toward Bethlehem to be born. The phrase "but now I know" seems to embrace both. Yet the poem ends with a question mark. In the drafts, no knowledge is claimed for the speaker regarding the beast; the beast itself is described as "knowing *its* hour come round."

argues, that they embody "Shelley's central insight; an insight of the Left that Yeats proceeds to appropriate for the Right."[53] But it is also true that Yeats's lines—"The best lack [originally 'lose'] all conviction, while the worst / Are full of passionate intensity"—not only echo the phrase Yeats underlined in book 11 of *The Prelude* ("I lost / All feeling of conviction") but are very close, poetically and politically, to Wordsworth's analysis of the political situation in revolutionary Paris in the autumn of 1792. Acknowledging the agitation of his "inmost soul," he speaks of

The indecision on their part whose aim
Seemed best, and the straightforward path of those
Who in attack or in defence were strong
Through their impiety.
　　(*Prelude* 10.130–33)

Though still an advocate of the Revolution at this stage of his recounting, Wordsworth is attacking, from his Girondin perspective of 1792, the Jacobin extremists. To the extent that Yeats's "worst" are those on the Left, his position is far more compatible with that of Wordsworth than with that of either Blake or Shelley. If Yeats has gone to the Romantics to appropriate an insight for the Right, therefore, he seems most likely (judging from the echoes in both canceled and retained lines of "The Second Coming") to have gone to the French Revolutionary books of *The Prelude*.[54]

In conclusion, I wish to emphasize that I am *not* saying that "The Second Coming" is "about" the French or the Russian Revolution. Nor, incidentally, is it about the Fascist or Nazi revolutions—though many, perhaps most, readers have taken it that way, and though Yeats himself, in a 1936 letter, cited the poem as evidence that he was not "callous," that "every nerve trembles with horror at what is happening in Europe, 'the ceremony of innocence is drowned'" (L 851). If the poem were "about" any one of these historical cataclysms, it could hardly accommodate, as it does, *all* of them. One of the most persuasive polemics directed against the kind of genetic study I have been engaging in here concludes by warning, "The search for the author's generative intention as context of the poem is a search for a temporal moment which must, as the author and the poem live on, recede and ever recede into the forgotten as all moments do. Poems, on this theory of their meaning, must always steadily grow less and less cor-

53. Bloom, *Yeats*, 320. "After Long Silence" (VP 523) ends: "Bodily decrepitude is wisdom; young / We loved each other and were ignorant."

54. There is also a passage in *The Excursion*, which Yeats read in 1915, that resembles these lines in "The Second Coming," especially in their earlier version: "The good are wavering & uncertain." In the Wordsworth passage (that speech of the Wanderer whose influence is detectable in Keats's *Hyperion*), the Wanderer announces that the wavering good deserve their defeat, but that the defeat is temporary. Though the "impious rule," and he bewails their triumph, yet "the law / By which mankind now suffers, is most just. / For by superior energies; more strict / Affiance in each other; faith more firm / In their unhallowed principles; the bad / Have fairly earned a victory o'er the weak, / The vacillating, inconsistent good" (*The Excursion* 4.298–309).

rectly known and knowable; they must dwindle in meaning and being toward a vanishing point."[55]

I sincerely hope that my "search" has not contributed, even slightly, to a diminution that would fly directly counter not only to my, but also to Yeats's, "intention." For there was, of course, method in his deletion of details during the process of revision. In *Waiting for Godot*, Yeats's fellow Irishman Beckett achieved symbolic resonance by avoiding all overt reference to the historical-political matrix of the play: the German Occupation and French Resistance. Similarly, Yeats, by canceling allusions to the Irish situation and all specific references to Burke, Marie Antoinette, Pitt, Marx, Germany, Russia, and so on, liberated his poem from those localized events destined to be assimilated like so many grains of sand in the desert of time. One suspects that Yeats would have enjoyed the effect on critics of this procedure, for Marxist critics in particular have been disturbed by the autonomy of art, by what Geoffrey Hartman has called art's "aristocratic resistance to the tooth of time." In a 1950 essay, the East German scholar Werner Krauss, disturbed by this "capacity of art-forms to outlast the destined hour," acknowledged the inability of Marxist theory to understand the phenomenon.[56] Had we world enough and time, it could also be shown how, in a similar universalizing process, Yeats stripped his vast archetypal image of the Sphinx-beast of most of its private associations and accretions, striving for a deliberate indefiniteness and vagueness.

As we have just learned from Wordsworth, all things have second birth; and there is a sense of rondure in considering that it may have been MacGregor Mathers, the occultist whose symbolic cards summoned up in Yeats the mental image that eventually became part of the Sphinx-beast of "The Second Coming," who also provided him with a horrible example of misplaced concreteness, as well as a living demonstration of the paradoxical virtues of vagueness. Yeats recorded his uncertainty concerning Mathers's prophetic dreams in the nineties of a new revelation to be inaugurated by "immense wars" and "anarchy": was it "an unconscious inference taken up into an imagination brooding upon war or was it prevision?" Yeats concluded that, whether prevision or inference, it was "vague in outline, and as he attempted to make it definite, nations and individuals seemed to change into the arbitrary symbols of his desires and fears" (Au 336–37). Reinforcing what Yeats may have learned from Burke about the advantages of generalization and the element of uncertainty and indefiniteness in "the Sublime," here was fair warning for a man who shared the apocalyptic temperament of Mathers, but who had no desire to appear either idiosyncratically arbitrary or ridiculous. The example of Mathers, I think, provides another clue to Yeats's abandonment in various drafts of "The Second

---

55. W. K. Wimsatt, "Genesis: An Argument Resumed," in *Day of the Leopards*, 38–39.
56. Krauss, "Literaturgeschichte als geschichtlicher Auftrag," in *Studien und Aufsatze* (Berlin, 1959), but my source is Geoffrey Hartman, "Toward Literary History," in *In Search of Literary Theory*, ed. Morton W. Bloomfield, 199.

Coming" of almost all those localized, limiting "definite nations and individuals."

Yet the manuscript versions do serve a legitimate purpose in indicating the original historical counterparts of generalized "mere anarchy" and in suggesting the sociopolitical nature of the beast-initiated response. When the darkness drops again, as it should, over the manuscripts, we can—without diminishing the power of the final version of "The Second Coming"—"know where its roots began," can answer, at least partially, the question Yeats himself thought important enough to ask near the end of his life: "Those masterful images because complete / Grew in pure mind, but out of what began?" (VP 571, 630)

No less a figure than Goethe has said that to be fully understood works of art must, to some extent, be caught "in their genesis."[57] But what matters—the sine qua non—is the received text, the completed poem. "The Second Coming" does, of course, transcend the minutiae of its genesis: the inter-association of "revolutionary crimes" and the responses to them of Burke, Wordsworth—and Yeats. On the other hand, the finished poem would be very different—in terms of imagery, attitude, and actual verbal details—if it had not had precisely those "roots" I have tried to explore and to explicate. It is one thing, after all, simply to be general and abstract, quite another to generalize after having delved deeply into, and worked through, materials that are concrete and specific.

The method of Yeats, who always insisted "mythology" be "rooted in the earth" (LTSM 114), clearly falls into the second category. In the case of "The Second Coming," the specific details of its political genesis have been buried; but the poet's rooting of his fears and cryptic prophecy in contemporary history—significant soil enriched by the responses of Burke and Wordsworth to the great upheaval of *their* era—surely contributed to the unique power of a poem in many ways Yeats's, and his age's, most central. Without that rooting, idiosyncratic theories and his obsession with what Joyce called Yeats's "gygantogyres" could easily have produced oracular bombast that would be truly "callous" and shapelessly vague. What we have instead is a poem whose deepest feeling is less visionary than human—whose apprehensive and genuinely troubled glimpse of imminent apocalypse, or transformation, or the loosing of a blood-dimmed tide of terror may constitute (to quote Shelley on the French Revolution) "the master theme of the epoch in which *we* live."

*   *   *

Yeats's own note to "The Second Coming" (in *Michael Robartes and the Dancer*, 1921) draws on the fictional correspondence between two of his personae. According to the notes accompanying the mathematical diagrams Robartes copied from the "*Speculum Angelorum et Hominum*" and gave to

---

57. Goethe, letter to Karl Friedrich Zelter, 4 August 1803.

Owen Aherne, "the mind, whether expressed in history or in the individual life, has a precise movement, which can be quickened or slackened but cannot be fundamentally altered." This movement can be expressed by a mathematical form, most frequently by the figure Yeats reproduces in the note: a double cone, the apex of each cone intersecting the base of the other.

On this figure can be plotted the tension in the individual soul between movement outward into the external world and inward into itself—the "objective" and "subjective" tendencies respectively, or what Yeats italicizes as the *primary* and the *antithetical*. The figure is true also, according to the Judwalis (the Arab sect from whom Robartes allegedly acquired this esoteric material), of history, "for the end of an age, which always receives the revelation of the character of the next age, is represented by the coming of one gyre to its place of greatest expansion and of the other to that of its greatest contraction." The revelation glimpsed in "The Second Coming" will sweep away what belongs to the outward gyre—"all our scientific, democratic, fact-accumulating, heterogenous civilization," the world of the Lockean swoon and the spinning jenny—and replace it with an *antithetical* civilization, ushered in by the birth of the rough beast. According to the Judwalis, "When the revelation comes it will not come to the poor but to the great and learned and establish again for two thousand years prince & vizier? Why should we resist?" (VP 823–25).

Their doctrine, whether applied to historical or individual life, is, the Judwalis contend, "not fatalistic because the mathematical figure is an expression of the mind's desire, and the more rapid the development of the figure the greater the freedom of the soul." This problematic relationship between fatalism and freedom, the nagging paradox at the crux of Yeats's mature thought, will be taken up in a largely though not exclusively Nietzschean context in Chapter 6. The subject of Chapter 5, more specifically poetic, is still legitimately related to these speculations. For the tension in the individual soul between *antithetical* freedom and *primary* subservience to the abstract "objective"—whether materialistic or spiritual—constitutes the debate at the antagonistic heart of Yeats's most characteristic poetry. In "Fragments," materialism is "refuted" by a deeper "truth" that comes "out of" occult and chthonic sources ultimately "sacred." In "The Second Coming," in which a vast image comes "out of *Spiritus Mundi*," our *primary* age, the world bequeathed us by the scientific revolution and the Enlightenment, is "refuted" by a beast-engendered reversal transvaluing the spiritual—at least in its dominant Western form, Christianity.

The final section of this discussion of the genesis of "The Second Coming" stressed the poem's "alteration" of its political and literary sources. But more than Romanticism is "revised" in "The Second Coming," the very title of which reveals its fusion of Christ's *parousia* with the advent of the Antichrist. Going beyond the alteration of Genesis in "Fragments" (the substitution of Locke for Adam and spinning jenny for living Eve), this variation on Christian Apocalypse is another—though more extreme—illustration of the daring with which Yeats alters his spiritual sources.

Yeats's typical procedure is dialectical, first polarizing opposites, then nudging or forcing them together; yoking, as it were, fragments of the truth into a more inclusive unity of being. For years he tried to unite poetry and religion. Unlike "others of my generation" in being "very religious," yet "deprived by Huxley and Tyndall whom I detested, of the simple-minded religion of my childhood, I had made," says Yeats, "a new religion, almost an infallible church of poetic tradition, of a fardel of stories and of personages, and of emotions, inseparable from their first expression, passed on from generation to generation by poets and painters with some help from philosophers and theologians" (Au 115–16).

Yeats's chief among "poets and painters" was Blake. But early Yeats's vision only *seemed* to ally him with Blake, whom he tried to turn into an occult mystic. As Hazard Adams, Harold Bloom, and George Bornstein have pointed out, Yeats creatively distorted Blake in order to ally himself with him. In fact, Adams notes that Yeats's early "poetic religiosity" is "almost the exact opposite of Blake's attempt to raise up art as a 'prolific' contrary to 'devouring' religion." "Traditional sanctity and loveliness" (VP 491), the Mallarmean "sacred book of the arts" Yeats longed for as the bible for his "infallible church of poetic tradition," remained an unattainable oxymoron; and, as Adams rightly asserts in *Philosophy of the Literary Symbolic*, "Yeats's later career displays a growing realization—and a decisive one—that a sacred book and a poetic book are two different things and that the sacred book of the arts is in fact a profane book that expresses the contrary of the "religious."[58]

It is also true that Yeats's antinomial vision demands fruitful conflict; that, in Blake's axiom, "without Contraries is no progression." The later Yeats continues to fuse contraries in the sense that he plays variations on, or alters or inverts rather than simply dispenses with, the "religious." It is part of the process of transformation described by Valéry in the passage used as epigraph to Chapter 1, with the emphasis here on the ways in which Yeats "rebuts, overturns, destroys and denies" the "religious," but "thereby assumes it and has"—visibly or invisibly—"used it."

The focus of the next chapter is the *antithetical* alteration of received "religious" texts—Platonic, Neoplatonic, and Christian—in the poetry of later Yeats. But we may begin—returning for a moment to Robartes and Aherne—by glancing at the fictional, and thus all-the-more revealing, genesis of Yeats's *A Vision*.

58. Adams, *Philosophy of the Literary Symbolic*, 188–89.

III

SINGING IN CHAINS

5

ALTERING SPIRITUAL PARABLES:
YEATSIAN VARIATIONS ON GHOSTLY PARADIGMS—PLATONIC,
NEOPLATONIC, AND CHRISTIAN

The swordsman throughout repudiates the saint, but not without vacillation. Is that perhaps the sole theme—"so get you gone Von Hügel though with blessings on your head"?
—Yeats, quoting "Vacillation" in a letter

Homer is my example and his unchristened heart.
—Yeats, "Vacillation" (VIII)

Sex, philosophy, and the occult preoccupy him. He strangely intermingles the three.
—Dorothy Wellesley on Yeats in old age

We must laugh and we must sing,
We are blest by everything,
Everything we look upon is blest.
—Self in "A Dialogue of Self and Soul"

Then you will no longer have any need of your God, and the whole drama of Fall and Redemption will be played out to the end in you yourself.
—Nietzsche, *The Dawn*

I. Overview

When Yeats had Michael Robartes first show Owen Aherne the occult diagrams and notes from which *A Vision* allegedly derived, the soiled and torn sheets "were rolled up in a bit of old camel skin and tied in bundles with bits of cord and bits of an old shoe-lace. This bundle, he explained, described the mathematical law of history, that bundle the adventure of the soul after death, that other the interaction between the living and the dead and so on" (V-A xx). The most engaging bundle, the third, involves "interaction" not only between the living and the dead, the flesh and the spirit, but also between ghostly paradigms and their embodiments in the living speech of poetry. Though he was exercising audacity of thought when, at the height of his poetic powers, Yeats pronounced two subjects alone worthy of a serious mind, "sex and the dead" (L 730), the hyperbole hardly undermined the connection between the two, a connection demonstrated in numerous poems and plays as well as in the fictional framework of *A Vision* itself.

In Cracow, where "Dr. Dee and his friend Edward Kelly had . . . practised alchemy and scrying," Robartes finds his own crystal connecting angels and men—the calf-bound "*Speculum Angelorum et Hominorum* by Giraldus"—propping up one end of the bed from which he has just been "thrown" while making love with "a fiery handsome girl of the lower classes." Yeats is responsible for the mutilated Latin of the title (as his occult friend Frank Pearce Sturm later pointed out, the last word should be *hominum*); but the old book on which, we are to believe, *A Vision* is ultimately based is itself mutilated—Robartes's "beggar maid" had torn out the middle pages "to light our fire."[1]

The interaction between *A Vision*'s ghostly paradigms and both lyrical and sexual embodiment is reinforced in this introduction attributed to Owen Aherne. Despite the angry protests of Aherne, a scandalized Christian, it is to one W. B. Yeats that Robartes proposes to entrust his manuscripts. Having spent "much toil" upon Robartes's "often confused and rambling notes," Aherne complains about them being given to a man "who has thought more of the love of women than of God." "Yes," replies Robartes, "I want a lyric poet, and if he cares for nothing but expression, so much the better, my desert geometry will take care of the truth" (V-A xxvi). But, again, it is a matter of interaction; as the creator not only of lyric poetry but also of *antithetical* Robartes and *primary* Aherne, and as at least co-producer of *A Vision*, Yeats was interested in both the truth of desert geometry and the moister oases of literary and sexual expression.

Obsessed with the spiritual in more than Giraldian and Judwali form, Yeats ranged speculatively through Platonism, Neoplatonism, and Christianity; Arabic and Indian philosophy; Buddhism and the spiritual implications of Japanese Noh drama; Irish mythology and folklore; Hermeticism, the Kabbala, Swedenborgian angelology, Theosophy, psychical experiment, astrology, automatic writing, and the Lord knows what. He had none of the positivist's embarrassment at getting his "truth . . . out of" such suspect sources as "a medium's mouth." This obsession and its eclectic variety have been viewed from a variety of critical perspectives. Though the study of Yeats's transactions with religions East and West, with spiritualism and the occult, has its own intrinsic fascination, there are times when even

---

1. V-A xvii, xviii. For Sturm's correction, see *Frank Pearce Sturm: His Life, Letters, and Collected Work*, ed. Richard Taylor, 93–94.

hardened Yeatsians share the exasperation expressed by one critic trying to make sense of the poet's arcane speculations: "A little seems too much, his business none of ours."[2] But if Yeats's business was to obey the mysterious inner voice that told him to hammer his thoughts into unity, the critic's must be a related quest for unity: the attempt to determine how Yeats's spiritual interests and esoteric learning enter into, and are altered by, the poetry.

Some readers, understandably less engaged by *gnosis* than by *poesis*, either ignore the spiritual content of the poems or, whether stoically or condescendingly, accept it as the crazy salad accompanying an otherwise substantial meal. Others, for whom the "mummy wheat" (VP 562) is the main course, tend to take the spiritualism straight, dismissing as mere decoration imagery not related to the "perennial philosophy." The result has been readings that, however learned, often strike us as tone-deaf. And the key is tone. Richard Ellmann, though perhaps too insistent that doctrine is always subordinated to poetic ends, was acute in drawing attention to the Yeatsian caveats inserted in religious passages. Gifted with so fine an ear, he made tone detection, the recognition of simultaneous assertion and skeptical hesitancy, easier for those who followed.

Sometimes too easy. In the autobiographical passage relating how scientific rationalism (the detested Huxley and Tyndall) had deprived him of the "simple-minded" Christianity of his childhood, Yeats described himself as "very religious" and, more persuasively, as "steeped in the supernatural" (Au 116). The man who spent years as an active member of both the Hermetic Order of the Golden Dawn (1890–1922) and the Society for Psychical Research (1913–1928), and more years working on the revelations brought to him by ghostly Instructors through the mediumship or interpretation or skillful performance of his wife, was clearly interested in more than what Robartes called "expression." During the Automatic Script sessions (1917–1922), Yeats repeatedly lamented his lack of formal philosophy—despite his Instructors' insistence that he defer such reading until the sessions were complete. "I give you philosophy to give you new images," declared one of the Controls; "you ought not to use it as philosophy."[3] Disobeying the Instructors who specifically told him they had come to give him "metaphors for poetry" (V-B 8), Yeats attempted to systematize their revelations. The result, *A Vision*, is, like Everest, unignorably there.

With the publication of *Yeats and the Occult* (edited by George Mills Harper), the annotated first edition of *A Vision* (co-edited by Harper and Walter Kelly Hood), James Olney's illuminating *The Rhizome and the Flower*, and, most recently, Harper's *The Making of Yeats's "A Vision": A Study of the Automatic Script*, the time is past when one could dismiss Yeats's

---

2. William York Tindall, *W. B. Yeats*, 27.

3. Unpublished prose; cited by George Mills Harper in a 1982 lecture ("The Authors Are in Eternity") at Le Moyne College, Syracuse. Now in Harper's *The Making of Yeats's "A Vision": A Study of the Automatic Script*.

occultism with W. H. Auden's "how embarrassing!" or T. S. Eliot's orthodox certitude: "Mr. Yeats's supernatural world is the wrong supernatural
world."[4] Not that we should swallow the occultism whole (the flaw in the
valuable work of F. A. C. Wilson and Kathleen Raine), failing to note how
it is usually altered or varied by its context in actual poems or plays—and
often even in the prose, discussing which Olney refers to "the asser-
tion/denial, give-with-one-hand/take-away-with-the-other and always-
have-it-both-ways strategy that Yeats practises whenever anything of the
occult is in question."[5] Besides, there is a good deal about Yeats's supernatural world that most of us still find bizarre or, worse, repellent. Yet there
is much that no longer seems as eccentric as it did to the generation of
rationalist critics who sang a premature requiem not only over the body of
Romanticism but over the world of spirit as well.

Neither ridicule nor unqualified acceptance of the esoteric Yeats will do.
Caught between the pull of these uncritical critical extremes, most readers
sense that, somehow, the spiritual "sources" and the poetry are no less
interdependent than the Yeatsian *antithetical* and *primary*, the Here and the
There, the dancer and the dance. That creative interplay seems not only a
central issue of Yeats criticism and the mainspring providing most of the
tension in his poetry, but also the very heart of Yeats's mystery, both as
man and as poet.

Far from claiming to have plucked out the heart of that mystery, I intend
simply to focus on a number of poems fleshing out ghostly paradigms in
particular embodiments. Presumably, Yeats would approve; speaking
through the Browningesque mask of Kusta Ben Luka, he acknowledged
that while the ultimate source of mysterious knowledge might be supernatural (a daemon or "Great Djinn"), the prophetic voice, like that of
Shelley's West Wind, had been altered, varied, made particular, by its medianic passage through human lips, in this case the lips of a beloved woman.
In his fullest poetic tribute to his wife, he tells us that the inspired voice had
drawn "A quality of wisdom from her love's / Particular quality" and that
all those Parmenidean "abstractions," all those "gyres and cubes and midnight things," were but "a new expression of her body / Drunk with the
bitter sweetness of her youth. / And now my utmost mystery is out" (VP
469). When he wrote those lines fusing "wisdom" and "expression," Yeats
must have believed that his own marriage embodied the mysterious truth
later placed in the mouth of his heterodox monk, Ribh: "Natural and supernatural with the self-same ring are wed" (VP 556).

The marriage of "natural and supernatural" is sometimes one of poetic

4. Auden, "Yeats as an Example," in *The Permanence of Yeats*, ed. James Hall and Martin
Steinmann, 309. Auden was being at least as playful as he was patronizing; Eliot, in the
austerely judgmental *After Strange Gods* (1934), was not.

5. Olney, "W. B. Yeats's Daimonic Memory," 595. See also Ellmann's "Assertion without
Doctrine," chap. 3 in *The Identity of Yeats*.

convenience, with Yeats's echoing of his spiritual heritage in order to alter it part of the pattern of transmutation examined by M. H. Abrams in *Natural Supernaturalism*, his study of the Western spiritual heritage as modified by the individual talents of writers of the Romantic movement. Yeats's displacement, internalization, to some extent secularization, of the supernatural sometimes involves what is most typical of Abrams's visionary Romantics: variations on Milton, the central poetic interpreter and transmuter of the Bible in English. Yeats's Miltonic interactions are with both the epic poet and the youthful Christian, the demythologizing anti-pagan of the Nativity Ode and the chaste Neoplatonist of *Comus*. But Yeats's alterations are more typically of Neoplatonism itself; in this he had help.

Learned in occult thought, Yeats also read with excitement and insight a philosopher who provided him with the self-assurance he would later need to "mock Plotinus' thought / And cry in Plato's teeth" (VP 415). The philosopher was, of course, Nietzsche, that strong enchanter whose affirmation of the earth and of human instinct, of autonomy and heroic gesture, Yeats pitted against Christianity as well as against Plato and Plotinus. By the late 1920s the resultant tension—between Soul and Self, Saint and Swordsman, the spiritual *primary* and the heroic *antithetical*, austere Neoplatonism and Homeric Nietzsche—proved as poetically energizing as the Nietzschean antitheses Yeats was echoing: "Plato versus Homer" and "Dionysus versus the Crucified."[6] Thus, my main though not exclusive focus here is on the work of the late 1920s, specifically 1926–1927, when, as Yeats rightly said, his poetry was "at its best" (LTSM 113). Much of the discussion adumbrates the 1927 poem I end with, "A Dialogue of Self and Soul." This poem, as a study of its genesis should reemphasize, is Yeats's central alteration of, or variation on, the spiritual tradition. Yeats's true career had begun with a table-turning dialogue, the poet siding with pagan Oisin, as he later does with Ribh, against a fire-and-brimstoning St. Patrick. Written almost forty years later, "A Dialogue of Self and Soul" is a poem in which Neoplatonism, Christianity, Milton, and the whole Body-Soul *débat* tradition become the recipients of Dionysian news from Yeats at his most Nietzschean, full of a self-redemptive astringent joy.

This is not to suggest that a poet who ran his course between extremities did not vacillate. He did, and in the poetry it is *not* true that, as Yeats said of occult thought, "all vacillation lessens power."[7] He had just reread all his lyric poetry, he wrote to Olivia Shakespear in 1932; thinking of the debate between Oisin and Patrick (VP 61–63) and of the more recent one between Heart and Soul in "Vacillation" (VII), he cited a line from the next and final section of that poem in order to clarify what he now thought of as the motif

---

6. The Nietzschean antitheses occur in the *Genealogy of Morals* 3.25 and *The Will to Power* §1052.

7. Quoted by Harper in "The Authors Are in Eternity."

dominating all his poetry: "The swordsman throughout repudiates the saint, but not without vacillation. Is that perhaps the sole theme—Usheen and Patrick—'so get you gone Von Hügel though with blessings on your head'?" (L 798). It is no accident that the section concluding with this courteous but patronizing dismissal of the Catholic theologian von Hügel should contain not only Yeats's most emphatically Nietzschean declaration, "Homer is my example and his unchristened heart," but also a terminal benediction by a man who believed in miracles and who believed that, at certain privileged moments at least, he "was blessèd and could bless" (VP 503, 501).

II. Poems of the Thirties

Before concentrating on the poems of 1926–1927, we might initiate a brief survey of related poems from Yeats's final decade by drawing out the canonical implications of "Vacillation" (VII).

"Vacillation" (1932) ends with the Poet blessing, yet repudiating, his necessary contrary, the Saint, here represented by von Hügel. The poem's penultimate movement, which "puts clearly an argument that has gone on in my head for years" (L 789), is a career-concentrating debate between the Saint (as "Soul") and the Poet (as, inevitably, "Heart"):

The Soul. Seek out reality, leave things that seem.
The Heart. What, be a singer born and lack a theme?
The Soul. Isaiah's coal, what more can man desire?
The Heart. Struck dumb in the simplicity of fire!
The Soul. Look on that fire, salvation walks within.
The Heart. What theme had Homer but original sin?

The debate, in effect "A Dialogue of Self and Soul" in stichomythy, confirms a point frequently made by Yeats's most perceptive readers. "His poetry," wrote Archibald MacLeish in a 1938 article admired by Yeats himself (L 908), is "no escape from time and place and life and death but, on the contrary, the acceptance of these things and their embodiment." His predilection for the debate form itself reveals Yeats's allegiances as provisional and subject to the countertruths of polar opposition; nevertheless, late Yeats, as Northrop Frye says, locates "the sources of creation . . . within man, in the corruption of the human heart," a heart that may be a rag-and-bone shop but that creates "translunar Paradise." It is not only that Yeats is, in one recent and accurate formulation, "committed to the paradox that in and through the profane, the sacred, the creative, and the valid are to be found in the here and now." The more profound point, made more than thirty years ago by the late Peter Allt, is that Yeats's "mature religious *Anschauung*" consists of "religious belief without any religious faith, . . .

notional assent to the reality of the supernatural" combined with "an emotional dissent from its actuality."[8]

The debate in "Vacillation" begins with Soul commanding Heart to "Seek out reality, leave things that seem." Heart does not dispute this "notional" distinction between Platonic-Plotinian "reality" and the mere semblance of phenomena; but the poet, emotionally dissenting, cannot simply "leave" the things of this world, complexities of mire and blood providing as they do the resinous fuel of his art. "What," cries Heart, "be a singer born and lack a theme?" To *sing* is the Yeatsian alpha and omega: the "European *Geeta*" he proposed to leave behind is "not doctrine, but song" (L 836); Crazy Jane's "body makes no moan / But sings on"; soul must "sing, and louder sing / For every tatter in its mortal dress," and, transfigured to a golden bird, "sing / To lords and ladies of Byzantium"; Cuchulain's soul, on the verge of assuming "a soft feathery shape," is "about to sing." Perhaps the most passionately life-affirming song from *Words for Music Perhaps* is that of one of Yeats's favorite if least likely personae: "'O cruel Death, give three things back,' / *Sang a bone upon the shore*."[9] Whatever the singer's form, the song goes on, its most frequent "theme" the antinomies and human love.

Soul next repairs to the Hebrew Bible and to the great symbolic act in which the lips of the prophet were cleansed, touched by the burning coal brought from the altar by one of the Seraphim: "Isaiah's coal, what more can man desire?" Though "desire" signals a leading question, there is, again, no denial that man's "unclean lips" can be purged of "sin" by the live coal borne from God's holy fire (Isaiah 6:5–7). But what happens to the purified tongue if it happens to be a singer's? Heart, unwilling to be consumed, is indignant, even appalled at the prospect: "Struck dumb in the simplicity of fire!"

Even when, in the nineties, he was most susceptible to the lure of the spiritual world, Yeats invoked the mystical Rose to "come near," but not "too near." Like half-converted Augustine in the *Confessions* ("Give me chastity, but not yet!"), Yeats wants to be left "a little space / Lest I no more hear common things that crave" and, "seek[ing] alone to hear the strange things said / By God" to the dead, "learn to chaunt a tongue men do not know" (VP 101). This hesitant embrace, even recoil—come near, yet leave me some human space—is rejected when, as at the turning point of the "Ode to a Nightingale," it threatens to become more than a half-embrace.

8. MacLeish, "Public Speech and Private Speech in Poetry," 59–70. Frye, "The Top of the Tower," 257–77. Paul A. Bové, "Cleanth Brooks and Modern Irony: A Kierkegaardian Critique." Allt, "Yeats, Religion, and History." See also Allt's earlier insistence, "W. B. Yeats," that Yeats was *not* a religious poet, but that Christians should read him despite his dangerous doctrines because he was above all an honest man.

9. VP 512, 407, 408, 521; VPl 1061. "Three Things" was a lyric "I like better than any I have done for some years" (LTSM 143).

The attraction and *antithetical* resistance in "To the Rose upon the Rood of Time" initiates Yeats's characteristic pattern, a Romantic dialectic of notional assent and emotional dissent climaxing in Heart's recognition of the fire's "reality" and a simultaneous drawing back from such occult or spiritual cleansing.

As usual, Yeats dramatizes the antithesis. "There are," he declared in *Per Amica Silentia Lunae*, "two realities, the terrestrial and the condition of fire. All power is from the terrestrial condition, for there all opposites meet and there only is the extreme of choice possible, full freedom. And there the heterogeneous is, and evil, for evil is the strain one upon another of opposites; but in the condition of fire is all music and rest" (Myth 356–57). But it is a music without poetic words, a condition *too* disembodied for a poet caught in "sensual music" and attracted to the fleshpots of language. For a singer to be "struck dumb in the simplicity of fire" would be to lose all "power," to sacrifice the antinomial tension from which his art springs. Ultimately, Yeats's "heart" (literally and symbolically) is not with "rest," stasis, the Eliotic "still point of the turning world," contemplation of what Diotima calls in the *Symposium* "beauty absolute, . . . pure and clear and unalloyed . . . simple and divine." In *A Vision*, though he recognizes the primacy and inclusiveness of the divine symbol of the sphere, Yeats has little to say of its repose, its "concord." He is, instead, engaged by and in the perpetual *agon* symbolized by his diagrams of dynamic conflict, wheel and gyre. Unlike Socrates' instructress, Yeats's Instructors "identify consciousness with conflict, not with knowledge," all conflict leading toward "a reality which is concrete, sensuous, bodily" (V-B 214). That emphasis, experiential and Romantic rather than Symbolist or occult, looks back to the *antithetical* quest for "life" rather than to the *primary* quest for "knowledge" (to cite the distinction, noted below, made by Yeats in annotating Nietzsche in 1902), and ahead to the celebrated declaration in one of the poet's final letters: "Man can *embody* truth but he cannot *know* it. I must embody it in the completion of *my life*" (L 922; italics added).

For such a poet to succumb to the condition of complete simplicity, to the spiritually refining fire of Isaiah, Dante, Eliot, would be to pay "not less than everything"—to recur to that phrase about "the costingness of regeneration" borrowed from von Hügel by Eliot following his implicit comparison of himself with the recently dead Yeats in the ghost-encounter in "Little Gidding." Human speech, which necessarily draws its concepts from our concrete, sensuous, bodily life, is both inadequate to theology and threatened by it. Yeats had feared, in the proof version of "To Ireland in the Coming Times," that "we, our singing and our love,"

Are passing on to where there is
In truth's consuming silences
No place for love and dream at all;
For God goes by with white footfall.

In the published text the austere "silences" became a considerably more appealing "ecstasy" and the dogmatic "there is" a qualified "may be," but the emphasis remained on the threat presented by such total transcendence, its spiritual "truth" consuming "our singing and our love."[10] Aware of this peril, and knowing that "meditations upon unknown thought / Make human intercourse grow less and less" (the case with MacGregor Mathers according to "All Souls' Night"), Yeats had Heart ask rhetorically in the draft of this line of "Vacillation": "Can there be living speech in heaven's blue?" (L 790).

Soul's final tactic, drawn from the Christian tradition, looks back, not to the hellfire threat of St. Patrick in his debate with pagan Oisin, but to Dante's refining flame, the fire that makes all simple. "Look," Soul commands with the imperiousness of his counterpart in "A Dialogue of Self and Soul"—"Look on that fire, salvation walks within." Heart's response—"What theme had Homer but original sin?"—sets against Plato, Plotinus, Isaiah, and Christ the great pagan poet (Homer's is an "unchristened heart") of love and war, Helen and Achilles, his "theme" culturally wrenched into another context so as to intensify the clash with Christian theology. Such "salvation" and sanctifying grace as Yeats's Homer finds he finds within all that human turbulence and passion held by orthodox Christians to derive from the primal sin of rebellion in Eden. Yet, paradoxically if predictably, Yeats makes his Homer a believer in original sin, another singer in chains.

"Homer . . . and his unchristened heart"—Yeats's own chosen "example"—is demonstrably Nietzschean, the fully ripened fruit of the diagram he had set up thirty years earlier in the margin of one of the Nietzsche volumes given him by John Quinn:

Night {	Socrates }	one god	night—denial of self, the soul
	Christ		turned towards spirit seeking knowledge.
Day {	Homer }	many gods	day—affirmation of self, the soul turned from spirit to be its mask & instrument when it seeks life.[11]

These crucial antitheses are solidly based on Nietzsche's anti-Christian distinctions between Dionysus and the Crucified, Homer and Plato, polytheism and monotheism ("Is not just this godlike, that there are gods but no God?"), between slave morality and master morality, between power issu-

10. The unpublished version of "To Ireland in the Coming Times" (in a bound proof copy of *The Countess Kathleen* [1892] in Sterling Memorial Library at Yale) is cited by Richard Ellmann (*Identity of Yeats*, 49).

11. This crucial diagram, to which I have been alluding throughout, was drawn by Yeats in the margin of the Nietzsche anthology compiled by Thomas Common, p. 122.

ing in "affirmation" and *ressentiment* issuing in "denial."[12] The diagram, along with much else in Yeats, confirms the poet's observation in his letter of gratitude to Quinn for bringing Nietzsche to his attention and for sending him (in mid-September 1902) copies of *Zarathustra*, *The Case of Wagner*, and the *Genealogy of Morals*: "I don't know how I can thank you too much for the three volumes of Nietzsche. I had never read him before, but find that I had come to the same conclusions on several cardinal matters. He is exaggerated and violent but has helped me very greatly to build up in my mind an imagination of the heroic life."[13] In terms of Yeats's alteration of spiritual parables, that imagination of the heroic life took as model the Nietzschean Homer and his unchristened heart—doubly exemplary for Yeats since this is the central line in the stanza of "Vacillation" he himself chose to represent his life's work in the *Oxford Book of Modern Verse*.

Nietzsche's iconoclastic daring and what Yeats called, in a finely tuned phrase, his "curious astringent joy" (L 379) confirmed and strengthened the poet's belief in what he described, in the title of a splendid 1926 article defending life and art against religious censorship, as "The Need for Audacity of Thought." That audacity took the form of an increasingly candid celebration of the body. In his preface to Tagore's *Gitanjali* (1912), Yeats quoted "that doctrine of Nietzsche that we must not believe in the moral or intellectual beauty which does not sooner or later impress itself upon physical things," for (as he later put it in "Michael Robartes and the Dancer") "all must come to sight and touch" (E&I 389; VP 386).

If we leave aside the remarkable triad of Solomon and Sheba poems (their relatively early sexual candor reflecting Yeats's reading of *The Arabian Nights*), audacity, physicality, and tonic variations on the spiritual come together most dramatically in Yeats's final decade—most prominently in the Crazy Jane poems, "Supernatural Songs," and the "Three Bushes" sequence. The genesis of the latter may be traced in Yeats's correspondence with Dorothy Wellesley, and it was she who best characterized Yeats in old age: "Sex, philosophy, and the occult preoccupy him. He strangely intermingles the three" (LDW 174). "We suck always at the eternal dugs," wrote Yeats of his own "mood between spiritual excitement and . . . sexual torture, and the knowledge that they are somehow inseparable" (L 731).

In all three of the sequences just mentioned, the spiritual is *varied*, not denied. The heroine of the first group insists, echoing Blake's "Less than all cannot satisfy man," that "Love is all / Unsatisfied / That cannot take the whole / Body and soul"; Ribh, the unorthodox monk of the "Songs," tells us that "Natural and supernatural with the self-same ring are wed" and reads his breviary in the incandescent Swedenborgian light provided by the

---

12. The parenthetical rhetorical question is Nietzsche's (*Zarathustra* 3.8); "affirmation" and "denial" are Yeats's accurate synopses of Nietzsche's contrasting "moralities."

13. Unpublished letter of 6 February 1903; cited by William Murphy in a footnote in his *Prodigal Father: The Life of John Butler Yeats, 1839–1922*, 596, n. 69.

sexual "intercourse of angels," the dead lovers, Baile and Aillinn. The Lady of the "Three Bushes" sequence prays that "The Lord have mercy on us" yet can ask, "If soul may look and body touch, / Which is the more blest?" The still more daring "Wild Old Wicked Man," "mad about women," travels "where God wills," yet turns from his opposite number, "the old man in the skies," to "choose the second best," forgetting the spiritual wisdom "no right-taught man denies," at least for a while, "Upon a woman's breast." Woman had been earlier praised for covering all she had brought "as with her flesh and bone"; what keeps "the soul of man alive" in "John Kinsella's Lament for Mrs. Mary Moore" is the old whore's ability to "put a skin / On everything she said." And in Kinsella's altered version of the prelapsarian "Eden's Garden" (found in "a book . . . the priests have got"), "No man grows old, no girl grows cold," while the most solemn of Nietzschean pronouncements on God is transformed into a question and audaciously debased: "What shall I do for pretty girls / Now my old *bawd is dead?*"[14] Yeatsian physicality is at its most blasphemously sensationalistic in the quatrain whose titular "Stick of Incense" is revealed to be that of St. Joseph, who "thought the world would melt" but, probing in Mary's "virgin womb," "liked the way his finger smelt" (VP 619).

Yeats is less repellently mischievous, indeed at his most winningly insouciant, in "News for the Delphic Oracle." Even in this poem's predecessor, "The Delphic Oracle upon Plotinus," Yeats had altered his Neoplatonic source. According to the oracle's report (in the Stephen MacKenna translation Yeats read), the soul of the swimming Plotinus, even amid the "roaring welter," the "bitter waves of this blood-drenched life," never lost sight of his spiritual goal: sleep "never closed those eyes; . . . tossed in the welter, you still had vision." Though Yeats responded to Plotinus's strenuous labor in this, one of his "favorite" passages (E&I 409), and ended his poem with an anticipatory glimpse of the Platonic "Choir of Love," he devoted his most sharply memorable line to the dimming, even the temporary obliteration, of spiritual vision: "Salt blood blocks his eyes."[15]

In "News for the Delphic Oracle," with "salt flakes on his breast," a kind of testimonial badge of honor rather than the vestiges of degradation, Plotinus finally arrives at the Blessed Isles; but he, along with the ultimate spiritual and poetic authority, is given strangely erotic news. As Daniel Albright seems to have been the first to notice, there also appears to be news for young John Milton.[16]

This poem, Yeats's most astringent—and funniest—alteration of his own indefinite, effete early pastorals, ends in sexual tumult:

---

14. VP 510, 556, 555, 573, 587–90, 345, 621. Nietzsche's "God is dead" first occurs in *The Gay Science* §125 and is repeated in "Zarathustra's Prologue" at the opening of *Thus Spoke Zarathustra*.

15. VP 530–31. Porphyry's "Life of Plotinus" accompanies the Stephen MacKenna translation of the *Enneads*, 1.22–24.

16. Albright, *The Myth Against Myth: A Study of Yeats's Imagination in Old Age*, 122–23.

Foul goat-head, brutal arm appear,
Belly, shoulder, bum
Flash fishlike,
Nymphs and satyrs
Copulate in the foam.

But its opening lines, first scribbled in Yeats's copy of Milton's poems,[17] are filled with sighing wind and water—a suspended calm echoing that in Milton's earlier bulletin for the Delphic Oracle, in which "the winds, with wonder whist, / Smoothly the waters kiss't" while "Birds of Calm sit brooding on the charméd wave." Young Milton's fatal news for the Delphic Oracle on the morning of Christ's nativity is that all the pagan "Oracles are dumb"; that Apollo himself "from his shrine / Can no more divine, / With hollow shriek the steep of Delphos leaving," to be replaced by the infant Christ, figured as "the mighty Pan," who has "kindly come" to live with the shepherds "below," his arrival accompanied by "such musick sweet / . . . / As never was by mortal finger strook." In Yeats's alteration (reminiscent of his unconscious but revealing substitution of "deep" for "high" in lines of Milton he often repeated to himself as a boy), "Thetis' belly listens" while

Down the mountain walls
From where Pan's cavern is
Intolerable music falls.[18]

Yeats has replaced messianic Christ—Milton's heavenly Pan attended by sweet immortal music—with the lusty, half-goatish earthy Pan and his all-too-mortal music, "intolerable" to spiritual orthodoxy, whether Neoplatonic or Christian or both. Like Blake in *Europe* and *Milton*, Wordsworth in the "Prospectus" to *The Recluse*, and Keats in the "Ode to Psyche," Yeats is echoing the Milton of the Nativity Ode in order to supersede him, though Yeats's naturalizing of supernaturalism goes well beyond any "wedding" of mind and nature dreamed of in Wordsworth's philosophy, even beyond the warm sexual union of Eros and Psyche in Keats's ode.[19] Both the Platonic Choir of Love and the youthful Milton's angelic harmony are rudely dispersed by Yeats's sensual music; what Milton calls in *Paradise Lost*

17. Reported by Albright; the book was given by Mrs. Yeats to the late Richard Ellmann.

18. Yeats is playing on "On the Morning of Christ's Nativity," stanzas 5, 19, 8. As a boy Yeats often "repeated to myself Milton's lines: 'Bosomed deep in tufted trees / Where perhaps some beauty lies'" (Mem 78). But Milton's lines ("L'Allegro," lines 78–79) have been altered, Milton's "Miltonic" adjective "high" yielding to a more Yeatsian "deep."

19. In the "Prospectus," Wordsworth is engaging primarily the Milton of *Paradise Lost*. But the Nativity Ode was endlessly rewritten by the great Romantics, most memorably by Blake in *Europe: A Prophecy*, by Coleridge in *Religious Musings* (both 1794), and, very differently, by Keats in the "Ode to Psyche."

"the barbarous dissonance / Of Bacchus and his revellers" here becomes the fallen but resonant basso profundo attending Pan's copulating minions. These nymphs and satyrs—their "belly, shoulder, bum" a crude triad replacing "Among School Children's" leaf, blossom, bole, and body swayed to music—seem a far cry as well from the decorous "lords and ladies of Byzantium," Yeats's repetition, in a finer tone, of earthly happiness and the sexual principle in "Sailing to Byzantium." In renouncing Byzantium as a "holy city," while affirming the ultimate interdependence of natural and supernatural from which the Byzantine poems derive their power, and, more immediately, by renouncing both the Classical Blessed Isles and the Christian version of Incarnation, Yeats in "News for the Delphic Oracle" *almost* debases love to lust (almost, for Peleus *is* in love and the Choir presumably sings of love), impertinently choosing not transcendent serenity beyond desire but a generative fecundity that would make Milton's or even Swedenborg's copulating angels blush—to say nothing of the virginal sibyl at the shrine of Apollo, the titular recipient of "news" actually intended for Plotinus and Porphyry.[20] Finally, since the infant in Thetis' belly is fetal Achilles, warlike antithesis to the infant Jesus and his kindly reign of peace, we have another endorsement of Yeats's Nietzschean cry: "Homer is my example and his unchristened heart."

The unchristened, Dionysian music of pagan Pan is part of the deep cascade of Plotinian defluction; rejecting the way up, accompanying copulation in the generative foam, it "falls . . . Down." In "The Circus Animals' Desertion," Yeats says he "must *lie* down"—if he is to remain a poet—where everything starts:

Those masterful images because complete
Grew in pure mind, but out of what began?
A mound of refuse or the sweepings of a street,
Old kettles, old bottles, and a broken can,
Old iron, old bones, old rags, that raving slut
Who keeps the till. Now that my ladder's gone,
I must lie down where all the ladders start,
In the foul rag-and-bone shop of the heart.

Yeats's Platonic or Neoplatonic ladder of "pure mind" starts and, for a gravitational poet who insisted on the "rooting of mythology in the earth" (LTSM 114), cyclically ends in the dregs and dreck composed of what seems to be the rubble of "Byzantium," whose moonlit or starlit dome and Emperor's pavement here become (via Swift's "Sweepings from Butchers

---

20. I owe the parenthetical qualification to Helen Vendler. For the Miltonic and Swedenborgian angels, see my "The Human Entrails and the Starry Heavens: Some Instances of Visual Patterns for Yeats's Mingling of Heaven and Earth," 378–83.

Stalls, Dung, Guts, and Blood") a "mound of refuse or the sweepings of a street," and of "A Dialogue of Self and Soul," whose consecrated sword wound in silken embroidery is reduced to "old iron . . . old rags."[21]

Lying down at the foot of the ladder, Yeats deliberately and perversely chooses what Pietro Bembo calls, in the exposition Yeats studied so carefully in Castiglione's *Book of the Courtier*, the "lower-most step" of the Platonic Stair of Love, the *scala coeli*. The old poet, at once defeated, degraded, and paradoxically triumphant, turns a passive fate into a chosen destiny by embracing what he once called, in contrasting his *antithetical* path to the *primary* way of Eastern mysticism, "a dynamic and substantializing force as distinguished from the eastern quiescent and supersensualizing state of the soul—a movement downwards upon life, not upwards out of life" (L 469). It is the direction of Oedipus, the "new divinity" proclaimed in the 1937 *Vision*, who "sank down body and soul into the earth," an earth "riven by love." Yeats would have the chthonic hero of Sophocles' *Oedipus at Colonus* balance Christ, who, "crucified standing up, went into the abstract sky soul and body." As "a man of Homer's kind," a Nietzschean Homer of course, Oedipus is "altogether separated from Plato's Athens, from all that talk of the Good and the One, from all that cabinet of perfection, an image from Homer's age" (V-B 27–28).

These introductory pages of *A Vision* seem relevant to the conclusion of "A Circus Animals' Desertion." Just three pages before contrasting descending Oedipus to ascending Christ, Yeats compares the Muses to "women who creep out at night and give themselves to unknown sailors . . . except that the Muses sometimes form in those low haunts their most lasting attachments" (V-B 24). At the end of "The Circus Animals' Desertion," the old man descends—in yet another version of "desecration and the lover's night" (VPl 989)—into the genetic matrix of his images. Into a haunt lower than Alexander Pope's "moving toyshop of [the] heart," Yeats's descent is to a "foul rag-and-bone shop of the heart" whose shopkeeper, "that raving slut / Who keeps the till," is a debased but still recognizable Muse. Milton's Urania may have become, less than Pope's "coquette," a Dublin Paudeen, but the painful, fruitful exchange between art and heart, experiential loss and imaginative gain, goes on. Nothing is got for nothing, but the poetic "till" keeps ringing.[22]

The raving "slut" with whom Yeats formed his most memorable attachment was Crazy Jane, whose original name ("Cracked Mary") suggests a blasphemous, "rent" variation on the Virgin Mary. In "Crazy Jane Talks with the Bishop," she tells her antagonist, a "religious" spokesman nevertheless fixated on "those breasts," where *her* God—not Jehovah, or even

---

21. See Swift's "A Description of a City Shower." I borrow "dregs and dreck" from Robert Lowell's "Waking Early Sunday Morning," in part a conscious reworking of the final stanza of Yeats's poem.

22. For the coquettish toyshop of the heart, see Pope's *Rape of the Lock*, canto 1.99–100.

Jesus, but Eros himself—has "pitched" (set up and, perhaps, darkened) his "mansion." "Love has pitched" his tent in the form of a "mansion," not up among the stars (the lofty "heavenly mansion" the Bishop borrows from Bembo and John 14:2 in order to cast disdain on her "foul sty"), but down, *inter urinam et faeces*: "in / The place of excrement."

Jane is no mere materialist, no denizen of the "excrement" left when Locke took away the living world. What she insists on—echoing and altering Augustine, Swift, and Blake in her excremental vision—is the beauty of both the physical and the ideal world, with "Love" the *tertium quid*, the "great spirit" or daemon mediating between them. These are the words of Diotima as reported by Socrates in the *Symposium*. When Jane cries out that "Fair and foul are near of kin, / And fair needs foul," she is in agreement not with Macbeth's witches but with Socrates' fabled "instructress in the art of love." When Diotima takes issue with Socrates' statement that the "mighty god" Love is "fair," he leaps to the dualistic conclusion that she is declaring Love "evil and foul."

> "Hush," she cried, "must that be foul which is not fair. . . . Do not insist . . . that what is not fair is of necessity foul, or what is not good, evil: or infer that because love is not fair and good he is therefore foul and evil; for he is in a mean between them."
>
> (*Symposium* 202–3)

As a daemonic mediator, Love yokes apparent opposites, creating unity out of division. In that "parable" from the *Symposium* altered by Yeats in "Among School Children," Plato's Aristophanes describes human nature as "originally one and . . . whole" until split in two by Zeus. In a Donne-like axiom of spiritual and genital punning, Jane plays a *felix culpa* variation on that tragicomic rending: "For nothing can be sole or whole / That has not been rent."[23]

Jane is herself a mediatrix between the physical and the transcendent, the latter a world she acknowledges and vitalizes with Blakean infant joy. What, at death, she shall joyously "leap" into (in "Crazy Jane and Jack the Journeyman") is the light lost when she entered this fallen world, the pristine radiance of Plotinus's eternity:

A lonely ghost the ghost is
That to God shall come;
I—love's skein upon the ground,
My body in the tomb—
Shall leap into the light lost
In my mother's womb.

23. Plato, *Symposium* 190–94. For some observations on Yeatsian punning and the influence of Donne, see James L. Allen, "Yeats's Use of the Serious Pun."

Jane will come to God as a *lonely* ghost, the terminus of her "flight of the alone to the Alone." These are, of course, the final words of the *Enneads*, words of Plotinus also recalled by Lionel Johnson at the climax of "The Dark Angel," a poem Yeats rightly admired: "Lonely unto the Lone I go, / Divine to the Divinity."

But Jane is still altering spiritual parables. *Her* transcendence is earned, not through a body-bruising, soul-pleasuring abstinence, but (since nothing can be sole or whole that has not been rent) by utterly unwinding, through experience (even though she knows that "The more I leave the door un-latched / The sooner love is gone"), what Blake called in *The Gates of Paradise* "the sexual Garments." Though "love is but a skein unwound / Between the dark and dawn," if left unwound, it would bind her to the earth, condemning her ghost, like Jack's, to "walk when dead." "Sexual abstinence," though it "fed" the "fire" of the Crazy Jane poems ("I was ill and yet full of desire"), seemed to Yeats, if voluntary, "a most needless trampling of the grapes of life" (L 814; V-A x). Love's skein is to be fully unwound, the passions exhausted. "If you don't express yourself," Yeats told an interviewer at this time, "you walk after you're dead. The great thing is to go empty to your grave."[24] Yeats confided to Olivia Shakespear, "I shall be a sinful man to the end, and think upon my deathbed of all the nights I wasted in my youth" (L 790); and he quoted with approval one of Blake's central convictions, a theory of "emanation" at least half a world away from that of ascetic Plotinus: "Men are admitted into Heaven not because they have curbed and governed their passions, but because they have cultivated their understandings. The treasures of Heaven are not nega-tions of passion, but realities of intellect, from which the passions emanate uncurbed in their eternal glory" (E&I 137–38). The repressed and repressive Bishop—still in the words of this passage from Blake's *A Vision of the Last Judgment*—is a representative of the "modern church," which "crucifies" the true imaginative Christ upside down; one of those who, "having no pas-sions of their own, because no intellect, have spent their lives in curbing and governing other peoples'."

III. *A Woman Young and Old*: "Among School Children"

The debate between the Bishop and Crazy Jane was rehearsed a few years earlier in the opening poem, written in 1926, of *A Woman Young and Old*, a sequence notable for its alteration, largely under the auspices of Donne, of Neoplatonic and Christian doctrine:

---

24. *W. B. Yeats: Interviews and Recollections*, ed. E. H. Mikhail, 2:203. The interview took place in 1931, the same year Yeats wrote "Crazy Jane and Jack the Journeyman." Yeats makes a similar observation in *A Vision* (V-B 236).

She hears me strike the board and say
That she is under ban
Of all good men and women
Being mentioned with a man
That has the worst of all bad names;
And thereupon replies
That his hair is beautiful,
Cold as the March wind his eyes.

"Father and Child," in its own minor key, is another confrontation between submission to, and defiance of, conventional moral "bans"—another *Winding Stair* dialogue in which a representative of Self or Heart rejects Soul's life-denying way to a heavenly mansion, choosing heroically to rage in the unchristened, passionate dark.[25] That might seem too heavy a theological burden for this slight lyric to bear—until we read it as a deliberate alteration of its precursor, George Herbert's "The Collar."

Not that the poem lacks an intrinsic religious dimension, from its title on. The child is "under ban," under quasi-ecclesiastical interdict, of "all good men and women"—to oppose the "all bad," the "all good": one collective Blakean Accuser of Sin. Against this accusatory village ethos we have, in the girl's unanswerable reply, the young man's beautiful hair and exciting eyes cold as the March wind—cold *and* passionate, a liberating herald of the coming spring. The girl's triumph in the poem is achieved by means of the heavily stressed beats on *hair, beautiful, cold, March wind,* and *eyes,* which provide, beneath the serenity of her response, the physical, pagan power of incantation and the aesthetic-erotic excitement that drive from the stage Father and his bourgeois ethics, with its hearsay notions of good and bad, its obsession with what the neighbors say.

The poem's literary-historical coup, however, is Yeats's dramatic assimilation, and Romantic alteration, of the spiritual parable in "The Collar." Herbert's first line ("I struck the board, and cry'd 'No more'") and crucial word ("Childe") are echoed in Yeats's title and opening line: "She hears me strike the board and say. . . ." Like "Father and Child," "The Collar" is a miniature drama (though Herbert recounts a past event) of the revolt of the heart against orthodox moral authority; and the imagery of its more explicit protest also centers on the sensuous (the natural plenitude of cordial fruit, wine, corn, and garlands gay) and on the wind: "My lines and life are free . . . / Loose as the wind."

All this, the speaker of Herbert's poem has told himself, he must set against the Collar; against "thy cold dispute / Of what is fit, and not," against "thy cage," "thy rope," "thy law," "thy deaths head." But, as the

25. The poems alluded to are "A Dialogue of Self and Soul," "Vacillation," "Crazy Jane Talks with the Bishop," and "The Choice."

mounting intensity of his protest and the proliferation of his rhetorical figures suggest, Herbert's speaker is overwrought. The "Childe" of the poem, he is as excessive, as hyperbolic, as the Yeatsian Father. At the very end Herbert's frantic persona is rebuked, his defiance stilled, by a single word—the still, small voice of God or of the inner self—and the submission, prefigured by the growing rant, follows instantly:

But as I rav'd and grew more fierce and wilde
      At every word,
Me thoughts I heard one calling, *Childe!*
      And I replied, *My Lord.*

Herbert's "Childe" ends, like Yeats's, with a "reply" that is calm, but, unlike Yeats's, it is also submissive. Herbert's was the more difficult lyric task, and his reversal is the more stirring and magnificent for it. Reversing *that* reversal, Yeats's poem revalues the moral tables by implicitly rejecting the yoke (whether "collar" or "ban") of the Christian God—at least as that ban is understood by the Father and the conventionally "good" men and women of the poem.

On the basis of the analogy with Herbert's semi-autobiographical poem, we may see adumbrated in "Father and Child," also semi-autobiographical, Yeats's own *un*submissive, *antithetical* position in his relationship to the God of formal theology, of whom, he admitted, he always wrote "coldly and conventionally" (Ex 305). The tables are also turned by the poet on the speaker, Yeats parodying himself as a Polonius-like tyrannic Father, a Blakean Urizen or "Nobodaddy," or as his own curbing and governing Bishop—whose "ban" (VP 508) against Crazy Jane and Jack the Journeyman is explicitly ecclesiastical, rooted in frustrated sexuality. Thus, Yeats accepts, in this Romantic anecdote for fathers, the Wordsworthian credo that the Child is intuitively wiser than the Father who would impose his demonstrative categories of thought and his conventional morality. Though he found Herbert's "austerity" and self-discipline admirable,[26] Yeats has rewritten his Christian ending: instead of triumphant submission, the Yeatsian triumph goes to Dionysian vitality, to the almost impersonal energy of what Walt Whitman called "the procreant urge of the world."

In other poems in this sequence, other spiritual parables are altered in accordance with that urge. The fifth poem, spoken by the child become a woman, is entitled "Consolation":

O but there is wisdom
In what the sages said;
But stretch that body for a while
And lay down that head

26. Among the few poets Yeats once recommended to Austin Clarke was Herbert, whom he singled out "for his austerity." See *Interviews and Recollections*, 2:350.

Till I have told the sages
Where man is comforted.

How could passion run so deep
Had I never thought
That the crime of being born
Blackens all our lot?
But where the crime's committed
The crime can be forgot.

A witty Yeatsian variation on both the Boethian consolation-tradition and on the old theme of *felix culpa*, "Consolation" pits the woman's carnal knowledge against the pessimistic "wisdom" of "the sages": the Neoplatonists and other magi of the occult tradition, as well as preachers of original sin. She accepts and subsumes the sages' wisdom by telling them all precisely "where" fallen man is comforted: a genital concentering again reminiscent of John Donne at his most blasphemous. The woman's consolation—a gloss on one aspect of the "theme" Yeats attributes to his Nietzschean Homer—turns conventional theology on its head by making original sin serve the ends of sexuality (rather as Byron had, his guilt-ridden Calvinism sweetening the forbidden fruit). It is precisely a belief in the lot-blackening "crime of being born" that intensifies the moment of sexual ecstasy by (and this is a nice Yeatsian twist on Neoplatonic defluction) making "passion run so deep." Finally, the enactment of that passion provides our mortal "consolation": for "where the crime's committed / The crime can be forgot."

The rondure here is wholly erotic. We "end where [we] begunne," to borrow the line concluding "Valediction: Forbidding Mourning," but with no hint of the background theme of resurrection detectable in Donne's womb image, no hint of the ultimate return to the sages' divine One, from whom we have departed by being born into the fallen, criminal cycle. Partial redemption occurs here on earth; and if the soul (to fuse Donne's "Valediction" imagery of "gold to ayery thinnesse beate" with related imagery from "The Extasie") is pure refined gold, the body is not, as the "sages" have perennially taught, worthless dross, but a metal necessarily baser than gold yet still valuable, even indispensable: strengthening alloy. We owe the bodily senses "thanks," says Donne, because they "convey" lovers to one another, "Nor are dross to us, but *allay*." The charming yet cruel girl of Poem II of *A Woman Young and Old* had set her suitor an impossible task: to "love" her archetypal, nonsensuous self, "the thing that was / Before the world was made" (perhaps echoing and altering a Donne sermon in which *God* is still as He was "before the world was made").[27] The

27. In sermon 23 (folio of 1640), Donne observes: "God did not plant a paradise for himself and remove to that as he planted a paradise for Adam and removed him to that; but God is *still where he was before the world was made*." *John Donne: The Sermons*, ed. G. R. Potter and E. M. Simpson.

mature woman of "Consolation" knows this world better and, even as she accepts the theological "wisdom" of the sages, informs *them* that the "crime of being born" can be "forgot" in returning to the scene of the crime, in the momentary ecstasy of sexual communion.

The terminal point of what, in their "Dialogue," both Self and Soul call "the crime of death and birth" comes in Poem IX of *A Woman Young and Old*, entitled "A Last Confession." In this monologue, hardly a contrite deathbed reception of the sacrament of penance, the old woman first declares that while soul-love brought her "misery," she had "great pleasure with a lad / That I loved bodily." From this celebration of a merely bodily love in which "Beast gave beast as much," the lady recovers. But even that recovery (verbally re-creating Blake's "Reunion of the Body & the Soul," the illustration Yeats and Ellis chose for the cover of their 1893 edition of Blake) projects sexual union into the Afterlife, "when this soul, its body off, / Naked to naked goes," to

Close and cling so tight,
There's not a bird of day that dare
Extinguish that delight.

Following Swedenborg and out-Miltoning the Milton who, in the most audacious angelological flight in *Paradise Lost*, has Raphael describe for a curious Adam the sexual intercourse of angels, Yeats here alters Christ (who ruled out marriage in heaven) and not only takes literally what his "ardent" (L 715) Plotinus meant strictly metaphorically (the reunion of the soul with the Divine One as an ecstatic heterosexual embrace), but also substitutes for the Divine Bridegroom of Christian mysticism a human lover. On this occasion, Yeats himself was, or pretended to be, taken aback by his own audacity: "Would it be less shocking if I put a capital to 'he' in the last stanza?" he asked Olivia Shakespear. It certainly would have been less shocking to traditional sensibilities had Yeats permitted God his assigned role of Celestial Bridegroom.[28] But, once again, in a pattern familiar to readers of young John Donne and of Swedenborg, supernaturalism is naturalized, "the Beatific Vision" made indistinguishable from "sexual love" (V-A xii), with Christian and Neoplatonic mysticism echoed in order to be altered rather than simply dismissed.

In *A Woman Young and Old*, "A Last Confession" (Poem IX) symmetrically balances "A First Confession" (Poem III). The sixth and central lyric

---

28. L 716. Mrs. Yeats identified the poem referred to as "The Friends of Youth" from *A Man Young and Old*. Though accepted by Wade and never challenged, this is inaccurate. Not only had that poem already been published; the letter (which has apparently not survived) makes it perfectly clear that the enclosed manuscript poem was one of those from the *Woman* series, "spoken when she is old." Of the two possibilities, only in the concluding movement of "A Last Confession" would the point about capitalization (that is, identification of the lover with God) make any sense.

of this concentrically structured eleven-poem sequence, "Chosen," eroti-
cizes its stanzaic model, Donne's "Nocturnall upon S. Lucies Day," by
substituting for projected communion after death a quasi-spiritual sexual
union here on earth. If questioned by some "new-married bride" as to her
"utmost pleasure with a man," the experienced old woman would choose
that moment of postcoital stillness

Where his heart my heart did seem
And both adrift on the miraculous stream
Where—wrote a learned astrologer—
The Zodiac is changed into a sphere.

Responding more to this occult astrology than to the poem as a whole,
critics have described this still moment as an "evasion," an "escape" or
"exemption" from time. Even Helen Vendler, a close reader primarily
concerned with the human and aesthetic implications of Yeats's System,
remarks in passing that the phaseless "sphere" of "Chosen" places the poem
in the nonhuman, discarnate realm. But this is to forget the lesson of Yeats's
master at the moment: "Donne could be as metaphysical as he pleased,"
noted an approving Yeats (Au 326), yet never seem "unhuman" because "he
could be as physical as he pleased." Yeats may have gone too far in believing "Nocturnall" to be an expression of Donne's "passion" for Lucy, the
Countess of Bedford (L 570), but as his own version of Donne's "poem of
great passion" (L 902), "Chosen" is less an occult hymn to the divine sphere
than an affirmation of the tragic cycle of human love in the mortal world, an
earth to which the poem's miraculous stream and "unhuman" sphere are
dragged down by their dramatic context. The personality and tone of the
woman speaker and Yeats's symbolic structuring alike suggest that no
"moment"—no matter how ecstatic, "miraculous," and apparently exempt
from time—is truly isolated from the temporal stream. Nothing in the
Woman Young and Old drafts transcribed by Jon Stallworthy is more thematically significant than the revelation that "Chosen" and "Parting," the moments of union and imminent separation, were originally a single poem, the
yolk and white of the one shell.[29]

The "learned astrologer" cited by the woman is the Neoplatonist Macrobius, whose speculations on zodiac and sphere had been brought to
Yeats's attention in January 1926 by Frank Pearce Sturm. Yeats alters Macrobius in two ways. First, as Sturm, that "learned mystic," pointed out,
Macrobius told how "the descending soul, when it reaches the contact point
of Zodiac & sphere," changes from sphere to cone—not the reverse, as
Yeats had it in what Sturm called his "vague" note in the 1929 Fountain

29. See Stallworthy, *Between the Lines*, 143–54. For other critical positions referred to in this
paragraph, see Helen Vendler, *Yeats's Vision and the Later Plays*, 69; F. A. C. Wilson, *W. B.
Yeats and Tradition*, 210–11; Giorgio Melchiori, *The Whole Mystery of Art*, 183; and Peter Ure,
W. B. Yeats, 81–82.

Press edition of *The Winding Stair*. Sturm corrected his friend with good-natured exasperation: "It would be folly to hope for accuracy in a poet, even in his philosophy." But the details were peripheral to the connection being suggested. For in the poem at least, Yeats knew what he was doing. By *seeming* to elevate the lovers' *seemingly* fused hearts to the status of Neoplatonic transcendence, Yeats is actually (and this is his second and significant alteration) laicizing the world of spirit, identifying occult perfection with the postcoital stillness of very human lovers.

Though he had played, seriously, with this erotic-spiritual fusion for many years, it is in "Chosen"—through a female persona who has evidently read Macrobius, along with *A Vision* and John Donne—that Yeats makes his strongest claim for sexual union as the symbol of the resolved antinomy: what Michael Hearne, the lovelorn Yeatsian hero of *The Speckled Bird*, called the reconciliation of "religion and the natural emotions," divine and human love. Or, to repeat, *seems* to. For the whole claim is qualified both by the lady's urbane wit and mock pedantry in citing a learned astrologer to a "new-married bride" and by the pivotal caveat—"did seem"—which, characteristically, puts all in doubt.

This qualifying tendency, Yeats's ability to seem to assert doctrine while denying neither what he called (comparing himself to Maud Gonne) his "more skeptical intelligence" nor his proud yet tragic sense of separation even within union, is displayed in another, and greater, poem of 1926, a poem in which Plato and Macrobius come in for more specific alteration.

Macrobius's role in "Among School Children" is minor and covert, part of the occult bones of the poem. Glossing the lines about the

> youthful mother, a shape upon her lap
Honey of generation had betrayed,
And that must sleep, shriek, struggle to escape
As recollection or the drug decide,

Yeats wrote: "I have taken the 'honey of generation' from Porphyry's essay on 'The Cave of the Nymphs,' but find no warrant in Porphyry for considering it the 'drug' that destroys the 'recollection' of prenatal freedom. He blamed a cup of oblivion given in the zodiacal sign of Cancer" (VP 828). While it is tempting to go along with those New Critics who found this note "fantastic" (Cleanth Brooks) or "crazy salad" (R. P. Blackmur), I remain primarily interested in the relationship between note and poem, between Yeats's esoteric sources and their embodiment in poetry.

What has happened in this stanza is actually rather mundane. First, as Thomas Parkinson has shown, a pentimento has occurred in the course of revision resulting in ambiguity as to who, mother or child, is betrayed, struggling, and recollecting: it is the child. Second, and also apparently without intention, Yeats has conflated his arcane sources. The translation of Porphyry's *De Antro Nympharum* used by Yeats was that of Thomas Taylor, who happened to append to it an extended footnote from the very passage

of Macrobius's *Commentary* on *Scipio's Dream* to which Yeats had been
directed by Dr. Sturm. Yeats found neither "warrant" *nor* cup of oblivion in
Porphyry; rather, conflating text and footnote, he fused Porphyry's honey
of generation—actually, Homer's, since Porphyry was writing an extended
gloss on the Cave of the Nymphs in *Odyssey* 13—with Macrobius's "starry
cup placed between Cancer and Lion" from which descending souls, in
varying degrees, "drink oblivion."[30] The result is an ambiguous chalice, an
intoxicating concoction that seduces potential mothers into coition and so
betrays infants into the world of generation—a process referred to by Yeats
in the drafts of this stanza as the "Degradation . . . / Of the soul betrayed
into the flesh."[31]

This stanza of "Among School Children," with the youthful mother's
proleptic vision of her son as an aged "shape," is bleak enough. Yeats's
occult sources, bleaker still, "honey of generation" notwithstanding, are
chiefly useful—as in "Chosen" and "A Dialogue of Self and Soul"—in
revealing how far Yeats had to come, and how well he succeeded, in subor-
dinating esoteric doctrine to human drama, allowing the tone and texture of
the poems themselves to supply the needed qualification of Neoplatonism,
with its cold, ascetic revulsion from material darkness and the degraded
flesh. Somehow, Yeats managed to transform his initial "curse against old
age" (L 719) and this degradation of the soul betrayed into the flesh into a
rhapsodic celebration of blossoming and dancing, with the inorganic disem-
bodiment of "old clothes upon old sticks" yielding to a "great-rooted blossomer" and a "body swayed to music." Though this final harmonious
integration was adumbrated by the apparent blending of "two natures . . . /
Into a sphere" back in stanza II, that was an occult and abstract icon; and the
need to "alter Plato's parable" only revealed the sphere as a premature and
inadequate emblem for the healing of division.

According to Aristophanes' sardonic parable of love (the myth later
played on by Crazy Jane), the primal androgyne, "originally one and . . .
whole," was cut in two "as you might divide an egg," with the two halves
ever after "longing to grow into one," thus "reuniting our original nature,
making one of two, and healing the state of man" (*Symposium* 190–94). In
"Summer and Spring," a poem written at the same time as "Among School
Children," the healing is psychological, intellectual, and, above all, sexual:

> when we talked of growing up
> Knew that we'd halved a soul
> And fell the one in t'other's arms
> That we might make it whole.

30. Taylor, *Thomas Taylor the Platonist*, 310.
31. The drafts have been transcribed by Thomas Parkinson, *W. B. Yeats: The Later Poetry*,
92–113 (97). Yeats's note to stanza V—dismissed by Brooks and Blackmur—is in the *Variorum*
(VP 828). Yeats's conflation of Porphyry and Macrobius was first noted by S. P. Rosenbaum,
"'Among School Children,' Stanza V."

In the greater poem, it is precisely that becoming sole and whole that is made problematic by the alteration. The Ledaean woman has told the Yeatsian speaker a tale

> of a harsh reproof or trivial event
> That changed some childish day to tragedy—
> Told, and it seemed that our two natures blent
> Into a sphere from youthful sympathy,
> Or else, to alter Plato's parable,
> Into the yolk and white of the one shell.

Yeats alters Plato's parable in a variety of ways. First, the "sphere"-like union does not encompass sexual intercourse, as it does in "Summer and Spring," "Chosen," and the Crazy Jane poems; the blending here is "from human sympathy." Second, there is, as in the "sphere"-like fusion of hearts in "Chosen," a subtle disclaimer: "it *seemed*." The third variation is tonal: what Plato intended satirically Yeats handles playfully, yet poignantly. Finally, there is the precise alteration itself: the change from the reunification of an egg divided into two halves, each consisting of both white and yolk, to "the yolk *and* white of the one shell."

That final alteration may be documented. In February 1926, a month before he began "Among School Children," Yeats received from Dr. Sturm, along with information on Macrobius's zodiac and sphere, an account of the "Eagle's Egg" in John Dee's *Monas Hieroglyphica* (1564). Though the Latin text, according to Sturm, is "crabbed and cob-webby like the mind of Dee, & needs a key which is lost if it ever existed," Dee seems to be saying (in Sturm's words), "The great work of dissolving the Eagle's Egg is accomplished when the white disappears in the yolk." In his response, written two weeks before he jotted down the prose "topic" from which "Among School Children" germinated, Yeats told Sturm that the "extracts from Dr. Dee interest me." He went on immediately to make the equation with his own lunar and solar symbolism: "One sees vaguely that the dissolving of the White in the Yolk is [☽] in [☉]—Phase 1—or whichever that was in his symbolism—the soul made divine" (*Frank Pearce Sturm*, 96-102).

In the first version of *A Vision*, published in January of this same year, Yeats had referred to "Sun in Moon and Moon in Sun" as "a single being like man and woman in Plato's Myth" (V-A 149). In the poem, however, that androgynous myth, the "sphere" emblematic of divine perfection, Dee's Eagle's Egg and Sturm's explication, fuse in an alteration in which the white does *not* dissolve into the yolk. Separateness (yolk *and* white) is preserved within union (the one shell).[32] The soul, *not* "made divine," remains

---

32. For a discussion of the Yeatsian epiphany as a reconciliation of opposites involving simultaneous unity and separateness, see Edward C. Jacobs, "Yeats and the Artistic Epiphany."

human. Here, as in "A Dialogue of Self and Soul," Self gets the last word; though Yeats longed for total unity with the Ledaean Maud Gonne, we are left, even in this image of communion, with the perpetual virginity of the soul. Even if here the seesaw is inclined toward integration, it is not Platonic and divine but Yeatsian and human and, therefore, not without its poignancy and pain.

This human rather than divine integration extends to the poem's rhapsodic conclusion where the sphere-like reconciliation, made somewhat less abstract in the yolk and white of the one shell, is fully concretized, transformed to the integrated, dynamic organicism Yeats had found in the Romantics and (in the year he wrote "Among School Children," 1926) in Whitehead's *Science and the Modern World*. Had he read *Being and Time*, published in the following year, Yeats would have discovered that he had, in this final stanza, anticipated Heidegger in resisting the abstract spatialization of thinking by putting Time back into Being, thus stressing the rich, concrete continuum of temporal life.[33] Yeats's specific continuum of leaf, blossom, and bole may derive from other Germans (Goethe and Hegel),[34] and the mutual flame of dancer and dance from Nietzsche and the French Symbolists; the result is pure Yeats:

Labour is blossoming or dancing where
The body is not bruised to pleasure soul,
Nor beauty born out of its own despair,
Nor blear-eyed wisdom out of midnight oil.
O chestnut-tree, great-rooted-blossomer,
Are you the leaf, the blossom or the bole?
O body swayed to music, O brightening glance,
How can we know the dancer from the dance?

Again, the division-healing reconciliation is human, not divine; the blossoming or dancing finds its local habitation (signaled, as in "Consolation" and "Chosen," by the word *where*) in a paradisiacal state "where / The body is not bruised to pleasure soul"—as it *is* bruised in the Platonism that reduces "nature" to "a spume that plays / Upon a ghostly paradigm of things," or in the religion of nuns wed to a Christ whose austere, candle-lit image in the chapel must "break hearts," and by implication bruise their celibate bodies, by remaining inanimate, unmoved and untouchable, maintaining "a marble or a bronze repose."

In contrast to the Symbolist icon in marble or bronze repose, the animated "body swayed to music" returns us to the third of Yeats's triad of philosophers in stanza VI: not to Plato, who saw nature as ephemeral foam playing on an Idealist paradigm, or even to "Solider Aristotle," playing his

---

33. Yeats was much concerned with such matters; see, for example, his annotations on Spengler's *Decline of the West*, recorded in O'Shea's *Descriptive Catalog*.
34. For the passages from Goethe and Hegel, see my Preface.

schoolmaster's strap on the bottom of young Alexander, but to the master of all who "learn to cipher and to sing," player Pythagoras, who

Fingered upon a fiddle-stick or strings
What a star sang and careless Muses heard.

All these forms of play are meticulously rule-governed, especially that of Pythagoras, who, measuring precisely the intervals between notes played on a stretched string (L 719), discovered the mathematical laws governing the acoustical relationship between pitch and harmony and thus, at a third remove from the harmony of the spheres and from Platonic "reality," created earthly music: music by a "mortal finger strook" and already distorted by having been passed on to poets through inspiring Muses who were "careless"—without human cares, but also casual auditors.

It is to this music—patterned but no "ghostly" paradigm—that the body of the final stanza sways. For all its ecstasy, such fingering and dancing are acts of creative "play" that are, Yeats insists in the solemn, stanza-opening word, "Labour." For the *locus* even of this idealized "where" remains the fallen world, characterized by the sweat of the brow rather than by the artless art of Paradise, the morning orisons of unfallen Adam and Eve, who praised their Maker in "unmeditated" prose or verse "More tuneable than needed Lute or Harp / To add more sweetness" (*Paradise Lost* 5.148–52). But we are Here, not There, and so require the mediation of fiddle-sticks and strings. Prelapsarian spontaneity, Milton's Adam is told, is "not to bee gotten by labour and learning," but it *can* be approximated by human art. Yeatsian "labour" subsumes that of schoolchildren and their teachers, mothers, lovers, and (above all) what Yeats elsewhere calls the "accustomed toil" of artists laboring deliberately at "this craft of verse," their "trade." Even this final blossoming and dancing is earthbound, indeed the fruit of "Adam's curse," though here that curse becomes a blessing, a labor that (in this poem of "compensation," "enterprise," and "labour") provides its own abundant recompense.[35]

IV. "The Second Coming";
"Two Songs from a Play"

Still, even this embrace of the continuum of life is a *projected* state of secular blessedness. One such projected paradise, in which bodies sway to a more sensual music as copulating nymphs and satyrs play in the spume of nature,

35. The Yeatsian allusions are to "All Things Can Tempt Me" and "Adam's Curse," which also stresses the "labour" of artists, beautiful women, and lovers. The "economic" language notable in both "Among School Children" and "A Prayer for My Daughter" is less indebted to Marx than to the Miltonic and Wordsworthian concepts of "recompense" in "Lycidas" and "Tintern Abbey."

is presented in "News for the Delphic Oracle," which emphasizes Yeats's ardent enlistment for the moment under the Dionysian half of Nietzsche's banner. The crucial influence of Nietzsche can best be demonstrated in the present context in three of Yeats's indisputably central poems, "The Second Coming," "Two Songs from a Play," and "A Dialogue of Self and Soul." These are, in their very different ways, transvaluations, or at the very least alterations, of Christian doctrine; all suggest apocalypses, the first two more or less public, the third more or less private.

The preceding chapter pursued the rough beast of "The Second Coming" through Yeats's drafts back to the French Revolutionary books of *The Prelude*. But Yeats did not find in Wordsworth's monsters come to "second birth" (or in Blake's Tyger or Shelley's Demogorgon) the Beast at the center of "The Second Coming," a fusion of Matthew 24 and the Book of Revelation. He found precedent for that fusion in Nietzsche's revaluation of Revelation. What forced Yeats to an agonizing reappraisal of the whole tradition of apocalyptic Romanticism and of his role in that tradition was precisely his excited reading of "Nietzsche, that strong enchanter." One major consequence was that he continued to invoke apocalyptic violence, but—and here he deviated from the Hebrew prophets and the author of the Book of Revelation, as well as from Blake and Shelley—Yeats became joyful in his contemplation of imminent destruction, refusing to see that destruction as prolegomenon to any promised millennium: the ignoble dream, in Nietzsche's phrase, of a safe "universal green-pasture happiness of the herd."

"I am no believer in Millenniums," Yeats confirmed in his 1930 diary (Ex 336). There was something facile in the millennial vision of the poets whose thought had shaped his life and early work. Yeats came to this perhaps unfortunate conclusion, his letters and essays show, in 1902–1903, and his transformed vision, further embittered by the loss of Maud Gonne to a man of action, seems largely attributable to the reading of Nietzsche begun at this time. It was then, he later noted in the preface to *The Resurrection*, that, rebelling against the myth of "progress," he began to imagine the "brazen winged beast" he later associated with "laughing, ecstatic destruction." This monster first appeared as the "wild beast" of apocalyptic "Laughter, the mightiest of the enemies of God," in the 1902 play *Where There Is Nothing*, written under the immediate influence of Nietzsche, and it was, Yeats tells us, "afterwards described" in "The Second Coming" (Ex 392–93).

The stirring of the rough beast inaugurates a pagan *parousia* conceived, Yeats acknowledged in his 1930 diary, as a "counterbirth" to that of "Christ" (Ex 311). If we are to believe anything at all in Yeats's central myth, that counterbirth, however terrifying, is the necessary gyre-reversing harbinger of the *antithetical* age to come, "its hour come round at last." However "troubled" the poet-prophet's vision may be, the note of breathless expectancy, even exultation, is unmistakable in the poem. "After us, the Savage

God," Yeats cried out in "The Tragic Generation" (Au 349). In part at least, he was recalling Nietzsche, who wrote in *Beyond Good and Evil*,

In late ages that may be proud of their humanity, so much fear remains, so much *superstitious* fear of the "savage cruel beast" whose conquest is the very pride of these more humane ages, that even palpable truths remain unspoken for centuries . . . because they look as if they might reanimate that savage beast one has finally "mortified." . . . Almost everything we call "higher culture" is based on the spiritualization of *cruelty*, on its becoming more profound: this is my proposition: That "savage animal" has not really been "mortified"; it lives and flourishes, it has merely become—divine.

(§229)

In this passage we find not only a key to the tone and imagery of "Nineteen Hundred and Nineteen" but also the irrepressible, titillatingly evil beast— rough, savage, divine—of "The Second Coming." That prodigiously bestial Antichrist, moving its slow thighs and slouching toward Bethlehem to be born, is more terrifying than its original in Revelation because there is no sign of the Christ who promised to return and subdue it. This is Yeats's most thorough, and Nietzschean, alteration of the Christian parable of apocalypse.

It is an alteration some readers, understandably, find hard to accept. Kathleen Raine has suggested that the notorious Aleister Crowley, who "believed himself to be a prophet of the Antichrist, under the sign of the Apocalyptic 'Great Beast,'" may have been an "aspect of Yeats's 'rough beast.'" She cites a passage by Crowley on a hawk-headed God "having spiral force" that is, as she says, "strangely reminiscent" of Yeats's gyring falcon—in fact, though she does not mention it, the Beast of "The Second Coming" was originally a "Great Falcon." Nevertheless, she concludes, "Whereas Crowley placed himself in the services of Antichrist, 'the Savage God' of the new cycle, Yeats's fidelity was to 'the old king,' to 'that unfashionable gyre,' the values about to be obscured, to the 'workman, noble, and saint' of Christian civilization."[36]

Yeats, who opposed Crowley in Golden Dawn politics, was obviously no self-styled Antichrist, and there *is* a humane and genuinely elegiac tone when he speaks of the "many ingenious lovely things" that must be obliterated, the "ceremony of innocence" that must be drowned, at the explosive flash points of historical reversal. But Kathleen Raine's allusive sentence—despite its gathering together of "The Tragic Generation," "The Black Tower," and "The Gyres"—simplifies, even distorts, Yeats's attitude

36. Raine, *Yeats, the Tarot and the Golden Dawn*, 33–35. Similar simplifications of Yeats's "Christianity" occur in Virginia Moore's *The Unicorn: William Butler Yeats's Search for Reality* and in Cleanth Brooks's chapter on Yeats in *The Hidden God*.

toward "Christian civilization," to say nothing of his complex and vacillating response to Christ and Christianity. "If reality is timeless and spaceless," Yeats wrote in his 1930 diary, everything having to do "with Christ, or angels or Deism" could be, not the "sentimental make-believe" he thought it was, but "a goal, an ultimate good." But his belief that reality is "also a congeries of autonomous selves" ruled out for him belief in "one ever-victorious Providence" (Ex 309). At the same time, Yeats remained fascinated by Christ. On one sheet of Automatic Script, he attempted to correlate the career of "*Primary* Christ" with his own scheme of lunar phases. The schema begins and ends with phase 1, from "Nativity" to "Crucifixion," with the "Transfiguration" providing the "Centre or Axis." No Resurrection is mentioned, though that is the miraculous event that provides the most electrifying moment in Yeatsian drama.[37]

A Dionysian interpretation, shaped in part by Yeats's reading of Nietzsche, *The Resurrection* begins and ends with songs that are not only among Yeats's most powerful and compelling poems but that also represent perhaps the most succinct statement of his ambivalence toward Christianity. In yet another instance of Yeatsian alteration, the "Two Songs from a Play" (as they are titled in the *Collected Poems*) alter Virgil's Fourth, so-called messianic, Eclogue as well as Shelley's own variation on Virgil in the final chorus to his lyrical drama, *Hellas*. Despite the obtuseness of anti-Romantic critics who persist in trying to reduce Shelley to a naive utopian optimist, his vision was sufficiently skeptical for him to end in near despair, altering Virgil by considering the *horror* of eternal recurrence ("must hate and death return?") and by crying out for termination: "Oh, cease!" He wants history to be transformed from the cyclical shape of pagan recurrence to the linear, apocalyptic paradigm, modeled on the Bible, in which history attains its zenith, then stops. In the songs accompanying the unfolding and folding of the curtain in *The Resurrection*, the Shelleyan premonition of eternal recurrence is assimilated by a twentieth-century poet who, his vision largely shaped by Blake and Shelley, has been enchanted by Nietzsche. The cyclical vision of *circuitus temporum* that appalled Shelley and, for Blake, constituted the ultimate nightmare, is here embraced by Yeats—though less with joy than with the astringency he found in the German prophet of Eternal Recurrence.

According to Virgil, the advent of the new Golden Age would be preceded by a cyclical return: a new race of greater heroes would be sent again to Troy; there would be another Jason and another Argo. Virgil's "second Argo" was made "loftier yet" by Shelley, but both millennial visions are denigrated by Yeats in contemptuous epithets emphasizing cyclicism, the ravages of time, the sense of deterioration and corruption in this modern Age of Iron:

37. See Harper, *The Making of "A Vision."*

Another Troy must rise and set,
Another lineage feed the crow,
Another Argo's painted prow
Drive to a flashier bauble yet.

Yeats's song had begun with an echo of Virgil unmediated by Shelley. The Roman poet's returning Virgin—Astraea or Justice, the last of the divinities to leave the earth at the end of the original Golden Age—was identified by Christian commentators with the Virgin Mary, mother of the child who was to usher in the Christian equivalent of the pagan Golden Age. Yeats identifies three pairs: Astraea and Spica, Athene and Dionysus, and Mary and Christ, with the first couple clearly lifted from Virgil's Fourth Eclogue, the messianic aspects of which were frequently referred to by Yeats (Myth 310, Ex 150, V-B 243–44). In *The Resurrection* he parallels the dying and resurrected gods, Christ and his "half-brother" (E&I 514) Dionysus. The play-opening song begins: "I saw a staring virgin stand / Where holy Dionysus died," and the virgin here (Athene) is fused, in the second stanza, with a formidable Virgin Mary:

The Roman Empire stood appalled:
It dropped the reins of peace and war
When that fierce virgin and her Star
Out of the fabulous darkness called.

With the steady Romans themselves shaken by a world-transforming birth, we are prepared for the consequences of Christ's death and resurrection:

In pity for man's darkening thought
He walked that room and issued thence
In Galilean turbulence;
The Babylonian starlight brought
A fabulous, formless darkness in;
Odour of blood when Christ was slain
Made all Platonic tolerance vain
And vain all Doric discipline.

The "formless darkness"—a phrase borrowed from the *Vita Maximi* of the fourth-century anti-Christian Neoplatonist Eunapius[38]—has modulated into man's "darkening thought," in pity for which Christ sacrificed himself. For Yeats, at least the Nietzschean Yeats, pity is a suspect emotion; and he was at best vacillating about Christ and Christianity. The stanza ends with three powerful lines epitomizing Yeats's dual perspective. On the one hand,

38. From *Vita Maximi*, as excerpted in *Select Passages Illustrating Neoplatonism*, ed. E. R. Dodds, 8.

as T. R. Whitaker puts it with characteristic precision, the divine sacrifice of Christ on Calvary rendered vain "the merely natural virtues of Greek culture and offered a superior mode of salvation," yet Yeats's images simultaneously evoke "the spectacle of a sober and restrained culture maddened like some beast by the odor of blood" (*Swan and Shadow*, 106). So a tolerant, disciplined, and rational culture is seen as driven into irrationality by the human blood of a crucified divinity. This is a paradox, or Pauline "folly," equally incomprehensible to Greek intellect, Roman power, and Yankee Christianity. (In "his favorite pose as poet-thinker," Yeats, a Robert Frost persona accuses, "once charged the Nazarene with having brought / A darkness out of Asia that had crossed / Old Attic grace and Spartan discipline / With violence.")[39] But the paradoxical mixture was simultaneously repellent and attractive to a poet torn between Doric discipline and the "return" of "the irrational," between Classical culture and uncontrollable mysteries on the bestial floor. In the final analysis, three strange bedfellows—Edward Gibbon, the Enlightenment author of *The Decline and Fall of the Roman Empire*; Nietzsche, the self-proclaimed Antichrist and prophet of Eternal Recurrence; and Yeats, the last of the great Romantic poets—concur that a religion at once spiritual and bestial, a revolutionary slave morality, rose up and, in a transvaluation of all values, overturned Greco-Roman culture: a reversal of Yeatsian gyres that stood the Classical world on its head.

In their curious way, the songs from *The Resurrection* confirm the messianic interpretations of the Fourth Eclogue. "Curious," because Yeats was less than enthusiastic about the victory of a religion that, he agreed with Eunapius, was a "formless darkness mastering the loveliness of the world," or as Yeats put it, that "fabulous formless darkness" that had "blotted out 'every beautiful thing' . . . by an act of power" (Ex 377, V-A 190). This is, again, the Nietzschean side of Yeats—the man who marked the final aphorism of *The Antichrist* with bold marginal strokes apparently approving Nietzsche's violent characterization of Christianity, "with its anaemic ideal of holiness," as a parasitical vampire that had sucked the blood of classical culture and perverted the ideals of *aretê*, *virtù*, *humanitas* itself. These were the vaunted "'humanitarian' blessings of Christianity!"—"the other world as the will to the negation of every reality; the cross as the rallying sign for the most subterranean conspiracy that has ever existed,—against healthiness, beauty, well-constitutedness, courage, intellect, *benevolence* of soul, *against life itself*" (*Antichrist* §62). Only in the final stanza of the second of the *Resurrection* "songs" (a stanza added in 1930) did Yeats, like Shelley, once again center things on "life itself," on the human: "Whatever flames upon the night / Man's own resinous heart has fed."

But even here Yeats maintains an ambivalence characteristic of modern

---

39. *The Poetry of Robert Frost*, ed. Edward Connery Lathem, 511: *A Masque of Mercy* (1947), an allusion noted by Terence Diggory in *Yeats and American Poetry*, 74.

man, torn between human images and the world of spirit. At the climactic moment of *The Resurrection*, the Greek, an idealist confident that Christ was a mere phantom, touches the risen god and falls back in shock: "The heart of a phantom is beating. Man has begun to die. Your words are clear at last, O Heraclitus. God and man die each other's life, live each other's death" (VPl 931). With the marvelous adjective "resinous" in the final line of the play-concluding song, we are also returned to divinity—not to Christ, however, but to Dionysus, whose heart was torn out of his side and borne away in the opening song, and whose Bacchantes carried torches of resinous pine. Though, in the play, Yeats had been a good Frazerian comparative mythologist in paralleling Dionysus and Christ, this final image of human suffering and creativity is pagan—Dionysian, not Christian. God has died so that man and his own resinous heart can achieve a godlike creative power. In this case, Yeats is completing Heraclitus with Nietzsche, who formulated his most profound "antithesis" as "Dionysus versus the Crucified": the pagan affirmation of creative/destructive/re-creative life versus what he conceived of as the Christian denial of life; "eternal fruitfulness and recurrence" versus "condemnation"; heroic, "tragic" humanism versus a weak, disinherited longing for "redemption" from life and a "curse" on earthly existence (*Ecce Homo* 4.9; *The Will to Power* §1052). For Yeats, too, *antithetical* revelation is an influx "neither from beyond mankind nor born of a virgin, but begotten from our own spirit and history," a "psychological" revelation that "is developed out of man and is man" (V-B 262, Ex 312–13).

Read in this light, Yeats's play-concluding song, even though that play's subject was Christ's resurrection, may constitute the twentieth-century poet's ultimate return of his own eclogue to Virgil—who was, after all, a pagan, not a Christian, *naturaliter* or otherwise. Yeats himself, though instinctively *antithetical*, continued to feel the pull of the *primary*. But while he never accepted the Nietzschean pronouncement of the death of God, Yeats always, as he admitted, wrote "coldly" when he tried to write of God. Remembering Nietzsche's opposition of life-affirming Homer to life-denying Plato and Christ, Yeats chose as his exemplar "Homer . . . and his unchristened heart." Still, that poem, reflecting the antinomies and personal ambivalence, is justly entitled "Vacillation."

"Vacillation," as we have seen, contains a crucial dialogue between Soul and Heart, dialogue being the inevitable form for so double-minded a man as Yeats. That double-mindedness is clear even in his—largely approving—annotations on Nietzsche and in the great dialogue in which he seems to side fully with Self in the conflict with Soul.

Annotating a passage from the *Genealogy of Morals*, Yeats indicated both his agreement with Nietzsche and the limitations of that agreement. First, summarizing a number of Nietzschean points, Yeats accused "Christianity" of "teaching men to live not in the continuous present of self-revelation but to deny self & present for future gain." This anticipates the affirmation of

Self in "Dialogue" and of the continuum of life itself in "Among School Children." More obviously, it looks forward to the Paudeens satirized in "September 1913," those middle-class Catholics, born "to pray and save," who

> fumble in a greasy till
> And add the halfpence to the pence
> And prayer to shivering prayer.

The two forms of life- and self-denial "for future gain" would have been more closely linked in a speech made in July 1913 had Yeats included in his diatribe against the "little greasy huxtering nation groping for halfpence in a greasy till" the phrase he told Lady Gregory he had added mentally: "by the light of a holy candle" (recorded in her book on Hugh Lane). But this was not to deny the existence of genuine spiritual light. In these annotations on the *Genealogy of Morals*, Yeats seems suddenly to have recalled that the conflict of opposites—the *antithetical* Homeric Day and the *primary* Platonic-Christian Night—must be preserved, not obliterated or ignored. He posed in the margin the symbolic question of an essentially *antithetical* man sufficiently drawn to the supernatural to resist his strong enchanter's atheism: "But why does Nietzsche think that the night has no stars, nothing but bats & owls & the insane moon?"[40]

V. "A Dialogue of Self and Soul"

It is to that preeminently spiritual stellar light, the constant Pole Star, that Soul directs Self in "A Dialogue of Self and Soul," and, again, it is Nietzsche who provides much of the *antithetical* resistance to the essentially Neoplatonic summons. In this case, we have hard (though hitherto undiscussed) evidence of Yeats's alteration of his spiritual sources, an alteration that preserves rather than obliterates opposites through a process of variation and assimilation issuing in fusion and something approaching unity of being.

In a series of congested notes intended to accompany *The Winding Stair and Other Poems* (1933), Yeats explained his now central symbolism. After discussing towers and winding stairs, he cited (accurately at last, thanks to Sturm) the passage behind the final lines of "Chosen." The "learned astrologer" was Macrobius, who, in his *Commentary* on Cicero's *Somnium Sci-*

---

40. Yeats's annotations in the Thomas Common anthology of Nietzsche, 124. Yeats's symbolic question about Nietzsche reducing the realm of the spiritual to a starless "night" with "bats and owls" refers to the "owls and bats whirring past" in *Zarathustra* 3:15 rather than to any specific statement in the *Genealogy* text he is annotating. Nevertheless, Yeats's noctural equation was accurate. Nietzsche would agree with the formulation of A. W. Schlegel: "In the Christian view, the contemplation of the infinite has annihilated the finite; and life has become a world of shadows, life has become night." Quoted by Arthur Lovejoy, *Essays in the History of Ideas*, 246.

pionis, spoke of the astrological "sign inimical to human life" and of the "descending soul by its defluction" being "drawn out of the spherical, the sole divine form, into the cone," or gyre. In the portion of the note here published for the first time, Yeats goes on to describe the opening movement of "A Dialogue of Self and Soul" as a "variation on Macrobius," a variation that

may be familiar, for I find this passage in those "Intimate Journals of Paul Gauguin" which have attained a popularity so alarming that our Board of Censorship has put them on the index. "The Colossus"—Balzac—"remounts to the pole, the world's pivot; his great mantle shelters and warms the two germs, Seraphitus, Seraphita, fertile souls, ceaselessly uniting, who issue from their Boreal Mists to traverse the whole universe, teaching, loving, creating."[41]

This is a creative fecundity at the opposite "pole" from what Yeats himself called in *Per Amica Silentia Lunae* "the straight line . . . of saint or sage" in *Séraphita*, Balzac's Swedenborgian novel culminating (despite the sublimated sexuality Gauguin detected) in an arrowlike ascent to, and mystical union with, God, as opposed to the "winding movement of nature," the *antithetical* "path of the serpent" (Myth 340). As it plays out in the opening movement of "Dialogue," the "variation" is *antithetical*, despite the fact that Soul's stair and Self's embroidery are both "winding."

My Soul. I summon to the winding ancient stair;
  Set all your mind upon the steep ascent,
  Upon the broken, crumbling battlement,
  Upon the breathless starlit air,
  Upon the star that marks the hidden pole;
  Fix every wandering thought upon
  That quarter where all thought is done:
  Who can distinguish darkness from the soul?

My Self. The consecrated blade upon my knees
  Is Sato's ancient blade, still as it was,
  Still razor-keen, still like a looking-glass
  Unspotted by the centuries;
  That flowering, silken, old embroidery, torn
  From some court-lady's dress and round
  The wooden scabbard bound and wound,
  Can, tattered, still protect, faded adorn.

My Soul. Why should the imagination of a man
  Long past his prime remember things that are
  Emblematical of love and war?

41. Yeats Archives, SUNY Stony Brook, 30.3.286.

Think of ancestral night that can,
If but imagination scorn the earth
And intellect its wandering
To this and that and t'other thing,
Deliver from the crime of death and birth.

My Self. Montashigi, third of his family, fashioned it
Five hundred years ago, about it lie
Flowers from I know not what embroidery—
Heart's purple—and all these I set
For emblems of the day against the tower
Emblematical of the night,
And claim as by a soldier's right
A charter to commit the crime once more.

My Soul. Such fullness in that quarter overflows
And falls into the basin of the mind
That man is stricken deaf and dumb and blind,
For intellect no longer knows
Is from the *Ought*, or *Knower* from the *Known*—
That is to say, ascends to Heaven;
Only the dead can be forgiven;
But when I think of that my tongue's a stone.

As a disciple of such Neoplatonists as Macrobius, Soul is unaware that Eternity is in love with the productions of time, that man's fall is also an alternate form of fulfillment and perfection, albeit profane. Thus Soul deplores the descent from the eternal sphere into the cone or gyre of "fallen" human life and austerely commands total concentration on reversing that descent and escaping from the gyre. The obvious "variation" is that mutinous Self, rejecting the imperious summons to "the steep ascent," sets up opposing gyre-symbols, the sword and silk-wound sheath "emblematical of love and war," and chooses rebirth rather than escape from the cycle of Mutability. (Whereas Spenser would, in the *contemptus mundi* tradition, finally "*cast away*" the "love of *things so vaine . . .* / Whose *flowering* pride, so *fading* and so fickle / Short Time shall soon cut down with his consuming sickle," doctrine-altering Self chooses another keen, curved weapon: Sato's sword, "unspotted by the centuries," bound in embroidery that is both "flowering" and "faded" yet protective and beautiful. What Self will finally "cast out" is not the love of "things" but "remorse," issuing in a final *affirmation* of "*every*thing.")

Despite the repeated admonitions by hectoring Soul to "fix" every thought "upon" the One, "upon" the steep ascent, the straight line of saint or sage, "upon" the occult Pole Star, "upon" the spiritual quarter where all thought is done, the recalcitrant Self remains diverted by the Many, by earthly multiplicity, by the sword bound and wound in embroidery representing the winding movement of nature, the path of the serpent. In the Ciceronian text Macrobius was glossing, the young Scipio "kept turning my eyes back to earth" despite the rhetorical question of his grandfather's spirit: "Why not *fix* your attention *upon* the heavens and contemn what is mortal?" Scipio, according to the synopsis of Macrobius, "looked about him everywhere with wonder, and when his eyes lighted on the earth, he fell into pleasant reveries. Hereupon his grandfather's admonition recalled him to the upper realms."[42]

Though the conflict between the Yeatsian Self and Soul is identical to that between the two Scipios, the Soul in Yeats's dialogue is a considerably less successful spiritual guide than the ghostly grandfather of the *Somnium Scipionis*. This is true despite the fact that Self, in the drafts, seemed more than half convinced of the essential validity of the Neoplatonic position. In the drafts of "Among School Children," Yeats referred—in that passage based on Porphyry and Macrobius—to the "degradation" of being "betrayed into the flesh." In the 1927 manuscripts of Self's peroration, part II of "Dialogue," the speaker sets himself to "count all that degradation to its source." All that degradation turns out to be (in the published poem) nothing less than "every event in action or in thought"; in short, the totality of that "crime," human life. The situation could hardly be grimmer. In the manuscripts, indeed, it was not Soul but *Self* who cried out: "Cannot the wisdom of the sages stop / That burning phantasy till it run pure / Or must I whirl upon the wheel of life once more?" Here the echo of King Lear's contrast between "a soul in bliss" and his own agony, "bound upon a wheel of fire," is reinforced by Self's lamentation that "Man's soul" must "groan" being "bound / Upon the wheel of life." This seems an echo as well (probably via Blake's *Vision of the Last Judgment*) of St. Paul on the whole creation groaning in pain and crying out for deliverance from corruption (Romans 8:21–22). Of course, the final choice of Self, and of *antithetical* Yeats, is—to quote his poem-synopsizing letter to Olivia Shakespear—"rebirth rather than deliverance from birth" (L 729).

The second movement of the poem, Soul's paradoxically physical "tongue" having been turned to stone, is all Self—revealingly called "Me" in the initial draft:

My Self. A living man is blind and drinks his drop.
  What matter if the ditches are impure?
  What matter if I live it all once more?
  Endure that toil of growing up;
  The ignominy of boyhood; the distress
  Of boyhood changing into man;
  The unfinished man and his pain
  Brought face to face with his own clumsiness;

42. Macrobius, *Commentary on the Dream of Scipio*, 3.7–4.1; 5.3–6.1; pp. 152–53, 155 in the translation by W. H. Stahl.

The finished man among his enemies?—
How in the name of Heaven can he escape
That defiling and disfigured shape
The mirror of malicious eyes
Casts upon his eyes until at last
He thinks that shape must be his shape?
And what's the good of an escape
If honour find him in the wintry blast?

I am content to live it all again
And yet again, if it be life to pitch
Into the frog-spawn of a blind man's ditch,
A blind man battering blind men;
Or into that most fecund ditch of all,
The folly that man does
Or must suffer, if he woos
A proud woman not kindred of his soul.

I am content to follow to its source
Every event in action or in thought;
Measure the lot; forgive myself the lot!
When such as I cast out remorse
So great a sweetness flows into the breast
We must laugh and we must sing,
We are blest by everything,
Everything we look upon is blest.

It is a Nietzschean choice, earning final ecstasy by accepting the eternal recurrence of all the "toil," "ignominy," "distress," "pain," "clumsiness," and "folly" of life and, altering Nietzsche, at once acknowledging and embracing the "impurity" of human life. The formula for "power" in *Thus Spoke Zarathustra* is *Selbstüberwindung*, self-overcoming. In "Dialogue," Self achieves a doubly Nietzschean victory. The first phase, in Yeats as in Nietzsche, is the recognition of inner "contradiction," the "bad conscience" of a "soul . . . willingly divided against itself," "burning" into itself an awareness of a contradiction between good and evil. This bad conscience, according to Nietzsche, must eventually be overcome, but its ultimate value is that it has been "the womb of all ideal and imaginative events and has thus brought to light an abundance of strange new beauty and affirmation—and perhaps *beauty itself*" (*Genealogy of Morals* 2.18).

Though "a disease as pregnancy is a disease," the "bad conscience" *is* a disease—"that is not subject to doubt" (*Genealogy of Morals* 2.19). The fruit of this dialectically necessary evil, this "pregnancy," is the "child" of innocence and affirmation, reborn in beauty. This "self-overcoming" takes the form not of an extirpation of the Self's passions but of a "sublimation" in which the Self-Soul dualism is at once preserved, canceled, and lifted up (Nietzsche's *sublimare* is identical, in German, to Hegel's famous *aufheben*).

As in Nietzsche's monistic synthesis—the subsuming, under Will to Power, of his earlier dualisms of impulse and reason, passion and spirit, chaos and order, Dionysus and Apollo—Yeats's dialectical triumph is over his own self-division. It is the victory, as Yeats wrote of Nietzsche, the sole representative of the phase of the hero in *A Vision*, of the man who "overcomes *himself*," thus attaining the *antithetical* "perfection that is from a man's combat with himself" rather than "with circumstance": the "simple distinction" upon which Yeats's ghostly Instructors built up their "elaborate classification" of human personality (V-B 127, 8–9). Self's victory, resembling that of Blake's Oothoon, heroine of a poem repeatedly echoed in "Dialogue," is over the severe moralism, the "bad conscience," that would reduce the body to an object of defilement and degradation. In Yeats's case it seems, above all, a triumph over his own Neoplatonism, even Gnosticism. This is *creative* self-overcoming, for "we make out of the quarrel with others, rhetoric, but of the quarrel with ourselves, poetry" (Myth 331).

Yeats's *psychomachia*, standing the Body-and-Soul debate tradition on its venerable head, plays a variation amounting to reversal not only on Cicero's dialogue and Macrobius's Neoplatonic commentary on it but also on Marvell's two Body-Soul dialogues, as well as his Neoplatonic poem "On a Drop of Dew," in which the drop, "Remembering still its former height, / Shuns" its beautiful "Mansion new" of green leaves and "purple flow'r." While the Yeatsian Self aligns himself with the "flowering" embroidery of "Heart's purple" and "drinks his drop," the Marvellian drop longs only to return to the clear heaven from which it has fallen. Yeats is also, I suspect, echoing the famous dialogue between the chaste Lady and Comus in Milton's *Maske at Ludlow*. Milton's Neoplatonic Attendant Spirit resembles the Yeatsian Soul, while the role of Self is anticipated by Comus, the advocate of the descending path. The wand and cup the enchanter inherits from his mother, Circe, provide the phallic and vaginal equivalents of Self's emblematic sword and sheath; the drink he offers the Lady comes from the same Heraclitean-Porphyrian source as the drop actually drunk by Self. Even Self's "frog-spawn of a blind man's ditch"—though it echoes the language of Edgar as Poor Tom in *King Lear*—has its thematic original in Comus's image of bountiful nature "thronging the seas with spawn innumerable." The characteristic variation is that what the Lady spurns as a blasphemous invitation to the banquet of sense is accepted with vitalistic relish by Self, who, drinking impure waters and pitching into fecund ditches teeming with spawn, glories in precisely what Milton's Lady condemns as "besotted" baseness.

Yet the spiritual tradition is not simply dismissed. For Yeats, the world of experience, however dark the declivities into which the generated soul may drop, is never utterly divorced from the world of light and grace. Indeed, the water imagery branching through Self's peroration subsumes, in effect, Comus's proffered cup of oblivion, the seas with spawn innumerable, *and* the "drops" from the water-spirit Sabrina's "fountain-pure," Milton's true

(Plotinian and baptismal) restorative liquid. Yeats can have *both* impure ditches *and* a pure fountain ("So great a sweetness flows into the breast") by playing yet another variation.

Soul's "fullness" that "overflows / And falls into the basin of the mind" refers to the Plotinian Plenum and the Hypostatic fountain of emanation. "What is full," wrote Plotinus, "must overflow," cascading down from the divine One through *Nous* (mind or intellect) to the generated soul (*Enneads* 5.2.4). Macrobius's description of the Neoplatonic hypostases—uncharacteristically succinct and "as good a summary of the Plotinian trinity as was possible in Latin"[43]—anticipates Soul's language in stanza 5 of "Dialogue" and adumbrates the conflict between the Yeatsian antagonists:

God, who both is and is called the First Cause, is alone the beginning and source of all things. . . . He, in a bounteous outpouring of his greatness, created from himself Mind. This Mind, called *nous*, as long as it fixes its gaze upon the Father, retains a complete likeness of its Creator, but when it looks away at things below creates from itself Soul. Soul, in turn, as long as it contemplates the Father, assumes his part, but by diverting its attention more and more, though itself incorporeal, degenerates into the fabric of bodies.

(*Commentary* 1.14.4)

This clarifies the position of the Yeatsian Self as perceived from Soul's perspective: viewed *sub specie aeternitatis*, Self is an emanation of, and a falling off from, the higher Soul. When the attention, supposed to be fixed on things above, is diverted below—to the "blade upon my knees" wound in "tattered" silk and, still further downward, to the "impure" ditches—the lower Soul (or Self) has indeed degenerated into the world of nature and the "fabric," the tattered embroidery or mortal dress, of bodies.[44] The connection between icon and ditch was stronger in the drafts, where Yeats wrote, "The *sword & silk* have made mankind *impure*." The published poem's "impure" ditches from which Self "*drinks* his drop," the "source" to which Self will "follow" every event in action or in thought, and the sweetness that "*flows* into the breast," though all "things below," can still be envisioned as part of a processional and cyclical continuum, the Neoplatonists' *circuitus spiritualis*. "What's water," asked Yeats, echoing Porphyry's synopsis of Heraclitus, "but the generated soul?" (VP 490).

Perhaps the degenerate "drop," like Marvell's "drop of dew" emblematic of the fallen but resolved soul, seeks to return (*epistrophé*) to the divine

43. H. F. Stewart's comment (*Cambridge Medieval History* 1:573), cited by Stahl in *Commentary on the Dream of Scipio*, 86, n. 10, 143, n. 4.

44. The poem with which Yeats intended to end his canon, "Politics," seems a final variation on the rejection of the Neoplatonic command to "fix the attention" (Macrobius) or "fix the gaze" (Plotinus) on things above—in this case, lofty international politics rather than the spiritual realm, though the distraction is still aesthetic and sexual: "How can I, that girl standing there, / My attention fix / On Roman or on Russian / Or on Spanish politics?" (VP 631).

source: Marvell's "clear Fountain of Eternal Day," the Plotinian Fountain
that is "Source of All." The "source" to which Self refers seems anything
but transcendent. But since, as the Neoplatonist Proclus says, the search for
the source is often pursued "subconsciously and thus randomly," Self can
be seeking blessedness even in that random "wandering / To this and that
and t'other thing" so harshly criticized by Soul. The quest goes on even in
the midst, not of the "steep ascent" urged by Soul, but of its polar opposite:
the descent down ("How could passion run so deep"?) to the cesspools
of the universe, the "impure" waters of defluction and the generated soul.
The paradox may be traced ultimately to Heraclitus, for whom the soul,
though generated *from* water, also finds both its death and its bliss *in* water.
A "dry soul is wisest and best"; yet, according to Heraclitus, once embodied, the soul is "connected with humidity"; it is at once "death" and "pleasure" for souls to "become moist," even though such a wet-souled man "is
drunk, . . . stumbling and not knowing where he goes" (Fragments 36, 77,
117, 118).

The aimless "wandering" of the Yeatsian Self, an *antithetical* drunkard
who drinks his drop, assumes precise yet paradoxical direction in the final
stanza, where Heraclitean Yeats has things both ways, finding pleasure *and*
blessedness:

I am content to follow to its source
Every event in action or in thought;
Measure the lot; forgive myself the lot!
When such as I cast out remorse
So great a sweetness flows into the breast
We must laugh and we must sing,
We are blest by everything,
Everything we look upon is blest.

Mere contentment suggests awareness that there may be another and
higher "source" external to the self. But here, following everything to the
"source" within, Self rejects the grim doctrine that "only the dead can be
forgiven," an acceptance of passivity so numbing that its mere utterance
turned Soul's tongue "to stone." Instead Self audaciously (or blasphemously) claims the power to forgive himself. In a similar act of self-determination, Self "cast[s] *out*" remorse, reversing the defiling image earlier
"cast upon" him by the "mirror of malicious eyes." Self's own passive
mirror has turned lamp and Christian redemption has been secularized,
with the autonomous Romantic imagination as redeemer. The sweetness
that "flows into" the self-forgiving breast displaces the infusion (*infundere:*
"to pour in") of Christian grace through divine forgiveness. And there are
Miltonic infusions Yeats may be echoing and altering. In *Paradise Lost*, the
Creator initially "infus'd" vital spirit; "self-begot" Satan "infus'd" bad influence into the "breast" of his associate angels; and Eve's sensuous beauty,

according to an ominously smitten Adam, "infus'd / Sweetness into my heart."[45] The Yeatsian infusion of sweetness into a self-forgiving breast is thus both redemptive and heretical: a confirmation of man's claimed autonomy, a prideful *non-serviam*, and a stubborn clinging to sensuous beauty, however painful.

In the germinal scribblings from which "Dialogue" emerged, adamant Soul, more Plotinian than Platonic, ruled out any place at all on man's "steep ascent" for the sensuous, for "love of women"—to which the equally extremist Self cried out, "Never enough of women!" The final influx of sweetness into that passionate breast is cognate with, but in a finer tone than, the earlier pitch down into impure ditch-water teeming with frog-spawn, with "the most fecund ditch of all, / The folly that man does / Or must suffer, if he woos / A proud woman not kindred of his soul." Though Milton's angel Raphael would still find Self "sunk in carnal pleasure" (*Paradise Lost* 8.593), the final thoughts of the Yeatsian "we" have been refined, the heart enlarged, by the spirit of love.

The final turn of the poem remains audacious—despite this sublimation, and despite precedent for Self's climactic assertion of internalized beatitude. "The kingdom of God is within you," says Jesus in Matthew and Luke, a saying taken up by the Inner Light tradition of Protestantism, celebrating the "divinity within" (*entheos*) or "paradise within" of internalized redemption and autonomous grace. Though both phrases appear in *Paradise Lost*, Milton is not Boehme, or his own Puritan contemporary Gerrard Winstanley (for whom there was no savior but the Christ in one's own heart), or Blake, or Wordsworth, who also speaks of "Divinity within." Indeed, the Miltonic context of that phrase is instructive.

Though Adam and Eve "feel / Divinity within them breeding wings / Wherewith to scorn the earth," this feeling overwhelms them not when they are in the prelapsarian state of grace but as the initial consequence of their fall—that is, at the "completing of the mortal sin / Original." Adam and Eve merely "fancy" that they experience divinity within; indeed, far from producing scorn of the earth, "that false fruit / Far other operation first displayed, / Carnal desire inflaming" (*Paradise Lost* 9.1003–13). In Yeats's "Dialogue," Soul calls for imagination to "scorn the earth." If the echo is an intended allusion, Yeats's point would be not only to remind us of the ironically carnal context of Milton's phrase but also to contrast the Miltonic with his own *antithetical* perspective on the consequences of the fall. Having been beckoned by Soul to "scorn the earth," Self instead embraces the earth and the "crime" of existence, glories in the fecund possibilities of Eternal Recurrence, and (in the climax of the poem), feeling divinity within, forgives himself the whole of his fallen, criminal "lot," even claiming that everything we look on is "blest."

This self-forgiveness and self-redemption, like the embrace of Eternal

45. *Paradise Lost* 7.236; 5.856–61, 694–96; 8.474–75.

Recurrence itself, reflect the impact of Nietzsche. He had been preceded by Behmenist hermeneutics, the heterodox Inner Light tradition, and such theological speculations as those of Lessing and of Schleiermacher at his most daring (as in his *Dialektik*); but it took Nietzsche, himself the son of a Protestant minister, to most radically transvalue the Augustinian doctrine that man can only be redeemed by the power and grace of God, a pre-destinarianism made even more uncompromising in the strict Protestant doctrine of the salvation of the elect as an unmerited gift of God. Unable to believe in "the dogmas of religion," but still needing "consolation" and even a form of "salvation," you find—not God's predestined grace—but, says Nietzsche (in a work Yeats read with care), your own "grace." He who has "definitively conquered *himself* henceforth regards it as his own privilege to punish himself, to pardon himself." Casting out remorse, we should love rather than despise ourselves: "Then you will no longer have any need of your God, and the whole drama of Fall and Redemption will be played out to the end in you yourself" (*The Dawn* §437, 79).[46]

In his own version of this sacred drama, affirming the absolute inwardness Rilke called *Weltinnenraum*, the Yeatsian Self also asserts an autonomy substituting Selfhood for Godhood. When, according to "A Prayer for My Daughter," the soul "recovers radical innocence," it

    learns at last that it is self-delighting,
Self-appeasing, self-affrighting,
And that its own sweet will is Heaven's will.

The same claim is made by the Self in "Dialogue." If, as Yeats rightly said, Blake's central doctrine is the "forgiveness of sins," the sweetness that "flows into" the self-forgiving "breast" (Blake also said, "All deities reside in the human breast" [MHH, plate 11]) confirms the uniqueness of the individual as the ultimate "source" of value.

Following the Inner Light tradition and emulating Blake, Yeats sometimes claimed a Christian sanction. Trying in 1896 to persuade his friend W. T. Horton that the Order of the Golden Dawn was *not* "anti-Christian" but indeed quintessentially Christian, he told him, "Progress lies not in dependence upon a Christ outside yourself but upon the Christ in your own breast, in the power of your own divine will and divine imagination, and not in some external will or imagination however divine. We certainly do

46. The second of these passages from *The Dawn* is also employed by M. H. Abrams in his brief discussion of "A Dialogue of Self and Soul" as the culmination of the secularization and internalization of the concept of redemption. Abrams emphasizes the role of Wordsworth in this tradition. With "no helper," says Wordsworth, man, keeping his "individual state," acknowledges "the sorrows of the earth"; but Wordsworth insists that, "centring all in love," his life, "in the end," is "all gratulant" (*Prelude* 13.185–91, 383–85). This theme is brought to conclusion, Abrams rightly notes, by the Yeatsian Self, who "sees his life and the world he looks upon as all gratulant, although not by a Wordsworthian but by a Nietzschean act of heroic self-forgiveness and self-redemption" (*Natural Supernaturalism*, 122).

teach this dependence only on the inner divinity, but this is Christianity." What it really "is," Yeats confirmed in a follow-up letter, is Blake's conviction of "the Divine Humanity" (L 261–63), "and that, as Blake said, 'God only acts or is in existing beings or men'" (E&I 352, LTSM 80). It is a conviction shared by a number of radical thinkers—most emphatically, and with least accommodation to Christianity, by Nietzsche, who dreamed dreams of the advent of a Superman, "once man ceases to flow *out* into a God" (*The Gay Science* §285).

The Nietzschean *Übermensch* is relevant here. Yeats believed that Nietzsche's thought "flows always, though with an even more violent current, in the bed Blake's thought has worn," and that "Nietzsche completes Blake and has the same roots," especially Blake in his "praise of life—'all that lives is holy,'" a Blake Yeats identifies with Nietzsche "at the moment when he imagined the Superman as a child" (E&I 130, L 379, Au 474–75). That occurs (see below, Chapter 6) in Zarathustra's speech on the threefold metamorphosis of the spirit, from burdened camel to defiant lion to the "sacred Yes" of the value-creating "child." In Self's peroration in "Dialogue," Yeats himself "completes" a presumably truncated Blake with Nietzsche by fusing childlike joy, which Nietzsche's Zarathustra shared with Blake, with the painful but finally ecstatic acceptance of Eternal Recurrence: Nietzsche's "highest formula of affirmation which is at all attainable," a doctrine anathema to Blake, for whom cyclicism was the final dehumanizing nightmare. That part of the "completion" is forced, but not Yeats's association of Nietzsche's "sacred Yes" with the final chant of Blake's Oothoon in *Visions of the Daughters of Albion*, an affirmation addressed to everything we look upon: "sing your infant joy! / Arise and drink your bliss, for every thing that lives is holy!" Self is a living man who, defying Neoplatonism, "drinks his drop," ending in a state of infant joy. Though this *antithetical* choice entails pain, Self finds, rather than everlasting pain, the bliss traditionally reserved for those who follow the ascending path:

We must laugh and we must sing,
We are blest by everything,
Everything we look upon is blest.

The radical autonomy of Self is tempered by the shift from the stanza-opening "I" to "such as I" to this four-times-repeated "we"—a progression suggesting a welcome expansion of ego, issuing in a final benediction somehow (as in Wordsworth and Coleridge) merging solipsism with widest commonalty and an all-encompassing reciprocity or "ennobling interchange."[47] It is also, if not a reconciliation of the previously sundered Self

47. I have in mind, along with the generous expansion of the ego to be found at many points in *The Prelude*, the shift in personal pronouns that takes place during the progress of the Immortality Ode. As Roger Cox has noted, the "I" of the first four stanzas of the ode "becomes 'we' in the fifth, and a 'new I' emerges in the last three. . . . The 'new I' of the poem's

and Soul, an absorption of the latter by the former, signaled by Self's commandeering of the theological vocabulary that Soul, like Crazy Jane's Bishop, tries to monopolize. The last word is "blest," and it is the word of Self, exercising redemptive imagination.

Thus "Dialogue" proceeds by what Blake called the prolific opposition of "contraries," not by wholesale obliteration of the opposite, which would produce no "progression." Laughing, singing, blest and blessing, the finished Self seems to embody that fusion spoken of by AE (George Russell). Of the poems in *The Winding Stair*, sent him as a gift by Yeats, he liked this one "best" of all. "I am on the side of Soul," he wrote acknowledging his friend's gift, "but know that its companion has its own eternal claim, and perhaps when you side with the Self it is only a motion to that fusion of opposites which is the end of wisdom" (LTWBY 2:560). Having acutely synopsized the central Yeatsian dialectic, Russell was tentatively noting its reflection in the poem's impulse, beneath the manifest debate of opposites, toward "fusion." In Yeats's version of Balzac's "two germs," those "fertile souls, ceaselessly uniting," Self resolves the debate with Soul by achieving "a transcendence, not of life, but rather of the terms of the conflict altogether."[48]

"Man can only love Unity of Being," Yeats wrote in his 1930 diary, explaining why such conflicts as those urged on us by discarnate spirits are "conflicts of the whole soul."

All that our opponent expresses must be shown for a part of our greater expression, that he may become our thrall—be "enthralled" as they say. Yet our whole is not his whole and he may break away and enthrall us in his turn, and there arise between us a struggle like that of the sexes. All life is such a struggle.

(Ex 302)

In "Dialogue," the spiritual "opponent" is a contrary part of the Self, "a part of our greater expression," and the quarrel with "others," now recognized as a quarrel with "ourselves," makes not "rhetoric" but "poetry." However deep the psychical division out of which such poems spring, Yeats's "masterful images"—root *and* blossom, tower *and* winding stair,

---

last section participates in the 'we' of the second part as the original 'I' had not." The "joyous affirmation" of the tenth and final stanza is possible only after the earlier introspection has "been transformed into a sense of solidarity with all men, and the poignant quality of the last two lines . . . depends almost entirely on the two lines which precede them: 'Thanks to the human heart by which we live, / Thanks to its tenderness, its joys and fears, / To *me* the meanest flower that blows can give / Thoughts that do often lie too deep for tears'" ("On Wordsworth's Immortality Ode"). A similarly effective use of the "we" occurs in Yeats's "Nineteen Hundred and Nineteen" (IV and V) and in "The Stare's Nest By My Window," section VI of "Meditations in Time of Civil War."

48. Norman Friedman, "Permanence and Change: What Happens in Yeats's 'Dialogue of Self and Soul.'"

sword *and* silk (its "heart's purple" perhaps itself a fusion of soul's blue and body's red), the "we" Self becomes—*are* masterful because "complete." As Yeats's essential spokesman in this, the greatest of his internal dialogues, Self incorporates rather than simply refutes the spiritual perspective. Since the night *has* spiritual stars, Self's way is not an out-and-out rejection of, but (as Yeats says) a "variation on," the Neoplatonic position—the position of Plotinus, Porphyry, Macrobius.

Still, the variation, part of naturalizing supernaturalism, remains radical. Self ends his great chant swept up in a moment of childlike joy, self-redemption, and secular beatitude that goes beyond Lear (who tells Cordelia that in prison they'll "pray and sing and tell old tales, and laugh"), beyond the Wordsworth of "Tintern Abbey" (for whom "all which we behold from this green earth / Is full of blessings"), and beyond Coleridge (from the heart of whose Mariner a "spring of love" gushed as he looked on the previously slimy water snakes and "blessed them unaware"). Yeats's alteration of the spiritual tradition goes all the way to a Blake completed by Nietzsche, whose exuberant Zarathustra, jumping "with both feet" into "golden-emerald delight," also jumps into a cluster of images and motifs we would call Yeatsian:

In laughter all that is evil comes together, but is pronounced *holy* and *absolved* by *its own bliss*; and if this is my *alpha* and *omega*, that all that is heavy and grave should become light; all that is body, dancer; all that is spirit, bird—and verily that *is* my alpha and omega: oh, how should I not lust after eternity and the nuptial ring of rings, the ring of recurrence?

(*Zarathustra* 3:16)

Both Zarathustra, who here replaces the Lord God of the Book of Revelation with his own alpha and omega, and the Yeatsian Self, who begins his excited reverie brooding on a personally chosen "consecrated" icon and ends claiming the power of self-redemption, vary the biblical Apocalypse in order to laugh and to sing their own autonomous revelation and absolution.

"To sing": that remains the sine qua non of "a singer born," an imperative projected even into the world beyond birth and death. Zarathustra's final "alpha and omega," that spirit should become bird, recurs not only in Yeats's projected reincarnation as a golden bird set on a golden bough "to sing / To lords and ladies of Byzantium," but also in his final fusion of opposites, "Cuchulain Comforted," the mysterious and beautiful *terza rima* poem dictated to his wife on his deathbed. In that Dantesque masterpiece we encounter for the last time Yeats's central, and remarkably Nietzschean, hero. Nietzsche had helped Yeats "very greatly to build up in my mind an imagination of the heroic life," a vision embodied in Cuchulain, who reflects the sovereignty of Nietzsche's noble man and who, in unpublished notes, shared with Nietzsche phase 12 of *A Vision*, the phase of the hero.

But in "Cuchulain Comforted," all's changed—though not utterly, since
the hero "strode" among the dead, still bore "arms," and "took up the
nearest" bundle of linen with the old heroic nonchalance of hand.

A man that had six mortal wounds, a man
Violent and famous, strode among the dead;
Eyes stared out of the branches and were gone.

Then certain Shrouds that muttered head to head
Came and were gone. He leant upon a tree
As though to meditate on wounds and blood.

A Shroud that seemed to have authority
Among those bird-like things came, and let fall
A bundle of linen. Shrouds by two and three

Came creeping up because the man was still.
And thereupon that linen-carrier said:
'Your life can grow much sweeter if you will

'Obey our ancient rule and make a shroud;
Mainly because of what we only know
The rattle of those arms makes us afraid.

'We thread the needles' eyes, and all we do
All must together do.' That done, the man
Took up the nearest and began to sew.

'Now must we sing and sing the best we can,
But first you must be told our character:
Convicted cowards all, by kindred slain

'Or driven from home and left to die in fear.'
They sang, but had nor human tunes nor words,
Though all was done in common as before;

They had changed their throats and had the throats of birds.

Among the dead, not in the Neoplatonic or Christian heaven but in the
pagan underworld, Yeats's slain superman joins timid spirits who, as cowards, are his polar opposites. *Antithetical* autonomy yielding to *primary* community, the equivalent of Self's transformation of "I" to "We," they together undergo metamorphosis—not simultaneously, but with Cuchulain
shortly to follow. Nietzsche might have been disturbed by this spiritual
transformation of the heroic life, with Cuchulain's enlistment in a commu-
nal sewing bee in which all "obey our ancient rule." He would, however,
have been in accord with the Yeats for whom even the ghostliest paradigm
is a reincarnated form. Though transfigured, chthonic Cuchulain remains
more an image than a shade; for they had "changed their throats and had the

throats of birds." Spirit has become bird, a miraculous bird that, not struck dumb in the simplicity of fire, is singing—inevitably and in keeping with the hero's prevision, in *The Death of Cuchulain*, of his soul as a "feathery shape . . . about to sing" (VPl 1060–61).

* * *

The preceding chapter takes for granted the impact of Nietzsche, "the crucial figure in Yeats's poetic life, if any single figure may be named." That is the verdict of Denis Donoghue (*William Butler Yeats*, 44), a judgment largely validated by the more extensive work of David Thatcher and—most recently and fully—of Eitel Friedrich Timm and Otto Bohlmann. Thanks to them (and to Richard Ellmann, Conor Cruise O'Brien, Erich Heller, Patrick Bridgwater, John Burt Foster, and others), it is no longer necessary to rehash all the evidence of Yeats's reading of Nietzsche in order to demonstrate what is obvious: that these were kindred spirits and that the poet found in his "strong enchanter" much that either shaped or confirmed his *antithetical* vision.[49] One indication of the centrality of this influence is the fact that, for Yeats, Nietzsche completed Blake and in part refuted Shelley, his two shaping spirits.

Unhappily, Yeats's copies of the books given him by John Quinn (including *Zarathustra*) have disappeared; but we have his revealing annotations in the Nietzsche anthology lent him by Quinn, along with other scattered marginalia, and there are a number of acute and memorable references in the letters and published prose. Privately, he conceded that Nietzsche was "exaggerated and violent," and in an unpublished passage in an early (circa 1918) version of *A Vision*, discussing the phase of the hero, he speculated on what lay beneath Nietzsche's "mask of lonely sublimity": "The typical figure of the phase is of course Nietzsche, neurotic, nervewracked, always on the verge of the madness that overwhelmed him, he cannot escape from the *antithetical* excess that has made possible his genius."[50] In the published version, however, we hear of the "awakening of his *antithetical* being," marked by "a noble extravagance, an overflowing fountain of personal life" (V-A 63).

The timing of Yeats's introduction to Nietzsche was critical. It coincided with his emergence from the Celtic Twilight, and his own post-Nietzschean characterization of it as "sentimental . . . unmanly . . . womanish" (L 434–35) suggests he would have agreed with Joyce's cruelly accurate pun in *Finnegans Wake*, "Cultic twalette." With his entrance into the public arena of the Abbey and the loss of Maud Gonne to a man of action, the initial

49. Thatcher's *Nietzsche in England 1890–1914: The Growth of a Reputation* remains an excellent examination. Timm's dissertation—"William Butler Yeats und Friedrich Nietzsche" (1980)—is a more penetrating study than Bohlmann's nevertheless useful *Yeats and Nietzsche*.

50. See the letter to John Quinn cited above (n. 13). The unpublished passage from the early version of *A Vision* is cited by George Mills Harper, "The Creator as Destroyer: Nietzschean Morality in Yeats's *Where There Is Nothing*," 119n.

"excited" reading of Nietzsche (L 379) toughened Yeats, enabled him (not without cost) to "get under foot" in his "heart" that "unmanly" tendency toward sentimental beauty, and validated his own growing glorification of aristocratic morality with its heroic virtues and *self-imposed* duties. Nietzsche's "curious astringent joy" and Zarathustra's "laughter from the heights" shaped Yeats's concept of tragic joy, from *Where There Is Nothing* and *The King's Threshold* on, from the "sweet laughing thoughts" of Anglo-Irish aristocrats and the "laughing lip" of Cuchulain (both in the 1910 *Green Helmet* volume) through the laughing, singing exultation of "Dialogue" to the harsh "tragic joy" and dread-transfiguring "Gaiety" of his most overtly Nietzschean poems, "The Gyres" and "Lapis Lazuli." As we shall see in Chapter 8, Nietzsche also contributed to the "lonely impulse of delight," and to the autonomy in general, of the death-foreseeing Airman as Yeatsian hero.

Yeats's central hero, Cuchulain, would be a very different figure had the poet not been acquainted with *Thus Spoke Zarathustra*, the *Genealogy of Morals*, and *Beyond Good and Evil*. Cuchulain was not only Yeats's closest equivalent to the Nietzschean *Übermensch* but also his own heroic "mask," a concept for which he is also largely indebted to Nietzsche, for whom "everything profound loves the mask," whose noble man, when not speaking to himself, "wears a mask," at once sword and shield protecting "a solitude within him that is inaccessible to praise or blame, his own justice that is beyond appeal" (*Beyond Good and Evil* §40; *The Will to Power* §962). With his stress on antithetical conflict and penchant for images of combat, his sense of discipline and drama, Nietzsche added hardness and virility to what Yeats had inherited from Wilde concerning mask and anti-self and so helped forge pervasive Yeatsian doctrine, as well as the poet's own Nietzschean "mask of lonely sublimity."

Discussing the relation between "discipline and the theatrical sense" in his 1909 diary, Yeats outlines the "condition of arduous full life": "If we cannot imagine ourselves as different from what we are and assume that second self, we cannot impose a discipline upon ourselves, though we may accept one from others. Active virtue as distinguished from the passive acceptance of a current code is therefore theatrical, consciously dramatic, the wearing of a mask" (Au 469). Nietzschean heroic discipline, self-overcoming, the wearing of a mask, the active will to power, the distinction between master morality and slave morality—all of which Yeats had read of with great excitement—here join with the poet's own distinction between self-disciplined, *antithetical* "personality" (the "created" mask) and passively accepted, *primary* "character" (the "imitative" mask). Divided into opposing spokesmen, this is the debate between Self and Soul, perhaps Yeats's most Nietzschean exercise in masking.

The drafts of "A Dialogue of Self and Soul" reveal that the eventually triumphant Self (originally "Me") had begun ("I know symbols too") by establishing, in opposition to Soul's "star, stair, and T[ower]," his own double icon emblematical of love, war, and eternal recurrence: "sword & silk" (the poem's title, in its original typescript). That genetic impulse survived all revision. Referring to the "razor-keen" sword bound in "Heart's purple," Self exclaims:

> all these I set
> For emblems of the day against the tower
> Emblematical of the night,
> And claim as by a soldier's right
> A charter to commit the crime once more.

The "soldier's right" reflects the resistant aspect of Cicero's soldier, youthful Scipio (though, as Soul cruelly noted, Self's imagination is that of "a man / Long past his prime"), and *antithetical* warriors both Homeric and Nietzschean: "soldiers—they obey life," Yeats noted in one margin of the Nietzsche anthology. In the most important of these marginal notes, that diagram worthy of his "Diagrammatists," the Judwali, Yeats also anticipated the setting of unpurged "emblems of the day" against those of "night." Aligned with Homeric "Day" and opposed to Socratic-Christian "Night" appears the bare original of Yeats's *antithetical* "variation on Macrobius" and his fellow Neoplatonists in "Dialogue": "*affirmation* of *self*, the soul *turned from spirit* to be its *mask* and instrument when it *seeks life*." As already noted in the discussion of "A Dialogue of Self and Soul," Nietzsche provided an impressive *antithetical* counterweight to the *primary* world of Plato, Plotinus, Macrobius, Gnosticism, and the "life-denying" aspects of Christianity. The diagram suggests even more: that, under the direct stimulation of Nietzsche, indeed synopsizing Nietzsche, Yeats formulated his true concept of the "mask" (this is his first theoretical use of the term) and of "self," that *antithetical* aspect of the soul "turned from spirit" and "knowledge" to seek and affirm "life." "I have often felt that Nietzsche could have become a stroke of luck and a happy discovery for a great poet . . . the source, that is, of a most highly erotic-crafty *irony* that moves playfully between life and intellect." By the time Thomas Mann wrote that (about the same time that Yeats inserted Nietzsche in *A Vision*), adding, "Nietzsche has not found, or not yet found, his artist," Nietzsche had in fact found not only Thomas Mann but also W. B. Yeats.[51]

Though he learned much about erotic irony and about masks and personae from Nietzsche, what attracted Yeats to the German philosopher was not so much his radical skepticism, pragmatism, and perspectivism (stressed by most contemporary readers, especially practitioners of deconstruction and related postmodern literary theories) as his vitalistic counter-Platonism, his pagan and Romantic exaltation of "life" over

---

51. Mann, *Reflections of a Non-Political Man*, 58. The book was written between 1915 and 1918.

"knowledge," heart over head, "will" over "reason," life-affirming Homer and Dionysus over life-denying Plato and Christ. Yeats also grasped more sophisticated aspects of Nietzsche, especially (and here Nietzsche anticipates Freud's insistence that we make ourselves in the struggle to break free of the tyrannizing past) the imperative to re-create Time's "it was" into a liberating "thus I willed it" (*Zarathustra* 2:20). The emphasis is inevitably on the "I" and its individual will to power. Yeats's "strong enchanter" is the Nietzsche who advocates heroic individualism, the prophet of active self-overcoming, self-creation, self-redemption, in opposition to salvation by passive accommodation to any imposed code or universal moral imperative. That struggle and eventual triumphant affirmation is what "A Dialogue of Self and Soul" celebrates.

Arguably Yeats's central poem, the one (as Lawrence Lerner once said) with the "most repercussions" in his other work, "A Dialogue of Self and Soul" constitutes Yeats's principal variation on, or alteration of, the spiritual tradition. His chief ally in the struggle to "overcome" the esoteric side of himself, a wrestling match whose outcome was by no means certain in the drafts, is the prophet of self-overcoming. And Nietzsche played an equally crucial role in another antithesis at the heart of "A Dialogue of Self and Soul": the tension between fate and freedom, necessity and autonomy. Inherent in the concept of a passive, imitative mask versus an active, creative mask, or the notion of a discipline either self-imposed or passively accepted, this tension between free will and determinism, and its possible resolution through tragic joy, is at the heart of Yeats's mature, and notably Nietzschean, vision. Since it is acted out in its most "consciously dramatic . . . wearing of a mask" in "A Dialogue of Self and Soul," I will have to risk some repetition in order to address the paradox, salient in both Nietzsche and Yeats, of exultant freedom within compulsion and constraint.

6

"PREDESTINATE AND FREE":
YEATS AND THE NIETZSCHEAN PARADOX OF EXULTANT FREEDOM
WITHIN COMPULSION AND CONSTRAINT

I murmured, as I have countless times, "I have been part of it always and maybe there is no escape, forgetting and returning life after life like an insect in the roots of the grass." But murmured it without terror, in exultation almost.
—Yeats, Introduction to *A Vision* (1925)

When Yeats exults in his mood of desperate optimism, as in "The Gyres," he strides to war with the God-Who-Is-History; *amor fati*, the strange device woven into Zarathustra's battle-flag, is also Yeats's motto. The Eternal Recurrence then indeed becomes a doctrine to cheer oneself up and gain the courage to face the "desolation of reality."
—Harvey Gross, *The Contrived Corridor: History and Fatality in Modern Literature*

One thing is needful. To "give style" to one's character—a great and rare art! . . . It will be the strong and domineering natures that enjoy their finest gaiety in such constraint and perfection under a law of their own. . . . Conversely, it is the weak characters without power over themselves that *hate* the constraint of style. . . . Such spirits . . . are always out to interpret themselves and their environment as *free* nature—wild, arbitrary, fantastic, disorderly, astonishing.
—Nietzsche, *The Gay Science* § 290

I. Determinism and Freedom

Neither my chapter title nor the epigraphs are intended to suggest that Yeats's encounter with this philosophic, historical, and stylistic paradox takes place solely in a Nietzschean context, still less that Nietzsche solved the "problem" for Yeats any more than he did for himself. The paradox has been stated ad infinitum; whether it *can* be resolved logically is another matter. Perhaps its only satisfying resolution is stylistic, specifically in poetic metaphor. The word *compulsion* in the title presents additional difficulties, since most philosophers—Aristotle, Aquinas, Hobbes, Leibniz, Hume, Locke, and Mill prominent among them—distinguish necessity from coercion or compulsion. Leaving that aside for the moment, the reconciliationist view that determinism is both true and compatible with free will has a long history. Among the most familiar formulations is that of Hume, a compatibilist who tried to salvage liberty by equating it with one's own desires, preferences, volition, while also insisting that since the will itself is determined, human actions are simultaneously free and causally determined.[1]

The most paradoxical form of determinism—the idea that freedom is the recognition of necessity, acceptance of the world as it "must" be—is germane here. This fatalistic view, rooted in Stoicism, is fully developed in Spinoza, for whom freedom means a development from "passive" to "active" powers through enhanced intelligence, the clarification of hitherto confused ideas leading to an adequate understanding of the causes of one's own behavior. "An emotion which is a passion," says Spinoza, "ceases to be a passion as soon as we form a clear and distinct idea of it" (*Ethics* 5.3). This concept of freedom is not only compatible with but *requires* determinism, since the "power" of the mind is increased "in so far as it understands all things as necessary." To have adequate ideas is to comprehend and be guided by "the law of one's own nature," but our power to sublimate the instincts and passions is, according to Spinoza, "far surpassed" by the power of external things. In any case, the final fruit of such an educational development is the attainment of at least a relative, practical freedom. Belief in free will is discarded as one of the illusions stemming from confused ideas, but one can attain a strictly limited freedom, even some degree of self-determination, within necessity and "human bondage."

It often comes down to a question of *tone*. Spinoza's stoical acquiescence, though it has its element of happiness, altogether lacks the *brio* of the joyous fatalism Nietzsche found in that partial Spinozist, Goethe, and that he strove to emulate in his own version of the stoic doctrine of *Amor Fati* in the specific form of an ecstatic embrace of the thought of the Eternal Recurrence, that psychological test of the mettle of any potential *Übermensch*.[2] In Yeats's own doctrinal System—the mélange of explicated symbolism, cyclical philosophy, and occultism that constitutes the Great Wheel of *A Vision*—true freedom is found, as it is in Spinoza and Nietzsche, in the recognition of necessity. For Yeats, the recognition issues, ultimately, in "tragic joy," a Nietzschean "gaiety transfiguring all that dread" (VP 564, 565). For the dread is there. Yeats knows, as well as Spinoza, how difficult it is for the passive to turn active, for "the mirror [to] turn lamp," for the

---

1. Hume, "On Liberty and Necessity," *An Enquiry Concerning the Principles of Morals* (1751), section 7.

2. Nietzsche, who refers to *Amor Fati* four times in his published work, calls it his "inmost nature" (*Nietzsche contra Wagner*, epilogue), the "highest state" of Dionysian affirmation a philosopher could attain (*Will to Power* §1041). One should not only "bear" what is "necessary," but "*love it*" (*Nietzsche contra Wagner*, epilogue). "I want to learn more and more to see as beautiful what is necessary in things" (*The Gay Science* §276).

Will to accept and somehow overcome all that is "forced upon [us] from without" (V-B 83). Yeats is also aware of the danger of being ground under by the dread of cyclicism itself, a tension played out in the exultant "Dialogue of Self and Soul" and in the untransfigured dread of *Purgatory*.

In theoretical discussions and, more importantly, in poems embodying the tension between freedom and necessity, Yeats is characteristically gyre-torn. As a consequence, and almost predictably, he founds his mature position on Kant's third antinomy in *The Critique of Pure Reason*. Like Kant, Yeats denies neither free will nor causality. Since the latter is needed for science and the former for ethics, freedom for Kant must be a special type of causality: a form of self-determination dictated by a determined will obeying, as in Rousseau, its own "inner laws." These are, according to *The Critique of Practical Reason*, moral laws residing within man's deeper "noumenal" self. If as phenomenon man is determined, as noumenon he is free.

That was a compatibilist solution not open to Nietzsche, for whom Kant's noumenal world of things-in-themselves was a pernicious figment, vestigial Platonism, that "*horrendum pudendum* of the metaphysicians." But, like so many of the German Romantics, Nietzsche seized on the idea, transmitted particularly through Kant, of the will's inner laws and the agent's self-sufficiency, a concept as applicable to aesthetics as to ethics.[3] Both he and Yeats avoid the sine qua non of most philosophers on the question—that freedom, though compatible with necessity, is impossible under external constraint—by arguing that the restraining laws to be obeyed are not external but inherent, thus leaving the agent (or a poem, for that matter) autonomous; in Aristotle's resonant term, "self-moved."

The Romantics—specifically, A. W. Schlegel in Germany and his English pupil and plagiarist, Coleridge—distinguish between the organic and the mechanical, between inner laws as a principle of autonomous form and those laws artificially imposed from without. The distinction is echoed in Yeats's synopsis of his Instructors' doctrine in *A Vision*: "By fate and necessity is understood that which comes from without, whereas the *Mask* is predestined, Destiny being that which comes to us from within" (V-B 86). Thus fate is imposed and *primary*, destiny somehow self-determined and *antithetical*. A related dichotomy informs Nietzsche's distinction between "master morality" and "slave morality," the former based on autonomy issuing in life-affirmation, the latter on enforcement from without, servile *ressentiment*, and consequent life-denial.[4] Yeats, self-schooled in the Romantic poets and theorists, read Nietzsche with equal insight and excitement. As his annotations on passages from *Beyond Good and Evil* and the *Genealogy of*

---

3. The evolution of the application of the language of autonomy—from theology through ethics to aesthetics—has been traced, with Kant as the pivotal figure, by M. H. Abrams, "Kant and the Theology of Art."

4. These are prominent features of passages (from *Beyond Good and Evil* §260 and part 1 of the *Genealogy of Morals*) that Yeats marked in the Thomas Common Anthology lent him by Quinn.

Morals reveal, he understood these central antitheses and was in essential agreement with Nietzsche's instinctive preferences. Poetically fusing Schlegel-Coleridge with Nietzsche in the opening stanza of "Ancestral Houses," Yeats celebrates aristocratic life as an overflowing fountain (Nietzschean, not Plotinian) that "rains down life" and mounts higher the more it rains,

As though to *choose* whatever shape *it wills*
And never *stoop* to a *mechanical*
Or *servile* shape, at *others'* beck and call.
     (VP 417; my italics)

Yet even this apparently uncompromising affirmation of the organic and of Nietzschean master morality, will to power, and autonomy is qualified by caveat ("As though"), recanted ("Mere dreams!"), and then reaffirmed ("And yet"). It is that characteristic pattern—powerful affirmation, opposition, reaffirmation—Yeats called vacillation. In fact, at this point one "must"—good determinist word—once again confront Yeats's crucial poetic sequence entitled "Vacillation," a work in which the antinomy, in the specific form of the tension between the predestinate and the free, is most explicitly embodied.

II. Compulsion and Choice

In Lady Gregory's *Vision and Beliefs*, Yeats wrote: "I was once at Madame Blavatsky's when she tried to explain predestination, our freedom and God's full knowledge of the use that we should make of it. All things past and to come were present in the mind of God and yet all things were free."[5] In this attempted reconciliation of divine omniscience and human freedom (God knows how man will freely choose) as in her insistence on the eternal present of God's vision, Madame had been preceded by Augustine, Boethius, Aquinas, Descartes, and subsequent theologians and philosophers taking an essentially Augustinian line. That "all things past and to come were present in the mind of God" is echoed in the refrain of Yeats's 1931 poem "Crazy Jane on God": "*All things remain in God.*" Yet Jane is nothing if not a spokeswoman for individual freedom. In the contemporaneous "Vacillation" Yeats addresses the paradox of predestination and freedom in its most personal form:

I—though heart might find relief
Did I become a Christian man and *choose* for my belief
What seems most welcome in the tomb—play a *predestined* part.
Homer is my example and his unchristened heart.

---

5. *Visions and Beliefs in the West of Ireland*, 1:127.

Though a reconciliationist at heart, Yeats sounds here almost like one of William James's "hard" determinists, applying to himself the doctrine he had applied, in "No Second Troy," to his femme fatale: "Why, what *could* she have *done, being* what she *is*?" No one can be other than what one is: Yeats could "choose" to be a Christian man except that in the sacred drama of life he is "predestined" to play the "part" of Homeric poet, a part that rules out Christian redemption.

The final line of the preceding section of "Vacillation" posed a rhetorical question: "What theme had Homer but original sin?" Yeats's unchristened Nietzschean Homer "sings," in tragic but ineradicable joy, of precisely what Christians interpret as the inevitable consequences of man's fall: a fall that, for the heirs of Augustinian predestination, involved the casting of man, the author of his own degradation, into a morass of sin from which he cannot save himself by his own power. Yeats yields to this helpless passivity in the ghostly play *Purgatory*, written not long before his own death, but utterly rejects it, as we've seen, in "A Dialogue of Self and Soul." There, Self overcomes the horror expressed in *Purgatory* to instead embrace Eternal Recurrence, at the same time claiming the power of *self*-redemption, a claim validated by an immediate influx of autonomous grace.

That victory of Self over Soul or, at least, the absorption of the latter by the former, is no less under Nietzschean auspices than the choice of "Homer . . . and his unchristened heart" as Yeats's "life"-seeking Nietzschean "example." The alliance with life-affirming Self is also emphatically personal. Yeats told Olivia Shakespear that he was writing a poem ("Dialogue," then called "Sword and Tower") that was "a choice of rebirth rather than deliverance from birth. I make my Japanese sword and its silk covering my symbol of life" (L 729).

Yeats seems to accept the darkest consequences of his choice in the poem entitled "The Choice." "My wife said the other night"—Yeats wrote Dorothy Wellesley after the death of George Russell—"'AE was the nearest thing to a saint you and I will ever meet. You are a better poet but no saint. I suppose one has to choose'" (L 838). In "The Choice," as in "Vacillation" and "A Dialogue of Self and Soul," the tension is between playing a religious or an aesthetic part: is Yeats to be saint or poet? Again, the choice is paradoxically enforced, the outcome no less predestined:

The intellect of man is *forced* to *choose*
Perfection of the life, or of the work,
And *if* it take the second *must* refuse
A heavenly mansion, raging in the dark.

So much for the "traditional sanctity" Yeats says (in the stanza that originally followed these lines) "We . . . last romantics . . . chose for theme" (VP 491). Yeats, who runs his course "between extremities" (VP 499), characteristically pushes matters to the extreme, maximizing for dramatic purposes the antipodal nature of the consequences of the choice. If one chooses to perfect the work rather than the life, to be poet rather than saint, one has no further options; the Homeric artist "*must* refuse" the heavenly mansion. This either/or reflects the one hint of "escape" from the Great Wheel as presented in the poem "The Phases of the Moon." Between Hunchback (phase 26) and Fool (phase 28), between deformity of body and of mind, the Saint (phase 27) draws his bow (a fusion of the burning bow of Blake's Los and of Balzac's seraph, shooting into his heavenly joy):

> The burning bow that once could shoot an arrow
> Out of the up and down, the wagon-wheel
> Of beauty's cruelty and wisdom's chatter—
> Out of that raving tide.

Though Yeats told Dorothy Wellesley he believed in the eventual "return of the soul to God" (LDW 177), the more *antithetical* poems give only modest credence to this possibility of release. Yeats tends instead to locate the poet in "the serpent's mouth," and he alters an ancient formulation: "If it be true that God is a circle whose centre is everywhere, the saint goes to the centre, the poet and artist to the ring where everything comes round again" (E&I 288, 287)—round again in ouroboric cycle, the great wagon wheel, the raving tide of generative life. The poet, playing his predestined part, must refuse a heavenly mansion, raging in the dark.

The imperative *must*, itself a paradoxical fusion of freedom and necessity, plays its own predestined part in another summing-up poem, "The Circus Animals' Desertion." At the end, the Yeatsian old man, now that his Platonic "ladder's gone,"

>   *must* lie down where all the ladders start,
> In the foul rag-and-bone shop of the heart.

More than bodily decrepitude compels the old man. He can do no other if he is to remain a poet—because the foul but fecund heart is a "shop" in which "that raving slut / Who keeps the till" is the Muse herself. He "must" lie down in this genetic matrix of his poetic images, but only if he chooses to continue to play his predestined part as poet—to side with the Heart rather than the Soul of "Vacillation," whose spiritual fire would purge but silence the poet. Just as Crazy Jane rejects the Bishop's "heavenly mansion" for the "mansion" Love has "pitched . . . in / The place of excrement," so the speaker of this poem chooses, perversely and because he "must," Bembo's "lower-most step" on the Platonic *scala*. "The Circus Animals' Desertion" ends with the Yeatsian speaker triumphant in defeat, standing proud

and stiff in the very act of seeming to "lie down" in submission and degradation. Again, he finds his limited freedom within his predestined role.

III. The Happy Prison

It is, of course, a venerable paradox, from Plato on, that service, rightly
chosen, is the only true freedom. Paul, who said we feel most falsely free
precisely when we are "slaves of sin," also speaks of the righteous as "God's
slaves" (Romans 6:15–22), and Augustine of bondage to God as perfect
freedom. The same formulation, with God replaced by the Muse-Goddess,
has been employed by writers from Apuleius to Robert Graves, who finds
his freedom in obeisant submission to the vagaries of the White Goddess,
Apuleius's Isis compounded with the *belle dame sans merci* of the Romantic
agony. For artists, the paradox of freedom within constraint is not only a
philosophic and Muse-matter but also a question of form: the relationship
between energy and order, "passion and precision" (VP 264), imagination
and what even Blake acknowledged as the necessary "outward circum-
ference" of reason (MHH, plate 4). The great prototype of the artist,
Daedalus, would have had no prison from which to escape had he not first
invented that restraining labyrinth. According to Pope's *Essay on Criticism*
(1.90–91), "Nature, like liberty, is but restrained / By the same laws which
first herself ordained." Artists who work within linguistic restraints, particularly poets, never tire of variations on the old formulas: Thomas Gray's
"constraint / To sweeten liberty," Shelley's "sweet bondage which is Freedom's self." Austin Clarke spoke to Robert Frost of the Houdini-pleasure
of loading oneself with chains and then getting out; Frost himself spoke of
having "freedom when you are easy in your harness" and of the writing of
"free" verse being like playing tennis without a net. Richard Wilbur has
reminded us that "the strength of the genie comes of his being confined in a
bottle."

In the context of the recurring Romantic metaphor Victor Brombert has
labeled "the happy prison," one recalls the famous variation on what Cor-
bière would have called the "*cage de la gâité*" of Wordsworth, whom "un-
charted freedom tires," and who, having "felt the weight of too much
liberty," found solace in the "narrow room" of the Miltonic sonnet; for "In
truth the prison, unto which we doom / Ourselves, no prison is." Coleridge, referring to Wordsworthian "Duty," speaks of "chosen Laws controlling choice" and, equating music with "Poetry in its grandest sense,"
defines both as "Passion and order aton'd! Imperative Power in obedience!"
In expressing the fertile tension between, on the one hand, the freedom of
vision, imagination, and strong emotion and, on the other, the confining
discipline of order, form, firm restraint, many writers have testified to the
joyful necessity, constructive rather than restrictive, of what Baudelaire
calls constricting form (*formes contraignantes*) or Camus, "cellular lyricism,"

a grace of containment. It was, significantly enough, *in* a poem that Nietzsche, who elsewhere advocates "dancing in chains," described himself as "in
most loving constraint, free."[6]

Here Nietzsche aligned himself with one of his favorite poets and thinkers, Goethe, who spoke of the interplay between "power and restriction . . .
freedom and measure."[7] "Measurement began our might," says Yeats in
"Under Ben Bulben," and might is precisely measured in those lines in
which the true visionary artist (ostensibly Robert Gregory, but actually, I
argue in Chapter 7, Yeats himself) is born to, and trained in,

>   that stern colour and that delicate line
> That are our secret discipline
> Wherein the gazing heart doubles her might.
>   (VP 326)

"Gazing," for Yeats, is internal as well as secret; the consequence of this
internal discipline, of submission to stern yet delicate restraint, is, as in
Nietzsche's gaiety in stylistic restraint, an augmentation of power. It is
another instance, Yeats would say, of Nietzsche completing Blake, whose
internalization of the stony law transforms it "from arbitrary commands to
the inner discipline of the free spirit."[8]

As early as 1901, Blakean Yeats had lectured his fellow adepti in the
Order of the Golden Dawn on the importance of inner discipline and obedience. He spoke of "greater things than freedom," the "cry" of "every
idler, every trifler, every bungler." In contrast, "the busy, the weighty
minded, and skilful handed, meditate more upon the bonds that they gladly
accept, than upon the freedom that has never meant more in their eyes than
a right to choose the bonds that have made them faithful servants of the
law."[9] Thirty-six years later, in no less important a place than the intended
"General Introduction for My Work," Yeats, who equated poetry with "the
fascination of what's difficult," noted, "Because I need a passionate syntax

---

6. Nietzsche's poem appears in the section on *The Gay Science* in *Ecce Homo*. He advocates
"dancing in chains" in *The Wanderer and His Shadow* §140 and claims, in *Beyond Good and Evil*
§226, "We dance in our 'chains' and between our 'swords.'" The Wordsworth poems referred
to are "Nuns fret not at their convent's narrow room" and the "Ode to Duty." Coleridge is
quoted from his poem "To William Wordsworth" and his *Notebooks* (ed. Kathleen Coburn),
2:3231. For a discussion of this metaphor in French literature, see Victor Brombert's *The
Romantic Prison: The French Tradition*. Discussing the acceptance of bounds implicit in Pindar's
image of the Pillars of Herakles, "the world's boundary," D. S. Carne-Ross says that Pindar
sees those pillars as "constructive" rather than "restrictive," a "grace of containment providing
man's energetic nature with the space within which it can flourish in the manner which is
proper to it" (*Pindar*).

7. Goethe, quoted by Karl Viëtor, *Goethe the Thinker*, 146.

8. The formulation is Northrop Frye's; see "The Keys to the Gates" in his *The Stubborn
Structure: Essays on Criticism and Society*, 183. The remark on "gazing," elaborated on in the
next chapter, is indebted to Denis Donoghue.

9. Yeats, *Is the Order of R.R. & A.C. to remain a Magical Order.*

for passionate subject-matter *I compel myself to accept* those traditional metres that have developed with the language. Ezra Pound, Turner, Lawrence wrote admirable free verse. I could not. I would lose myself, become *joyless*" (VP 260, E&I 522). This gladly accepted bondage or disciplined joy—Nietzschean "gaiety . . . in constraint," what Yeats called, borrowing the term from Coleridge, "shaping joy"—is often embodied, in Yeats as in Nietzsche, in the imagery of dance. After telling us in this passage that the merely personal rots unless it is "packed in ice or salt" and that "ancient ice is best packing," Yeats adds: "Imagination must dance, must be carried beyond feeling into the aboriginal ice . . . a poem 'cold and passionate as the dawn.'"[10] "Cold and passionate": like "terrible beauty," this is another Yeatsian oxymoron for the Apollonian-Dionysian fusion that resulted in his pouring, for example, the teeming images of "Byzantium" into so intricate a stanza, or the sexual and mythic violence of "Leda and the Swan" and "Her Vision in the Wood" into, respectively, a Shakespearean-Petrarchan fused sonnet and his favorite "traditional" stanza, *ottava rima*.

Yeats seems to have been first attracted to Nietzsche by this Apollonian-Dionysian antithesis (L 402, 403). He was impressed by Nietzsche's conception, in *The Birth of Tragedy*, of chaos ordered, Dionysus rhapsodized yet harnessed by Apollo. In Nietzsche's later thought, the "Dionysian" subsumes the Apollonian, but his earlier formulation was based on his understanding of the bipolar fusion of Apollo and Dionysus in the Greek spirit. At the end of his "Untimely Meditation" on history, having reminded us of Apollo's oracle, "Know yourself," Nietzsche asserts, "Thanks to that Apollonian oracle, Hellenic culture was no mere aggregate. The Greeks gradually learned to *organize the chaos* by following the Delphic teaching and thinking back to themselves, . . . a parable for each one of us" (*Untimely Meditations* 2.10). But the chaos must be organized, not extirpated in the plucking out Nietzsche called (in *Twilight of the Idols* 5.1) Platonic-Christian "castratism." As Zarathustra puts it, "One must still have chaos within oneself to be able to give birth to a dancing star" (*Zarathustra* 1:prologue 5).

The ideal represented by the *Übermensch*—the result of *Selbstüberwindung*, self-overcoming—is passion under control, a power-enhancing self-mastery ever aware of the forces stirring under restraint. Nietzsche's presiding example is Goethe: a "stylized human being" who attained "noble form" by overcoming his own "romantic" impetuosity with "classical" Apollonian severity (*Untimely Meditations* 2.8). Later, when Nietzsche's "Dionysian" came to mean passion under control, the chief exemplar of the Dionysian was Goethe, a "spirit who has become free" *within* constraint. In his own words (in his poem *Die Geheimnisse*), amid life's internal storm and outward tide (*innern Sturm und assern Streite*), Goethe heard a difficult, mysterious promise:

---

10. E&I 522–23; the final phrase is a self-quotation, from the poem "The Fisherman." For "shaping joy," see E&I 255 (compare Nietzsche, *The Will to Power* §495).

Von der Gewalt, die alle Wesen bindet,
Befreit der Mensch sich, der sich überwindet
(From the compulsion that all creatures binds,
 Who overcomes himself, his freedom finds.)

Selbstüberwindung is Yeats's ideal as well. We see it in his admiration of self-controlled Parnell; in his account of Nietzsche, the "hero" who "*overcomes himself,* and so no longer needs . . . the submission . . . or . . . conviction of others to prove his victory"; in his historical speculations, for "a civilization is a struggle to keep self-control . . . like some tragic person . . . who must display an almost superhuman will" (V–B 127, 268). We see it as well, of course, in his determined effort to attain "self-possession" and, above all, in his art. Writing to Dorothy Wellesley, he explained (alluding to Lear's plea for sanity) the secret of the leashed power of this ideal:

We have all something within ourselves to batter down and get our power from this fighting. I have never "produced" a play in verse without showing the actors that the passion of the verse comes from the fact that the speakers are holding down violence or madness—"down Hysterica passio." All depends on the completeness of the holding down, on the stirring of the beast underneath.
   (LDW 86)

This more vigorous version of Keats's "Might, half slumb'ring on its own right arm" addresses the paradox of freedom within necessity in the specific form of compulsion and constraint. Echoing Goethe and sounding much like the Yeats of the letter to Dorothy Wellesley and of the "General Introduction," Nietzsche spoke, in *Beyond Good and Evil* (§ 188), of "the compulsion under which every language so far has achieved strength and freedom—the metrical compulsion of rhyme and rhythm":

All there ever has been on earth of freedom, subtlety, boldness, dance, and masterly sureness . . . in the arts just as in ethics, has developed only owing to the "tyranny of . . . capricious laws"; and in all seriousness, the probability is by no means small that precisely this is "nature" and "natural"—and not that *Laisser aller*.   Every artist knows how far from any feeling of letting himself go his most "natural" state is . . . and how strictly and subtly he obeys thousandfold laws precisely then ["in the moment of inspiration"].

(Though Nietzsche believed that man orders "nature," he knew too that much in nature functions with astonishing mathematical precision.) True thinking, he continued a few pages later, combines a "bold and exuberant spirituality that runs *presto*" with a "dialectical severity and necessity." Such thinking is "light, divine, closely related to dancing and high spirits."

Artists seem to have more sensitive noses in these matters, knowing only too well
that precisely when they no longer do anything "voluntarily" but do everything of
necessity, their feeling of freedom, subtlety, full power, of creative placing, disposing, and forming reaches its peak—in short, that necessity and "freedom of the will"
then become one in them.

(*Beyond Good and Evil* §213)

"Aesthetic man"—wrote Nietzsche in a brilliant discussion of Heraclitus—and "only" aesthetic man, an experienced observer of the forces at
play both in the world and in the "birth of art objects," can see "how the
artist stands contemplatively above and at the same time actively within his
work, how necessity and random play, oppositional tensions and harmony,
must pair to create a work of art."[11] When the creative pairing of necessity
and freedom, discipline and passion, order and energy, pattern and play, is
perfect, one cannot be distinguished from the other. The constant emphasis
by both Nietzsche and Yeats on dancer and dance culminates, in "Among
School Children," in the climactic image of a unified "Labour" in which
"body is not bruised to pleasure soul" but has instead been transfigured into
a oneness in which flesh and spirit, performer and performance, can no
longer be distinguished:

O body swayed to music, O brightening glance,
How can we know the dancer from the dance?

We cannot because, as Nietzsche puts it in the opening section of *The Birth
of Tragedy*, the Dionysian dancer, "on the brink of taking wing as he
dances," has attained a dynamic, mystical unity: "No longer the *artist* he has
himself become a *work of art*."[12]

IV. "Dialogue" Revisited

Then there is the even more rhapsodic, and perhaps no less division-healing, conclusion of "A Dialogue of Self and Soul," a poem that is precisely a
celebration of joy within compulsion, as well as the embodiment of Yeats's
most crucial creative pairing, of Blake with Nietzsche. Yeats believed, as
we have seen, that "Nietzsche completes Blake and has the same roots." In
Self's peroration in "Dialogue" Yeats himself "completes" Blake with
Nietzsche by fusing that childlike joy common to Blake and Zarathustra
with the difficult but finally exultant acceptance of Eternal Recurrence, a

11. Nietzsche, *Philosophy in the Tragic Age of the Greeks*, trans. Marianne Cowan, 62. See
below, Section VII of the present chapter.
12. *The Birth of Tragedy* 1. In her sole reference to Yeats in *Beyond Nihilism: Nietzsche without
Masks*, Ofelia Schutte remarks that "Among School Children's" final stanza "vividly captures
the Dionysian vision," the "subject-object distinction that makes discursive thought is suspended as the dynamic unity of life is perceived" (26–27).

Zarathustrian embrace that would have appalled that enemy of cyclicism, Blake. In forcibly completing Blake in this way, Yeats forces upon *us* consideration of the relationship between cyclical recurrence and not only the present general subject—free will and determinism—but also the specific paradox of freedom, even joy, within constraint.

Self begins his final speech having turned a deaf ear to Soul's imperious summons to fix his "wandering" thought "Upon the breathless starlit air, / Upon the star that marks the hidden pole." Rejecting the "steep ascent" of spirit, Self has preferred to focus downward on life, brooding on the consecrated blade upon his knees. Its tattered but still protective wrapping ("That flowering, silken, old embroidery, torn / From some court-lady's dress and round / The wooden scabbard bound and wound") makes the double icon "emblematical" not only of "love and war" but also of the ever-circling gyre, the *eternal* "round." When Soul's tongue is turned to stone with the petrifying realization that, by his own austere lights, "only the dead can be forgiven," Self, blind to the Neoplatonic light but anything but dumb, takes over the poem. He begins by playing an *antithetical* "variation" (Yeats, we saw, specified it as a "variation on Macrobius") on Soul's Plotinian fountain, the Plenum or "fullness" that "overflows" from the spiritual quarter:

A living man is blind and drinks his drop.
What matter if the ditches are impure?

He then adopts a Nietzschean gesture ("What matter if I live it all once more?"), a gesture immediately undercut by the litany of grief that Nietzschean Recurrence, the exact repetition of the events of one's life, would necessarily entail—from the ignominy of boyhood to the finished man among his enemies, all that "toil" leading up to the crucial question of how to overcome passive acceptance of a "discipline" imposed by others. Soul's tongue may be turned to stone, but other forces still have palpable designs upon the assaulted Self:

How in the name of Heaven can he escape
That defiling and disfigured shape
The mirror of malicious eyes
Casts upon his eyes until at last
He thinks that shape must be his shape?

Though they have gone unnoticed, the Yeatsian interactions here are brilliant. In the System's terminology, which would be understood perfectly by Spinoza, this is the struggle of the individual soul, failing to establish its "chosen Image" against the Body of Fate, all that is "forced upon [it] from without" (V-B 94, 83). The gleam of the "malicious eyes" that cast upon Self a distorting lie so powerful that he falls victim to it is borrowed from the first stanza of Browning's most compelling quest-poem. Childe Roland's

> first thought was, he lied in every word,
> That hoary cripple, with *malicious eye*
> Askance to watch the working of his lie
> *On mine*, and mouth scarce able to afford
> Suppression of the glee, that pursed and scored
> Its edge, at one more victim gained thereby.

Even closer to Self's temporarily mistaken belief that that "defiling" shape "cast upon" him by mirroring eyes "must be his shape" is the mistaken, masochistic cry of Blake's Oothoon for her "*defiled* bosom" to be rent away so that she "may *reflect* / The image" of the very man (the moralistic sadist Theotormon) whose "loved" but unloving "eyes" have cast upon her precisely this "defiled" shape—one of Blake's, and now Yeats's, grimmest ironies.

Self's eventual casting out of this defiling mirror-image is effected by completing Blake with Nietzsche. The defiling and disfigured shape temporarily accepted by Self is that servile shape at others' beck and call rejected in favor of the Homeric-Nietzschean fountain-image in which aristocratic "life overflows," raining down more life that "mounts" as though to "choose" the shape it "wills," never stooping to a "mechanical / Or servile shape" imposed from without, by "others." In contrast to Soul's Plotinian "fullness" that "overflows / And falls into the basin of the mind," striking man "deaf and dumb and blind," this autonomous fountain—emblematic of master morality and the will to power—is life-affirming. The next lines of "Ancestral Houses" confirm Yeats's linking of Nietzsche, depicted in *A Vision* as an "overflowing fountain of personal life" (V-B 126), with Nietzschean

> Homer [who] had not sung
> Had he not found it certain beyond dreams
> That out of life's *own self-delight* had sprung
> The abounding glittering jet.

But in "Dialogue," the consecrated sword—"still like a looking-glass / Unspotted by the centuries," a mirror in which clear self-perception is possible—has been forgotten for the moment, and it is not yet time for the defiling "mirror" of malicious eyes to be replaced by a creative "lamp" in that moment when life-affirming, self-delighting "sweetness flows into the breast," transforming servile "character" to active, creative "personality." At this stage, poor Self even wonders what would be gained if he should honorably "escape" that defiling distortion only to end up a truly "finished man," a Lear in old age's "wintry blast" (another echo, incidentally, of Blake's *Visions of the Daughters of Albion*).

At this point, having analeptically and proleptically rehearsed the painfulness of his life, Self recovers his audacity, recommitting himself to Eternal Recurrence—not only "once more" (itself an echo of Zarathustra's "Was *that* life? Well then! Once more!"),[13] but many times:

I am content to live it all again
And yet again, if it be life to pitch
Into the frog-spawn of a blind man's ditch,
A blind man battering blind men;
Or into that most fecund ditch of all,
The folly that man does
Or must suffer, if he woos
A proud woman not kindred of his soul.

I am content to follow to its source
Every event in action or in thought.

As Yeats's wording confirms, what we have here is a tracing, *within human life*, of the ghostly Return phase of the posthumous Meditation as explained in book III of *A Vision* ("The Soul in Judgment"). The *Spirit* "must live through past events in the order of their occurrence; because it is compelled by the *Celestial Body* [by which Yeats means the Divine Ideas in their Unity] to trace every passionate event to its cause until all are related and understood, turned into knowledge, made a part of itself" (V-B 226). Still "a *living man*," Self is content to follow every event in action or in thought to quite another "source," as the substitution of "source" for the more deterministic "cause" may suggest—not back via the *epistrophé* that returns us to the Neoplatonists' "Source of All" *atop* the Plotinian fountain of emanation, but to the Self as *internal* "source" of *its own* thoughts and actions. Departing from his own Systematic determinism, and varying the *circuitus spiritualis* of his Neoplatonic sources, Yeats here has Self embody the theory philosophers call, appropriately enough, "self-determination," a libertarian theory traceable, according to Cicero's *On Fate*, back to Carneades, whose essential position was restated in Thomas Reid's well-known 1788 study, *Essays on the Active Powers of Man*. The Yeatsian Self seems in this final stanza to embody such active powers, that "creative activity" ascribed to autonomous "selves" in C. A. Campbell's self-determinist *Selfhood and Godhood* (1957). Indeed, after casting out the servile shape cast upon him by malicious eyes, Self asserts an autonomy actually *substituting* Selfhood for Godhood. The sweetness that "flows into" the self-forgiving human "breast" (where, Blake said, "all deities reside") confirms, as noted

13. *Zarathustra* 3.2 ("On the Vision and the Riddle").

in Chapter 5, the unique individual as the ultimate "source" of value. It is a conviction shared by Emerson, Thoreau, Feuerbach, Kierkegaard, and, of course, Nietzsche, who prophesied the advent of a *Super*man, once man "ceases to *flow out* into a god."

Once the Yeatsian Self casts *out* bitter remorse, *antithetical* sweetness flows *in*, a vacuum-filling sweetness so great that "We must laugh and we must sing, / We are blest by everything, / Everything we look upon is blest." In his 1909 diary, after noting Blake's preference for embodied happiness over abstract intellect and after slightly misquoting Blake's "praise of life—'all that lives is holy,'" Yeats adds of this preference: "Nietzsche had it doubtless at the moment when he imagined the 'Superman' as a child" (Au 474–75). Blake's repeated axiom about the holiness of everything is given to Oothoon at the climactic moment of *Visions of the Daughters of Albion*. Her recovery from self-deception in the course of the poem is synopsized in Self's speech, from the opening "A living man is blind and drinks his drop," through the temporary acceptance of an externally imposed defiling shape, to the concluding childlike chant. Oothoon's final affirmation (plate 8:9–10) is addressed to everything we look upon:

> sing your infant joy!
> Arise and drink your bliss, for every thing that lives is holy!

But there is still the need to "complete" Blake with Nietzsche. Blake's poem ends with Oothoon's personal liberation qualified, circumscribed as it is by the "margind ocean" beside which the Daughters of Albion continue to wail in their cycle-bound tragedy. They begin and end the poem "Enslav'd" (the opening word), bound, like Oothoon's God-tormented pseudolover, to the tyranny of nature symbolized by the "margind" Atlantic, its waves black and "incessant." Self is also bound to incessant cycle and to waters of generation even more impure. But Yeats Nietzscheanizes Blake in order to transform the Romantic poet's nightmare of cyclicism into an ecstatically embraced vision of joy and freedom *within* the admittedly painful confines of Eternal Recurrence.[14]

Nietzsche, to return to Yeats's words, "imagined the 'Superman' as a child" in the first of Zarathustra's speeches on the "steps" to the *Übermensch*, a parable on the three metamorphoses of the spirit embodying both the dialectical tension between compulsion and freedom and the Blakean proverb that "the thankful receiver bears a plentiful harvest." First the "reverent" spirit must resemble a camel, submitting freely to the fascination of what's difficult and to the burden of the past ("What is most difficult," asks

---

14. In (understandably) attacking Eternal Recurrence as promulgated in "The Great Year of the Ancients" section (book IV) of *A Vision*, Harold Bloom observes: "Nietzsche is a formidable antagonist for Blake when he insists upon the heroism necessary to endure the idea of Eternal Recurrence, but Yeats is manifestly less formidable when he adopts the Nietzschean principle that there is no redemption from recurrence" (*Yeats*, 279).

the camel-like spirit that would "bear much, that I may take it upon myself and exult in my strength").[15] The next stage is that of the tradition-defying lion, who "would conquer his freedom and be master in his own desert." But for the ultimate task, not only the preservation and destruction but also the genuine *creation* of values, the child is needed; for "the child is innocence and forgetting, a new beginning, a self-propelled wheel, a sacred 'Yes.' For the game of creation, my brothers, a sacred 'Yes' is needed: the spirit now wills his own will, and he who had been lost to the world now conquers his own world" (*Zarathustra* 1.1).

Yeats, anticipating the coming *antithetical* change in the external world, called in 1930 for "a new beginning, a new turn of the wheel" (Ex 337); three years earlier he had put in the mouth of Self not only this internalized celebration of the wheel, recovery of self-determination, and sacred Yes, but also the delighted laughter of Zarathustra as he reaches on the Merry-Go-Round of life for "the nuptial ring of rings, the ring of recurrence," for "in laughter all that is evil comes together, but is pronounced holy and absolved by its own bliss." Thus "We must laugh and we must sing." Bound to the wheel of recurrence, "we" are no longer bound to King Lear's wheel of fire, but, like Lear and Cordelia in the old man's projection of their life in prison, we *will* "sing like birds i'th cage," another happy prison in which "we'll live, / And pray, and sing, and . . . laugh." Though it obviously echoes Lear's words, Self's prayer is one of secular beatitude and *self*-absolution. We laugh and sing because, along with "remorse," Soul's "only the dead can be forgiven" is also "cast out"—a doctrine of numbing passivity and fatalistic acceptance rejected in favor of autonomous grace and self-forgiveness. Having followed to its source every event in action or in thought, Self can "Measure the lot; forgive myself the lot!" (Even here, the tension between freedom and fate is maintained. The repeated "lot," deriving from Plato's Myth of Er, is the "fate" we "choose" between incarnations. In "Chosen, the female speaker is adamant in insisting, "The *lot* of love is *chosen*.") In any case, with this deliberate, painful, and finally re-demptive measuring of every past action and thought, Yeats goes beyond the innocent "forgetting" of the Zarathustrian child to what Nietzsche called a "*second* taste" or *recaptured* "innocence of becoming" (*Unschuld des Werdens*). Out of prolonged exercises in self-mastery, one emerges trans-formed, still loving life, but differently: "the love of a woman who raises doubts in us." Strangest of all, says Nietzsche, is that "afterward one has a different taste—a *second* taste. Out of such abysses . . . one returns newborn, having shed one's skin . . . with gayer senses, with a second dangerous innocence in joy, more childlike and yet a hundred times subtler than one has ever been before" (*The Gay Science*, preface 4).

This is the condition of the newborn Self at the conclusion of "Dialogue."

---

15. "Be secret and exult," Yeats advised a defeated Lady Gregory in a Nietzschean poem of consolation, "Because of all things known / That is most difficult" (VP 291).

Having pursued the winding "path of the serpent," Self ends in the *recovered* "radical innocence" of "A Prayer for My Daughter," in *"organiz'd* innocence," Blake's equivalent of Nietzsche's shed skin and "second . . . innocence," or what Hart Crane calls "an *improved* infancy." All would agree for once with Blake's bête noire Francis Bacon: "It is not possible to join serpentine wisdom with the columbine innocency, except we know exactly all the conditions of the serpent"—as the shepherd does who, obeying Zarathustra's cry to bite off the head of the serpent hanging out of his mouth, jumps up transformed—"one changed, radiant, *laughing*" (*Zarathustra* 3.2). In reintegrating the sundered self, experience is not to be deferred or evaded but embraced; since knowledge, "the hand that inflicts the wound," is, in Hegel's homeopathic metaphor, "also the hand that heals it," restored unity of being must take the form of putting on "knowledge with . . . power" (VP 441), Wordsworth's "Knowledge not purchased by the loss of power."[16]

Self augments his power by assuming prerogatives traditionally reserved to God. It is in part true, as Robert Langbaum argues in "The Self as God" chapter of *The Mysteries of Identity*, that the thoughts of later Yeats about reincarnation and the "supernatural confirmation of identity" reflect his reading of Indian philosophy and religion and that "Balzac showed him how he could absorb such insights while remaining European." Yeats's citation of Gauguin's quotation from *Séraphita* in the unpublished note to "Dialogue" may confirm Balzac's role. But, Yeats claimed, "all Nietzsche is in Balzac" (see Chapter 4, note 32), and the tonality and progression of the poem itself, from near collapse to fierce affirmation and a recaptured childlike joy in Recurrence, suggest that Yeats was "remaining European" in proclaiming the Self as God by adhering closely to that "good European," Nietzsche. To that strong enchanter's sacred Yes and astringent joy, Self adds Nietzschean self-forgiveness and self-redemption. This constitutes an audacious rejection not only of Soul's morbid conviction but also of Augustinian predestination, with its insistence that fallen man can only be redeemed by the power and grace of God; can be saved, not by the exercise of his own free will, but by being divinely chosen. Nietzsche radically transvalued Augustinianism as promulgated, and made even more uncompromising, by Luther and, especially, Calvin in the strict doctrine of the salvation of the elect as an unmerited gift of God. You must find, says Nietzsche in a passage cited earlier, not God's predestined grace but your *own* "grace"; then you "no longer have any need of your God, and the

16. *The Prelude* 5.425, echoed in Yeats's "Leda and the Swan." This overloaded paragraph begins with two of Blake's Proverbs of Hell; Blake says elsewhere that unorganized innocence is finally an impossibility. Hart Crane's phrase is from "Passage" in *White Buildings*. Bacon is cited from *Works*, ed. Spedding et al., 3:431. Hegel's famous image occurs in *The Logic of Hegel*, trans. W. Wallace, 56. For more of the same—following in the line of Geoffrey Hartman's "Romanticism and Anti-self-consciousness" and Abrams's *Natural Supernaturalism*—see my article entitled "On Truth and Lie in Nietzsche," 72–73, 89–90.

whole drama of Fall and Redemption will be played out to the end in you yourself." Having unwittingly killed God, man can become his own deity through the power of imagination, making possible a Dionysian innocence of becoming, a transformation into an autonomous self—radiant, laughing, blessed, and blessing.

Self's triumphant chant, more Nietzschean than Blakean, is, depending on one's perspective, blasphemously presumptuous or exhilarating, persuasive or a kind of glorious whistling in the dark. But is it an illustration of *autonomy*, given its encircling round of compulsive reenactment? For the constraint is still there: "I am *content*." (So was Shylock, who uses precisely these words, under compulsion, at the end of the scene Yeats once said he found most "moving" [L 465] in *The Merchant of Venice*.) Furthermore, we "must" laugh and we "must" sing; and we must also remember that acceptance of Nietzschean Recurrence means the rending reenactment of all that suffering which the poem itself, looking before and after, summons up: all that "toil," "ignominy," "distress," "pain," "clumsiness," "folly," and the defilement cast upon us before we cast out "remorse." Remorse can be cast out, but not the painful memories of events—events we must, again and yet again, "Endure."

V. Recurrence and Sexuality

Nietzsche's Zarathustra, too, was painfully aware of the full implications of Recurrence, a thought that initially filled him with terror and even nausea before he embraced it—"laughing." It is precisely this darker, nightmare side of Eternal Recurrence that we encounter in Yeats's 1938 play *Purgatory* in the form of the tormenting dream of the old man's dead mother, a dream she seems condemned to repeat, barring the unlikely intervention of God, through all eternity. As an intimate countertruth to "A Dialogue of Self and Soul," the play enacts the grimmest possible version of the determinism inherent in Nietzsche's Eternal Recurrence—a tragedy encompassing not merely the old man, twice a murderer and yet helpless to end "all that consequence," but also the tortured spirit of his mother, who renews her self-degradation each time she reenacts her original transgression. She cannot escape because in her ghostly repetition of the initial sexual act with her corrupt and corrupting husband, she renews both her "remorse" (that remorse "cast out" by the autonomous Self in "Dialogue") and her "pleasure"; thus she can find no redemption except in the possible but hitherto unexercised "mercy of God." The play ends with the old man's anguished prayer:

O God,
Release my mother's soul from its dream!
Mankind can do no more. Appease
The misery of the living and the remorse of the dead.
    (VPl 1049)

But all the imaginative weight falls on the horror-stricken realization a moment earlier ("how quickly it returns") that his mother, her soul still unpurified, "must animate that dead night / Not once but many times!" "Again and yet again," as Yeats had put it in two manuscript drafts,[17] doubtless deleting that formula as an unwanted, but highly significant, echo of precisely what Self had been "content" to accept—just as he had deleted from "Dialogue" passages at odds with Self's eventual vitalistic embrace of Recurrence. (In the drafts, as we saw in chapter 5, it was not Soul but Self who, "bound upon the wheel of life," cried out: "Cannot the wisdom of the sages stop / That burning phantasy till it run pure / Or must I whirl upon the gyre [the wheel] of life once more?") As an impressed but resisting T. S. Eliot said, not without horror, in his Memorial Lecture on Yeats a year or so later, the play gives us a Purgatory without purgation. Though a Nietzschean Recurrence with no exit, this was nevertheless a reflection of what Yeats once acknowledged to be his own convictions about this world and the next.

The repetition of "again" and associated words, not only at the end of *Purgatory* but throughout *Last Poems*, confirms Yeats's final obsession with Recurrence, on both sides of the grave. Though Yeats claimed that "the eternal circuit may best suit our preoccupation with the soul's salvation, our individualism," and denied the fatalism of his System (Ex 355, VP 824), that System, a play like *Purgatory*, poems like "The Gyres" and even the more gloriously Nietzschean "Dialogue of Self and Soul," do raise, in the most extreme form, the classical problem of the seeming incompatibility of freedom and determinism. Despite his emphasis on *antithetical* "freedom," "the realization of myself as unique and free" (Ex 305), Yeats does *not* locate that freedom outside what Blake deplores as the circle of Destiny.

Caught in this tension, Yeats was naturally attracted to Kant's discussion of the "antimonies," a passage Yeats marked and to which he devoted considerable thought. In *A Vision*, Yeats's spokesman claims to "found" himself upon "the third antinomy of Immanuel Kant, thesis: freedom; antithesis: necessity." "But," Robartes goes on, "I restate it. Every action of man's declares [both] the soul's ultimate, particular freedom, and the soul's disappearance in God; declares that reality is [both] a congeries of beings and a single being" (V-B 52). Since Yeats believes the contradiction is "constitutive" rather than merely "regulative" (LTSM 131), there is a further alteration: the replacement of Kant's mental ordering apparatus with a larger category. "This antinomy is not an appearance imposed upon us by the form of thought," says Robartes, "but life itself which turns, now here, now there, a whirling and a bitterness."

Robartes asserts that "after an age of necessity" (associated with Platonic-Christian truth, goodness, democracy, and peace, along with rationalistic mechanism, science, and abstraction) there "comes an age of freedom"

---

17. Quoted from the *Purgatory* manuscripts, as transcribed by Curtis Bradford, *Yeats at Work*, 299, 300.

(associated with such Nietzschean-Homeric antitheses as fiction, evil, art, aristocracy, particularity, and war). After asking if our age of necessity has not "burned to the socket" as the prolegomenon to its end or transformation, Robartes makes an observation directly relevant to Self's choice to commit the crime of death and birth again and yet again. The antinomy, says Robartes, cannot be solved by death; indeed, "death and life are its expression. We come at birth into a multitude" (the Platonic Many, the "this and that and t'other thing" to which Self's attention wanders in "Dialogue") and "after death would perish into the One." Would, that is, "did not a witch of Endor call us back, nor would she repent did we shriek with Samuel: 'Why hast thou disquieted me?' instead of slumbering upon that breast" (V-B 52). In short, even if, like the reluctant spirit of Samuel raised up for Saul by the witch of Endor (1 Samuel 28:15), we wanted to be left in the serenity of death, such *antithetical* characters as Robartes would not be permitted to "perish" into the Plotinian One, losing all individuality ("To die into the truth," as Yeats said of Platonism, "is still to die"). In fact, as believers in the irresoluble antinomy, soldiers in the creative clash of opposites, *antithetical* men do not seek the quiet of Sheol from which "disquieted" Samuel was roused. The only serenity they desire is to slumber on the breast of that occult, sacrilegious, and unrepentant Muse who, far from summoning us to the "breathless starlit air," "call[s] us back" to the crime of death and birth, to life's fecund ditches, offering us, as the witch offered predestined Saul, human consolation.

Robartes's biblical-poetic images are clarified by the sustained speculations on the antinomy recorded in Yeats's 1930 diary. There are "two conceptions" of reality, he notes, and since human reason "cannot reconcile" them, he accepts like a good Kantian—or Schleiermachian—both. "I am always, in all I do, driven to a moment [even here the language is semi-determinist] which is the realization of myself as unique and free, or to a moment which is the surrender to God of all that I am." This parallels Schleiermacher's description (in *On Religion: Speeches to Its Cultured Despisers*) of the soul's two impulses: on the one hand, the desire "to establish itself as an individual" and, on the other, "the fear to stand alone over against the Whole, the longing to surrender oneself and be absorbed in a greater." He adds: "Every soul shares in the two original tendencies of spiritual nature."

But unlike Schleiermacher, at least the Schleiermacher of "dependence" on the infinite Other, Yeats resists the "surrender to God of all that I am." The personal "I am" enlists, if not Yeats's exclusive, certainly his deepest, allegiance. After admitting that he has always "failed" when he "would write of God, written coldly and conventionally," he adds: "Could those two impulses, one as much a part of truth as the other, be reconciled, or if one or the other could prevail, all life would cease." While Plotinus— "compelled" to take this position "by his epoch"—"thought of man as reabsorbed" into God as "final reality," Yeats's ultimate reality must maintain the "antinomy" between what he calls (preserving the honorific noun at all cost) "human and divine freedom," the two freedoms "unthinkably, un-imaginably absorbed in one another." The language, as usual in Yeats, has become sexual. "Surely," he continues, "if either circuit, that which carries us into man or that which carries us into God, were reality, the generation had long since found its term." If men are "born many times," as, Yeats says, "I think," the process must originate in this antinomy between human and divine "freedom." Yeats sees this, his variation on Kant's third anti-nomy, as a Heraclitean process, each freedom dying the other's life, living the other's death: "Man incarnates, translating 'the divine ideas' into the language of the eye, to assert his own freedom, dying into the freedom of God and then coming to birth again. So too the assertions and surrender of sexual love, all that I have described elsewhere as the antithetical and pri-mary" (Ex 305–7).

So we are called back, incarnating many times, to slumber, and more than slumber, on the breasts of women less occult than the witch of Endor. As we have seen, the woman of "Consolation," while she does not deny their "wisdom," tells the occult sages "where man is comforted," and "Me," the prototype of Self in the initial draft of "Dialogue," had cried out, "Never enough of women," reminding us of the wild old wicked man of *Last Poems* who acts out the antinomy between divine and human freedom. "Mad about women," he "travels where *God wills*," yet turns from "that old man in the skies" to "*choose* the second best," forgetting the spiritual truth "no right-taught man denies," at least temporarily:

I forget it all awhile
Upon a woman's breast.

VI. Joyous Fatalism

Yeats either chooses the second best or leaves no room for choice at all. The latter is the perfectly understandable view of those disturbed by the fatalistic elements of his vision—and that includes not only instinctive opponents like D. S. Savage and admirers with deep reservations (Frye and Bloom for example), but even friends. To "follow in the wake of Yeats's mind," wrote AE reviewing the first edition of *A Vision*, "is to surrender oneself to the idea of Fate and to part from the idea of Free Will."[18] Martin Buber—who,

18. Russell's review is reprinted in his *The Living Torch*. Bloom's attack, discussed below, is in the mode established in Savage's "The Aestheticism of W. B. Yeats": since the "static, deterministic nature of the cosmic process" elaborated in Yeats's system "precludes progress of any kind, even individual striving, . . . moral effort is redundant." The individual, like every-thing else, "is regulated automatically by the cosmic mechanism, and there is no possibility of really changing or improving things." The article is reprinted in Savage's *The Personal Princi-ple*. Between Savage and Bloom was Northrop Frye. In the first of his three major essays on the relationship of *A Vision* to Yeats's symbolism ("Yeats and the Language of Symbolism," 1947), Frye notes the "romantic pessimism" of *A Vision's* "cyclic fatality." In the preface to his 1976 collection, *Spiritus Mundi*, Frye objects more strenuously to the "irresponsible fatalism" of the "Yeatsian system." Such partially valid emphases are not to be dismissed. They are,

as a young man, was enthralled enough by Nietzsche to translate the first part of *Zarathustra* into Polish—has stressed the distinction between what he calls "the dogma of process" and freedom's "most real revelation of all, whose calm strength changes the face of the earth—reversal." Though Buber's earth-changing "calm strength" recalls Yeats's and Nietzsche's images (in "Long-legged Fly" and "The Stillest Hour" chapter of *Zarathustra*) for quiet, world-transforming thought, their reversals take place within a scheme of cyclical recurrence, within Buber's dogma of process. I've cited Buber here because his statement is employed as the ultimate weapon by Yeats's most formidable opponent on this issue. Harold Bloom's charge, in the final pages of his study of Yeats and the Romantic tradition, is that Yeats, betraying the Blakean-Shelleyan ideal of freedom, is instead entrameled in determinism. "Rationally and humanely, Yeats ought to be appalled" by his prophecy in the poem "The Gyres," but "he repeats 'What matter?' because of his faith in his own myth as an explanation of the blood-dimmed tide. Whatever this gesture is, it is not artistic freedom, but the darkest of bondages to the idols of determinism" (*Yeats* 471, 436).

Though he has since moved considerably closer to the Gnosticism he deplored in Yeats in 1970, Bloom was then thinking of, among other things, the difference between the visions of Blake and Yeats. To quote M. H. Abrams's characteristically lucid synopsis in *Natural Supernaturalism*:

Blake's redemption [is] figured as a circling back of divided man to his original wholeness; he breaks out of his ceaseless round of wandering in what Blake calls "The circle of Destiny"—the cyclical recurrences of pagan history—into a "Resurrection to Unity" which is the full and final closure of the Christian design of history.

(259–60)

Yeats had been taught by both his major traditions, Romantic and occult, to desire wholeness and unity, whether of culture or of individual being. But his individual genius lay in the projection of the plight of "divided man"— with his own divided allegiance instinctively, and increasingly, with the singer of unchristened Homeric heart who refuses a heavenly mansion and who, despite Soul's badgering, instinctively chooses the ceaseless round of wandering, the cyclical recurrence not only of pagan history but also of Friedrich Nietzsche. He could not, therefore, wholeheartedly embrace any "full and final closure," certainly not one embodying "the Christian design of history." The Christian revelation, Yeats wrote in his 1930 diary, *could* be

---

however, often countered by the poems themselves, which were written by a poet, not a dogmatist. Yeats, notes Daniel Harris, is less the "servant of his system" than such readers as Bloom claim. "What needs to be studied in detail is the conflict *within* the poems between" the theories in *A Vision* and the "relentless insistence upon individual freedom and responsibility." *Yeats: Coole Park and Ballylee*, 113, n. 61.

"a goal, an ultimate Good." "But," he continued, "if I believe that [reality] is also a congeries of autonomous selves I cannot believe in one ever-victorious Providence" (Ex 320). So, despite his dual heritage, and despite the powerful transcendental pull of one side of, say, the Byzantium poems, Yeats remains caught in the ceaseless round of wandering, the cyclical recurrence acted out, at its grimmest, in that gnomic ballad of Blake's that so profoundly influenced *A Vision*, "The Mental Traveller."

This denial of revelation through reversal; the insistence on eternally recurring reversals rather than one unique and final apocalyptic reversal; his "bondage," in short, to the antinomies and to the endless cycle of time: it is this that defines, at least for certain champions of Christian or humanistic apocalyptism, Yeats's failure of nerve, of vision, of spirit, of humanity. But *is* Yeats's vision one of mere bondage to the idols of determinism, a passive surrender to Moira (Fate), to the cyclical coils of Ananke, an "antihumanist" submission to the nightmare of Recurrence? As we have seen, Yeats annotated and shared Coleridge's indignation at being reduced to "the mere quicksilver plating behind a looking-glass." It was *this* passive "mirror" that had, Yeats said, to "turn lamp," to become active and creative. Whatever we make of his vision, it *is* active and creative; at its best, and in most of the actual poems, it is less subservient and darkly antihumanistic than heroic, tragic, and—since it is at once Greek and Nietzschean—necessarily paradoxical.

Like the Greek tragic hero who paradoxically "chooses his fate," the Nietzschean *Übermensch* is he who has (in Karl Löwith's succinct formulation, one Yeats would endorse) "overcome himself by accepting voluntarily what cannot be otherwise, thus transforming an alien fate into his proper destiny." Yeats, fusing Blake's Prolific and Devourer with Nietzsche's Dionysian and Apollonian, declares, "*Fate* is known for the boundary that gives *Destiny* its form and—as we can desire nothing outside that form—as an expression of our freedom" (V-B 136). In the 1930 diary, history is viewed as a "necessity," which, when accepted and comprehended, "takes fire in someone's head and becomes freedom or virtue" (Ex 336)—a remark anticipated in the passages cited earlier from *Beyond Good and Evil* by Nietzsche, who, in turn, was anticipated not only by Spinoza and Goethe but also by the colleague he so admired at Basel. According to Jakob Burckhardt, "Contemplation . . . is our freedom in the very awareness of universal bondage and in the stream of necessities." As Yeats insisted, poets of active imagination "desire whatever happens, being at the same instant predestinate and free, creation's very self" (Au 273).[19]

What Bloom calls the darkest of bondages to the idols of determinism is for Nietzsche *Amor Fati*, "that one wants nothing to be different. . . . Not

---

19. Löwith's formulation is taken from "Nietzsche's Revival of the Doctrine of Eternal Recurrence," in Löwith's *Meaning in History*. Burckhardt is quoted in Erich Heller's *The Disinherited Mind*, 85.

merely bear what is necessary . . . but *love* it"; as Yeats says, "we desire whatever happens," and "would not change that which we love."[20] Though, according to notes in *The Will to Power* (§§552, 55), Nietzsche planned an "attack on determinism," he can hardly be said to have escaped an enemy that on other occasions he seems to embrace. Yet the bondage of Nietzsche and Yeats is neither all "dark" nor opposed to what Bloom calls "artistic freedom." Even on the level of technique, Nietzsche talks of gaiety in compulsion, of "dancing in chains," of the true freedom of the artist being owed to "determinism" in the form of metrical compulsion. Yeats's position, even his imagery, is strikingly similar; artistically, it is certainly true that, within tight stanzaic and metrical constraint, Yeats achieves both a remarkable concentration of power and considerable prosodic variation.

A related "test" is presented by the thought of Eternal Recurrence: who can bear it, asks Nietzsche, and, finally, rejoice in it? Eternal Recurrence—the "same dull round" for Blake; a horror to be escaped even if history has to be abolished for the Shelley of the final chorus to *Hellas*—is a terrible test for Nietzsche and Yeats. But both—at least in their masks as Zarathustra and Self—ultimately accept, even embrace, it, with that dread-transfiguring gaiety that is Yeats's highest tribute to the astringent joy he found in Nietzsche—rejoicing, as Yeats says, in the midst of tragedy.

Ultimately, the only resolutions of the tension between freedom and determinism may be poetic images paradoxically combining them: Dylan Thomas's "Time held me green and dying / Though I sang in my chains like the sea"; the falling ascent at the end of Rilke's *Duino Elegies*; the graceful, "ambiguous undulations" of Wallace Stevens's casual flocks of pigeons "as they sink, / Downward to darkness, on extended wings"; Hart Crane's seagull's wings dipping and pivoting, "Shedding white rings of tumult, building high / Over the *chained* bay waters *Liberty*."[21] All three of these images of flight and descent come from poets significantly influenced by Nietzsche.

Yeats has his own avian icon, not so much the gyring falcon as the swan on the historical wind, its vitality stimulated by adversity, since, as Nietzsche says, "Resistance that must be continually overcome . . . is the measure of freedom." Yeats's image (in "Nineteen Hundred and Nineteen") is that of the "solitary soul" of the man who can "read the signs, nor sink unmanned," and who therefore may—like a swan, "breast thrust out in pride"—"play or . . . ride / Those winds that clamour of approaching night." Rather than sink unmanned, the noble man finds his freedom, even athletic joy, playing or riding the winds of predestined history, especially when that history is adverse. Says Nietzsche, "The ages in which . . . freedom and the classic type of the sovereign man is attained—oh no! They

20. Yeats, Au 273, V-B 274; Nietzsche, *Ecce Homo* "Why I Am So Clever" 10.
21. Thomas, "Fern Hill"; Rilke, *Duino Elegies* X; Stevens, "Sunday Morning"; Crane, "Proem" to *The Bridge*.

have never been humane ages!"; and again, "Out of life's school of war: What does not destroy me makes me stronger." Speaking of this type of "*sovereign man*"—a strong, self-controlled spirit such as Goethe—Nietzsche wrote: "Such a spirit who has *become free* stands amid the cosmos with a joyous and trusting fatalism, in the *faith* that only the particular is loathsome, and that all is redeemed and affirmed in the whole—*he does not negate any more. Such a faith is . . .* the highest of all possible faiths: I have baptized it with the name of *Dionysus*."[22]

VII. The Fire Gaze

This joyous and trusting fatalism, another instance of gaiety within compulsion, is closer to the halcyon than to the hysterical side of Nietzsche, whose first glimpse of the vision of Recurrence came high in the Engadine, "6000 feet beyond man and time."[23] This visionary moment is memorably recaptured by Yeats at the conclusion of *A Vision*. Discussing Blake and Nietzsche in terms of his own dialectic between turbulence and stillness, he describes "such men" as "full of morbid excitement and few in number, unlike those who . . . have grown in number and serenity. They were begotten in the Sistine Chapel and still dream that all can be transformed if they be but emphatic; yet Nietzsche, when the doctrine of the Eternal Recurrence drifts before his eyes, knows for an instant that nothing can be so transformed and is almost of the next gyre" (V-B 299).

That will be a time when, as Yeats says, men once again "see the world as an object of contemplation, not as something to be remade" (V-B 300): an anti-Marxian vision that was more than momentary in Nietzsche. Though mere resignation is hardly Nietzschean, he embraced *Amor Fati*: "that one wants nothing to be different, not forward, not backward, not in all eternity"; and he did see life as eternally cycling, yet eternally remaining itself: "The world also lacks the capacity for eternal novelty."[24] Nietzsche was therefore in diametrical opposition to the assumption underlying the last and most famous of Marx's "Theses on Feuerbach," that the important thing was not to "interpret" the world but "to *change* it." For this, as Ernst Nolte has said, "does not merely envisage a political revolution or even a superficial dynamism: it postulates a change of 'reality,' of the essential structure of the world. The possibility of denying and refuting such a change, of detesting and unmasking its champions, is the passionate and compelling need controlling all Nietzsche's thought."[25]

It is a passionate and compelling need in later Yeats as well. Writing to Dorothy Wellesley after her poem "Horses" had been attacked in a Decem-

22. *Twilight of the Idols* "Skirmishes of an Untimely Man" 49. For the passages from Nietzsche cited earlier in the paragraph, see *The Will to Power* §44 and *Twilight of the Idols* "Maxims and Arrows" 8.
23. *Ecce Homo* (section on *Zarathustra* 1.)
24. *Ecce Homo* 2.10; *The Will to Power* §1062.
25. Nolte, *Three Faces of Fascism*, trans. Leila Vennewitz, 554.

ber 1936 issue of the Communist paper *The Daily Worker*, Yeats advised her to be secret and exult. In any case, the real enemy was the political lust to change reality's deep structure:

> Joy is the salvation of the soul. You say we must love, yes but love is not pity. It does not desire to change its object. It is a form of eternal contemplation of what is. When I take a woman in my arms I do not want to change her. If I saw her in rags I would get her better clothes that I might resume my contemplation. But these communists put their heads in the rags & smother.
>
> (LDW 114–15)

Yeats's position here is Nietzschean not only in its affirmation of redemptive joy, critique of pity, and contempt for Marxism but also in its minutest particular. "Man is necessity down to his last fibre, and totally 'unfree,'" wrote Nietzsche; "that is if one means by freedom the foolish demand to be able to change one's *essentia* arbitrarily, like a garment—a demand which every serious philosophy has rejected with the proper scorn."[26]

I am quoting, again, from Nietzsche's splendid pages on his, and Yeats's, favorite pre-Socratic philosopher. When Yeats imagines Nietzsche, the doctrine of Eternal Recurrence drifting "before his eyes," he may well be recalling Nietzsche's Heraclitus looking at the world with "the all-encompassing eye of the artist," taking "the same contemplative pleasure in it that an artist does when he looks at his own work in progress." This is to see the world, as Nietzsche repeatedly says in *The Birth of Tragedy*, "as an aesthetic phenomenon." To the Heraclitean vision, says Nietzsche, "all contradictions run into harmony, invisible to the common human eye, yet understandable to one who, like Heraclitus, is related to the contemplative god. Before his fire-gaze not a drop of injustice remains in the world poured all around him." Not a drop of injustice: "One must know," wrote Heraclitus, "that war is common, and justice [Dike] strife, and that all things come by way of strife and necessity" (Fragment 80). Echoing this passage, Yeats described his own antinomial and necessitarian vision as enabling him to "hold in a single thought reality and justice" (V-B 25).

Nietzsche goes on, in his meditation on Heraclitus, to elaborate that "sublime metaphor," the world-child at play, by means of which Heraclitus masters the contradictory impulses. That elaboration anticipates the amoral Dionysian vitality of Nietzsche's own antithesis-resolving Eternal Recurrence—he acknowledged in *Ecce Homo*, "This doctrine of Zarathustra might in the end have been taught already by Heraclitus." It also seems to anticipate, and to fuse, the "radical innocence" recovered by the "self-delighting" soul and the amoral "murderous innocence of the sea," those apparent

---

26. *Philosophy in the Tragic Age of the Greeks*, 63. For Nietzsche's critique of pity, see (for example) *The Will to Power* §367,368.

opposites in Yeats's "A Prayer for My Daughter." It looks forward as well to the Zarathustrian vision expressed in "Lapis Lazuli," the belief—beyond politics, beyond good and evil—that "All things fall and are built again, / And those that build them again are gay." The Heraclitean metaphor also resolves the seeming incompatibility of freedom and determinism, randomness and necessity, creative liberty and conformance to "inner laws," both in the world and in the work of art:

In this world only play, play as artists and children engage in it, exhibits coming-to-be and passing away, structuring and destroying, without any moral additive, in forever equal innocence. And as children and artists play, so plays the ever-living fire. It constructs and destroys, all in innocence. . . . Transforming itself into water and earth, [the aeon] builds towers of sand like a child at the seashore, piles them up and tramples them down. From time to time it starts the game anew. An instant of satiety—and again it is seized by its need, as the artist is seized by his need to create. . . . The child throws its toys away from time to time—and starts again, in innocent caprice. But when it does build, it combines and joins and forms its structures regularly, conforming to inner laws.

Only aesthetic man can look thus at the world, a man who has experienced in artists and in the birth of art objects how the struggle of the many can yet carry rules and laws inherent in itself, how the artist stands contemplatively above and at the same time actively within his work, how necessity and random play, oppositional tension and harmony, must pair to create a work of art.

(*Philosophy in the Tragic Age of the Greeks*, 61–62)

The vision here attributed to Heraclitus and later "baptized . . . with the name of Dionysus" also reflects the vision of the titan who perhaps came closest to, and certainly helped to shape, the ideal of the *Übermensch*. For Goethe, nature itself is a "mobile order," an interplay of polarities, "of power and restriction, of caprice and law, of freedom and measure." At the age of seventy-nine, four years before his death, speculating on this interplay of forces—the inner ones desiring autonomy, the external ones having determinative effect—Goethe spoke of how they can reach a balance "within" us:

If we contemplate ourselves in every situation of life, we find that we are externally conditioned, from our first to our last breath; but that all the same the highest freedom has been left to us to develop within ourselves, in such a way that we can place ourselves in harmony with the moral order of the universe, and, no matter what hindrances may offer, thereby achieve peace with ourselves.

Having struck, in a more optimistic tone, the essential note of Spinoza, Goethe immediately returned to his master's darker emphasis on the power of those external "hindrances": "This is quickly said and written, but it merely stands before us as a task, to whose completion we have to devote our days throughout life."[27]

VIII. Tragic Joy

It was to the completion of this "task" that Nietzsche—also conscious of Spinoza as "a *precursor*, and what a precursor!"—devoted *his* days, providing we drop Goethe's adjective "moral," remembering that what "enchanted" Nietzsche when he first encountered Spinoza was, among other things, his presumed denial of "the moral world-order." That he had turned to Spinoza in late July 1881—when the idea of Eternal Recurrence, which "overcame" him in August, was in gestation—was, he told a friend in an excited postcard,

inspired by 'instinct.' Not only is his over-all tendency like mine—namely to make knowledge [*Erkenntnis*] the *most powerful* affect—but in five main points of his doctrine I recognize myself: this most unusual and loneliest thinker is closest to me in precisely *these* matters: he denies the freedom of the will, teleology, the moral world-order, the unegoistic and evil.[28]

For Nietzsche, the task was to endorse these denials in his own vocabulary of fierce affirmation; to prepare the way for the *Übermensch*—a noble type, of whom Goethe was proleptic, strong enough to affirm existence in all its tangled totality of pain and pleasure. By actively and joyously *loving* a passively determined fate (*Amor Fati*), Nietzsche would break down the contradiction between freedom and determinism. If "the most extreme fatalism is identical with chance and creativity," Zarathustra can claim, in the chapter "On Redemption," that "Every 'it was' is a fragment of an enigma, terrifying chance, until such time as the creative will says in addition: 'but that is just what I wanted!'"

One Yeatsian equivalent of Zarathustra's redeeming "until," the will's "revenge" against the assertion of Time, is the pivotal "unless" in "Sailing to Byzantium." Time's victim, "an aged man," is a paltry fragment of an enigma

unless
Soul clap its hands and sing, and louder sing
For every tatter in its mortal dress,
Nor is there singing school but studying
Monuments of its own magnificence.

27. Letter to Count C. F. M. von Bruhl, 23 October 1823; cited by Viëtor, *Goethe the Thinker*, 148.

28. This 30 July 1881 postcard to Franz Overbeck ends: "In *summa*: my lonesomeness . . . is now at least a twosomeness." Quoted by Walter Kaufmann, *Nietzsche: Philosopher, Psychologist, Antichrist*, 4th ed., 140. For Nietzsche's other references to Spinoza, all laudatory, see Kaufmann, 246–47 n.

More than a simple longing for a purely transcendent, imperishable bliss, this is an "addition" of the "creative will": the will to "make my soul, / Compelling it to study / In a learned school," run by "singing-masters" whose "singing school" consists of "studying monuments of unageing intellect" (VP 416, 407). This is poetry's revenge, the will's revenge against Time's "it was." My connection of Yeats's "unless" with Zarathustra's "until" is also prompted by the fact that the hand-clapping, singing soul is a direct echo of Blake, and that just this fusion of infant joy and discipline (associated by Yeats with Blake and Nietzsche at the moment he imagined the Superman as a child) underlies the praise of life and earned capacity for self-redemption expressed by Self in his laughing and singing embrace of Eternal Recurrence in "Dialogue."

As to the thought of Recurrence: what is most needful, for both Nietzsche and Yeats, is the transformation of dread into deep delight, of terror and negation into the sacred and universalizing Yes of existence itself, through what Yeats—thinking of Romantic delight and of the tragic joy of Nietzsche's Zarathustra, "laugh[ing] at all tragic plays and tragic seriousness"—celebrates as "Gaiety transfiguring all that dread" (VP 565). "I would go so far," says Nietzsche in *Beyond Good and Evil* (§294), "as to venture an order of rank among philosophers according to the rank of their laughter—rising to those capable of *golden* laughter."

But quite aside from the question of dread, acceptance of the thought of Eternal Recurrence is more than a laughing matter. A difficulty esoteric Yeats sometimes acknowledged and at other times evaded through creative misreading—namely, does not the unique soul lose its individuality in returning to the unity of the Plotinian One?—is also relevant to Nietzsche's very different doctrine of the Return. Does not the autonomous self, by uniting itself with the fatalism of Eternal Recurrence, sacrifice its own identity? At this point, Nietzsche simply goes beyond traditional logic, shattering such reconciliationist positions as those of Kant and Hegel. The thought of the Eternal Return, like all great poetic symbols, "melts the glaze of metaphysical antitheses and volatilizes logical contraries."[29] Organizing the chaos, it gathers everything up into what Yeats calls, at the end of *A Vision*, the "Completed Symbol"—in Nietzsche's case, the antithesis-resolving dance described by Zarathustra in the "Yes and Amen Song" that shatters "The Seven Seals": "that heavenly *need* that *constrains* even accidents to *dance star-dances*."

Zarathustra, who "would believe only in a god who could dance," goes on in this climactic chapter (3.16) to claim for himself "a dancer's virtue," adding, in a passage cited earlier, that he has often jumped, "laughing," into golden-emerald delight, a laughter in which evil becomes holy, "absolved by its own bliss." Zarathustra's "alpha and omega" is that "all that is heavy and grave should become light; all that is body, dancer; all that is spirit,

---

29. The phrase is Michael Haar's from "Nietzsche and Metaphysical Language."

bird." Thus the "eternity" he lusts after is that of "the nuptial ring of rings, the ring of recurrence."

We have no inclination to resist—any more than Yeats seems to have resisted—the imagery of this passage of *Zarathustra*. When Nietzsche tries to have it both ways in his own voice, the antitheses and contraries seem so violently yoked that we *do* resist. Believing his theory of Recurrence "the completion of fatalism," Nietzsche also identifies "free will as nothing but fate to the highest power." Yeats did refer, as in a letter to Olivia Shakespear, to events being "fate unless foreseen by clairvoyance and so brought within the range of free will" (L 727), but he stopped short of claiming, as Nietzsche once did, that "I myself am fate and condition existence from all eternity." This is his most grandiose of various assertions about aligning ourselves with fate. Once fate has struck "we should seek to love it." Even "before fate strikes us we should guide it"—at once Nietzsche's secularized version of cooperating with divine grace and an internalization of the Hegelian-cum-Marxist imperative to lead, rather than vainly cut ourselves off from, the inevitable march of historical process.[30]

Yeats, too, despite his apparently rigid machinery of lunar phases, spinning gyres, and Great Wheel, also manages a number of more-than-reconciliationist maneuvers, even when it comes to the dogma of historical process. At the critical point of his exposition of the "Great Year," he produces from his hat the mysterious Thirteenth Cone, described earlier in *A Vision* as "that cycle which may deliver us from the twelve cycles of time and space. . . . Within it live all souls that have been set free" (V-B 216). There had been other gestures toward freedom in the "Soul in Judgment" chapter, most notably in the Purification, the penultimate stage between death and rebirth, where the Spirit is said to be "at last free." It has substituted for the Neoplatonists' "Whole" its "own particular aim," becoming "self-shaping, self-moving, plastic to itself as that self has been shaped by past lives" (V-B 233). But as Yeats's language of "shaped" freedom suggests, not even this stage brings complete deliverance. That is achieved only in the Thirteenth Cone, the phaseless sphere described by Yeats as his "substitute for God" (Ex 320).

At the critical point just mentioned, the conclusion of book IV of *A Vision*, Yeats is discussing the approaching *antithetical* influx and its "particular" manifestation. His concluding sentence begins: "Something of what I have said it must be, the myth declares, for it must reverse our era and resume past eras in itself. . . ." The two "musts" and the authoritative "declares" are balanced by the characteristic vagueness of the opening "something" and the slightly ambiguous status of "*the myth.*" The sentence concludes: "what else it must be no man can say, for always at the critical moment the *Thirteenth Cone*, the sphere, the unique intervenes." As exam-

---

30. For the Nietzsche passages cited, see Ivan Soll, "Reflections on Recurrence," 333.

ple, Yeats brings onstage his own most celebrated animation of the predestinate yet unique and mysterious:

> Somewhere in sands of the desert
> A shape with lion body and the head of a man,
> A gaze blank and pitiless as the sun,
> Is moving its slow thighs, while all about it
> Reel shadows of the indignant desert birds.
>   (V-B 263)

The Nietzschean rough beast slouching toward Bethlehem to be born may be less thrilling to us than it was to Yeats, whom it excited as well as troubled. Nevertheless, with this intervention of the unique and unpredictable, a desperate but saving freedom rushes back into what had seemed an utterly deterministic universe.[31] It is hardly an intervention to be welcomed with open arms. But whatever the poet's attraction to the gyre-reversing beast, an attraction mingled with trepidation and elegiac grief for the lost "ceremony of innocence," Yeats's final commitment *is* to "the unique," a commitment that can take more poignant forms than attraction to the "vast image out of *Spiritus Mundi*." Gazing at quite another image, the Municipal Gallery portrait of his late friend Augusta Gregory, he acknowledged not only the cold comfort of general theory in the face of particularized human grief but also a despairing skepticism regarding Zarathustra's assertion of the return of the *"identical and selfsame* life":

> And I am in despair that time may bring
> Approved patterns of women or of men
> But *not* that *selfsame* excellence again.
>   (VP 602)

A poem set in and just outside the Municipal Gallery, and also intimately connected to "The Second Coming," may be Yeats's most straightforward account of freedom and joy within deterministic bounds. In "Demon and Beast," one of his less discussed yet most winning poems, Yeats finds a privileged moment. Though he has "long perned in the gyre" between bestial hatred and demonic desire, he is liberated for "certain minutes at the

---

31. Bloom insists that Yeats is not saved from determinism by the "desperate freedom . . . imported into *A Vision* as the thirteenth sphere" (*Yeats*, 470). A counterargument would seize on this intervention of the unpredictable. As William Barrett has noted in "Determinism and Novelty," determinism must assert predictability "down to the last detail—lock, stock, and barrel, and even down to the last scratch on the barrel. Anything less than this, and the thesis of determinism must crumble. Determinism cannot afford to leave any loose ends lying around. Small and great are inextricably linked in the happenings of nature and history; an unpredictable detail might trigger an enormous explosion, and empires and battles do sometimes hang on a straw" (47).

least," in which he sees his "freedom won" and a Blakean-Zarathustrian
solar joy all about him: "all laugh in the sun." In this state of "aimless joy,"
he discovers that the play of seagull and "stupid happy" duck could "rouse
[his] whole nature." Yet this freedom is poignantly finite, subject to "natural" constraints. Indeed, it seems what Kant would call a noumenal state
attained only, in this instance, because the speaker is growing old,
"mellowing" enough to make possible a brief liberation from the deterministic gyre of the passionate phenomenal world. Despite this momentary
epiphany, Yeats, aware of the limits imposed by Nature, is

> certain as can be
> That every natural victory
> Belongs to beast or demon,
> That never yet had freeman
> Right mastery of natural things,
> And that mere growing old, that brings
> Chilled blood, this sweetness brought;
> Yet have no dearer thought
> Than that I may find out a way
> To make it linger half a day.
> (VP 401)

It is a joyous freedom all the more precious because of its transience and
natural limitation.

IX. Freedom in Fetters

As "Demon and Beast" confirms, the realm of the "natural" is not the arena
in which the free man achieves "victory" or "mastery." His power is ex-
ercised, not in the phenomenal, external world ("Demon and Beast" ends
with the exultant rhetorical question, "What had the Caesars but their
thrones?"), but in the noumenal, internal world. Indeed, the greatness of
man exists precisely in the *agon* between "natural" determinism and "human" power, a dualistic paradox well expressed by the American thinker
most valued by Nietzsche. "Though Fate is immense," wrote Emerson, "so
is Power," and if "Fate follows and limits Power, Power attends and antag-
onizes Fate." Though we "must respect Fate as natural history" ("never yet
had freeman / Right mastery of natural things"), "Man is not order of
nature," consisting merely of "belly and members" and such "ignominious
baggage," but "a stupendous antagonism, a dragging together of the poles
of the Universe."

Despite the "dragging together" epitomized by man, Emerson accepts
Cartesian dualism to the extent that he instinctively refuses to treat human
consciousness as part of the extended universe of mindless physical particles—whether the molecules of our own "belly and members" or of the rest

of physical nature. He might agree with the modern scientist that at the fundamental level of micro-elements everything is determined. But if "Fate is immense, so is Power," our stubborn denial (even in the face of the physical-mechanistic conception of nature on which the past three centuries of science is based) that we are totally subject to Fate, a vestigial sense of ourselves as agents somehow capable of conscious, intentional, voluntary behavior.

Like most of us, Emerson sees human freedom as limited but not abolished by the determinism of physical nature. Thus the antagonism between Fate and Power is perceived as the *agon* at the heart of human existence, and of human creativity. The same might be said of the *primary-antithetical* antagonism at the heart of *A Vision*. Though much in the Yeatsian *agon* would appall Emerson, what he would applaud is that, having created his own System, Yeats was not, at least in the best of the poetry that flowed from it, enslaved by it. Far from condemning him to the grim fatalism most of the theory entails, the System, paradoxically, brought him freedom of contemplation and augmented power. We find that freedom and power in the poems and in the magnificent concluding section of *A Vision*, "Dove or Swan," the central belief, or supreme fiction, of which is that "the acceptance of history is at one with freedom and creativity." That is the accurate synopsis of Whitaker, who adds the crucial truth that the System "heralded a surge of creative activity beyond any he had yet known" (*Swan and Shadow*, 93, 96).

Indeed, the year that opened with the publication of *A Vision*, 1926, might fairly be called Yeats's *annus mirabilis*, marked by masterworks embodying the power-enhancing tension of the antinomy and expressing *human* rather than divine "freedom." That should make us believe the Instructors' insistence that they came to bring Yeats "metaphors for poetry." While he disobeyed them and sought to systematize their revelation, the creative energy shaped by the System—Yeats's own working out of the concept of imaginative energy made more powerful under constraint— makes us largely believe, and for the rest *want* to believe, Helen Vendler when she makes the humane case that the esoteric process of purgation outlined in *A Vision* is essentially a series of metaphors about the aesthetic process, the creation of poems and plays.[32] If it is by *those* fruits that most of us know the System, we can suspect that, even for esoteric Yeats, what mattered was less the deterministic machinery than the creative substance of the vision, not the "skeleton in my cupboard," as he called *A Vision*, but the poetic body swayed to music.

"All that is body, dancer": that was the consummation Zarathustra devoutly wished. It is a body disciplined, yet at creative play; and it was this "athletic joy" (L 435) of power under control, of gaiety in constraint, that

---

32. This is a central thesis of Vendler's *Yeats's* Vision *and the Later Plays.*

was paramount among Nietzsche's life-affirming gifts to Yeats. Nietzsche described himself in a poem as "in most loving constraint, free." In the poem that serves as epilogue to both editions of *A Vision*, Yeats offers *primary* and *antithetical* versions of fettered freedom. The first is Florence Farr's raveling out of "some learned Indian / On the soul's journey"—how the soul finally plunges into the *primary* sun where, being both Chance and Choice, it is "free and yet fast." Yeats himself has other "mummy truths to tell," having less to do with the posthumous soul (or with the submission of Browning's Andrea Del Sarto to "God's hand" by which, though "so *free* we seem, so *fettered fast* we are") than with the human mind and its freedom:

Such thought—such thought have I that hold it tight
Till meditation master all its parts,
Nothing can stay my glance
Until that glance run in the world's despite
To where the damned have howled away their hearts,
And where the blessed dance;
Such thought, that in it bound
I need no other thing,
Wound in mind's wandering
As mummies in the mummy-cloth are wound.

The final stanza of "All Souls' Night" leaves Yeats caught up in a meditation the "religious" would call death, the "empiricist," madness (theirs is the "world" Yeats spites in envisioning as components in his system of opposites nonempirical but still physical realms "where" the damned "howl" and the blessed "dance"). But if neither of these be right, what is joy? It must be identified as a creativity in which the artist, recognizing what Hazard Adams calls "the enclosure of his openness," is simultaneously bound in his symbolic thought and master of it, capable of exercising power over it.[33] The *antithetical* poet, though "in it bound," is also able to speak with Nietzschean assertiveness of "*I* that hold *it* tight / Till meditation *master* all its parts." Though bound, Yeats is wound in his own "mind's *wandering*" (as in "Dialogue") and so is fast and yet free.

As epilogue, this fittingly culminates the reflexive paradox with which *A Vision* began: a paradox implicit in the ironic joke behind the volume's prefatory poem, "The Phases of the Moon," in which Robartes and Aherne, who mock meditative Yeats and withhold from him the occult wisdom he seeks and "will never find," are themselves his puppets, part of the mythic phantasmagoria he has created. As their master, Yeats is a Mental Traveler at once wound in, yet outside and above, the world the poem *describes and completes*. For Yeats gets the last laugh. "The light in the tower window was

33. Adams, *Philosophy of the Literary Symbolic*, 323. I also borrow from Adams the terminology *he* borrowed from the opening movement of "Vacillation."

put out" not because Yeats gave up his occult meditations in baffled despair but because he finished his poem! Like the Heraclitean artist described by Nietzsche, Yeats—involved and detached, bound and free—is above all *creative*: a creativity frequently marked by the irony, skepticism, and solemnity-checking sense of the comic present in the very poems, "The Phases of the Moon" and "All Souls' Night," that flank—and balance—*A Vision*.[34]

We end as we began, with paradox—freely but necessarily. And with images. For we are left with that Nietzschean artist who "stands contemplatively above and at the same time actively within his work," a work that is the fruit of "necessity and random play"; and with the poet who is at once, according to Yeats, "predestinate and free, creation's very self." It is creation's very Self—believing in a redemptive interchange between himself and the fated totality of everything that lives—who laughs and sings: "We are blest by everything, / Everything we look upon is blest." We "must" laugh and we "must" sing because, like Lear and Cordelia, we "sing like birds i' the' cage," constrained yet all-affirming, an affirmation and redemption reciprocated by the whole of existence itself. Such a Goethean spirit who has "become free," says Nietzsche, "stands amid the cosmos with a joyous and trusting fatalism, in the faith that only the particular is loathsome, and that all is redeemed and affirmed in the whole." It is a fatalism, Zarathustra adds, that subsumes chance and chaos—including even the most bestial intervention of what Yeats calls "the unique"—and "constrains" them as well to "dance star-dances." As above, in the starry heavens, so below in the human entrails: we must, in Zarathustra's resplendent image, have "chaos within," a chaos organized and sublimated by the discipline of autonomous inner laws, if we are to "give birth to a dancing star."

* * *

It is not impossible to reconcile what is logically, but not *psycho*logically, incompatible—certainly not for image-creating poets such as Yeats and, at his best, Nietzsche's Zarathustra. And evidently not for philosophers. Kant defends the causality of freedom in the third antinomy of the first *Critique*, seized on and restated by Yeats, and, more fully, in *The Critique of Practical Reason*. And it was not a poet but a philosopher, Dickenson Miller, who published between the first and second editions of *A Vision* a now-famous

---

34. In "The Balancer: Yeats and His Supernatural System," Richard Moore emphasizes Yeats's "strong sense of irony, even the 'Puckish humor' in his invocations of 'spirits from the Vasty Deep.' There is a definite spicing of Hotspur . . . in this gloomy Glendower" (385). The article focuses on "All Souls' Night" as "a richly comic poem" combining "classic deadpan," gentle mockery, and "tipsy" humor, "a marvelous mixture" of awe and "nonchalant dismissal," "Celtic bravado" and "noncommittal skepticism" (388–94). Once, imaginatively "sterile for nearly five years," Yeats "only escaped at last when I had mocked in a comedy my own thought" (Myth 334; the "comedy" was *The Player Queen*, made farcical at the suggestion of Ezra Pound).

essay whose title neatly synopsizes the reconciliationist paradox: "Free Will as Involving Determinism and Inconceivable Without It."[35]

This paradoxical compatibility of fatalism and freedom is incarnated in Yeatsian heroes who "choose" their "fate," looking unflinchingly, even exultantly, into the face of death. In "A Deep-sworn Vow," an "excited" Yeats presents himself at the critical moment "when I look death in the face." The notebook version of the poem is prefaced by four lines transcribed (by Yeats's American poet-friend Agnes Tobin) from a fragment by another friend, Arthur Symons. Symons's concluding couplet—"I die of rapture yet I see that soon / The fated sisters shall my web have spun"—would be fully applicable to the "doom-eager" (VPl 571) Yeatsian hero if "yet" were changed to "for."

In a related poem in this same volume, *The Wild Swans at Coole*, an Irish Airman foresees his death. His monologue opens:

I know that I shall meet my fate
Somewhere among the clouds above . . .

The balancing of "I know" with the less certain "somewhere" anticipates the Yeatsian speaker's mixture of certitude and residual mystery in "The Second Coming," where the claim to clairvoyance—"I *know*" what rough beast, "its hour come round at last, / Slouches towards Bethlehem to be born"—is undercut both by the punctuation (that final line ends with a question mark) and by the admission, earlier in the poem, to the same locational uncertainty expressed in the Airman's second line: "*Somewhere* in sands of the desert."

In *A Vision*, as we just saw, Yeats cited this and the following four lines of "The Second Coming" to illustrate both his vatic certainty as to the coming *antithetical* influx and his human *un*certainty regarding the "critical moment" of its arrival and the nature of its "particular" manifestation. Always, "the unique intervenes"—fortunately, since this loophole saves the System from its own determinism, allowing maneuvering room for the ambiguous undulations of freedom and creative individuality. Since what "drove" the Airman to his fateful tumult in the clouds was "a lonely impulse of delight," he stands as another example of exultant freedom within constraint. At the

35. For one of the best contemporary defenses of "scientific determinism" as compatible with "the ability to do otherwise inherent in freedom of action," see Adolf Grünbaum, "Freewill and Laws of Human Behavior." While self-determinists like C. A. Campbell insist that libertarianism and determinism are incompatible, critics like Grünbaum salvage compatibility by, on the one hand, distinguishing determinism from both fatalism and external compulsion and, on the other, denying that introspection reveals indisputable evidence of freedom of action in the Campbellian sense. Still more recently, John Searle has argued for, at best, a "modified form of compatibilism." But while "psychological libertarianism" may be compatible with "physical determinism," this "does not give us anything like the resolution of the conflict between freedom and determinism that our urge to radical libertarianism really demands." Our scientific conception of micro-physical reality "simply does not allow for radical freedom." *Minds, Brains and Science*, 97–98.

same time determined and autonomous, his fate "foreseen" and so "brought within the range of free will," he would seem to reenact two related paradoxes: that of the Greek hero choosing his fate and that of Nietzsche's *Übermensch* voluntarily and exultantly embracing what cannot be otherwise, thus transforming an alien fate into his proper destiny.

But this particular hero's "proper destiny" is—I will be arguing in the next two chapters—a question more open than the poems that celebrate him would seem to assert. The "Irish Airman" was modeled on the only son of Augusta Gregory, Yeats's onetime patron and later colleague and dear friend. A man of action killed *in* action in World War I, Robert Gregory became the subject of four poems and, ostensibly, the very epitome of the Yeatsian hero. Under close scrutiny, however, the two central Gregory poems, "An Irish Airman Foresees His Death" and "In Memory of Major Robert Gregory," become increasingly problematic, their intrinsic ambiguity deepened when they are read in a widening gyre of functional contexts.

The first three are manifest. To begin with, there is the immediate context Yeats carefully, even cunningly, prepared for the two poems, which appear back-to-back among the mutually illuminating lyrics clustered in the opening pages of the 1919 edition of *The Wild Swans at Coole*. Then there is the context established by the magniloquent yet ambivalent prose "Note of Appreciation," the obituary Yeats published in the London *Observer* of 17 February 1918, just twenty-five days after Gregory, a volunteer in England's Royal Flying Corps, had been shot down on the Italian front. A third context is provided by the 1920 poem addressed to the Airman's ghost, the bitterly revisionist "Reprisals," which Yeats held back from publication only at the urgent request of Lady Gregory. The fourth and final context is that with which this study as a whole is concerned: that of Yeatsian interaction with his precursors and their texts.

Though the Airman monologue should not be reduced to a mere pendant to the elegy, both poems must be read in the context of the Gregory cluster and, ultimately, in the context of Yeats's own inherited tradition. Thus, the company in which the death-foreseeing Airman is enlisted is, finally, not the Royal Flying Corps but Yeats's own company, its heroic tradition quarried in part from Shakespeare, Nietzsche, Homer, and Castiglione, and later declared Anglo-Irish. Above all, it is the visionary company that provided the youthful Yeats with his first "idols"—the solitary and triumphantly self-destructive band of Romantic questers. "An Irish Airman Foresees His Death" is, for example, thematically and verbally shaped by lines in the passage that most haunted Yeats in Shelley's *Alastor*, a poem whose questing Visionary early Yeats chose as his "chief of men." Similarly, the central aesthetic tribute of "In Memory of Major Robert Gregory"—Gregory's elevation to the status of "great" artist—is a dream dependent on the dead man's right to membership in another platoon in the visionary company: that of Blake and his disciples, Palmer and Calvert, covertly alluded to in the pivotal ninth stanza. The elegy's remarkably dense fabric of echoes and allusions extends, appropriately, to the Renaissance and, surprisingly, even to the Restoration. For Gregory's status as multitalented Renaissance Man—"As 'twere all life's epitome"—is rendered problematic by what I take to be an echo of Dryden's famous description, in *Absalom and Achitophel*, of inconstant, mercurial Zimri, a man "so various that he seemed to be / Not one, but all Mankinds Epitome." Such interactions suggest that there is more to these two poems than meets the delighted eye, with most of the subtler reverberations so agitating the fulsome surfaces as to register a profound ambivalence regarding Gregory's life, accomplishments, and chosen fate.

In what follows, I take a few deliberate steps along the road of excess in stressing the poet's ambivalence in the elegy (and to a lesser extent in the anonymous Airman's monologue). Yet there can be little doubt that, as a second son to Augusta Gregory, Yeats experienced mixed feelings toward her actual son—a multifaceted man whose remarkable athletic skills and military prowess surely inspired envy as well as admiration in a sedentary man. Further, as Torchiana remarks, "one senses some vague animosity in Gregory towards Yeats: twitting him on his scholarship, putting the gloves on with him at the Arts Club and then stretching him flat, mysteriously capsizing a boat with Yeats and himself in it" (*Yeats and Georgian Ireland*, 66).

I am not quite saying that Yeats, instead of getting angry, got even. But the praise with which the elegy for Gregory is brimming is qualified not only by its very excess but also by a network of caveats and covert allusions. Overtly, the elegy is lavish tribute; but as an elegist, after all, Yeats was in the best possible position, not only to silence the envy in his thought, but also to stretch flat or mysteriously capsize the man of action who was his ostensible hero. In the secret recesses of the Gregory elegy, as in *Meditations in Time of Civil War*, Yeats turns away from the temporarily envied man of action, back into the tower, there to continue his contemplation and evocation of poetic images, "daemonic images" whose half-read wisdom "suffice the ageing man as once the growing boy."

IV

YEATS. GREGORY. AND TRADITION

7

"OUR SECRET DISCIPLINE":
THE GAZING HEART'S DOUBLING OF POWER
IN "IN MEMORY OF MAJOR ROBERT GREGORY"

He had so many sides: painter, classical scholar, scholar in painting and in modern literature, boxer, horseman, airman . . . that some among his friends were not sure what his work would be.

  —Yeats, obituary for Robert Gregory

Soldier, scholar, horseman, he,
As 'twere all life's epitome.
What made us dream that he could comb grey hair?
  —Yeats, Gregory elegy

A man so various that he seem'd to be
Not one, but all Mankinds Epitome.
. . . every thing by starts, and nothing long . . .
  —Dryden, *Absalom and Achitophel*

Immodicis brevis est aetas, et rara senectus.
  —Epigraph (from Martial) to Cowley's elegy "On the Death of Mr. William Hervey"

We dreamed that a great painter had been born
To cold Clare rock and Galway rock and thorn,
To that stern colour and that delicate line
That are our secret discipline
Therein the gazing heart doubles her might.
  —Yeats, Gregory elegy

I. Preliminaries

Yeats rarely ranked his own poems, but he placed "In Memory of Major Robert Gregory," as of 1918 at least, "among my best works" (L 650).

Though seconded by his perceptive friend Sturge Moore and by a majority of subsequent readers, that evaluation has not been universally accepted. George Brandon Saul detects in the elegy "something too studied—too suggestive of a constructed courtesy . . . undoubtedly sincere, the sincerity yet seems poured into a mould of duty." That sternest of reason's defenders, Yvor Winters, finds the poem bereft of study or mold. Though "commonly described as one of the greatest poems in our language," it is structurally "loose," its writing "slovenly," and its praise of Gregory—who "appears to have been no Sidney, but a charming and admirable young man who dabbled in the arts"—"exorbitant," "excessive." While he rightly thinks this wintry onslaught itself excessive, Harold Bloom agrees that what is "weakest" in the poem is "Gregory himself, more an Edward King than a Sidney." (As Bernard Knox has written of Pindar's celebrations, "public praise is a dangerous medium," provoking resistance when it "exaggerates beyond the limits of credibility.")[1]

In response, Denis Donoghue, for whom Yeats's elegy is an "incandescent tribute to the antithetical life," dismisses any impugnment based on the judgment that Gregory was "not the remarkable man that Yeats took him to be," an argument he pronounces "sordid." The conventional rejoinder to the sordid argument of unjustified praise (if it *were* justified, Winters dryly observes, "we should have heard of Gregory's accomplishments from other sources") is that it is poetically irrelevant.[2] Whatever his actual character and qualities, Robert Gregory has been changed utterly; he has become, in the words of a later Coole Park poem, "another emblem there!"—in this case, the Renaissance Man reborn, a hero of universal genius and Castiglionian *sprezzatura*.

But what if, as Marjorie Perloff argued twenty years ago, the "passionately warm praise of Gregory is undercut by a slight tinge of skepticism" *in the poem itself*? What, indeed, if the very fulsomeness of the praise was secretly intended by ambivalent Yeats to evoke protest on the part of those outside the Coole Circle? What if, as I suggest in my conclusion, Yeats—"using against the edifice the instruments or stones available in the house"—was deconstructing his own "constructed courtesy" and "mould of duty"? In a study complementary to his well-known essay "Explicitness in Augustan Literature," Irvin Ehrenpreis has more recently stressed "acts of implication" and "covert meaning" in the works of four major writers beginning with Dryden. Yeats's elegy for Gregory, its covert meaning residing in part, I believe, in its interaction with Dryden, seems to me essentially an act of implication so clandestine that the poem appears to be remarkable for its *e*xplicitness.[3]

    1. Saul, "In . . . Luminous Wind," in *The Dolmen Press Centenary Papers MCMLXV*, ed. Liam Miller. Winters, *The Poetry of W. B. Yeats*, 15. Bloom, *Yeats*, 193. Knox, *New York Review of Books* (24 October 1985):43.
    2. Donoghue, *William Butler Yeats*, 80. Winters, *The Poetry*, 15.
    3. Perloff, "The Consolation Theme in Yeats's 'In Memory of Major Robert Gregory,'" 317. The edifice-and-stones image is that of Jacques Derrida, "The Ends of Man," in *The Structuralist Controversy*, ed. Richard Macksey and Eugenio Donato, 56. The Ehrenpreis book

In the most handsome tribute bestowed on the elegy, Frank Kermode has proposed it as the first poem "in which we hear the full range of the poet's voice. . . . After it, for twenty years, Yeats's poems, whenever he is using his whole range, are identifiable as the work of the master of the Gregory elegy."[4] That full-ranged work is notable for the ability of the Yeatsian speaker to have things both ways: to be, for example, at once terrified and titillated by the Rough Beast; to celebrate an austere, transcendent Byzantium and yet leave his golden nightingale singing of the world of temporal process; to defeat, in dialogue, the Neoplatonic spokesman of the Soul and yet end with the unreconstructed Self singing that everything we look upon is "blest," and so on. Ostensibly straightforward tribute, the Gregory elegy is no less a reflection of Yeatsian ambivalence; but for reasons unique to this poem that ambivalence had to remain covert. Praising the Gregory elegy for "a perfect articulation and lucidity which cannot be found in any other modern poem in English," Alan Tate said some forty years ago that he "would select this poem out of all others of our time as the most completely expressed."[5] The poem as I see and hear it is anything but completely expressed. There is an undertow, a dark countertruth, agitating the lucid, laudatory surface: a mixture of feelings characteristic of that full range of the Yeatsian voice of which Kermode speaks. What is less characteristic is the depth and concealment from which that dark voice resonates.

The reason for secrecy was personal, not generic. Yeats would not be worried about the impropriety of offending the dead in an elegy. He had been critical of the martyrs in the first of his group-elegies, "Easter 1916," and was, in "In Memory of Eva Gore-Booth and Con Markiewicz," initially so critical of the dead sisters as to "endanger" the elegy to a degree Helen Vendler has described as "unheard of before Yeats." But not after, since the innovator later became a victim of his own innovation. Auden's "In Memory of W. B. Yeats" is, like Galway Kinnell's "For Robert Frost," a "typically modern poem," wrote Charles Molesworth, "in the way it refuses to follow the ordinary 'rules' for elegiac praise and insists on an honesty that threatens to dislocate the very discourse of the poem and move down to the level of verse epistle or even satire."[6]

Auden and Kinnell were free to candidly qualify their praise of the dead; what made it impossible for Yeats to act as both mourner and overt judge in the Gregory elegy was, of course, the living presence of Lady Gregory, whom he venerated, and of Gregory's widow, with whom he had long had

---

is *Acts of Implication: Suggestions and Covert Meaning in the Works of Dryden, Swift, Pope, and Austen.*

4. Kermode, *Romantic Image*, 30.

5. Tate, "Yeats's Romanticism: Notes and Suggestions," in *The Permanence of Yeats*, 115.

6. Vendler, "Four Elegies," in *Yeats, Sligo, and Ireland: Essays to Mark the 21st Yeats International Summer School*, ed. A. Norman Jeffares, 221. Vendler didn't treat the Gregory elegy in her essay "because of its length" and because she decided it was "more a single elegy than a group elegy," her particular subject and a subgenre of which Yeats had become the master (private letter, 28 October 1981). Molesworth, *The Fierce Embrace: A Study of Contemporary American Poetry*, 100.

the somewhat strained relationship of a too-frequent house guest. At Margaret Gregory's request, and possibly to avoid "quarrelling" (line 15), Yeats inserted in the finished poem a stanza answering to her objection that he "had not said enough of Robert's courage."[7] But it was Augusta Gregory he was most concerned not to offend. She, after all, was the Gregory who really mattered in Yeats's life. Robert, to whom Yeats was not particularly close, is introduced, even in his own elegy, as "my dear friend's dear son," just as, twenty years later, among the dead looking out from their pictures in the Municipal Gallery, Robert was "Augusta Gregory's son" (VP 325, 602). Soon after hearing of Gregory's death, Yeats wrote John Quinn, "I feel it very much for his own sake, still more for his mother's"; in a letter written two weeks later, he was anxious that the prose Appreciation he had printed in *The Observer* of 17 February 1918 had been well received by Lady Gregory: "I hope you thought my little essay on Robert was right" (L 645–47).

Printed in full by Kermode in his chapter on the elegy in *Romantic Image*, stressed by D. J. Gordon and Ian Fletcher in their discussion of Gregory and the elegy, as well as by Peter Sacks in his excellent chapter on the poem in *The English Elegy*,[8] this "Note of Appreciation" is as delicately balanced a seesaw as the poem itself. Writing about three weeks after Gregory was killed in action in Italy, Yeats opened his Appreciation by observing that he knew of

no man accomplished in so many ways as Major Robert Gregory. . . . His very accomplishment hid from many his genius. He had so many sides: painter, classical scholar, scholar in painting and in modern literature, boxer, horseman, airman . . . that some among his friends were not sure what his work would be. To me he will always remain a great painter in the immaturity of his youth.

Yet, he added in the final paragraph, Gregory "often seemed led away from his work by some other gift." He has noticed, says Yeats, that "men whose lives are to be an ever-growing absorption in subjective beauty"—that is, Yeatsian *antithetical* types—sometimes "seek through some lesser gift, or through mere excitement, to strengthen that self which unites them to ordinary men. It is as though they hesitated before they plunged into the abyss." Yeats suspected that the final months of Gregory's life, which the airman told G. B. Shaw had been his happiest, "brought him peace of mind, an escape from that shrinking, which I sometimes saw upon his face, before the growing absorption of his dream, the loneliness of his dream, as from his constant struggle to resist those gifts that brought him ease and friendship" (UP 2:430).

Though he concludes on a note of integration and fulfillment—"Leading

7. Yeats records this objection in an unpublished note (Berg Collection, New York City Public Library).

8. D. J. Gordon and Ian Fletcher, *W. B. Yeats: Images of a Poet*; Peter Sacks, *The English Elegy: Studies in the Genre from Spenser to Yeats.*

his squadron in France or in Italy, mind and hand were at one, will and desire"—Yeats has subtly raised two questions. Was Gregory a universal genius or a jack-of-all-trades, master of none? Was he a true hero or a versatile escapist who shrank from plunging into that abyss of the self in which the *antithetical* man finds his true work in life? As gravely elaborated paean, the prose tribute would, Yeats hoped, be found "right" by Lady Gregory (whether he thought it right himself is problematic; he never reprinted it). As its subtleties indicate, however, the desire to console and please Lady Gregory obliterated neither uncertainties about her son nor Yeats's own painful honesty.

The poet's problem as I see it was how, without offending, to register those uncertainties in the poem. Given his relationship to Lady Gregory, his elegy for her son became one of those occasions when, to quote R. P. Blackmur, "the revelation . . . in Yeats's mind . . . was not and could not be given in the words of the poem."[9] There remained to him the more indirect methods of caveat and allusion.

The embedded disclaimer, taking away with his left hand what he gives with the right, is almost a Yeatsian signature. Discussing this "contemporary" mixture of belief and skepticism, Richard Ellmann (*Identity*, 144) notes that in those poems "where he comes closest to committing himself to a belief he does not fully hold, [Yeats] introduces a *caveat* at the crucial moment." Such a caveat is introduced, I believe, in the opening line of this poem's crucial stanza: "We *dreamed* that a great painter had been born." In addition, I will be arguing, practicing what is referred to in that ninth stanza as "our secret discipline," Yeats conducts, largely through allusion, a hidden agenda.

In speaking of his philosophy, Yeats distinguished between exoteric and esoteric, what was for publication and what was to remain private (L 916). In the Gregory elegy he has things, uniquely, both ways. For Yeats subversively qualifies almost to recantation the praise lavished on Gregory in a poem meant to be published—both to the Coole Circle and to the world at large. His principal secret weapon is allusion, language borrowed for a covertly destructive purpose. The result is to make the elegy as ambiguous as the prose tribute, and its secret hero not the elegized but the elegizer—as we might suspect, given the history of the genre and what various critics have called Yeats's maintenance in this elegy of his "aristocratic composure," his assumption of the "egotistical or Wordsworthian sublime," the poem's tone of "proud self-involvement," Yeats's "maneuvering himself into a central position from which the world and the events of history seem curiously dependent on *him*," awaiting "his ceremonies of integration and his conferrals of meaning."[10] Combining the centrality of the poet with his

9. Blackmur, "The Later Poetry of W. B. Yeats" (1936), in *Form and Value in Modern Poetry*, 33–58 (47).

10. A. G. Stock, *W. B. Yeats: His Poetry and Thought*, 119. Ronald Snukal, *High Talk: The Philosophical Poetry of W. B. Yeats*, 149. Sacks, *English Elegy*, 273

network of allusions, I conclude that the genuine heir of those others in the visionary company (Blake, Palmer, Calvert) who truly practiced "our secret discipline," a discipline practiced in this very poem, is not Gregory but Yeats, who, like Milton in "Lycidas," is here marshaling his powers for future accomplishment—unlike Gregory, who might have "published all" to be a world's delight but of course did not. Finally, Yeats can afford to claim that "all my heart" was taken by a thought of Gregory's death—at the end of a long poem the slain hero entered only halfway through—because he has, in a sense, *two* hearts, the curious consequence of that "secret discipline / Wherein the gazing heart doubles her might."

Before turning to the poem's likely allusion to Dryden's Zimri, we might briefly explore two borrowings that have been noticed, both slight but perhaps illustrative of Yeats's secret discipline in action.

When Robert Gregory finally does enter his own elegy, in stanza VI, he is "my dear friend's dear son" and, in the refrain repeated in stanzas IX, X, and XI, "Soldier, scholar, horseman, he." Though drawn from the English Renaissance and thus, like the designation of Gregory as "Our Sidney," appropriate to a modern Renaissance Man, these Shakespearean allusions, traced to their context, tap a reservoir of contrasts between youth and age and between the contemplative and active lives: material obviously at the heart of the elegy.

A. Norman Jeffares's suggestion (*Commentary*, 161) that "my dear friend's dear son" echoes John of Gaunt's "This land of such dear souls, this dear dear land" (*Richard II* 1.2.56–57), is enhanced by Gaunt's reference in the preceding line to "blessed Mary's *son*" and by the fact, unremarked by Jeffares, that aged Gaunt's famous speech begins with criticism of Richard's "rash fierce blaze," which "cannot last . . . / For violent fires soon burn out themselves" while "Small show'rs last long." Yeats's central image in the elegy similarly contrasts long-lasting wetness to a short-lived, self-consuming blaze:

Some burn *damp* faggots, others may consume
The entire combustible world in one small room
As though dried straw . . .

Did Gaunt's repeated "dear" float into Yeats's mind *in context*, lodging there because, beneath the honorific surface of the elegy, he was being critical, playing older but wiser Gaunt to Gregory's fiery young Richard? Gaunt's "dear land" (ironically, the same England *Irish* Gregory died for) and the violent fire that threatens it are united in the person of the king; similarly, Gregory is at once "dear son" and violent, self-destructive blaze, consuming himself rather like Gaunt's "cormorant" which, "consuming means, soon preys upon itself."

Of course, Richard II was no man of Gregorian action. He was, in Yeats's illuminating comparison, an "unripened Hamlet" to Henry V's "ripened

Fortinbras" (E&I 108). Though the Yeatsian speaker of the elegy eulogizes impulsive Gregory and so seems a meditative Hamlet to the dead man's Fortinbras, the litany of praise for Gregory, thrice repeated and triadic— "Soldier, scholar, horseman, he"—echoes praise not of Fortinbras but of Hamlet: Ophelia's litany of his Renaissance virtues as "soldier's, scholar's, courtier's" (Hamlet 3.1.151). Is Gregory a Fortinbras? a Sidneian Hamlet? or, as the elegy claims, an Anglo-Irish Sidney, a genuine balance of action and thought? Though Yeats applauds Gregory's "mind" in the equestrian stanza (VIII), his replacement of Ophelia's "courtier" with "horseman" makes Gregory essentially a man of action: two-thirds, to be half-seriously precise.

Of course, Yeats responded to precisely this penchant for action. In the Shakespeare essay just cited, he spoke of that Fortinbras who "came from fighting battles about 'a little patch of ground' so poor that one of his captains would not give 'six ducats' to 'farm it,' and who was yet acclaimed by Hamlet and by all as the only befitting king" (E&I 107–8). In the elegy, following Hamlet by implicitly and explicitly contrasting himself to a non-introspective warrior, the Yeatsian speaker implies that all occasions do inform against him: while he tediously burns damp fagots, Major Gregory has been consumed in the exciting flare. When, in the Gregory-poem immediately following this elegy, the Irish airman speaks of himself as driven to his fatal tumult in the clouds by a nonchalant "impulse of delight," he is like the Fortinbras described by Hamlet, "Exposing what is mortal and unsure / To all that fortune, death and danger dare, / Even for an eggshell" (4.4.51–53). But in this excessive praise and self-reproach, Hamlet, like Yeats in *his* excessive praise and self-reproach in the elegy, protests too much. If Fortinbras is courageous and honorable, he is also reckless, even foolhardy—another "rash fierce blaze." So was Robert Gregory. The contrast is that Hamletesque Yeats, unlike Shakespeare's Hamlet, *survives* Gregory's Fortinbras, taking, despite the bleakness of the poem's final stanza, covert comfort from that fact.

It is a curious, almost Rochefoucauldian, situation when, as I am suggesting, the consolation theme in an elegy partially coincides with the cause of grief, the death. But Yeats, a man of masks, here seems to me Janus-faced. As a dutiful celebrator who yet had private reservations and the furtive pride of a survivor, he is, like Hamlet's uncle, a man to double business bound; in this case, the doubling of his own power through practice of a secret discipline wherein his gazing heart doubles her might—to some extent, at the dead man's expense.

II. Possible Sources in *Absalom and Achitophel*

Though I may seem to have been as reckless as Gregory, riding "a race without a bit" (VIII) in these speculations on Yeats's interactions with Shakespeare, they are grounded in the elegy's borrowed language. One expects a sense of the poetic past—and thus allusion—in so traditional a genre as elegy. Yeats was "immensely learned in poetry," wrote Helen Vendler of Yeatsian elegy; "when he touched any genre he knew its lineaments," but "like all great poets," he "re-invented every traditional form he touched" ("Four Elegies"). "In Memory of Major Robert Gregory" is surely a reinvention of the traditional elegy. But despite its innovations (a procession of mourned rather than mourners; a nontraditional consolation theme; the delayed entry of the hero; and so forth), it is unlike his other elegies, unlike his other poems, in that here Yeats borrows almost as much as he invents.

To begin with, he borrows his stanza form—from Abraham Cowley's "On the Death of Mr. William Hervey."[11] Not only does he borrow his refrain from Ophelia, he also adapts rather than invents *all* the terms of praise lavished on his soldier, scholar, horseman, "Our Sidney." Gregory's powers of loving perception are, I shall suggest, borrowed from Thomas Hardy (stanza VII), while the tribute to the mental powers of the horseman (VIII) adapts Cowley's praise of his scholarly friend. Virtually all the verbal details of the splendid stanza that follows (IX) are borrowed, from sources as scattered as Thomas Chatterton, Samuel Palmer, Fulke Greville, and the Countess of Pembroke, whose elegy for her brother, the real Sidney, heralded him as "the world's delight," something better than the limiting "*a* world's delight," and that only potentially.[12]

But what of the supreme praise bestowed on Gregory: the apotheosis of this multitalented Renaissance Man ("and all he did done perfectly") as "all life's epitome" (X, XI)? I believe that both phrases are borrowed from Dryden's *Absalom and Achitophel* and that, by implicitly comparing Gregory to Dryden's all-too-versatile Absalom and Zimri, Yeats smuggled into his ostensible celebration the same uncertainties and reservations he had expressed, with equal tact and subtlety, in the prose "Note of Appreciation." Famous as *Absalom and Achitophel* is, it seems an unlikely source for Yeats,

---

11. The debt has been frequently noted, perhaps first by J. J. Cohane in "Cowley and Yeats." Of the several Yeats poems employing Cowley's stanza, the Gregory elegy is closest, differing in only slight metrical variations from Cowley's

5 5 5 4 5 3 4 5
a a b b c d d c

With "Adonais" in mind, Peter Sacks perceptively remarks: "Yeats seems to have crossed the form of Cowley's stanza with the syntactic momentum of another elegist he admired, Shelley" (*English Elegy*, 269).

12. Yeats's echo of the Countess's contribution to the Astrophel elegies (with its "Sidney is dead, dead is my friend, dead is the world's delight") was first remarked by Marion Witt, "The Making of an Elegy: Yeats's 'In Memory of Major Robert Gregory.'" See also Sacks, *English Elegy*, n. 31 to Gregory chapter, for the echo of Fulke Greville. In her essay on the poem, Marjorie Perloff notes the qualification implicit in Yeats's substitution of "*a* world" for "*the* world": "The speaker is saying something like this, 'It is not, of course, a fact, but to us, to our charmed circle, Robert seemed to be another Sidney'" ("Consolation Theme," 317). Daniel Harris speaks of "a limitary epithet ('*Our* Sidney') containing just enough irony to reveal the speaker's knowledge of illusion" (*Yeats: Coole Park and Ballylee*, 127).

who, as a Romantic, was usually critical of the major Restoration and eighteenth-century poets. He does, however, quote from *Absalom and Achitophel* on at least one occasion (VPl 950) and would presumably not have been reluctant to exploit the poem if it served his purposes.[13] Indeed, in the case of the Gregory elegy and its transaction of double business, Yeats's clandestine purposes would have been served not only by *Absalom and Achitophel* but also by Dryden's two most celebrated elegies.

In the first of these, "To the Memory of Mr. Oldham," Dryden's "young friend" has died at the age of thirty, having earned the palm of priority in satire but too young and "betrayed" by "too much force" to have mastered "the numbers of thy native tongue." His "fruits," though "generous," were "gathered ere their prime," and their very force and "quickness" seem in part ironic since Oldham is no longer among the forceful quick. Like survivor Yeats, survivor Dryden casts the benefits of artistic maturity in an ironic mold: "maturing time / But mellows what we write to the dull sweets of rhyme." But the point has been made. Young Oldham's achievement has been praised (he is, in an allusion to the footrace at the memorial games for Anchises in book 5 of *The Aeneid*, a victorious Euryalus to Dryden's Nisus); but it has also been qualified by a poet who, surviving, goes on maturing his art. While the note on which the poem ends is genuinely elegiac ("But fate and gloomy night encompass thee around"), this second Virgilian echo (*Aeneid* 6.866) reveals Dryden as an Augustus mourning a Marcellus destined never to be fulfilled. Though Oldham is "Marcellus of our Tongue" and Gregory, in what Peter Sacks calls Yeats's similarly "Augustan device of allusion" (*English Elegy*, 285), "our Sidney and our perfect man," neither emerges as the primary artist. In both "To the Memory of Mr. Oldham" and "In Memory of Major Robert Gregory," the mature man and *true artist* is the elegist, not the elegized.

In the second elegy, the ode "To the Pious Memory of the Accomplished Young Lady Mrs. Anne Killigrew," Dryden uses the death of an undistinguished poet and painter as the occasion to speak about his true subject, the arts themselves in the present age. Like the versatile and restless Gregory, Killigrew sought about for various arts to master. Not content with poetry, "To the next realm she stretched her sway, / For Painture near adjoining lay" (92–93). As in the Gregory elegy, emphasis falls on painting; but Mistress Killigrew could not rest with that. Again like Gregory, she consumed the entire combustible world, a flare destined to burn brightly and briefly:

---

13. The allusion is to *Absalom & Achitophel*, line 150: "Great wits are sure to madness near allied." Though he sees Dryden as a falling off from Shakespeare (E&I 225) and an extension of the Roman rigidity of Milton ("Pope and Dryden" are so depicted in an unpublished notebook begun 7 April 1921), Yeats *did* like to quote Dryden's rendering of Lucretius's thought that "the tragedy of sexual intercourse is the perpetual virginity of the soul" (V-B 214, LDW 192, and the famous conversation with John Sparrow reported by Jeffares in *William Butler Yeats, Man and Poet*, 267).

Thus nothing to her genius was denied
    But like a ball of fire, the further thrown
    Still with a greater blaze she shone,
And her bright soul broke out on every side.
What next she had designed, heaven only knows;
To such immoderate growth her conquest rose
That fate alone its progress could oppose.
    (143–48)

While the remaining three stanzas are resonantly elegiac, rising to the sublime crescendo of the apocalyptic finale, it is hard to take the lines just quoted *altogether* seriously. The artistic claims made for Anne Killigrew are so patently hyperbolic that they have the paradoxical effect of focusing us on Dryden's real subject: civilization, the arts, *decorum*. The "immoderate" Killigrew—God only knows what she would have turned to next!—is, like Gregory, an example of the condition Martial described in the line Cowley employed as epigraph to his elegy for Hervey as one of "*immodicis*," being *too* variously talented.

Though more genuinely talented than Anne Killigrew, Robert Gregory is also overpraised in Yeats's elegy; and of course he was nothing if not *immodicis*. Yeats borrowed his stanza form from the elegy to which Cowley prefaced this epigraph from Martial; he may have borrowed the rarest word in his own elegy—the astrological "trine" (line 39)—from Dryden, whom Yeats associated with Cowley (V-B 295) and who, expatiating on Killigrew's birth, asserts that on that auspicious occasion even the most "malicious" planets "were in trine" (41–43); that is, 120 degrees apart and thus favorable in their influence. The use of "trine" and the fire imagery are not the only things the two elegies have in common.

This brings us back to Dryden's greatest poem. Yeats's dilemma, if he was to be honest about Gregory and about himself, was to celebrate his friend's son and still delicately insinuate his own reservations. On the purely intrinsic evidence provided by the Gregory elegy itself, I think Yeats found in *Absalom and Achitophel* ways of registering the uncertainties that qualified his admiration of Robert Gregory without introducing into this most polite and politic of poems that "discourtesy" the elegy itself attributes to death.

While the author of *Absalom and Achitophel* was writing allegorical-biblical satire and Yeats was writing elegy, the two poems are equally triumphs of tact. Dryden had to criticize "Absalom" (the king's attractive son, the Duke of Monmouth) without offending his royal parent Charles II, who, as "David," is as "indulgent" in the poem as Charles was toward his son in real life. Dryden accomplished his difficult task by hinting at Absalom's flaws short of direct attack, by suggesting that his very virtues ("so beautiful, so brave," so accomplished in the arts of war and peace) constituted a hidden weakness that could be exploited to lead him astray. "It is typical of Dryden's handling of Absalom," notes Earl Miner, "that he should present him with seeming favor . . . and yet by numerous means make clear his strongest objections."[14] Miner's parenthetical remark ("not that any careful reader could possibly be taken in" by Dryden's praise) does not extend to Yeats's handling of Gregory since no unambiguous criticism of the "dear son" could be made without hurting the loving mother.

Nevertheless, Dryden's portrait of Absalom, a panegyric that yet conveyed criticism, would have served Yeats admirably as a model, for he too implies in the prose Appreciation that Gregory's very versatility may have been, as Gordon and Fletcher say, "a dubious gift, of uncertain issue" (*Images of a Poet*, 32), a judgment reflected, I would add, in the caveats in the poem itself. Furthermore, the possible debt to Dryden's satire is not restricted to the character of the king's son. Yeats would have found two other portraits relevant to his own of the multitalented Gregory, the first negative, the second positive.

The apogee of Yeats's exaltation of Robert Gregory is his emergence from the flare as "all life's epitome." Only once, I believe—and never elsewhere in poem or play—does Yeats use the word *epitome*. But in *Absalom and Achitophel*, in a sketch Dryden thought "worth the whole poem," the character Zimri is presented as

A man so various, that he seem'd to be
Not one, but all Mankinds Epitome.[15]

"Zimri" was George Villiers, Second Duke of Buckingham, a clever but finally ineffectual man in the first rank of the Opposition. He was, Dryden continues,

every thing by starts, and nothing long:
But in the course of one revolving Moon,
Was Chymist, Fidler, States-Man, and Buffoon;
Then all for Women, Painting, Rhiming, Drinking;
Besides ten thousand freaks that dy'd in thinking.
(lines 548–52)

Robert Gregory was no buffoon, lecher, or sot; but the list of Zimri's dubious accomplishments is not that far removed from the list of accomplishments in the elegy and in the prose Appreciation, a catalog so various— "painter, classical scholar, scholar in painting and in modern literature, boxer, horseman, airman"—that "some" of his friends were justifiably unsure "what his work would be." Doubtless one of the reasons Yeats chose

14. Miner, *Dryden's Poetry*, 133.
15. *Absalom and Achitophel*, lines 545–46. The only other Yeatsian use of the word I can recall (a remark in *Autobiographies*) may in fact echo Dryden, though it makes mankind the epitome: "The wholeness of the supernatural world can only express itself in personal form, because it has no epitome but man."

Cowley's elegy on Hervey for his stanzaic model was the poem's epigraph: "*Immodicis brevis est aetas, et rara senectus.*" Life is short and old age rare for those who are *immodicis*, "too variously accomplished."[16] Gregory was as "various" as Buckingham, Dryden's opinion of whom was shared, incidentally, by Bishop Burnet, who punningly thought him "full of mercury," "true to nothing for he was not true to himself"; he had "no steadiness . . . could never fix his thoughts." Though that would seem too harsh a verdict to pronounce on Robert Gregory, some who knew him thought him an "uneasy man," lacking focus and purpose.[17] Just beneath the surface of Yeats's prose tribute the dark undercurrent is that mercurial Gregory *did* scatter his excessive talents and that, lacking single-mindedness of purpose, he escaped into war and death, turning away in the process from the true struggle—that labor which blossoms into self-knowledge and perfection of the work.

While Yeats surely suspected that Gregory might be *immodicis*, "every thing by starts, and nothing long," it would be perverse to turn the dead warrior into a Zimri-like villain, or to suggest that such was Yeats's intention. His elegy, though covertly ambiguous, even hinting at the meniscus analogy (another drop of praise will overflow into its opposite), is still elegy, not satire, and Yeats remains ambivalent. Indeed, if his Gregory resembles Zimri and Absalom (compare Yeats's "And all he did done perfectly" with Dryden's observation in line 27 on Absalom: "whate'er he did was done with so much ease"), he also resembles one of the heroes of Dryden's poem: the son of James Butler, Duke of Ormonde and Lord Lieutenant of Ireland. As a distant relative of William Butler Yeats himself, Ormonde's son would have had appeal, an appeal reinforced by the fact that the man had died after a brief but distinguished military career and so was the subject of elegy in *Absalom and Achitophel*. Dryden presents him

> with every grace adorn'd,
> By me (so Heav'n will have it) always Mourn'd,
> And always honour'd, snatcht in Manhoods prime.
>   (lines 831–33)

16. Though he sees no ambivalence in Yeats's praise of Gregory, Frank Kermode does offer an interesting mini-history of the term. "The Roman poet is using the word *immodicis* with a pathetic irony; normally it means 'one given to excess,' but Martial is lamenting the death of a beautiful and accomplished slave-boy. For Cowley's purposes one could translate the line, 'For men of genius life is short, and old age rare,' but for Yeats's one would have to recover the original idea of excess: 'To those who are too accomplished . . . ' or even 'too variously accomplished'" (*Romantic Image*, 40).

17. Burnet's judgment and venereal pun are cited in a note on Dryden's portrait of Buckingham in a standard contemporary anthology: *The Oxford Anthology of English Literature*, 1:1617n. The judgment of Gregory as an "uneasy man" came up during interviews conducted by Gordon and Fletcher.

Robert Gregory, a "dear son" and "perfect man" who did everything "perfectly," consumed the entire world "in one small room." Similarly, Ormonde's son, allotted but a swift race and short time, nevertheless "All parts fulfill'd of Subject and of Son." Granted but a "Narrow Circle" and "Scanted in Space," he was "perfect" in his line (lines 838–39).

If I am correct in speculating that *Absalom and Achitophel* enters "In Memory of Major Robert Gregory" as part of a hidden agenda, it is intriguing to picture Yeats—at once judicious and sympathetic, skeptical and admiring—posing character against character, weighing and balancing the portraits of the king's son, of Buckingham-Zimri, and of Ormonde's mourned and honored son as aspects of the dead son of Lady Gregory. Though denizens of a deep subtext, Dryden's characters may be—like the antithetical speakers of the first Gregory elegy, "Shepherd and Goatherd," and like the trio presented in this poem (Johnson, Synge, and Pollexfen)—portions of the multifaceted Robert Gregory: a man so various that he too seemed to be all life's epitome, and yet a man of accomplishment who never quite accomplished the one definitive thing; a hero who may have been but a flaring thing, or who really may have completed himself in the scanted space of one small room, all parts fulfilled.

The conclusion one comes to will in large part be determined by one's response to the self-consuming straw-fire of stanza XI, the life- and work-finishing flare from which Gregory emerges as "all life's epitome." To undercut that apotheosis by referring it, as I have, to Dryden's Zimri would seem to sacrifice something timelessly true to the merely factual, of which art, the poem, knows nothing. Mine, it may be complained, is the "sordid" argument, focusing on the actual Gregory or even the Gregory of the prose Appreciation rather than on criticism's proper object: the heroic Renaissance icon, the Romantic Image, of the *poem*.

My response is that *this* image is less important than the Image-maker and his motivations. The Gregory elegy, like all elegies, does a good deal more than shape a commemorative image of the deceased; it serves "as a self-definition of the elegist." I am quoting the commentary on Yeats's first group-elegy, "Easter 1916," by Helen Vendler ("Four Elegies"), who adds that this is true of "any other poem." It is true of even so "impersonal" a poem as that biblical-political satire *Absalom and Achitophel*, in which we find, as Miner says, "a personal engagement that even the closed metaphor could not keep out." All of Dryden's major poems of the 1680s, he continues, "however public they are, possess an intense personal drive to discover what is meaningful to John Dryden" (*Dryden's Poetry*, 143). Miner finds the "personal force" behind those great poems best expressed in four lines (301–4) from one of them, *Religio Laici*:

If others in the same glass better see,
'T is for themselves they look, but not for me:

For MY salvation must its doom receive,
Not from what OTHERS but what *I* believe.

Yeats's version is also in two couplets:

The friends that have it I do wrong
When ever I remake a song,
Should know what issue is at stake:
It is myself that I remake.
   (VP 778)

The issue at stake in the Gregory elegy, another exercise in self-defini-tion, is Yeats's own life and artistic development (song and self being insep-arable) seen in the flaring light of Gregory's. Ostensibly, Yeats does not fare well; but that self-judgment, most explicit in the "flare" stanza, is qualified by much else in the poem, in fact by the straw-fire itself, a symbol compli-cated by the same ambivalence suggested in discussing the three portraits in *Absalom and Achitophel.*

III. Damp Faggots and Self-Consuming Flame

It is in stanza XI that Gregory becomes all life's epitome:

Some burn damp faggots, others may consume
The entire combustible world in one small room
As though dried straw, and if we turn about
The bare chimney is gone black out
Because the work had finished in that flare.
Soldier, scholar, horseman, he,
As 'twere all life's epitome.
What made us dream that he could comb grey hair?

Most readers have agreed that this is, in the words of Balachandra Rajan, "the poem's central symbol," to be read as "the blaze of total accomplish-ment." For Ronald Snukal, the blackout achieved here is, as in "Lapis Lazuli," the best way Yeats has of communicating "the ability of men to give expression to their fullest selves even while being consumed by the world." As that flaming consummation, as epitome, as something "wrested from the realm of accident into that of meaning," Robert Gregory "literally explodes into another dimension, into the autonomous world of the soul."[18] Yet shortcomings are detectable in that swift blaze.

Even Peter Sacks—who finds in Yeats's fire imagery "Gregory's death and the brevity of his life . . . transformed to a source of consolation" and who observes that Yeats is "describing a state close to the traditional condi-

18. Rajan, *W. B. Yeats: A Critical Introduction,* 108–9; Unterecker, *Reader's Guide,* 133; Snukal, *High Talk,* 154.

tion of ecstasy, which in turn implies transfiguration"—adds that Yeats revises his sources in a way that is "disturbingly original," "harsh," a "startling and bleak revision of an entire legacy" that deliberately turns from the "idealizations" we find in the regenerative fire imagery of Spenser's "Astrophel," Milton's "Lycidas," Cowley's elegy for Hervey, or Shelley's "Adonais." For Yeats "stresses only the conflagration, implying neither transcendence nor trace." The transfigurative ecstasy is "only for the instant," and "even Yeats's praise of Gregory as 'all life's epitome' expresses [the] contradiction" between the "satisfaction" of the "elegiac transaction" and its "disastrous cost." Sacks specifically notes how Yeats's synecdoche is here a trope "which cannot conceal that from which it turns": "the honorific *epitome*, even while it seems to encompass and signify 'all life,' cannot disguise its original relation to a 'cutting short' (*epitemnion*). . . . For all its claim to totality, the epitome, like the vehicle of any synecdoche, is inevitably partial and abbreviated" (*English Elegy*, 291–94).

There are, in short, clear reservations even in this pivotal stanza. "For while he admired the all-consuming flare of Gregory's life, Yeats saw the incompatibility with his own life and practice as a poet," a recognition, Sacks rightly adds, "crucial to the elegy" (294). Indeed, Yeats's "others" in this stanza's opening line is reminiscent of Dryden's "OTHERS," whose vision is quite different than what Dryden believes or finds needful for his own salvation. Yeats's ambivalence, subtly registered in the stanza itself, may be illuminated by a cluster of glosses.

Gaunt's denigration of the violent but short-lived blaze is glossed by a Yeatsian comment in an undelivered 1910 lecture. Of the Rhymers, the friends of his youth, Yeats said, "Life existed for them in a few intense moments that when they were gone left darkness behind them." This was the consequence of carrying out the Paterian program: the exaltation of the intense, passing moment. But Yeats's somber remark sounds less like Pater's rhapsodic "conclusion" to *The Renaissance* (and even he insisted on the need to "*maintain* this ecstasy," to "burn *always* with this hard, gemlike flame") than George Herbert's conclusion to his poem "The Windows" in *The Temple*. Does the momentary "flare" in the Gregory elegy also resemble the "flaring thing" in Herbert's poem, the spectacular but superficial and unsteady blaze that goes quickly out, plunging the temple—in this case, the Coole Circle—into darkness?[19]

19. Yeats's undelivered lecture, "Friends of My Youth," in *Yeats and the Theatre*, ed. Robert O'Driscoll and Lorna Reynolds, 80. In the famous "conclusion" to *The Renaissance*, Pater comes to a conclusion based on a string of premises: If "art" gives "nothing but the highest quality to your moments as they pass, and simply for those moments' sake"; if "every moment" provides "some mood of passion or insight or intellectual excitement," but "for that moment only"; if "not the fruit of experience, but experience itself, is the end"; if "a counted number of pulses only is given to us of a variegated dramatic life"; then we have few questions—"How shall we pass most swiftly from point to point, and be present always at the focus where the greatest number of vital forces unite in their purest energy?"—and a single, celebrated answer: "To burn always with this hard, gemlike flame, to maintain this ecstasy, is success in life." *The Renaissance: Studies in Art and Poetry*, 139, 236.

Such negative possibilities seem reinforced by the recurrence of the straw-fire image in another prose passage, again on the Rhymers. Whatever their shortcomings, they possessed "conscious deliberate craft" and "scholarship," and so, though themselves they could not save, the Rhymers helped save Yeats by teaching him that "violent energy, which is like a fire of straw, consumes in a few minutes the nervous vitality, and is useless in the arts. Our fire must burn slowly, and we must constantly turn away to think, constantly analyze what we have done, be content to have little life outside our work" (Au 318). These sentences from "The Tragic Generation," written one to three years after the Gregory elegy, seemed to Marjorie Perloff to pass at least retrospective judgment on Gregory's straw-fire: "Whereas Gregory's work, still in its immaturity, 'had finished in that flare,'" the speaker—"the confident and proud artist who has evidently survived the 'nervous vitality' of youth"—has managed "to follow the creed presented by Yeats in 'The Tragic Generation'" ("Consolation Theme," 320). She takes the contrast between the wasteful blaze and the slow-burning fire as confirmation of her earlier point that the Yeatsian speaker "is consistently presented as one who has heroically survived the turmoil and temptations of the fledgling artist to achieve the Unity of Being denied to Robert Gregory in his lifetime" (307–8).

Though Perloff adds that the speaker of the elegy, unlike the author of "The Tragic Generation," makes "no explicit judgment as to the relative value" of the two emblematic fires (310), she seems open to the objection of Daniel Harris. The evidence for her contention that the true creative artist burning his damp fagots is elevated at the expense of the quickly consumed fledgling artist is, he complains, "not the poem," but the prose passage.

Despite the same central image of fire burning through straw, the poem speaks not of Gregory's "nervous vitality" but of an energy everywhere controlled by judgment and courtesy. Hardly a wasted passion "useless in the arts," his intensity has produced a perfection both personal and aesthetic; the speaker's romanticism makes Gregory's deep visionary understanding more significant than its embodiment in paintings. The poem acknowledges what the prose ignores: Gregory belonged to a different order of humankind. And instead of showing a Yeats deliberately burning a slow fire to avoid early exhaustion, it depicts a speaker who feels condemned to his "damp faggots" and is, if anything, jealous of Gregory's blaze.

(Coole Park, 136)

On the overt level of the poem this seems irrefutable. But while Harris's reading is in accord with the accepted one, with the advantage of seeming utterly intrinsic, it fails, I think, to take into account the elegist's thematic and tonal ambivalence. Another intrinsic critic, William Pritchard, also dismisses the passage from "The Tragic Generation," not because it is irrelevant or in opposition to the poem, but because we don't need it here to see that the poet, burning damp faggots like the rest of us, has nevertheless preserved himself, has made something out of experience maybe less glamorous but surely more enduring than any "flare" set off by Gregory. Yet this self-preservation isn't presented as a triumph, and more is asked of the reader here than in earlier poems: while he must give his admiration to Gregory—the image—he must also imagine experience through the complex, depressed, and extraordinarily *tonal* world of the man who remains behind. . . . Nobody gets a cheer at the end of the poem. There is no convenient outlet for one's mixed feelings about heroic life, the art that celebrates it, and the artist who suffers, with whatever discretion, to create it.[20]

It would be hard to improve on the precision of Pritchard's own tonality here. But to hold that there *is* a muted triumph of the double-hearted Yeatsian speaker is not to deny these "mixed feelings" and this suffering, "with whatever discretion," of the true creative artist. For they are the themes, not only of the passage in "The Tragic Generation" and, more subtly, of the elegy, but also of the poems Yeats placed immediately before and after the elegy.

In both "The Tragic Generation" and the elegy Yeats appears as one whose fire burns slowly; and the prose passage emphasizes, as does Yeats's prose Appreciation of Gregory, the artist's *work* and the need not to be distracted from it or extinguished before it is achieved. Despite the pejorative implications of burning damp fagots, Gregory's variegated energies, even when focused in a single blaze of Paterian "purest energy," may still signal the opposite of total accomplishment. That blaze may really *be* "useless in the arts"; Yeats, like Dryden, may mean it when—as artist, not merely as aging man—he refers to "others." For the fire that "must burn slowly" is "*our* fire," the fire of the true artist engaged in "*our* secret discipline," the discipline of artists who have learned to "conserve *our* vitality" (Au 318). Chief among the slow burners of damp fagots in the elegy is Yeats himself, whom we encounter tending the "fire of turf in th'ancient tower" in the opening stanza. He is also, in a related image in his earlier group-elegy, "Easter 1916," one of those "around the fire at the club," telling his companions mocking tales and gibes about the "vivid"-faced men of action soon to die in the blaze of the Easter Rising, "bewildered" heroes who were in fact dead when Yeats wrote the poem.

Yeats, in short, is a survivor, with all the mixed emotions that entails. On the one hand, there is what Sacks (insisting on the relevance of the "Tragic Generation" passage to the elegy) refers to as the Yeatsian "preference for a bounded and therefore conserved vitality, . . . the reduction or displacement of life in the interests of work"; on the other, there is the poem's attempt to come to terms with Yeats's "inability, as a poet, to make the kind of

---

20. "The Uses of Yeats's Poetry," in *W. B. Yeats: A Critical Anthology*, ed. Pritchard, 361.

'plunge' into action and into unity of being for which he had celebrated Gregory. This, as much as Gregory's death, has been the poem's true object of mourning" (*English Elegy*, 295).

This inability, as well as the poet's painful consciousness of his own increasing age, are at the heart of the whole Gregory cluster. We encounter Yeats as a more than fifty-year-old leaf shuffler in the "dry" woodland paths of the poem immediately preceding the Gregory elegy, a man whose heart has "grown cold" in the nineteenth autumn that has inexorably come upon him since he first made his count of the wild swans riding the brimming lake of the Gregory estate. While the work is said to have "finished" in Gregory's flare, the passage of time in "The Wild Swans at Coole" brutally accelerates in the middle of Yeats's count, the swans suddenly mounting and scattering "before I had well finished." In contrast, Airman Gregory took wing like the swans, perishing before *he* was caught in the arithmetic of bodily decrepitude, before *his* heart could grow cold. He is, and has, "finished"—and, apparently, finished well. But to die in a flare is still to die. Knowing the elegy tradition, the speaker asks at the end of the flare stanza, "What made us dream that he could comb grey hair?" For as we are reminded by Wordsworth (ironically, Yeats's own Shelleyan image of genius withering into dotage), the good die first, and they whose "hearts are dry as summer dust, / Burn to the socket."[21] They also linger in the littering leaves when "woodland paths are dry," or, like the Yeatsian speaker in "Men Improve with the Years,"

> grow old among dreams,
> A weather-worn, marble triton
> Among the streams.

The titular assertion of this poem—a poem carefully placed immediately after the Gregory elegy and the Irish Airman poem in *The Wild Swans at Coole*—is questioned at its center; the discerning but aging artist, aesthetically contemplating a "lady's beauty," is

> Delighted to be but wise,
> For men improve with the years;
> And yet, and yet,
> Is this my dream, or the truth?
> O would that we had met
> When I had my burning youth!

---

21. *The Excursion* 1.500–502. Wordsworth's lines, slightly misquoted, later provided the epigraph to Shelley's *Alastor*, in which form they remained a shaping presence in Yeats's thought and work; see my discussion, above, of the Riversdale poems and, below, of "An Irish Airman Foresees His Death."

This poem's relationship to the elegy has been neatly synopsized by Hugh Kenner: "Dried straw, damp faggots; . . . a 'burning youth' followed by water" in the form of a weather-worn statue set amid the streams and fountains of "Major Gregory's mother's garden."[22] Ostensibly, the Gregory elegy celebrates burning youth, relegating "grey hair," old men "grown sluggish and contemplative," and the burning of damp fagots (both burning *and* watery) to an unspectacular, and decidedly un-Paterian, longevity. But that men do improve with the years seems a viable countertruth. To cite an example of a premature death both burning and watery: the difference between Airman Gregory and cautious Yeats resembles that between young Icarus, who flew too near the burning sun, so that the wax holding his wings melted and he fell to his death in the sea, and old Daedalus, who, surviving, escaped to Sicily to live out his life creatively. In "Men Improve with the Years," Yeats's self-mocking irony mingles with honest ambivalence ("And yet, and yet") as to what is "dream" and what "truth": precisely the "mixed feelings" referred to by Pritchard, indeed, the very question lurking at the covert heart of the elegy. We might apply the method of Hans-Georg Gadamer by reconstructing the "question" to which the work itself is an "answer."[23] To put the unspoken words in the elegist's mouth: "I am praising consummately gifted but swiftly consumed youth at the expense of mundane longevity. But is this my dream, or the truth? Do I really believe, albeit with mixed feelings, in what I appear to be denigrating: the fruit of experience, the gifts improved by the years?" From the dilemma of choosing between subjective dream and objective truth Gregory escaped through death; the inability to escape such a choice becomes "the implicit and deepest theme of the elegy," according to Harold Bloom, who adds that Yeats must "found all his art upon an intense vacillation in choosing" (*Yeats*, 196). One consequence is that what Sacks calls "the poem's true object of mourning," Yeats's inability to plunge into the Gregorian flare, is also its source of consolation.

Though a corpse would be even less capable than an old man of possessing the beautiful woman contemplated in "Men Improve with the Years," perhaps the Gregorian option, that of the man of action, is the right one after all—at least if one would be a candidate for elegy. Since "In Memory of Major Robert Gregory" brings the Renaissance into the modern world we may add to the gloss from Shakespeare's Gaunt countertruths from two other Renaissance favorites of Yeats: Ben Jonson and John Donne. In "To the Immortal Memorie," his Sidneian ode on Morison and Cary,

---

22. Kenner, "The Sacred Book of the Arts," an essay collected in Kenner's *Gnomon* but here quoted from the anthology cited in n. 20 (p. 222).

23. A procedure proposed by Gadamer in his central work, *Truth and Method*. For Gadamer, texts—though inexhaustible and ever open to "understanding otherwise"—are nevertheless constrained by the role they play in a continuing "tradition," within which the texts' questions and answers, and our own questions and answers, take place.

Jonson asks rhetorically, "What is life, if measured by the space, / Not by the act?" (lines 21–22). This recalls the life-epitomizing intensity, and the one small room, of Robert Gregory, while the description of Yeats's "dear friend's dear son" as soldier, scholar, and horseman who did everything "perfectly" resembles Jonson's description of Sir Henry Morison, dead at twenty-one:

Hee stood, a Souldier to the last right end,
A perfect Patriot, and a noble friend,
But most, a vertuous Sonne.
All Offices were done
By him, so ample, full, and round,
In weight, in measure, number, sound,
As, though his age imperfect might appear,
His life was of Humanitie the Spheare.
    (lines 43–52)

In the light of Jonson's praise of Morison, all longevity seems a Pollexfen-like sluggishness, and the slow burning of damp fagots something other than human life:

It is not growing like a tree
In bulke, doth make a man better bee;
Or standing long an Oake, three hundred yeare,
To fall a logge at last, dry, bald, and seare.

To the old, dry, bald log—an image of old age that seems to have found its way into several of Yeats's major poems[24]—Jonson contrasts a short-lived but perfect flower:

A Lillie of a Day
Is fairer farre, in May,
Although it fall, and die that night;
It was the Plant and flowre of light.
In small proportions, we just beauties see:
And in short measures, life may perfect bee.[25]

24. The poet of impotent middle age walking the dry woodland paths at Coole is encountered again, now past autumn, walking the same lakeside wood, "Now all dry sticks under a wintry sun, / And in a copse of beeches there I stood" (VP 490). The old man is as much dry sticks as the copse he stands in. Lacking compensating spirit, an aged man is but a paltry thing, "a tattered coat upon a stick," or, like the great philosophers of "Among School Children," "old clothes upon old sticks to scare a bird." The decrepit crone of "Her Vision in the Wood," now "too old for a man's love," refers to herself in her opening words as "Dry timber."
25. "To the Immortall Memorie and Friendship of that Noble Paire, Sir Lucius Cary and Sir H. Morison," lines 65–74. The resemblance between Jonson's lines and Yeats's eleventh stanza was first noted by T. McAlindon, "Yeats and the English Renaissance," but he restricts his comparison to this one stanza. (Yeats's great verbs in "The Second Coming"—*troubles* and *vexed*—may also be indebted to this Jonson poem.)

That such is the case with "our perfect man," whose short-lived flare consumed all in the small proportions of "one small room," is the ostensible claim of the Gregory elegy. A similar claim is made by Yeats in the peroration of his 1911 appraisal of Lady Gregory's nephew, John Shawe-Taylor, who died at forty-five. It may be that Ireland "should mourn that which is gone from it" in the early deaths of Shawe-Taylor and Synge, wrote Yeats. "And yet it may be that the sudden flash of his [Shawe-Taylor's] mind was one of those things that come but seldom in a lifetime, and that his work is as fully accomplished as though he had lived through many laborious years" (E&I 345). Like Morison and Cary, those "two so early men," Synge and Shawe-Taylor may have sown the proper seeds and (to cite the final line of Jonson's ode) "got the harvest in."

Since Yeats here has Synge as well as Shawe-Taylor in mind, and since it accords with the overt claim made for Gregory (whose "work had finished in that flare"), this prose passage seems more immediately relevant to the elegy than that on the aesthetically "useless" fire of straw. Thus, while Harris criticizes Perloff for bringing into the poem the prose passage from "The Tragic Generation," he himself cites *this* passage (*Coole Park*, 136). Both seem to me relevant. As in the case of the proposed interaction with *Absalom and Achitophel*'s heroes and villains, I imagine vacillating Yeats weighing and balancing, playing with, on the one hand, the possibility of the rare sudden flash producing work as fully accomplished as the labor of many years and, on the other, the probability that such bursts of violent, short-lived energy will prove useless in the arts, requiring as they do slow-burning concentration.

Of course, there is another kind of concentration in the flare stanza, a measured rather than "measureless consummation" (stanza III). To "consume / The entire combustible world in one small room" is to ram with life, and death, in a more than Shakespearean or Jonsonian gesture (Myth 360). The trope of concentering, of forceful microcosmic contraction of the whole world, is one Yeats learned from Blake and, above all, from Donne, whose work he had mastered with the help of H. J. C. Grierson. "The world's contracted thus," the "old foole" of a sun is told by the audacious lover at the conclusion of "The Sunne Rising": "Shine here to us, and thou art every where; / This bed thy center is, these walls, thy sphaere." The lovers of "The Canonization," burnt by self-consuming tapers, will, since "a well-wrought urne" as well becomes the greatest ashes as do half-acre tombs, "build in sonnets pretty roomes." This contraction—similar to the sun's between "these walls" and to Gregory's consummation of the entire world "in one small room"—reaches its fullest intensity at the end of "The Canonization," where we, the readers of the poem, address the dead lovers directly. Since you did "the whole worlds soule contract, and drove" that variegated world (countries, towns, courts) into the glasses of your eyes, those concentering eyes became mirrors that "did all to you epitomize."

Because they gaze on each other ("glance that mirrors glance," as Yeats echoed the image in a draft of "Among School Children"), the lovers' mirroring eyes become (in Yeats's line in the elegy) "As 'twere all life's epitome." Even if this line, as well as the world-contracting flare itself, is partially indebted to Donne, there is enough in the Gregory elegy to argue that the debt balances without canceling the parallel between versatile Gregory and Dryden's Zimri, men so *immodicis* that they seemed to be not one but "all Mankinds Epitome," men "everything by starts, and nothing long." The problem remains: if Gregory's work really was fully accomplished, if "the work" *had* "finished in that flare," we must still ask, "What work?" *He* produced no well-wrought urn. The fire in his small room *did* build "pretty roomes" (the Italian word for which, *stanza*, Donne here plays on), but they are the elegiac stanzas borrowed from Cowley by Yeats, not by Gregory, who "had the intensity / To have published all to be a world's delight," but of course did not. The poem does seem to supply an answer to the question—what work?—in the stanza just quoted, IX. But we must lead up to that, the elegy's central passage, by first considering the context Yeats prepared for the introduction of Gregory into the poem.

IV. The Companionable Dead: Stanzas I-VIII

The first five stanzas set the scene—at night, in the almost finished tower—and name the friends unable to sup with "us," that is, with Yeats and the new wife for whom he was restoring Thoor Ballylee. They might not be compatible, but not a friend he would bring this night "can set us quarrelling, / For all that come into my mind are dead." The first is the scholar-poet Lionel Johnson, who, "much-falling," brooded upon sanctity until his classical learning (which he loved better than mankind, though "courteous to the worst") "seemed" a blast upon the apocalyptic horn bringing "a little nearer to his thought / A measureless consummation that he dreamed." The caveats ("seemed . . . dreamed") combine with the Coleridgean "measureless" to reveal the impossibility of Johnson's dreams. Synge, on the other hand, found in the Arans an objective correlative for *his* solitude. Dying, he chose the living world for text, coming

>   towards nightfall upon certain set apart
> In a most desolate stony place,
> Towards nightfall upon a race
> Passionate and simple like his heart.

Echoing the word introduced with calculated casualness in stanza II's reference to the "affections of our *heart*," this establishes what will be the key term for this poem, as it is for "The Circus Animals' Desertion."

Yeats next turns to his maternal uncle, "old George Pollexfen." He may, in "muscular youth," have been "well known to Mayo men / For horsemanship," but Pollexfen's obscurity, especially in comparison with Johnson and Synge, and his dubious ability to show "by opposition, square, and trine," how horses and men alike are completely subject to astrological influence, make him less than fit to swell a progress in this procession of the mourned. Yeats has introduced these men as "Discoverers of forgotten truth / Or mere companions of my youth." The reservation following instantly upon the grandiose assertion may go beyond mere discrimination among the friends to suggest an ambivalence about the real accomplishments of those friends, perhaps even of Synge, who found life only as he neared death. Such a recoil from assertion would adumbrate Yeats's covert doubts, or at least vacillating feelings, about Robert Gregory. In any case, the introduction of Pollexfen, a kind of caveat in himself, makes us wonder about the company being prepared for Gregory. A warrior cut down in his prime may seem marked less by "square, and trine" than by "opposition" to an old man "grown sluggish and contemplative"; yet, while we hardly need this poem to tell us who Johnson and Synge were, we would, without Yeats's elegies, know no more of Gregory than we do of George Pollexfen. As unpublished horseman, Gregory has more in common with him than with the authors of "The Dark Angel" and *The Playboy of the Western World*.

Following a transition that may echo Ben Jonson's observation that Morison and Cary "grew a portion" of each other, Yeats finally allows Gregory to enter his own elegy:

They were my close companions many a year,
A portion of my mind and life, as it were,
And now their breathless faces seem to look
Out of some old picture-book;
I am accustomed to their lack of breath,
But not that my dear friend's dear son,
Our Sidney and our perfect man,
Could share in that discourtesy of death.

For all its tenderness, the stanza is an assertion of the survivor's power. While the dead are depicted as active, their faces only "*seem* to look / Out" at Yeats. The Last Duchess of Browning's poem, "Looking *as if* she were alive," is but a painted picture to which "none puts by / The curtain I have drawn for you, but I." In opening for us his "old picture-book," Yeats does not, like Browning's possessive Duke, indiscriminately reduce everything to so many controllable *objets d'art*. But the imperious artist does exercise control, here transforming the breathless dead into breathless artifice. In the inspired moment, by creative fiat, the artist, a mouth that, in that moment of inspiration, "has no moisture and no breath / Breathless mouths may summon" ("Byzantium"). That is what Yeats did in the opening stanza when he announced "*I'll name* the friends that *cannot* sup with us," and he continues to exercise a survivor's power over the dead throughout the poem. As Frank Kermode has recently remarked, "when Yeats surrounds himself with ghosts he is always the boss" (*London Review of Books*, 5 June 1986, p. 10).

But if the breathless faces of the first three companions are subtly reduced to a "portion" of the speaker's mind and life, Gregory himself could hardly be ushered into the poem with a greater show of decorum. He is our "perfect man" because, as the elegy goes on to claim, he recapitulates in himself the learning, vitality, and equestrian skills possessed singly by his dead predecessors in the poem, who are but portions of this, the complete man. The marvelous phrase in which Gregory finds his own bitter portion, coming to "*share* in that *discourtesy* of death," reminds us of the host-and-guest civilities with which the poem opened and of Johnson's "courteous" manner. More importantly, it reduces death itself to a boorish interloper in these neo-Renaissance ceremonies, and, simultaneously, makes Gregory both a victim of death and, literally, a sharer in its "discourtesy." He has in effect been made impolite by his own mortality.

The paradox of the perfect courtier made discourteous is stressed in the Miltonic "for" (compare "Lycidas": "*For* we were nursed upon the self-same hill") that opens stanza VII and in the final word of its closing line, "welcomer":

For all things the delighted eye now sees
Were loved by him: the old storm-broken trees
That cast their shadows upon road and bridge;
The tower set on the stream's edge;
The ford where drinking cattle make a stir
Nightly, and startled by that sound
The water-hen must change her ground;
He might have been your heartiest welcomer.

The stanza seems to me a subtle variation on the landscape poignantly imagined as left behind by the speaker in "Afterwards," the poem with which Thomas Hardy concluded his recently published *Moments of Vision* (1917). Had Yeats read "Afterwards"? Did he, like his friend Lennox Robinson, associate Hardy's "lovely poem" with the local scenery and with the ghost of an observant Gregory?[26] In both poems, the scenes modulate from dusk to night, with shadows, storm-broken trees (Hardy's are "wind-warped"), and similar nocturnal rituals: Yeats's timid water hen is disturbed when drinking cattle "make a stir / Nightly"; Hardy imagines his spirit passing "during some nocturnal blackness . . . / When the hedgehog travels

26. In Robinson's case, Augusta Gregory and Coole Park. "I had been re-reading the day before [a 1947 visit to Coole] Thomas Hardy's lovely poem 'Afterwards' . . . [which ends] 'He hears it not now, but used to notice such things.' Lady Gregory noticed such things and I am sure her spirit haunts, in a happy haunting, those grassy paths through her beloved woods." Robinson, introduction to *Lady Gregory's Journals*, 12–13.

furtively across the lawn." In both instances we have a surviving "gazer" or "delighted eye" that "now sees," with Hardy's "gazer" imagined as thinking, "To him this must have been a familiar sight." Yeats's opening and closing statements about the dead man would constitute a positive response to Hardy's question concerning his posthumous self: "will the neighbours say, / 'He was a man who used to notice such things?'" "All things the delighted eye now sees / Were loved by" Gregory, responds the most distinguished of that dead man's neighbors.

Like Hardy, Yeats creates an intimate yet mysterious world of eye and ear. Hardy's speaker, always alert to a change in sound, wonders if any will say, "He hears it not now, but used to notice such things." Gregory loved the ford where, startled by a sudden "sound," the water hen "must change her ground"—a homely echo of the emotional displacement caused by the death of the hero, who has certainly changed *his* ground, from the familiar neighborhood of Coole and Thoor Ballylee to a foreign grave in Italy. And the elegist, or so he will tell us at the end of the poem, was also startled into changing *his*. He "had thought" to do one thing, pursuing a routine, almost arithmetical plan, "until imagination brought" (in lines echoing this stanza's "*heart*iest *welcomer*") "A fitter *welcome*; but a thought / Of that late death took all my *heart* for speech." That sudden and climactic thought is prefigured by the disruption at the ford; and again, Hardy's poem is relevant, for death, implicit in Yeats's seventh stanza, is explicit in "Afterwards," where the final sound, cut by "a crossing breeze," is the speaker's own "bell of quittance . . . heard in the gloom."

The eye is still more central. Yeats begins with the "delighted eye" that "sees," and this stanza has been widely read as observant prelude to the ninth stanza's projection of Gregory as "great painter" of such visionary landscapes as that surrounding Thoor Ballylee. It has even been suggested (by Harris, *Coole Park*, 133) that Yeats intended the description of stanza VII "to resemble Gregory's sepia drawing of the tower and its environment." But that drawing (reproduced in Hone's biography of Yeats), though it does have storm-broken trees, is a rather poorly executed daylight scene, allusion to which could hardly support the case made—and subtly unmade—for Gregory as great painter. The hidden artists of the "great painter" stanza include Blake's disciple Samuel Palmer, alluded to throughout IX and here in VII as well, since this austere yet intimate scene, a coldly beautiful nocturnal, re-creates Palmer's famous *The Lonely Tower*. That superb illustration to Milton's "Il Penseroso" was celebrated by Yeats as "The lonely light that Samuel Palmer engraved, / An image of mysterious wisdom won by toil" (VP 373), and he referred to it again in "My House," a poem that repeats most of the details of this stanza of the elegy. The hidden artist of stanza IX, Palmer's rather than Gregory's companion in "our secret discipline," is Yeats himself—who is, of course, also the anonymous observer, the Emersonian transparent eyeball, in VII. Marjorie Perloff remarked that the "delighted eye" that "still sees the beautiful forms of nature is the eye of an artist less versatile but infinitely greater than Robert Gregory" ("Consolation Theme," 321), to which I add that it is the eye of a visionary artist who, like the Palmer of at least the Shoreham years rather than unfocused Gregory, submitted himself to the secret discipline and triumphantly won his images of mysterious wisdom "by toil."

Thomas Hardy, too, had what he calls in "Afterwards"—in a sublime stanza harking back to the Wordsworth of "Tintern Abbey" and the Immortality Ode—"an eye for such mysteries."[27] Altering B. L. Reid's contention that the scene of stanza VII of Yeats's elegy is "newly poignant because now it is lost to Robert Gregory," Daniel Harris declared, "The real point is that the speaker has assimilated Gregory's courteous perception, his passionate love, and in so doing has kept his affections alive."[28] Altering both, I suggest that the poignancy reflects that of the scene imagined lost in "Afterwards," and that it is the courteous perception and passionate love of Wordsworthian Hardy, another artist infinitely greater than Robert Gregory, that Yeats has covertly "assimilated." The "delighted eye" of the elegy is that of a man whose moments of vision have been intensified by thoughts of death but who is still alive: the precise case of the speaker in "Afterwards," as it was of Hardy's precursor—the elegiac Wordsworth for whom clouds that gather round the setting sun "take a sober colouring from an eye / That hath kept watch o'er man's mortality"; the Wordsworth who imagines himself where he "no more can see" the "wild eyes" of the sister with whom he stood "together on the banks of this delightful stream." As the language confirms, Wordsworth influenced Yeats as well—not only in Yeats's projection of his own disappearance or death in the poem preceding the elegy, in which he imagines the wild swans "delight[ing] men's eyes" when he is "gone," but also here in the elegy itself, where his "delighted

27. That Hardy is of this visionary company is demonstrated by the sublime penultimate stanza of "Afterwards," which, modulating from "hearing" to "watching," focuses on the inherited capacity of the eye to see not only familiar sights but also the mysteries inherent in the visible:

If, when hearing that I have been stilled at last, they stand at the door,
    Watching the full-starred heavens that winter sees,
Will this thought rise on those that will meet my face no more,
    'He was one who had an eye for such mysteries?'

Echoing both "Tintern Abbey" and the Immortality Ode, Hardy is Wordsworthian here. Winter "sees" the same starlit heavens the survivors are "watching," though not the deeper mysteries for which the dead man "had an eye." The Immortality Ode modulates from a similar pathetic fallacy to the deeper truths of the humanized and humanizing "eye"; from the thought that "The Moon doth with delight / Look round her when the heavens are bare," to the more profound transference in which the clouds that gather round the setting sun "Do take a sober colouring from an eye / That hath kept watch o'er man's mortality." The "eye" of Yeats's seventh stanza, though it looks round with the apparent "delight" of the Wordsworthian moon, has kept a similar "watch" o'er man's morality. It is the eye of an artist who, like Wordsworth and Hardy rather than Gregory, matured and, living, took the dead for text by writing an elegy that, as Lionel Trilling said of the Immortality Ode, is not merely about dying young or growing old, but about "growing up."
28. Reid, *W. B. Yeats: The Lyric of Tragedy*, 113; Harris, *Coole Park*, 133.

eye" drinks in the natural scene at "the stream's edge," a scene from which Gregory has departed.

That *Gregory* is gone is almost a betrayal of Romantic "delight." That he "*might* have been" this scene's heartiest welcomer may be as accusatory as it is elegiac. Had he not thrown his life away on an airman's impulse of "delight" he might still be here, as a welcomer greeting the scene with "delighted" eye—as mere observer at first, until imagination brought a fitter welcome, enabling him to transform the external landscape into the visionary art that stanza IX contends was his proper work, and so to have actually published all to be a world's "delight." But that dubious contention is undercut even here in VII, the details of which seem far less indebted to Gregory, whose eye produced that decidedly unvisionary drawing, than to Hardy, who, like Yeats and Palmer, "had an eye for such mysteries." Whether or not I am correct about the possible borrowing of tone, stance, and scenario from Hardy, the effectiveness of Yeats's verbal, as opposed to Gregory's graphic, description and the revealing use of the verb *published* in IX confirm that the precisely rendered details of stanza VII are the fruit, not of the painter's, but of what Ford Madox Ford called (in the title of his 1913 comparison of Yeats's poetry with that of Hardy) "The Poet's Eye."[29] We may have here no more than a remarkable analogue. But, if I am correct about an interaction with Hardy, the ostensible tribute to Gregory's attentive love of nature is actually a quiet *hommage* to the nature-loving observer who imagines himself dead in "Afterwards."

Initially, this seventh stanza was followed immediately by the "great painter" stanza. With the insertion of the present eighth stanza, requested in proof by the dead man's widow, Gregory's physical skill and courage were elevated at the expense of whatever aesthetic connection may have been intended between Gregory as perceptive observer and as potential great artist. As an insertion, the present eighth stanza is, though exciting, disruptive, suggesting the same kind of divided attention in multitalented Gregory that made his true work so difficult to determine. While his daring horsemanship rounds out Gregory's aristocratic attributes and is part of the Yeatsian heroic ideal, its celebration, superb in its own way, is also slightly trivializing—hardly the effect intended by Gregory's widow.

On the surface, these lines seem to embody the hero as noble rider:

When with the Galway foxhounds he would ride
From Castle Taylor to the Roxborough side
Or Esserkelly plain, few kept his pace;
At Mooneen he had leaped a place
So perilous that half the astonished meet

29. Ford Madox Hueffer (later, Ford), "The Poet's Eye. III." Ezra Pound, living with Yeats at Stone Cottage at the time, may have drawn Yeats's attention to this brief commentary by Ford, an equally admired friend of Pound's.

Had shut their eyes; and where was it
He rode a race without a bit?
And yet his mind outran the horses' feet.

Some readers—following their own instincts, or treating the stanza as the
afterthought we now know it to have been—have found these lines inferior,
omittable, even "childish."[30] Though it fleshes out the final item in Gregory's triad of accomplishments and links Gregory's horsemanship with Pollexfen's (V), the stanza was added only because Mrs. Gregory did not think
Yeats had said "enough of Robert's courage." Had Margaret Gregory detected any other holding back on Yeats's part, any other failure to say
"enough"? Yeats had no doubt of Gregory's physical courage, either on
horseback or in the cockpit of his war machine; that he entertained doubts
about a deeper courage in Gregory is clear from the prose Appreciation,
where Gregory is numbered among those subjective men who nevertheless
"hesitated to plunge into the abyss" of their own dream. Though we might
think that the Irish airman whom "a lonely impulse of delight" drove to
tumult in the clouds had done just that, Yeats's abyss-image recalls the now
celebrated climactic sentence of his undelivered 1910 lecture, "Friends of
My Youth": "Why should we honour those that die upon the field of battle,
a man may show as reckless a courage in entering into the abyss of himself."[31]

Spenser raised a related question in "Astrophel"—that otherwise unre-
served eulogy to the dead warrior Sidney that provided the model for
"Shepherd and Goatherd," Yeats's first attempt at an elegy for Gregory:
"What need perill to be sought abroad, / Since round about us it doth make
abroad?" (lines 89–90). This is the very question raised in "Reprisals," the
1920 poem Yeats withdrew when Lady Gregory told him its publication
would "give pain" to Robert's widow, and a variant of it may be implicit in
this poem as well.[32] For the real challenge facing Gregory—the need to find
himself and his true work—was precisely the one he escaped by seeking
abroad, whether in tumultuous clouds or in reckless horsemanship, for
"perill." At Mooneen he "leaped a place / So perilous" that half the specta-
tors shut their eyes, an exploit also recounted in Lady Gregory's autobiography, *Seventy Years.* But that reckless riding may have covered up
Gregory's internal failure of nerve: to leap *over* an external obstacle or abyss

30. Witt, in "Making of an Elegy." She finds the "adolescent praise of Gregory's foolhardy
horsemanship . . . puzzling." But the interpolation of this "unhappy eighth stanza" produces
only a disrupting "ripple" in the poem's "emotional flow" (117). Kermode prefers the poem
without the stanza: "Its omission leaves us with a clearer development from the landscape of
Thoor Ballylee to the greatness of the painter of cold Clare rock, stern colour and delicate line.
The poem is probably improved by the change" (*Romantic Image,* 40). My suggestion is that
Yeats deliberately disrupted the aesthetic theme, just as Gregory had in his own life.
31. Ronsley, "Yeats's Lecture Notes for 'Friends of My Youth,'" *Yeats and the Theatre,* 81.
32. On "Reprisals," see below, Chapter 8, section III.

takes a courage less reckless than that required of a man entering *into* the abyss of himself.

Was it because he lacked that ultimate form of Yeatsian courage that Gregory's wartime service could be described, even in the public tribute Yeats was so anxious Lady Gregory should think "right," as a mind-easing "escape" from "loneliness"? For the recent author of *Per Amica Silentia Lunae* and the future author of *A Vision*, Gregory was a man caught between the pull of subjective (*antithetical*) solitude and objective (*primary*) comradeship. Retreating from absorption in their dream, certain *antithetical* men "seek through some lesser gift, or through mere excitement, to strengthen that self which unites them to ordinary men." Gregory as boxer or bowler, as fine shot or horseman, even as airman, was prompted less by a "lonely" impulse of delight or desire to escape from "ease and friendship" than by mere excitement and, precisely, the need for comrades. Gregory himself was quite specific on this point. "I joined up out of friendship," he told Yeats after enlisting (first in the 4th Connaught Rangers in 1915, transferring the next year to the Royal Flying Corps). In his draft of the Irish Airman poem, Yeats scribbled at the right: "Robert said to me 'I see no reason why anyone should fight in this war except friendship. The England I care for was dead long ago.'"[33] If that was his motivation, it entailed a "*shrinking*"—something never dreamed of by Gregory as horseman or airman—from the deeper "loneliness" of the artist's subjective abyss, the fruitful void in which he encounters his true self, his work. The escape into action, ostensibly praised in the elegy, seems to involve the sacrifice of a greater for a "lesser gift," one such lesser gift being Gregory's equestrian skill. He was "never the amateur," Yeats insisted of Gregory in the prose Appreciation. Nevertheless, while he and George Pollexfen were superb horsemen, both *were* amateurs, performing for what has been called (Perloff, "Consolation Theme," 318) the "limited audience" of Mooneen and Esserkelly. In that sense, stanza VIII, for all its fine release of pent-up energy, may reaffirm the coterie-limitation inherent in the epithet "*Our Sidney.*"

There may be hidden limitation even in the stanza's final line, which would be more persuasive if what Peter Ure called its "shifting of key"[34] were less abrupt. Coming at the last moment, after seven lines recounting Gregory's daring but reckless riding, the ostensibly laudatory "and yet his mind outran the horses' feet" might imply that his thinking was even less disciplined than his horsemanship—an implication reinforced, I believe, by allusion.

A possible "ironic variant on the theme of Stanza V, for in its astrological

---

33. See Gordon and Fletcher, *Images of a Poet*, 30. Mary FitzGerald drew my attention to the unpublished draft of the Irish Airman poem.

34. Ure, *Towards a Mythology: Studies in the Poetry of W. B. Yeats*, 39. Ure's second chapter focuses on the Gregory elegy as an example of Yeatsian mythologizing.

fantasies, Pollexfen's 'mind' also 'outran the horses' feet,'"[35] the line also rings an ironic change on what would seem to be its rhythmic and syntactic original: "Nor could his Ink flow faster than his Wit," one of Cowley's stanza-ending lines in the poem that provided Yeats his stanzaic model. But if Yeats's tribute is an echo, it has been displaced from the literary arena, where ink immortalizes intellect, to the racecourse, where horses and riders share the vitality, speed, and *transience* of healthy animals. "To each species of creature," wrote a Renaissance humanist echoing Cicero's *De Finibus*, "has been allotted a peculiar and instructive gift. Galloping comes naturally to horses, flying to birds. To man only is given the desire to learn." Gregory both flew and galloped. A quick study whose ever-changing mind outran his capacity to concentrate, he "rode a race without a bit," an accomplishment for a fearless rider, but not for a man who needed to curb, control, direct his undisciplined runaway talents. If, as Kermode suggests, Yeats "liked the motto of Cowley's poem," he must have liked it because he thought Gregory *immodicis*, too *variously* accomplished—like Dryden's Zimri but unlike Cowley's focused friend William Hervey, who, crowding learning into his "short Mortalitie," sought "Knowledge . . . only." While it is best to both act and know, the afterthought of VIII induces skepticism, especially if it is a secondhand tribute adapted from praise of a true humanist scholar. As such, Yeats's stanza-ending line allies Gregory with "horseman" Pollexfen rather than with those men of "mind" and "ink," Johnson and Synge; indeed, the displaced "ink" prepares us for "published," in the final line of the next, and crucial, stanza.

V. Gregory as Artist: Stanzas IX-X

We dreamed that a great painter had been born
To cold Clare rock and Galway rock and thorn,
To that stern colour and that delicate line
That are our secret discipline
Wherein the gazing heart doubles her might.
Soldier, scholar, horseman, he,
And yet he had the intensity
To have published all to be a world's delight.

On the covert level, stanza VII was a verbal landscape, based in part I believe on Hardy's "Afterwards"; the climactic compliment of VIII covertly denied Gregory Hervey's mind-immortalizing "ink"; here in IX we realize that work in a medium other than paint has been on the speaker's mind all along. Though to publish means to promulgate, to make publicly known, it almost always means to issue to the public *written* work—as in Yeats's only other use of the word in his poetry, when, in this same volume, he depicts

35. Perloff, "Consolation Theme," 318.

himself as a man "who has published a new book" (VP 350). Noting that *"published,* of course, applies more sensibly to Yeats's rather than Gregory's work," Peter Sacks suggests the elegist may be "obliquely drawing attention to his own performance—a traditional gesture—here reminding us that he, too, can give delight as well as receive it, as earlier in 'all things the delighted eye now sees'" (*English Elegy,* 290). The very choice of "published" suggests that the gesture is more than oblique, as is the link, through the repetition of "delight," with his own "delighted eye" in VII, an eye that registered details transformed into verbal art in *this* "published" poem. On the other hand, Gregory's publication—and it was only *potential*—was that of a great "painter." If he was more than perceptive observer (VII), more than fearless horseman (VIII), he must, we are told, have been an artist born to put on canvas "cold Clare rock and Galway rock and thorn." But this very line is *verbal* art; and, again, it sounds borrowed, a replication of that famous line loved by Keats for its sound pattern: "Come with acorn cup and thorn."

The line is from Thomas Chatterton. In his prose Appreciation of Gregory, Yeats referred to "The Le[e]ch Gatherer," that is, "Resolution and Independence."[36] In terms of our hidden agenda, it seems pertinent that Wordsworth's poem is one in which a young man is given "human strength, by apt admonishment" (line 112), from an old man who has endured, a lyric of crisis "in which a poet saves himself for poetry, and by implication for life."[37] Since he had this poem in mind in writing of Gregory, Yeats might also, like Wordsworth in "Resolution and Independence," have "thought of Chatterton, the marvelous Boy, / The sleepless Soul that perished in his pride." "To me, he will always remain," said Yeats of Gregory in the prose Appreciation, "a great painter in the immaturity of his youth, he himself the personification of handsome youth." But Gregory was a chronologically mature man when he was killed, twenty years older than the considerably more accomplished Chatterton, who took his own life at seventeen.

Another Romantic reference in the prose Appreciation is immediately relevant to the language of this stanza. Yeats refers to Gregory's stage decorations, which, "obtaining their effect from the fewest possible *lines* and *colours,* had always the grave distinction of his own imagination"—borrowed language repeated in stanza IX's "stern colour" and "delicate line." Though Yeats does not, in the poem, reveal the school of visionary

36. "The Leech Gatherer" was an alternate title for "Resolution and Independence" (Arnold used it in his popular edition of Wordsworth). Yeats cited the poem in the prose Appreciation as an example of the "great lyric poetry" with which true visionary artists "share certain moods" (UP 2:430).

37. Harold Bloom's description, *Oxford Anthology of English Literature,* 2:168. Elsewhere, discussing Yeats's Chinamen and their "ancient glittering eyes" that are "gay," I have noted that their ancestors are Western and include "the ancient mariner with his glittering eye and Wordsworth's leech-gatherer—that 'oldest man . . . that ever wore grey hair,' the light flashing 'from the sable orbs of his yet vivid eyes.'" Keane, "The Human Entrails and the Starry Heavens," 386.

painters he has in mind, he does in the prose Appreciation: it was that of Blake and his disciples, Samuel Palmer and Edward Calvert, artists whose work Yeats was studying at the Bodleian Library at Oxford when word reached him of the death of Robert Gregory. They enter the elegy—again, covertly—through allusion to Palmer's discussions of the aesthetic theories he shared with Calvert and their master; specifically, his repeated insistence on sparing use of austere color and the importance of "line." In a passage that seems to have provided the original for most of Yeats's words in stanza IX, Palmer claims, "We scarcely miss the *colours* where *line* pervades everything in its *mysteries* and its *might*. The *precision* of its delicacy clears things up." Yeats's "gazing heart doubles her *might*" when engaged in "our secret discipline" of "stern colour" and "delicate line" because what is being painted is, in Palmer's words, "addressed not [to] the perception chiefly but the IMAGINATION." The result is landscape that is visionary rather than corporeal or representational, subjective rather than objective, internal rather than external, Blakean rather than Lockean; landscape projecting (as Yeats put it in the Paterian prose Appreciation) "moods" that are "a part of the traditional expression of the soul."[38]

"I know," Palmer declares with visionary certitude, that there is an artistic "mastery" that shall "command truth itself to look as we would have it, and to *echo* the pulses of the *heart*" (*Memoir*, 165; italics added). The "gazing heart doubles her might," then, by being echoed in a scheme of things remolded nearer to the heart's desire through a severe discipline and imperious mastery capable of commanding truth itself. Palmer is thinking above all of his master, of Yeats's "William Blake / Who beat upon the wall / Till Truth obeyed his call." Yeats's Cuchulain—modeled in part on the autonomous man of Blake's completer, Nietzsche—would say at the end of his life, "I make the truth"; Yeats himself, having mastered *his* chosen art, announces, "I have come into my strength / And words *obey* my call" (VP 256, 576; VPl 1056).

The title of that poem is "Words"; and "words alone are certain good." The art celebrated in stanza IX of the Gregory elegy is, on the covert level, more verbal than visual—hence "our" secret discipline and the otherwise odd verb "published." The fusion of painters and poets, initially suggested by the illuminating example of Blake, reflects the repeated linking of the two arts in Palmer, who wrote that if he loved any "secular thing" better than art it was literature: "Surely the direction of a *line* or the gradation of a *colour* are not more interesting than the structure of a paragraph" (*Memoir*, 72; italics added). Palmer's words are echoed in the prose Appreciation, where Yeats, speaking of what as "a man of letters" he cared for in visionary landscape, adds that one understood by "something" in Gregory's "se-

---

38. UP 2:430. Yeats's reading of Palmer (who is cited almost verbatim in "Under Ben Bulben") was first related to the elegy by Marion Witt ("Making of an Elegy," 117–20). She does not, however, speculate on the *function* of the echoing. The passages cited are from A. H. Palmer, *Samuel Palmer: A Memoir*, 57, and *The Life and Letters of Samuel Palmer*, 359; my italics.

lection of *line* and of *colour* that he had *read* his Homer and his Virgil and his Dante." But to read is not to publish, and the function, covert if not overt, of "published" at the end of stanza IX is to diminish the man who had the intensity to "have published all," but did not.

Even as painter, Gregory's status is undermined from the outset by caveat: "We *dreamed* that a great painter had been born." Sacks (*English Elegy*, 288) raises and dismisses the possibility that this opening "we dreamed" is Yeats's "recognition that Gregory never in fact lived to fulfill his potential." One cannot say that, Sacks insists, after reading Yeats's statement in the obituary: "To me he will always remain *a great painter* in the immaturity of his youth." Sacks italicizes "a great painter," though one might, with equal justice, emphasize "immaturity." Does the "we dreamed" primarily celebrate, elegize, or impugn Gregory? Is it not a case of all three, and is this not the "puzzle" in the elegy referred to by Harold Bloom, who finds the "heart of the poem" in the lines about "the Blake-Palmer-Calvert tradition," a great tradition "Yeats and Lady Gregory dreamed that the slain hero had been born to paint in"? The lines about the power-doubling secret discipline seem to Bloom, as they do to me, "the most deeply moving lines in the poem," but, he adds, "they make the choice for Gregory that he did not live to make for himself," and that "much else in the poem" (Bloom does not say what) makes us "doubt he would have made" (*Yeats*, 196). This links up with his opening assertion that while Gregory, "more an Edward King than a Sidney," is the "weakest" thing in it, what "saves the poem is that Yeats's career matters more to it than Gregory's," a "saving formula strenuously employed" by Milton in "Lycidas" (193–94).

I believe that Yeats's implicit defense of his own career and poetic development is *so* strenuously employed in this poem that he did not *really* "make the choice for Gregory" that he seems to make in stanza IX. Ostensibly, the slain hero is included in "our secret discipline," but Yeats's allusions in this stanza, both visual and verbal, combine with subtle disclaimers to exclude Gregory from the visionary company; even to suggest, when integrated into the rest of the allusive network comprising the poem's hidden agenda, that Robert Gregory is not the heir to that great tradition, but a man who failed to measure up to its stern standards. Yeats praised (even kept one of) Gregory's paintings of the Clare coast and the Burren Hills, paintings in which, he said, Gregory had found "what promised to grow into a great style, but he had hardly found it before he was killed." This remark, in a dated footnote added to "Ireland and the Arts" in 1924 (E&I 209), is in accord with the consensus on Gregory recorded by Gordon and Fletcher: "There is agreement that he did not devote himself to painting with a singleness of purpose, except perhaps in the few years just before the war when he seemed to work more assiduously and systematically" (*Images of a Poet*, 32). Even this is hedged with caveats ("perhaps . . . seemed") that put all in doubt; and Gordon and Fletcher sum up the feeling of acquaintances: Gregory "had talent," but "not enough." It seems likely that, for all the "austerity, "sweetness," and "majesty" (E&I 209, L 946) Yeats professed to find in Gregory's art, he and Lady Gregory were imposing rather than discovering when they "dreamed" that a great painter had been born.

In "Nineteen Hundred and Nineteen," the plural "we" wonders if "we were crack-pated when we dreamed." The plural "we" of the elegy certainly was crack-pated in succumbing to the spirit-sealing slumber that "made us dream" that Gregory would live to comb gray hair, and we recall Lionel Johnson and the impossible consummation *he* "dreamed." Whatever Lady Gregory's dreams, and she "hoped very early that her son might prove to be a distinguished painter,"[39] Yeats opens and closes this stanza by deconstructing the dream. In addition to the framing caveats, the body of the stanza alludes to a line of truly disciplined artists with whom the merely talented Robert Gregory had little in common. The true heir of that visionary legacy is not the man who might have published all and who had already inherited Coole Park, but the man who published much, this elegy included, and who was then in the process of completing the restoration of Thoor Ballylee. The Gregory elegy, the first poem in which the tower is named, "shifts the center" of attention, as Harris says (*Coole Park*, 127), "from Coole to Thoor Ballylee and implicitly names the tower's inhabitant heir to the aristocratic legacy." At its deepest level, the poem implies that disciplined Yeats is also the heir to the *artistic* legacy to which undisciplined Gregory was born.

The completeness of the shift to Thoor Ballylee is confirmed in the next stanza, ostensibly a celebration, reminiscent of Dryden on Absalom and, especially, Jonson on Morison, of Gregory's versatility and *sprezzatura*:

What other could so well have counselled us
In all lovely intricacies of a house
As he that practised or that understood
All work in metal or in wood,
In moulded plaster or in carven stone?
Soldier, scholar, horseman, he,
And all he did done perfectly
As though he had but that one trade alone.

Once again, it is Peter Sacks who best articulates the root in elegiac tradition, here Yeats's inclusion of "the familiar motif of the departed guide. As the use of *counselled* confirms, Yeats can here overtly defer to the younger man, thus performing, however mildly, an elegiac gesture which otherwise might have been unconvincing coming from an older, famous poet to a man 'in the immaturity of his youth'" (*English Elegy*, 291). The stanza has

39. *Images of a Poet*, 32. "And," Gordon and Fletcher add, "it is certainly not by accident that in the portrait which she commissioned from Shannon in 1906 he should be shown, formally, as a painter. Whether his mother's hopes were a stimulus to him, or a burden, we do not know."

factual as well as generic justification (it was Gregory who suggested that Yeats restore the tower, even recommending specific renovations). Yet the tribute to his mastery of all skills substantiates Gregory's artistic greatness by claiming that, had he lived, he would have done an excellent job in counseling in the decoration of a house! Unless he is to be thought of as the equal of Thomas Jefferson, working out every detail of the design of Monticello, this is a curious and tenuous claim to greatness. The implication, as Perloff notes ("Consolation Theme," 319), is that Gregory is "less the true artist" than a "glorified interior decorator," a "gentleman of impeccable taste upon whom one calls when designing one's home." The fact that the home he would be working on is Thoor Ballylee, "My House," the tower Yeats here introduces into his poetry and that, in "Blood and the Moon," he was to explicitly "declare . . . *my* symbol," places Gregory in a decidedly ancillary role, a sort of subcontractor to the truly great artist, Yeats himself. As decorator of the Yeatsian tower, Gregory becomes, like Johnson, Synge, and Pollexfen, "a portion of *my* mind and life." The man who had, as we are told in the prose Appreciation, designed costumes and scenery "for *my* 'Shadowy Waters'" when it was staged at the Abbey; the man whose "designs" Yeats wanted to incorporate in "a refurbished edition of *my* collected poems" (L 578), becomes the man who is called on, not as "great painter," but as mere consultant to "us."

Even the highest tribute in stanza X seems slightly suspect. "All" he did was done perfectly, "As though he had but that one trade alone." On the surface this paean to Renaissance *sprezzatura*, its shift from "all" to "one" reversing Dryden's "not one, but all," indicates Gregory's power to channel his "complex totality into simplicity," issuing in a "unified multiplicity" (Harris, *Coole Park*, 135). Yet the line subtly reminds us that the real Gregory's problem was precisely that he did not have "one trade alone," that one trade that, kindling his talent into genius, might have become "his work."

VI. Yeats's Heart-Doubling Secret Discipline

In the full context of the poem as I have been reading it, the apotheosis of the flare, in the central image already examined, can only seem problematic: more spectacular but less enduring than the domestic peat-fire with which the poem began. Juxtaposing the commonplace with the mythological, the homely with the hieratic ("a fire of turf in th' ancient tower"), Yeats has indicated from the outset that, far from rambling, he is modeling "calculations that look but casual flesh" (VP 610). With a similarly calculated casualness, he achieves rondure with the twelfth and final stanza, whose details of wind and shaking shutter return us to the tower and the opening thoughts of the friends who cannot sup with us beside that fire of turf:

I had thought, seeing how bitter is that wind
That shakes the shutter, to have brought to mind

All those that manhood tried, or childhood loved
Or boyish intellect approved,
With some appropriate commentary on each;[,]
Until imagination brought
A fitter welcome; but a thought
Of that late death took all my heart for speech.

Yeats's concealed art is particularly subtle in the conclusion. He had rationally "thought" to do one thing, he tells us, "but" something intervened,
an *emotional* "thought" so piercing as to disrupt his rational scheme. For the
bard of "Lycidas," who had also put off direct confrontation of the most
painful loss, the procession of mourners and the elaborated details of the
floral arrangement for the laureate hearse were intended to "interpose a little
ease." But that was to have "our frail thoughts dally with false surmise."
Yeats's plan of orderly progression, precise apportionment in a procession
of the mourned, was, we are to believe, a similarly false surmise based on
frail thought. Yet the very repetition (a "*thought* of that late death") suggests
the continuity of a deeper, no less artistically deliberate, scheme.

Indeed, he begins and ends this "artless" final stanza by saying things that
are not quite true. Despite the opening "I *had* thought," he has in fact made
"some appropriate commentary on each" of the three dead friends. Similarly, his attempt to persuade us that his elegy has been co-opted by a
thought of that late death comes at the conclusion of a poem that is, especially by Yeatsian standards, quite long; that the titular hero (unnamed in
the poem itself) had not entered until line 46; and that had reached line 95
before the elegist was so overcome as to be rendered speechless. The gesture
recalls Jonson on Morison: "thou fall'st, my tongue" (line 44). But tongue
and tenacious memory have been, for twelve stanzas, unfallen enough to
earn that criticism of Tennyson's *In Memoriam* Yeats heard directly from
Paul Verlaine (and recorded in the same section of *Autobiographies* in which
the fire of straw is judged aesthetically useless). Tennyson was "too noble,
too *anglais*," complained Verlaine; "when he should have been broken-
hearted, he had too many reminiscences" (Au 342). A master of double
effects, Yeats has had his reminiscences *and* his broken-hearted conclusion.
Larger than both, he has assumed in the elegy what Keats called "the
egotistical or Wordsworthian sublime," the Yeatsian persona remaining at
the center of the poem to become not merely, as Ronald Snukal says, "as
thematically important as Gregory," but considerably more important.[40]

40. *High Talk*, 149. In this the poem does not, as Snukal thinks, "differ from traditional
elegies." (Milton, however discreetly hidden in the "mantle blue" of his shepherd persona,
remains at the center of "Lycidas," and Shelley is thematically more important than Keats in
"Adonais.") Nor does Yeats assume the stance of the egotistical sublime "in order to come to
grips" with the greatness of his friends, particularly that of Robert Gregory. "From a stand-
point less grand," Snukal argues, "it would be impossible to freely acknowledge greatness; one
would have to become either a naïve flatterer or a skeptic" (155). I find the greatness in the
poem mostly Yeats's. Tempering the "flattery" of at least two of his dead friends with "skepticism" (in Gregory's case largely covertly), he has things both ways.

Yeats's mind, T. S. Eliot observed about the time this poem was written, is "extreme in egoism," a "just" remark, William Pritchard has recently added, "even if directed at the closing moments of the Gregory elegy, where it is hard to avoid feeling that we are being invited to admire the grieving poet for his wise and handsome subordination of words to inexpressible grief."[41]

"Wise" is double-edged, this final self-reflexive stanza constituting, as Graham Martin has said, "a reminder to the reader that a poem is what he has been reading," a "most deliberate" poem in which a "scheme" has been "overcome . . . by an allegedly spontaneous uprush of feeling."[42] We are entitled to be skeptical that the sudden memory of Gregory's death "took all" the speaker's heart for speech. To have "all" the heart taken would be to undergo a simplification through intensity too extreme for so deliberate and ambivalent an elegist. But it is an elegist who has, nevertheless, managed to say something that, while not quite true, is yet so poignant, so filled with that "direct and exalted simplicity" Theodore Spencer attributed to the mature Yeats and Dryden,[43] that we willingly suspend disbelief for the moment. However we judge the ultimate sincerity of the rhetorical coup, we are left, in the speaker's final line and a half, with the unanswerable grief of monosyllables, fulfilling the monosyllabic toll of "What made us dream that he could comb grey hair?" with what Kermode calls "clustered consonants grievously impeding utterance" (*Romantic Image*, 39). A calculated and calculating poem, this elegy is sophisticated enough to make rhetorical use of the Romantic notion that the surprised heart has reasons reason knows not of, and of the truism that our best-laid plans are, like the startled water hen, subject to sudden "change." How could it be otherwise in an elegy?—"But O the heavy change now thou art gone, / Now thou art gone, and never must return." Just as that funereal toll abruptly cuts across the pleasant memories in the opening movement of "Lycidas," so Yeats's utterance-impeding ending knowingly reflects the emotion that cuts across frail thought.

This may be true even on our "covert" level. To the vacillating calculus of the analytic intellect, to what on the level of the secret discipline has been another Yeatsian counting of good and bad, the speaker cries, as he does in "Easter 1916," "enough!" What if Robert Gregory's impressive but never completely developed gifts bewildered him till he died? Yeats writes it out in a verse. Though in neither poem does the Yeatsian speaker become *wholly* elegiac chorus, these final heart-broken lines make us look again at the world- and self-consuming fire of the preceding stanza and wonder if Gregory may not, after all, have been "changed, changed utterly." Even if so, however, it will not have been in that blaze and blackout, but through

41. Pritchard, "W. B. Yeats: Theatrical Nobility," in his *Lives of the Modern Poets*, 70. Eliot's remark comes from "A Foreign Mind," his review of Yeats's *The Cutting of an Agate*.

42. Martin, "The Wild Swans at Coole," in *An Honoured Guest: New Essays on W. B. Yeats*, ed. Denis Donoghue and J. R. Mulryne, 71.

43. "Antaeus, or Poetic Language and the Actual World," a 1943 essay posthumously collected in Spencer's *Selected Essays*, ed. Alan Purves, 21.

the transforming power of art—and not Gregory's but Yeats's, the verbal art of the poet-survivor.

Whether or not men in general "improve with the years," great artists tend to; certainly Yeats did. Indeed, his art had with this, for some his first indisputably great poem, attained a new level of maturity: an accomplishment marked by that seamless interweaving of the colloquial and the hieratic, the seemingly casual and the calculated, the intimate and the resonantly public, which was to shape such later artfully rambling works as "A Prayer for My Daughter," "Among School Children," "All Souls' Night," "Lapis Lazuli," "The Circus Animals' Desertion," and "The Municipal Gallery Revisited." The Gregory elegy is the direct precursor of all these poems, and I believe that Yeats's placement of it among his best works took into account its particular variety of concealed calculation. That his art had improved this elegy itself demonstrated to be "truth," not "dream." Yet, for most of the elegy, Yeats allowed his dream of the wasteful virtues of aristocratic recklessness, of the swift, violent energy of burning youth, to dominate that deeper truth. "Allowed" it, because if my argument is valid, Yeats realizes throughout the poem that, like his Connemara "Fisherman," the hero of the elegy is "a man who does not exist, / A man who is but a dream," and that, in the words of "The Circus Animals' Desertion," "It was the dream itself enchanted me" (VP 348, 630). But enchantment is impermanent, and neither the idealizing dream of Renaissance-Man accomplishment nor that of premature, heroic death can utterly abolish or destroy the truth grasped by the mature man. In the final analysis it was, I would say, Yeats's "boyish intellect" that "approved" young Gregory, not what "manhood tried," for that involves considered judgment, a putting to the proof.

It is just this kind of trial that occurs, largely clandestinely, in the elegy. By covertly weighing the relative values of the swift flare of burning youth and slow-burning longevity, of *immodicis* as opposed to the concentrated single-mindedness that constitutes "our secret discipline," our "one trade alone"; by mingling the contemplative artist's admiration, even envy, of the man of action with a measure of criticism; by ostensibly celebrating Gregory as fellow artist while at the same time delicately undermining, in fact co-opting, the imagined "great" painter's claim to greatness, Yeats balances paean with skepticism, affirmation with caveat, decorum with honesty, and so produces a public poem with a private agenda, a "secret discipline."

In this ninth stanza, the mighty heart of the poem, Yeats, in doubling the power of the heart, paradoxically undermines in advance the alleged monopolizing of the heart in the poem's final lines: the taking, in Yeats's (and Blake's) favorite word, of "all" the heart. The word had certainly been prepared for. Gregory saw and loved "*all* things" now delighted in by the survivor; he might, it is asserted in the final claim of the ninth stanza, "have published *all*"; could, in the next stanza, have counseled us in "*all* lovely intricacies of a house" because he "practised or . . . understood / *All* work."

No wonder the speaker establishes Gregory—"*all* he did done perfectly," the man who consumed "the *entire* [originally "*all* the"] combustible world"—as "*all* life's epitome" and ends by claiming that a thought of the late death of this paragon "took *all* my heart for speech." But "took *all*" is a familiar Yeatsian hyperbole. He was exaggerating when he said, in "The Circus Animals' Desertion," that the art emblematic of Maud Gonne "took all my love," just as he was when, at the other extreme, he said in 1911 that Maud "took / All" till his youth was gone, and when, in the very next poem, he claimed he "took all the blame out of all sense and reason" (VP 316). He is also fibbing when he declares that the death of Gregory—character isolated by an impulsive deed and here set upon the painted stage of heroic elegy—"took all" his "heart" for speech: a fiction preempted *in the poem* not only by the doubling of the heart but also by the fact that Gregory took only a "share" of discourteous death and, as another of those friends who seemed a "portion" of the mind and life of the elegist, only half of his own elegy.

Read in this context of measurement, stanza IX shows how "all" can be doubled. Yeats can seem to be sincerely wholehearted in his final elegiac grief for Gregory—indeed, Peter Sacks has brilliantly demonstrated how the final phrase is "even more deeply elegiac than it at first appears," how the final "sacrificial movement from desire to language" and the "archaic image of offering up the heart" rein Yeats in "at the very core of the genre" (*English Elegy*, 297). At the same time, I would add, the elegist has judiciousness and power to spare because *he* is the genuinely "great" artist of the poem, born to and trained in "that stern colour and that delicate line / That are our secret discipline / Wherein the gazing heart doubles her might." Just as the consequence of that discipline, that stern yet delicate restraint, is an augmentation of "might" (here, as in Yeats's final credo, "measurement began our might"), so the paradoxical final fruit of secrecy is publication—in this case, both world-delighting and, to a considerable but necessary extent, world-misleading. For if the present argument is valid, the elegy itself practices the secret discipline it preaches. Its true theme goes beyond the elegiac occasion to assert the magnified power of the mature survivor and disciplined poet. But if the sincere yet cunning mourner, half his doubled heart in hiding, was to console his dear friend and, as poet, have "all" his elegiac cake and eat it too, the secret had to be kept not only from Lady Gregory but from most of us: the audience reading what Yeats, not Gregory, "published."

It is oxymoronic that secrecy should be published; but as R. P. Blackmur observed in a passage cited earlier, there are times when "the revelation . . . in Yeats's mind . . . was not and could not be given in the words of the poem." Such elegies

as "Easter 1916," "In Memory of Major Robert Gregory," and "Upon a Dying Lady" may have buried in them a conviction of invocation and revelation; but if so it is no concern of ours: we are concerned only . . . with the dramatic presentations . . . and with the technical means . . . whereby the characters are presented as intensely felt. There is no problem in such poems but the problem of reaching, through a gradual access of intimacy, full appreciation; here the magic and everything else are in the words.[44]

I have been engaged with precisely the problem of reaching, through a gradual access of intimacy, full appreciation of a poem in which, I believe, there are just enough words (caveats for the most part) to convince even a purely intrinsic critic that the "buried . . . revelation" is our concern—as it was Yeats's. Whatever inferiority the elegiac speaker may have felt comparing himself to a man who was all life's epitome, one who saw, loved, understood, practiced, and, finally, heroically consumed "all," himself included, the poem also makes it clear that that man did not *publish* all, or, in fact, anything.

The implication, again, is that what matters most is not Gregory's but Yeats's career. As so often in Nietzschean Yeats, it may come down to a question of the will to power; here, as in "Blood and the Moon," "power" is "a property of the living." Ultimately, it is not the self-mocking speaker—the burner of damp fagots, the impotent triton among the streams—but the man whose passionate intensity coincided with extinction who is truly impotent. It is the survivor, many-minded and crafty Odysseus, who, at the edge of that blood pool Yeats thought "an ancient substitute for the medium,"[45] invokes the shade of Achilles—that prototype of heroes extinguished early, who tells Odysseus he would rather be a slave alive than king among the dead. Similarly, it is William Butler Yeats, the survivor, who opens the Gregory elegy by summoning the breathless and impotent dead:

Now that we're almost settled in our house
I'll name the friends that cannot sup with us
Beside a fire of turf in th' ancient tower.

Daniel Harris, who describes this fire as a "cheerless smolder of turf," concludes that the elegy, returning to this setting in the final stanza, ends in despair: Yeats's "desolation, extending beyond Gregory's death, is grief for the futility of his [Yeats's] life, now bitterly revealed in Gregory's splendor." The tower again stands "chill and cavernous upon barren ground," with no "resurgent hopes of new fruition" (*Coole Park*, 129, 137). Coldly eloquent as this is, I would argue that while much is taken, much abides; that the man we meet in this elegy is the mature Yeats, finally married, almost settled in the tower that was to be his sometime home and central symbol: the Yeats who has, at fifty-two, come into his strength, poetically

44. Blackmur, "The Later Poetry of W. B. Yeats," 47.
45. *Odyssey* 11.34ff.; Ex 366.

and personally; who has grown up, not simply grown old, and with more than "hopes" of new fruition, as the elegy itself demonstrates. Despite the bond of friendship established with the dead, the survivors ("we" and "our" and "us") as well as the peat-fire (which may be more warming than "cheer-less") are in sharp contrast to the dead who cannot sup with us: "*cannot*," because they are in the cold grave, two of them dead young, the lesser because he chose a blaze that purchased momentary unity of being at the price of self-destruction and, perhaps, self-betrayal. Even, as I said earlier, if we accept Gregory's transfiguration as one of accident into art, the trans-forming artist is Yeats, the living man who has endured, not to gloat over the dead, but to exercise poetic control over them.

Around fires at the club or fires of turf, Yeats survived to "name" dead friends or to celebrate, and criticize, dead heroes by "writ[ing] it out in a verse" ("Easter 1916"). For as he'd said in his canon-opening poem, "words alone are certain good," and dead heroes would be forgotten had they not been commemorated in art. "Warring kings," great men of action who were also "word be-mockers," ironically survive only in the potent words of poets:

Where are now the warring kings?
An idle word is now their glory,
By the stammering schoolboy said,
Reading some entangled story:
The kings of the old time are dead.
   (VP 65)

The point in bringing in "The Song of the Happy Shepherd" is not only to raise the obvious rhetorical question—who would remember the dead war-rior and minor Irish squire Robert Gregory were it not for Yeats's ele-gies?—but also to reinforce my argument that commemoration can be si-multaneously ironic and power-asserting, as in the lines just quoted and in their probable source, Shelley's "Ozymandias." The shattered visage half-buried in the greatest of the Gregory elegies tells that its poet read well the features of the actual Robert Gregory, and that some of these "survive" in the poem because Yeats, like the Shelleyan sculptor, had a "hand that mocked them." In both cases, though far more gently in Yeats's, it is a mockery that, covertly, goes beyond mimesis, covertly because the artist who carved the likeness of the pharoah had even more urgent motivation than Yeats to avoid offending his noble patron.

That Yeats risked offending Lady Gregory at all (for there are those detectable caveats) testifies to his honesty and to an ultimate allegiance—to art and to his most secret heart. We are told, in the early poem just cited, not to "hunger fiercely after truth" if it is something external, the truth of others; for, as with the Dryden of *Religio Laici*, salvation derives "not from what OTHERS but what *I* believe." Yeats's formulation in "The Song of the Happy Shepherd"—"there is no truth / Saving in thine own heart"—is Sidneian: "'Fool,' said my muse to me, 'look in thy heart and write.'" In the Gregory elegy, in the critical exercise of "our secret discipline," the "gazing heart doubles her might." Like the Milton of "Lycidas," Yeats gathers that secret might for future accomplishments—accomplishments that will be public, indeed recognizable, in Kermode's phrase, as "the work of the master of the Gregory elegy." But as "gazing" quietly confirms, the initiating augmentation of power is private. Discussing this word (as used here and repeatedly in the poems, plays, and prose), Denis Donoghue reminds us, "'Gazing' is a strict term for Yeats . . . the gaze is purely internal and secret."[46] In Yeats's elegy for Gregory, the gaze is directed "into the abyss of himself," and it is himself that he remakes in the exercise of a heart-doubling secret discipline to which, *as artist*, he owes an allegiance deeper than that to the aristocratic legacy, to Robert Gregory and his widow, or even to his own "dear friend," the dead man's grieving mother.

VII. Critical Epilogue

Advocates of intentionality as the key to assigning a work a single coherent meaning argue that understanding authorial intention allows us, in one extreme formulation, "to eliminate in the act of reading any potential incoherencies and ambiguities which cannot be resolved within our appreciation of the whole." Thus we are advised, in reading *Paradise Lost*, to dismiss, say, the relative unattractiveness of God or the appeal of Satan as "unintended negative consequences of the author's positive intentions."[47] Those resistant enough to my reading of the Gregory elegy to forego their own doubts about ascertaining authorial intention might wish to dismiss my network of caveats and backtracked allusions as precisely this. But I believe Yeats's intentions were divided. Even if the "negative consequences" were *not* consciously intended, to ignore their subversive implications would be to risk throwing the baby out with the bathwater; to "rule out of court," as Jonathan Culler says, "precisely those facts and elements that deconstruction finds most interesting and revealing: elements which are indissociable from a particular project yet work to undermine that project."[48]

But since I find the undermining *intended*, I must (at the risk of protesting too much, and so resembling the double-minded, and double-hearted, ele-

46. Donoghue, *William Butler Yeats*, 81, 82.
47. Ralph Rader, cited by Jonathan Culler, "Issues in Contemporary American Critical Debate," in *American Criticism in the Poststructuralist Age*, ed. Ira Konigsberg, 16–17. In *Validity and Interpretation* (1967) and *The Aims of Interpretation* (1976), E. D. Hirsch distinguishes between "meaning," which is unalterably fixed by the author's probable intentions, and "significance," which can vary. Meanings are stable and determinate, while significances, assigned by readers, are changeable and so of secondary importance—a distinction reminiscent of Northrop Frye's between the objective "analysis" and subjective "evaluation" of a work. In both cases, the model seems to be the old distinction between "primary" and "secondary" qualities.
48. Culler, "Issues in Contemporary American Critical Debate," 17.

gist) add that I do not think of this chapter as a deconstructionist exercise. Certainly, to swing to the subjectivist extreme, I do not believe that texts are deconstructible into utter indeterminacy, mere grounds for "freeplay." My intentions have not extended beyond "de-sedimentation," by which Jacques Derrida seems to mean not much more than the dredging up of latent meanings. Nor, while I may seem, like reader-response or psychoanalytic critics, to have "generated" meanings from my own response to the poem, do I think I am the only begetter of "my" version of the Gregory elegy. I may be suffering under the objectivist "illusion" that there *is* a "text in this class"; but while I have speculated about "sources" and done a good deal of reading between the lines, I would like to think that the author is present, overtly and covertly, and that he is the creator of the text I have described—a text that is more than what reception theorists Roman Ingarden and Wolfgang Iser call a set of "schemata" that the reader must actualize.[49]

Thus my reading of the elegy participates modestly in the Americanization of deconstruction. Like Paul de Man and J. Hillis Miller, I am arguing that the text under scrutiny is *self*-deconstructive and that I am merely elucidating, retrospectively repeating, what Yeats himself spirited into the elegy, however slyly. An inevitably immodest and irritating consequence is the implicit claim to have deciphered a poem that several generations of readers, not even aware of their gullibility, have simply been leafing through. But of course I have myself been one of those readers and may well—all passion for iconoclasm temporarily spent—have rejoined their ranks by the time these words are in print. If so, however, I will retain much of the skepticism conveyed here. I am not sure I "believe" every detail of my own argument any more than I "believe" every detail of Jack Stillinger's skeptical "The Hoodwinking of Madeline." At the same time, I can no more return to the Gregory elegy with an untroubled and innocent response than can most post-Stillinger readers to "The Eve of St. Agnes."

Such skepticism, however, does not require the abandonment of the notion of determinate meaning, which "does not involve the claim that every work has a univocal meaning: a work can include local or even systematic ambiguities as part of its determinate meaning; in this case, a work's true meaning includes a particular ambiguity. Nor is there a claim that we can necessarily discover a work's true meaning."[50] My procedures in determining a covert level of meaning in the case of the Gregory elegy

---

49. See the Polish theorist Ingarden's *The Literary Work of Art*. Wolfgang Iser, of the Constance school of reception-aesthetics, places greater emphasis on the different ways different readers actualize a work—though the text must be so construed (or "normalized") as to be internally consistent. See his *The Act of Reading: A Theory of Aesthetic Response*. American reception-theorist Stanley Fish refuses to find any immanent meaning, though he argues for chaos-preventing "interpretive strategies" shared by knowledgeable readers. See *Is There a Text in This Class? The Authority of Interpretive Communities* (1980).

50. Culler, "Issues in Contemporary American Critical Debate," 13–14.

will seem dubious to some, but those procedures have, I believe, less to do with me than with this inherently self-contesting, allusive and elusive, text.

Thus, while Harold Bloom is the Newreader to whom I am probably closest, my reading of the elegy does not seem to me an instance of creative misreading, willful misprision. Bloom would say that, exercising my Nietzschean will to power over the text, I have created a meaning of my own by deliberately swerving away from Yeats's officially declared meaning. But I am not, I think, *deliberately* misreading—even though Yeats's ostensible meaning has been universally endorsed, even by those readers (Winters, Perloff, Bloom himself) with reservations about the poem, or Gregory, or both. I do, however, see the elegy in terms of a struggle for power, a variation on what Bloom darkly describes as the war for imaginative space waged by a living poet against the oppressive dead—this elegy, like all others, being primarily about the elegist and survivor.

To add a final caveat of my own. The only thing certain about my argument is that "'Tis strange." "More strange than true," responds Shakespeare's skeptical Theseus in the final act of *A Midsummer Night's Dream*. I may be one of those whose "shaping fantasies" fabricate more than cool reason ever apprehends. But whatever the validity of my individual points, it seems statistically improbable that these intertextual interactions, borrowings, and embedded disclaimers should converge to tell a reasonably consistent and therefore plausible tale: a story of ambivalence and even covert undermining that is both internally coherent and corresponds to external reality: Yeats's divided feelings about Robert Gregory, personally and in terms of the direction of his talents. In any case, it *is* certain that Theseus is both limited and dead wrong. As Hippolyta points out, taken "all" together, the very consistency of the strange stories "More witnesseth than fancy's images / And grows to something of great constancy."

8

THE LONELY CROWD: THE IRISH AIRMAN
IN YEATS'S VISIONARY COMPANY

A lonely impulse of delight
Drove to this tumult in the clouds.
  —Yeats, "An Irish Airman Foresees His Death"

A restless impulse urged him to embark
And meet lone death on the drear ocean's waste.
  —Shelley, *Alastor*

I was asked why a certain man did not live at Boar's Hill, that pleasant neighbor-hood where so many writers live, and replied, 'We Anglo-Irish hate to surrender the solitude we have inherited', and then began to wonder what I meant. I ran over the lives of my friends, of Swift and Berkeley, and saw that all, as befits scattered men in an ignorant country, were solitaries.
  —Yeats, preface to Gogarty's *Wild Apples* (1930)

All those that manhood tried, or childhood loved
Or boyish intellect approved. . . .
  —Yeats, "In Memory of Major Robert Gregory"

According to Nietzsche, "Homer would not have created Achilles nor Goethe a Faust if Homer had been an Achilles or Goethe a Faust."[1] A complex and calculating artist who, with the help of Nietzsche, also created an heroic anti-self, Yeats is at his most audacious, even reckless, when he adopts this heroic mask, ruffling in a manly pose for all his timid heart. At such moments he can be majestic. He can also be histrionic, a victim of simple hero worship succumbing to what his boyish intellect approved. On such occasions Yeats presents us with the spectacle of the born survivor vicariously setting the sails of his heroes for shipwreck.

But ambivalence breeds ambiguity. While Yeats believed that "the heroic act was the act that combined the greatest degree of self-sacrifice with the

---

1. *Genealogy of Morals* 3.4.

greatest degree of self-realization,"[2] and while his Cuchulain is both "self-assertive" and "self-immolating" (L 425), he also often registers covert but detectable reservations about heroic self-sacrifice. The "balance" of "Easter 1916," to take the most obvious instance, stems from ambivalence toward the martyred heroes. Whereas one of those heroes, Padraic Pearse, had invoked Colmcille ("If I die it shall be for the excess of love I bear the Gael"),[3] Yeats asks: "What if excess of love / Bewildered them till they died?" Yet he wrote out in a verse the terrible beauty of their sacrifice, the transformation of comedy into tragedy, of motley into garments of re-demptive green. In a July 1916 note he remarked: "The late Dublin re-bellion, whatever one can say of its wisdom, will long be remembered for its heroism. 'They weighed so lightly what they gave,' and gave too in some cases without hope of success" (VP 820). Yeats quotes himself ("September 1913") to acknowledge his error in declaring Romantic Ireland dead and gone, yet refuses, as in the Easter poem, to elevate the Rising to the realm of thought's crowned powers: "Whatever one can say of its wisdom."

Wisdom is a *primary* quality for Yeats, and to value it, even in a subordinate clause, creates conflict with the ecstatic *antithetical*. In "An Irish Airman Foresees His Death," Yeats, apparently trying to have it both ways, puts in the not quite breathless mouth of his heroic speaker words meant to express both ecstasy *and* wisdom. That it is a world-weary wisdom clashes with the impulse of delight at the poem's heart; that it is there at all reminds us that the antinomies are always present, suggesting, here as well, something of the tension agitating "In Memory of Major Robert Gregory."

I. Explication

Robert Gregory's ambivalent elegist concludes bereft of "speech." Appropriately, the words of the poem immediately following are not "his." The dramatic speaker is an anonymous fighter pilot at or very near the moment of his rendezvous with death:

I know that I shall meet my fate
Somewhere among the clouds above;
Those that I fight I do not hate
Those that I guard I do not love;
My country is Kiltartan Cross,
My countrymen Kiltartan's poor,
No likely end could bring them loss
Or leave them happier than before.
Nor law, nor duty bade me fight,

2. Peter Ure, "The Hero on the World Tree: Yeats's Plays."
3. Cited by George Dangerfield, *The Damnable Question: One Hundred and Twenty Years of Anglo-Irish Conflict*, 220.

Nor public men, nor cheering crowds,
A lonely impulse of delight
Drove to this tumult in the clouds;
I balanced all, brought all to mind,
The years to come seemed waste of breath,
A waste of breath the years behind[,]
In balance with this life, this death.

"An Irish Airman Foresees His Death" would seem to be as autonomous as its speaker's impulse: freed from all external motivation, totally self-expressive. To respond to this poem it is not necessary to know who wrote it, let alone on whom, if any one, the Airman was modeled; it is "*an* Irish Airman," and that suffices. A poem is almost always, at least initially, best read "closely," in terms of how its components interrelate to produce a little world with its own equilibrium. This poem, so deliberately "balanced" throughout, lends itself to such an approach. Indeed, it challenges the critical orientation dominant in the preceding chapters, a "contextual" approach to be resumed, however, once the Airman's monologue has been subjected to intrinsic analysis.

The poem's internal equilibrium is firmly grounded in its syntax and structure: sixteen lines running together four iambic tetrameter quatrains, with the Airman's utterance falling into two balanced eight-line sentences. That is not, however, our initial impression of the poem's movement. Yeats's punctuation, always precarious, seems particularly so in these two Gregory poems. In the final stanza of the elegy he used a semicolon rather than a comma after "each"; here he omits the comma we mentally place after the penultimate line. At two points in the poem where we might expect periods we find semicolons—after "the clouds above" (2) and "this tumult in the clouds" (12). But, as the repetition hints, *these* are not cases of careless punctuation. The effect of the first semicolon is to link the Airman's foreknowledge of his fate with the swift disclaimer of conventional motivation; the isolated hero goes calmly to his death "among the clouds above" harboring neither hatred of those he fights nor love for those he guards, violent emotions literally beneath him. The second semicolon forges a link between seeming opposites: delighted "impulse" and calm deliberation in which all is brought to "mind." In short, though tense with paradox, the poem establishes its own internal unity of being. It mithridatically heals its own apparent breaches, balancing—through meter, syntax, diction, tone, and even punctuation—such traditional antinomies as freedom and fatalism, excitement and gravity, delight and sadness, impulse and reason, heart and head, ecstasy and wisdom, action and contemplation, in short, Romanticism and Classical Stoicism. For example, the monologue opens as it closes: totally self-possessed. The reversal at the end, in which the Romantic sublime yields to fatalistic stoicism, itself reverses the opening; for the Airman's reverie begins on a note of monosyllabic stoical certitude tempered by

Romantic mystery: "I know that I shall meet my fate / Somewhere among the clouds above." The predestined meeting will take place "somewhere," at once unspecified and portentous, though inevitably it will be among the clouds "above" mundane concerns.

A similar mixture of personal involvement, detachment, and laconic reservation governs the Airman's use and omission of personal pronouns. He begins with a barrage of first-person "I's" (six, three couplings, in the opening twenty-nine-word quatrain); begins the next two lines with "my" (referring now not to his "fate" but to his country and countrymen); then goes three lines before telling us, "Nor law, nor duty bade *me* fight." It is not until the opening of the final quatrain that the "I" returns: "I balanced all." More remarkable is the absence of personal pronouns in the concluding three lines (not *my*, but "*this* life, *this* death") and in those two lines that are the poem's glory: "A lonely impulse of delight / Drove to this tumult in the clouds." The *drive* here is both noun and verb (the root of "impulse"— *inpellere*—means "to drive"), and the ellipsis both intensifies the trochaic inversion and accentuates inner joy as the agent rather than "me" as an object being acted upon. The omission of "me"[4] makes the impulse "lonely" in that archetypal sense in which Yeats often uses the word. It is only one of the paradoxes of this succinct poem that the nameless Airman's most personal statements are simultaneously the most impersonal, with an absence of ego implicit in his very claim to autonomy.

In the lines preparing the way for that impulse, the Airman reveals himself—more paradoxes—as both rooted and deracinated as well as a blend of "eighteenth-century" and "Romantic" qualities. The rhetoric leading up to the climactic rapture of the Romantic sublime is notably Augustan: precise, restrained, disciplined. The double-balanced, end-stopped lines may even begin by echoing Samuel Johnson's question in an Ecclesiastean poem relevant to this one: will "Britain hear the last appeal, / Sign her *foes'* doom, or *guard* her *favorites'* zeal?"[5] The "last appeal" of such black-and-white patriotism would be the last refuge of a scoundrel to the solitary Airman: "Those that I *fight* I do not hate, / Those that I *guard* I do not love."

Though this Anglo-Irish autonomy and cold, measured appraisal must have astonished British readers at the time (the poem was written in June 1918 and published the following year), we can understand how an "Irish" pilot might neither hate the Germans he fought nor love the Englishmen he guarded in the Great War. But his commitment to *no* cause, his clear-headed, even indifferent freedom from all illusions, penetrates closer to home:

My country is Kiltartan Cross,
My countrymen Kiltartan's poor,

---

4. Compare Soul's elision in the opening line of "Dialogue": "I summon [you] to the ancient winding stair."

5. "The Vanity of Human Wishes," lines 91–92. As Johnson's title suggests, this is a poem related not only to Juvenal but also to Ecclesiastes.

No likely end could bring them loss
Or leave them happier than before.
Nor law, nor duty bade me fight,
Nor public men, nor cheering crowds.

Not utterly alienated, he *is* an Irish airman; even if his Kiltartan country and countrymen enter the poem primarily to reveal his assumption of the irrelevance to them of any conceivable outcome of the war, they at least serve, in a characteristically Yeatsian way, to actualize him in a context of countryside and neighbors, to give him a local habitation and, almost, a name. Yet these homely associations and even the regional allegiance are momentary. The war in which he has enlisted is meaningless to Kiltartan's poor, as, indeed, it is to the Airman himself, whose solitude verges on solipsism.

The Airman had followed his opening declaration about foreseeing his death with a negative catalog (not, not, no, nor, nor, nor, nor), a classically rhetorical dismissal of all those external, conventional factors—hate, love, war objectives, law, duty, orating politicians, the easily swayed mob—that did *not* impel him to fight. Responding line by line, the reader is being directed to ask the inevitable question: what, then, did? When the delayed answer finally comes, the whole weight of affirmation falls on two lines strong enough to bear the burden. The poem's curious balance—cold passion and measured recklessness, laconic heroism and astringent exultation, fatalism and autonomy—comes to thrilling life, vitalized by that "lonely impulse of delight" that seems to permanently capture the mystique of flyers driven like solitary birds to their fated "tumult in the clouds." These lines are of course the emotional center of the poem, as Yeats was perfectly aware. Joseph Hone reports that, coaching Clinton Baddeley for a 1937 BBC reading of "An Irish Airman," Yeats made him speak the two crucial lines "as though he was experiencing the physical sensation of flight. . . . 'Ecstasy, Baddeley!' he would cry, and repeat the lines lovingly to himself" (Hone, *W. B. Yeats*, 461).

Masterfully interlacing consonants and vowels, these two lines are acoustically worthy of the heroic tradition they tap—Homeric, Shakespearean, Castiglionian, Nietzschean, Anglo-Irish, and, above all, Romantic. But even within the limits of a popular ethos, the lines are telling. We have seen enough war movies to respond to that stereotypical mixture of fatalism and joyful energy apparently endemic to devil-may-care combat pilots, especially in World War I. And novels and films from *A Tale of Two Cities* to *Casablanca* have familiarized us with heroes both intensely alive in the face of death and intriguingly disillusioned. In the context of the Great War, there is the self-portrait of Siegfried Sassoon, thrilled by combat in a war he suspected was meaningless, and, particularly relevant to the Airman's final lines, the disenchanted, isolated Hemingway hero, driven by an impulse to the moment of truth, acting with grace under pressure, seeking only to die in his own way—all in language as simple, declarative, and, finally, enigmatic as the Airman's.

Yeats's Irish Airman is of their company, all of them shaped in part by the ancestral figure of the Byronic hero, the most influential of solitary and self-destructive Romantic individualists. But the most admirable of such heroes sacrifice for love, and even Byron gave away his "breath" for a cause in which he believed. The Airman believes in nothing but the exhilarating impulse. Consequently, our admiration of his fatal drive—toward adventure? excitement? death? attainment of his vision?—is likely to be subtly qualified by nagging doubts that the lonely quest, however thrilling in itself, may be so exclusively individualistic as to be, by implication, socially irresponsible, an evasion as much as an epitomization of human life. Again the Hemingway hero comes to mind, or perhaps Hemingway himself, alienated from the quotidian world, charting his dangerous and, finally, immature course between purely individualistic delight and despair. In a related sense, the Airman, as I suggest in the subsequent discussion of Tennyson's dramatic monologue, is a sort of Ulysses *redivivus*.

The Airman's lonely impulse may be one of "delight"; everything else is a sad waste time stretching before, though not after. For the lethal impulse—a solitary, alienated urge to both self-realization and self-destruction—drives him to "*this* tumult in the clouds," and "in balance with this life" is "*this* death." The shift from the opening "I know that I *shall* meet" to the immediacy of the double "this" marks the difference between anticipated and—the only word that seems accurate—*achieved* death. Further, the closing lines of the poem demand that "this death" be interpreted as not only expected but also desired, a consummation devoutly to be wished. Those closing lines, with their measured and measuring calm, are not only deliberate but also profoundly disillusioned—still heroic in a Byronic or Bogartian sense, yet far from the motivating impulse of delight.

Reread in the rather gray light of these final lines, the impulse itself seems problematic:

I balanced all, brought all to mind,
The years to come seemed waste of breath,
A waste of breath the years behind[,]
In balance with this life, this death.

The balanced composure and throwaway gesture are attributes of the aristocratic Yeatsian hero. But the abrupt tonal shift from momentary rapture to a measuring disillusionment; the somber verdict pronounced on "all" by a man who sees things, unflinchingly and cold-eyed, not as they ought to be, but as they are; the austere, fatalistic, disillusioned voice; the reduction of "life" to the metonymy of "breath"; even the chiastic structure: all point to the nuclear passages of Ecclesiastes, which, along with Revelation, was Yeats's favorite biblical text as a boy.

The Airman's chiasmus—"The years to come seemed waste of breath, / A waste of breath the years behind"—synopsizes the Preacher's "the thing that hath been, it is that which shall be; / And that which is done is that which shall be done," while the repeated "all" and "waste of breath" echo the philosophy-epitomizing motto with which Ecclesiastes begins and (almost) ends: "vanity of vanities! All is vanity" (1:9, 1:2). "Vanity," occurring thirty-eight times, is of course the keynote of the book, forcing upon us the sad wisdom that existence is as insubstantial and fleeting as a breath. Indeed, the Hebrew word used, *hebel*, means "breath," so that the book's formula for this life, perhaps even for "spirit" itself (also *hebel* rather than the usual *ruach*), is literally "breath of breaths." Perhaps Yeats had *not* "forgotten all my Hebrew."

But what has happened to the impulse of "delight"? Does its driving power extend, as Raymond Cowell suggests, even to the waste-of-breath lines, making mere time, even death itself, irrelevant? Does the impulse redeem from cold calculation a decision ultimately born, as Hugh Kenner says, of an "explicit disenchantment"? John Middleton Murry, reading Yeats's volume as the "Swan Song" of a worn-out poet who had failed to subdue his dreams or to build a new world from them, quoted the Airman's monologue as if it were spoken by the poet himself: "Now, possessing neither world, he sits by the edge of a barren road that vanishes into a no-man's land, where is no future, and whence is no way back to the past."[6]

Though this confuses persona with poet, it does contain an element of truth. As in Ecclesiastes and Tennyson's "Ulysses," texts in which credible language has been put in the mouths of others (both ancient kings, Solomon and Odysseus), the Airman monologue mingles dramatic impersonation with the expression of at least part of the author's personal attitude toward life. No one would deny that isolation and disenchantment are tonal elements of both the Airman poem and the volume in which it appeared; but so is the impulse of delight, an impulse inseparable, in the Airman, from his drive toward death. We might even synopsize his "case" in a single sentence employing, however "reductively," the terms of Freudian psychoanalysis. The Airman has leaped from the "pleasure principle" (he is a solipsistic man-child seeking self-delight) right over the adult stage of the "reality principle" (though a reasoning "realist," he is asocial, unadjusted to the surrounding world of countrymen, law, and duty) all the way to the "death drive"—a masochism that the ego, undeterred by the primary "ego-instinct" of self-preservation, unleashes on itself but that is still motivated by pleasure. Whether driven by an impulse of delight or by a death wish, the narcissistic Airman longs for a blissful, preconscious state hermetically sealed off from the external world.

This, it is hardly necessary to say, is only a part of the poem, and far from the most obvious part; nor are the poem's paradoxes to be reconciled under

6. Murry, "Mr. Yeats' Swan Song." Cowell's remarks, focused on the Gregory elegy rather than on the Airman poem, appear in his *W. B. Yeats*, 55; Kenner's in "The Sacred Book of the Arts," in *Gnomon*, 9–29.

Freudian or any other extra-literary auspices. The reader must come back to
the conflicted tonalities as bridged by the internal balancing act of the poem
itself. The final quatrain, which begins "I balanced all, brought all to
mind," performs a *volte face*, a shift *away* from the "unthinking," "irrational" heroic act stressed by every critic of the poem. We move, in fact, from a
"lonely impulse," a solitary and mysterious instinctual drive without conscious thought, to an act of *total* consciousness; "all . . . all." Insisting that
"the ways of nature are to be conquered, not obeyed," John Stuart Mill (in
"On Nature") attacked the "modern" (that is, Romantic) sentimental exaltation of "instinct at the expense of reason," a near-divinization so sweeping that "almost every variety of unreflecting and uncalculating impulse
receives a kind of consecration." The greater Romantics, Wordsworth's
"one impulse from a vernal wood" notwithstanding, were more than rational without being irrational; Yeats, more susceptible to the lure of the
irrational, protects his Airman's impulse overtly by adding to it precisely
the reflection and calculation whose absence Mill deplored.

Unlike the elegy's *contrast* between swift flare and slow-burning fagots,
this attempt to have it *both* ways, to balance the hero's instinctual impulse
with rational calculation, suggests a "Yeatsianizing" of Robert Gregory that
takes a very different form than, say, the poet's identification of Airman
Gregory with the hawklike and impulsive Cuchulain. In another poem in
The Wild Swans at Coole, Yeats contrasts the impulsive Maud Gonne, who
has not "lived in thought but deed" and so has "the purity of a natural
force," with himself, "whose virtues are the definitions / Of the analytic
mind" (VP 353). Writing to Robert Gregory regarding the "one serious
quarrel" he ever had with Lady Gregory (an occasion on which his defense
of her against attack had struck mother and son alike as inadequate), Yeats
explained that, through "analysis," he had destroyed in himself "instinctive
indignation." Indeed, his instincts in general had been "reasoned . . . away,
and reason acts very slowly and with difficulty and has to exhaust every side
of the subject." As a result, he had often not done the "natural and sometimes the right thing." Objective balancing of the evidence or "self-distrust-
ful analysis of my own emotion destroyed impulse." On this point he found
his and the Gregorys' "attitudes toward life . . . unreconcilable."[7] The line
given the Airman, "I balanced all, brought all to mind," seems an attempt
to reconcile the "unreconcilable": not only Romantic impulse with reason
but also divided, analytic Yeats with the Gregorys, whose instinctual attitude toward life had, like Maud's, that "purity of a natural force" Yeats
admired, envied, and—in a mixture of Chance and Choice—left to "others"
to embody.

In the poem, the bridge flung over the chasm between unmediated impulse and the mediations of mind is the verb itself. "Balanced," reinforced
by the final line's "in balance with," establishes the necessary link between

---

7. Mem 252–53, 257. This is a draft of a letter that may not have been sent.

impulsive delight, the act of soaring among the clouds, and rational deliberation, even calculation. The verb conveys a state of equilibrium, a thematically crucial equilibrium replicated in the rhetorical balance of the final
quatrain itself, with its parallels, repetitions, and dominant chiasmus. The
balancing is of past and projected future and, ultimately, of "this life, this
death." The man who calmly speaks these lines seems himself "balanced,"
possessing the mental and emotional stability to come to such a decision, as
we say, "on balance": considering everything, "all" in "all." We see him in
our mind's eye paradoxically holding the balancing scales of his own fate,
the "fate" he knows from the outset he must "meet." Fate's scales can
symbolize both divine justice and the human power to decide; in Homer,
Zeus weighs in his golden scales the "dooms" (keres) of opposing parties in
the Trojan War, yet even doomed Achilles chooses his fate. The doomed
Airman, weighing the alternatives of to be or not to be, finds a fearful
symmetry, a correspondence between life and death in which both are,
because equivalent, equally significant or insignificant.

At the same time, the mental weighing is itself balanced by the Airman's
aristocratic nonchalance and by the aeronautical appropriateness of the verb.
As an *Airman*, the hero is—to employ an "Anglo-Irish" simile from a poem
Yeats wrote two years later—"Like any rock-bred, sea-borne bird: / Sea-
borne or *balanced on the air*" (VP 397). In short, with "balanced" we are back
to fated yet delighted maneuverings "in the clouds"—a poise, as Thomas
Hardy once said, "actuated by the modicum of free will conjecturally possessed by organic life when the mighty necessitating forces—unconscious or
other—that have 'the balancings of the clouds', happen to be in equilibrium,
which may or may not be often."[8] Almost as rich as Hopkins's windhover-
verb, "buckle," the Airman's "balanced" makes his equipoise that of an
aviator as well as that of a thinker who claims to "know" his fate and to
have "brought all to mind." As we are told of the falcon-warrior Cromwell
in the ode in which Marvell is himself balanced on the historical wind: "So
much one man can do, / That does *both act and know*." If "sensations," by
themselves uncontrollable, are accompanied by "knowledge," wrote Keats,
we have "wings" to balance our flight; "our shoulders are fledged, and we
go thro' the same air and space without fear."[9]

II. "Reprisals"

Sensation and thought, action and contemplation, that fusion of passion and
reverie that constitutes Yeatsian "tragic joy": this is what we find, in a
variety of precarious balances, in the heroic tradition that is the Airman's

8. From Hardy's "Apology" to *Late Lyrics and Earlier* (1922), in *Collected Poems*, ed. James
Gibson, 557–58.

9. *Letters of John Keats*, ed. Hyder Rollins, 1:277. The poems referred to are Hopkins's "The
Windhover" and Marvell's "Horatian Ode on the Return of Cromwell from Ireland," whose
imagery of falcon and falconer Yeats imported into "The Second Coming."

ultimate context. But there are also *immediate* contexts. Two of them, the Gregory cluster in *The Wild Swans at Coole* and the prose Appreciation, have already been touched on in the discussion of "In Memory of Major Robert Gregory." The third, the unpublished poem "Reprisals," offers a revisionary context that may cast doubt on the Airman's "balance" of sensation and thought, action and contemplation.

"By reducing the entire war to an occasion for Robert Gregory's 'lonely impulse of delight,' Yeats brings his hero to a moment of perception that balances 'all' and that makes significant (because equivalent to each other) 'this life, this death.'" Though John Unterecker's synopsis (*Reader's Guide*, 134) is admirably succinct, it raises as many questions as it resolves. What are the implications of "reducing" the World War to a personal occasion? In rejecting Sean O'Casey's *The Silver Tassie* for the Abbey, Yeats told the playwright, "The mere greatness of the world war has thwarted you; it has refused to become mere background, and obtrudes itself upon the stage as so much dead wood that will not burn with the dramatic fire. . . . the whole history of the world must be reduced to wallpaper in front of which the characters must pose and speak" (L 741). One can take issue, as O'Casey did, with this even as dramatic theory; in "real life," should war be reduced to wallpaper before which the dramatic, combustible hero struts his stuff? Since nothing is got for nothing, at what human price is the heroic gesture purchased in the world we actually experience? Finally, just how "significant" is "this" particular life and death? Such questions, again literally beneath the Airman, are addressed, obliquely or directly, in the revisionist poem just mentioned.

"Reprisals" is a disillusioned acknowledgment of *mis*perception on the part of the survivors who applauded Gregory's heroic death, especially the survivor who put words in the dead man's mouth in the Airman monologue. Thus the recantation colors, if it does not invalidate, the solitary impulse that drove the Airman to *his* "moment of perception," one that may *not* have properly balanced quite "all." The poem—written in November 1920[10] and in the same *a b a b* tetrameters as the Airman monologue—begins with Yeats counting, not wild swans at Coole or "feathered balls of soot" at Thoor Ballylee (VP 424), but un-Byzantine mechanical birds:

Some nineteen German planes, they say,
You had brought down before you died.
We called it a good death.

The laconic judgment at once sums up matters, insinuates minute caveats ("they *say*," "we *called*"), and prepares us for reversal. It comes immediately, initiated in the same line:

10. The Berg Collection version, dated 23 November 1920, is a near-final draft.

We called it a good death. Today
Can ghost or man be satisfied?

The then/now contrast emphasized by the opening of the rhetorical question is followed by a twelve-line sentence that curves from one kind of death and one kind of war to another: from the solitary heroics of aerial combat—Gregory had been "particularly successful," Yeats wrote John Quinn, "in single combat with German planes" (L 945–46)—to the unheroic atrocities inflicted on tenants whose master was not there to protect them. The sentence begins with a weighing image recalling, and reductively glossing, the Airman's "balancing" of life and death in the poem written two and a half years earlier:

Although your last exciting year
Outweighed all other years, you said,
Though battle joy may be so dear
A memory, even to the dead,
It chases other thoughts away,
Yet rise from your Italian tomb,
Flit to Kiltartan cross and stay
Till certain second thoughts have come
Upon the cause you served, that we
Imagined such a fine affair:
Half-drunk or whole-mad soldiery
Are murdering your tenants there.

Though conceded, Homeric battle joy is diminished in advance by the opening "although," which prepares us for the second conjunction, "yet," calling for the dead man to rise from his foreign tomb and return home, not (as the audacious Spenserian verb "flit"[11] indicates) to rest in perpetual peace, but just long enough to become as disillusioned and embittered as those who never left. He is to stay "till," in the final prepositional reversal, he is sufficiently exposed to the brutalities inflicted by the soldiers for whose country he fought and died in the Great War to have (in Yeats's wry understatement) "certain second thoughts" about the "cause" he served, and which "we / Imagined such a fine affair"—a "fine affair," the colon insists, causally related to the present murder.

The mockery of "we" includes self-mockery, as it does in a greater poem written a year earlier, the closely related "Nineteen Hundred and Nine-

11. The verb appears twice within four lines in the "Mutabilitie Cantos": "Watry foules," like everything else in inconstant nature, "*flitting* still do flie, and still their places vary"; and the "Ayre," a "thin spirit," is felt to "*flit* still" (7.21–22). Yeats knew these Cantos well, and the cluster—birds, flying, air, spirit—would make the reminiscence especially appropriate to the ghost of an Airman.

teen"; Yeats is acknowledging that *he* was wrong in his "fine" thoughts. That "It was the dream itself enchanted me" (VP 630) might serve as epigraph for all the ostensibly hero-worshiping Gregory poems—especially, and bitterly, for "Reprisals," which goes on to particularize those murdered tenants. Yeats dwells on the aged and their reverence for the aristocratic tradition of Coole Park, on marriage, on the bringing of children into the world. All these organic, conservative, generational continuities of life are now—to employ the imagery of a directly relevant poem—ceremonies of innocence drowned in the blood-dimmed tide of mere anarchy:

Men that revere your father yet
Are shot at on the open plain.
Where may new-married women sit
And suckle children now? Armed men
May murder them in passing by
Nor law nor parliament take heed.

Yeats's language, emphasizing the revision of the earlier poem, establishes "Reprisals" as a palinode. The Airman's enforced "second thoughts" would reveal, too late, that he was wrong in his former airy assumptions about the inconsequence of the war to "Kiltartan's poor." One "likely end" of the world conflict, Allied victory, has led to this guerrilla war in Ireland, and another end, *his* (the fate he foresaw), has brought his Kiltartan tenants a double "loss," leaving them considerably un-"happier than before." The Airman's earlier aloofness from politicians and the crowd as well as his heedlessness of conventional institutions—"Nor law, nor duty bade me fight"—has also come back, less than three years later, to haunt his ghost. The mobs and contemporary politics he disdained now slouch to Kiltartan in the form of a collective rough beast—the Black and Tans, whose casual slaughters are greeted with impunity: "Nor law nor parliament take heed." The nursing mother—historically Ellen Quinn of Gort, murdered by the Tans in passing—is here a symbolic sister of Marie Antoinette, brutally assaulted (in the first draft of "The Second Coming") by the "mob" Yeats had read of in Burke's polemic against the French Revolution. Again, "there's no Burke to cry aloud, no Pitt," because Robert Gregory, the Anglo-Irish heir apparent of chivalric Burke, is not there to defend Ellen Quinn or his other tenants.[12] That he is not is essentially his own fault; the title suggests that, at a secondary level, these "reprisals" are a direct consequence of the impulse that drove him from Kiltartan Cross. Seven years earlier, in "To a Shade," the ghost of another betrayed Anglo-Irish hero was told to "gather the Glasnevin coverlet / About your head till the dust stops your ear." Yeats's final advice to the ghost of betrayed and culpable

12. See above, Chapter 4.

Gregory in "Reprisals" is even more bleak and disillusioned than that given Parnell:

Then close your ears with dust and lie
Among the other cheated dead.

Very much against his own wishes and only at the strong request of Lady Gregory, who understandably feared it would cause Robert's widow pain, Yeats did not publish "Reprisals." (The poem first appeared in print thirty years after Gregory was shot down—by an Italian pilot, in error, as it later turned out, though neither Yeats nor Lady Gregory was aware of that final irony.)[13] It was tolerable to have the World War (which detached Yeats dismissed as a "bloody frivolity" to which we should not attribute much "reality") depicted as meaningless aside from providing the hero with a theatrical backdrop for his lonely impulse, or even, as in the elegy, omitted altogether—though this may have been a contributing factor in Margaret Gregory's protest that Yeats had not said "enough about Robert's courage." It would have been *intolerable* for the dead man's pro-English widow to be told that the heroic gesture itself was meaningless—even irresponsible. And there would have been personal salt in the wound: the reminder of Gregory's statement to George Bernard Shaw to the effect that his "last exciting year / Outweighed all other years." As his obituary "Appreciation" reveals, Yeats was aware of the letter of condolence to Lady Gregory in which, having visited Robert at his flying station in France, Shaw quotes him as saying, "The six months he had been there had been the happiest of his life." (In the unpublished variant of lines 5–6 of "Reprisals": "'I had more *happiness* in a year / Than in all other years,' you said.") Shaw continued: "An amazing thing to say considering his exceptionally fortunate circumstances at home; but he evidently meant it. To a man with his power of standing up to danger—which must mean enjoying it—war must have intensified his life as nothing else could; he got a grip of it that he could not through art or love. I suppose that is what makes the soldier."[14]

As depicted in the Airman's "lonely impulse of delight" and in the "battle joy" of "Reprisals," Robert Gregory's martial rather than marital or artistic excitement reflects not only Gregory's character but also Yeats's accurate

---

13. First published in an Ulster poetry quarterly, *Rann*, in Autumn 1948, the poem is now available in VP (791). In an unpublished letter of 3 November 1920 acceding to Lady Gregory's request that the poem not be published, Yeats added: "I think the poem good . . . I hope your objection is entirely on public or local grounds and not on any personal dislike to it." Quoted by Elizabeth Cullingford, *Yeats, Ireland and Fascism*, 108. The Gregory children reported in 1981: "With sorrow we learned only recently that the Royal Flying Corps records state that he was shot down in error by an Italian pilot. Such are the ironies of war." Colin Smythe, ed., *Robert Gregory 1881–1918*, 5.

14. Lady Gregory quotes Shaw's letter in Chapter 29 (entitled "My Grief") of *Seventy Years*. She seems to have thought Yeats's repetition of Shaw's point to be the aspect of "Reprisals" *most* potentially disturbing to Margaret Gregory.

post-Nietzschean reading of the *Iliad*, where, "even in the midst of carnage, life is in full tide and beats forward with a wild gaiety." George Steiner's word to depict the tonality of the *Iliad*—gaiety—intentionally telescopes the direct lineage of heroic tragic joy: from Homer through Nietzsche to Yeats.[15] Placing the Airman poems in their full context requires synopsizing that aspect of Yeats's heroic tradition emphasizing pride, tragic "gaiety," aristocratic autonomy, and what Robert Tracy alliteratively synopsizes as "energy, ecstasy, elegy," before addressing the more complex tradition of the solitary Romantic questers, all those "lost adventurers" of whom the Irish Airman may or may not be a "peer."[16]

III. The Airman as Yeatsian Hero

The eagle's nest of the Yeatsian heroic ideal, one aspect of which is epitomized by the joyfully fatalistic gesture in the face of death, consists of twigs dropped layer upon layer. What he later found confirmed in Nietzsche and Homer, Yeats first encountered in Byron's *Manfred*, one of Nietzsche's own prototypes for the *Übermensch*, and in the tragic heroes of Shakespeare. Driven to his death by an impulse of delight, the Airman is, like "Hamlet and Lear, . . . gay, / Gaiety transfiguring all that dread" (VP 565). Robert Gregory's own mother, according to an approving Yeats, declared, "Tragedy must be a joy to the man who dies," and he himself repeatedly celebrated .Shakespeare's lonely and fatalistic heroes for their "ecstasy at the approach of death" (E&I 523, 255).

Yeats might have been thinking above all of the Hamlet of act 5, that "soul lingering on the storm-beaten threshold of sanctity," in whose presence Yeats felt "delight" (Au 522). Hamlet is associated with Gregory through the refrain of the elegy, and the Airman would seem to share what Nietzsche's heir Rilke (as quoted in an essay by William Rose) called the "true death" experienced by Hamlet. Yeats was close enough to his own death when he read Rose's essay to be stimulated to write (though not, as he claimed [L 913], in the margins of the essay) a first version of his own Airman-like heroic epitaph: "Cast a cold eye / On life, on death." Yeats was "annoyed" by certain points attributed to Rilke, but not by his notion of *Hamlet* as a progression of critical moments leading up to the hero's recognition of, and "final union" with, his own death as the existential

---

15. George Steiner's introduction to *Homer: Twentieth Century Views* is germane to this chapter since he repeatedly cites or alludes to Yeats. Earlier, in *The Death of Tragedy*, passages of which reappear in this introduction, Steiner had rightly remarked a direct line leading back from Yeats through Nietzsche to Homer, references to whom (though Steiner would have no reason to know this) crop up in Yeats only after his reading of Nietzsche.

16. Browning, "'Childe Roland to the Dark Tower Came,'" 1.195. Robert Tracy has explored Yeats's identification of Gregory with Cuchulain and Anglo-Irish impulsive heroism. The one flaw in his perceptive essay is that, like other commentators, he describes the Airman's direct action as "unthinking," in effect neglecting the speaker's bringing "all to mind." "Energy, Ecstasy, Elegy: Yeats and the Death of Robert Gregory," 45.

completion of life.[17] The theory was anticipated in the Airman's monologue and, twenty years later, dramatized in the great deathbed poem "The Man and the Echo," in which Yeats, like Hamlet and in Hamlet's words, rejects suicide: "There is no release in a bodkin." What is needful is that man's "intellect" grow "sure / That all's arranged in one clear view." Balancing "all," bringing "all to mind," finding "this life" in balance with "this death," the Airman, too, is in effect saying with Hamlet,

we defy augury. There is a special providence in the fall
of a sparrow. If it be now, 'tis not to come; if it be not
to come, it will be now; if it be not now, yet it will
come. The readiness is all.
   (5.2.208–11)

The magnificent nonchalance of that, so like the Airman's inclusiveness and "balance," appealed powerfully to Yeats, for whom Hamlet—especially in Henry Irving's famous strutting performance, to which his father took him when he was a boy—remained a lifelong image of plumed "pride" and "heroic self-possession" (UP 2: 507, VP 625, Au 47). The same was true of Coriolanus, whose speeches J. B. Yeats read to his impressionable son and to whom Yeats always responded "with delight, because he had a noble and beautiful pride." It was a pride purely personal, beyond nationalistic considerations—the creation of a poet "too full of life," Yeats wrote in 1903, to concern himself with externally imposed "duty," that "wisdom . . . Nietzsche has called an infirmary for bad poets."[18]

   Though the Anglo-Irish heroes who died for Romantic Ireland *were* nationalists, their "headlong" pride is also Nietzschean and Coriolanean:

The pride of people that were
Bound neither to Cause nor to State,
Neither to slaves that were spat on,
Nor to the tyrants that spat,
The people of Burke and of Grattan
That gave, though free to refuse—
   ("The Tower," III)

17. L 917. For Rilke, influenced by Nietzsche's Zarathustra on "Free Death" (1.21), each person is born with his death inside him "like the core in a beautiful apple" and needs to die that particular death. As Yeats rightly notes, Rilke found most disturbing mere "mass death" or any end that robbed the individual of this unique, conscious fulfillment. (Rilke, incidentally, practiced what he preached. Refusing drugs to alleviate the intense pain of the final stages of his fatal leukemia, Rilke experienced his own death to the full.)
18. UP 2:297, 302. In the first article ("The Freedom of the Theatre," 1902), Yeats adds that such is our "delight" that "for the moment" it seems of "little importance" that Coriolanus "sets all Rome by the ears and even joins himself to her enemies." The allusion in the second piece (a 1903 review of Lady Gregory's *Poets and Dreamers*) is to the "Famous Wise Ones" section of *Zarathustra*.

This negative catalog (neither . . . nor . . . neither . . . nor) recalls that of the aristocratic Anglo-Irish Airman, bound neither to Cause nor to State, committed solely to his own delighted impulse. That serenely joyful autonomy was, later Yeats decided, quintessentially Anglo-Irish—"the essence of volition," as Berkeley called it in his *Commonplace Book*. In the thirties, Yeats connected Berkeley's observation with a line from an Irish poem ("a joy within guides you") and with a line ("An aimless joy is a pure joy") from one of his own, in which Tom O'Roughly promises to dance a measure on his friend's grave, a poem placed immediately before Yeats's pastoral elegy for Robert Gregory in *The Wild Swans at Coole*. Yeats suspected that another analogous text was Berkeley's source: "Berkeley must have been familiar with Archbishop King's *De Origine Mali* which makes all joy depend 'upon the act of the agent himself, and his election'; not upon an external object. The greater the purity the greater the joy" (E&I 408).

"Caught up in the freedom of self-delight" (E&I 314), the Airman seems an agent guided by a joy within. Of the external objects he dismisses, we can say that, historically, "law" did not compel Gregory to fight since the Irish Conscription bill, which Yeats had joined Maud Gonne in vigorously opposing, never became law—and Gregory was, in any case, over the draft age. The detached dismissal of "public men," "cheering crowds," and, above all, "duty," taken together with the affirmation of the solitary impulse, amount to so many Yeatsian gestures in scorn of an audience. But long before those gestures were "Anglo-Irish," they were part of a heroic code Yeats's "boyish intellect approved," a code intellectually confirmed in his middle and late thirties.

The casually defiant, autonomous nobility he thrilled to in certain of Shakespeare's heroes and in Byron's Manfred, Yeats found again in his "counteractive to the spread of democratic vulgarity," Nietzsche, an aristocratic influence soon buttressed by that of Castiglione, to whose *Courtier* Yeats was introduced by Robert Gregory's mother. Their celebrations of the independent nobleman of magnificence and open-handed magnanimity at once reaffirmed and tempered the image of haughty Coriolanus and shaped the later myth that Yeats—extrapolating from Lady Gregory and, to a somewhat lesser extent, her son—projected outward to re-create an Anglo-Irish aristocracy that never was, on sea or land.

The lineage of nobility is clear in Yeats's 1903 annotations in the Nietzsche anthology lent him by Quinn. In the *Genealogy of Morals*, basing himself on the "stern" cardinal principle of "noble morality," Nietzsche declares that one has "only obligations to one's equals, that one may act toward beings of a lower rank . . . according to discretion or 'as the heart desires.'" Underlining "only obligations" and "to discretion," Yeats responded in the right-hand margin of the Thomas Common anthology: "Yes, but the necessity of giving remains. When the old heroes praise one another, they say 'he never refused any man.' Ni[e]tzsche means that the lower cannot create anything, cannot make obligations to the higher" (p.

111). As his comments here and elsewhere confirm, Yeats is clarifying Nietzsche, not rejecting him, as some have argued. He *knows* what "Nietzsche means": that the "noble type of man," like the *Übermensch*, "regards *himself* as the determiner of worth" (a passage marked by Yeats); has a "solitude within him . . . inaccessible to praise or blame, his own justice that is beyond appeal" (*The Will to Power* §962). Internally motivated, he has "no business but dispensing round / [His] magnanimities" (VP 404); but he gives out of his own superabundant power and sense of noblesse oblige, not because, any more than lofty Coriolanus or Manfred, he is obligated by a "duty" imposed from below. While the Airman, with disdain if not contempt for the masses, is such a "higher man," Lady Gregory is even closer to the ideal of those who "gave, though free to refuse." Yeats revered her for never having lost her "sense of feudal responsibility, not of duty as the word is generally understood, but of burdens laid upon her by her station and her character, a choice constantly renewed in solitude" (Au 395). After her son had volunteered, Augusta Gregory asked Yeats, "Why has Robert joined?" "I answered, 'I suppose he thought it his duty.' She said, 'It was his duty to stay here. He joined for the same reason I would have had I been a young man. He could not keep out of it.' She was right." Since Yeats was planning to read "An Irish Airman Foresees His Death" on the occasion for which he re-created this conversation (a 1937 BBC broadcast),[19] one wonders about his suggestion of "duty," specifically dismissed by his Nietzschean Airman as a factor. Lady Gregory was "right" about the motivation of her son, a "born soldier" as Yeats was planning to say in this same broadcast. Her own "choice . . . renewed in solitude" was to shoulder her "feudal responsibility"; her son's, or at least the Airman's, was solitude itself, the purely individualistic excitement of a lonely impulse.

Feudal responsibility is not all the Airman dismisses. He also shuffles off this mortal coil, dismissing not only his past life but even "the years to come" as " a waste of breath." The source in Ecclesiastes is reinforced by the actual circumstances of Robert Gregory, which were, as Shaw noted, "exceptionally fortunate." That Gregory was a happily married landed aristocrat, a man of varied mental and physical accomplishments (painter, scholar, horseman, boxer, aviator), would be so much grist for the mill of the Preacher, a master of *reductio ad absurdum* who relentlessly hammers home his central paradox: that which is full is empty. The most substantial, most "solid" existence, one filled with all a man could desire in terms of fortune, accomplishments, even knowledge, is all vanity, breath of breaths. "What then?" sings Plato's ghost in Yeats's own litany of accomplishment, the poem of a man who, while not attuned to this world only, adopts the stance not of a Saint but of a heroic Solitary, sharing the sad wisdom of Ecclesiastes that "there is no enduring remembrance" (2:16) even for those

---

19. 3 July 1937—not read, however, by Yeats, but by Margot Ruddock and V. C. Clinton-Baddeley; text quoted by Torchiana, *Yeats and Georgian Ireland*, 67–68.

who have brought their work to perfection. The hero of "Nineteen Hun-dred and Nineteen" is

He who can read the signs nor sink unmanned
Into the half-deceit of some intoxicant
From shallow wits; who knows no work can stand,
Whether health, wealth, or peace of mind were spent
On master-work of intellect or hand,
No honour leave its mighty monument.

Such a man "Has but one comfort left: all triumph would / But break upon his ghostly solitude." He resembles Browning's Childe Roland, his "hope / Dwindled into a ghost not fit to cope / With that obstreperous joy success would bring," a hero who no longer tries to rebuke "the spring / My heart made, finding failure in its scope." Coming out of the same mixed tradition, the self-destructive Solitary driven by a lonely impulse to his preordained death among the clouds finds himself more truly and more strange in a defeat that is paradoxically a triumph, but not one that would obstreperously break upon his ghostly solitude. It is all in the final gesture, one found first in Shakespeare and confirmed for Yeats by Nietzsche. The Airman's metonymy of breath in fact prefigures Yeats's own Nietzschean self-reminder in "Vacillation": "call those works extravagance of breath / That are not suited for such men as come / Proud, open-eyed and laughing to the tomb."

But Yeatsian tragic joy—which can become shrill, callous, melodrama-tic—seems "balanced" in the Airman. His exultation in the face of death, balanced as it is by that cold appraisal of life as an extravagance of breath, is, Yeats might say, "an ecstasy that is one-half the self-surrender of sorrow and one-half the last playing and mockery of the victorious sword before the defeated world" (E&I 254). That playing and mockery, a poetic form of Russian roulette, is at the heart of the Airman-mystique. The "world" may be defeated symbolically, but the reckless hero must die. Even the Irish Achilles, Yeats's own Cuchulain, representing "creative joy separated from fear" (L 913), eventually dies in battle, but in youth, before his "critical moment" has come, he is spared by the Red Man, who, instead of behead-ing him, declares:

I choose the laughing lip
That shall not turn from laughing, whatever rise or fall,
. . . .
The hand that loves to scatter; the life like a gambler's throw.
   (VPl 163)

Here are the wasteful virtues that earn the sun; the acting out of the Nietz-schean imperatives to "laugh" in the face of death, to "live dangerously!"

and "set your sails for shipwreck"; the Castiglionian *sprezzatura* and spend-thrift gesture Yeats associated with his Anglo-Irish heroes who—anticipating the "balancing" if not the solipsism of the Airman—"weighed so lightly what they gave" ("September 1913").[20]

Trotted out often enough, this can become lightweight stuff; what helps maintain the grave distinction of the Airman is that, guided by Nietzsche, Yeats found this heroic nonchalance, even indifference, in Homer as well. Achilles, one of the Airman's as well as Cuchulain's ancestors, knows that he, too, shall "meet" his "fate"—sometime, "somewhere":

> even I have also my death and my strong destiny,
> And there shall be a dawn or an afternoon or a noontime
> When some man in the fighting will take the life from me also.

He is speaking to Lycaon, whom he is about to kill and whom he has just lectured on the proper heroic attitude of self-possession, reticence, and cold-eyed composure in face of the inevitable: "So, friend, you die also. Why all this clamour about it?" (*Iliad* 21.110–12, 106).

He would not have had to lecture the Airman, a reticent aristocrat of superior and detached viewpoint exhibiting the Yeatsian "self-possession" (the equivalent of "style" in art) that arises "out of a deliberate shaping of all things, and from never being swept away, whatever the emotion, into confusion or dullness" (E&I 253). The Airman's monologue ends on a note of deliberate, inhuman calm—the tone of fated Achilles rather than of clamorous Lycaon or his brother Hector. Hector's very human "problem" is that he is *not* detached. Though both heroes are destined to die in a war that they, like the Irish Airman, realize is intrinsically meaningless, the Trojan champion is fighting for something beyond himself—for the family and city he loves and defends. Self-absorbed Achilles fights for no cause other than to exact personal vengeance on the killer of his friend; the man who confronts Lycaon and Hector now that Patroclos is dead is truly a solitary—as is the lonely Airman, who fights unmotivated by anything but his own impulse of delight.

In *The Wild Swans at Coole*, "Achilles" is one of those "who have lived in joy and laughed into the face of death" (VP 366). The laughter, as always in Yeats, is demonstrably Nietzschean ("he who climbs the highest mountains," says Zarathustra, "laughs at all tragic plays and tragic seriousness"), but the "tragic joy" is authentically that of Homer. The adjective bows before, but is not obliterated by, the noun: the vision *is* tragic. "The poet of the *Iliad*," as George Steiner has finely said, "looks on life with those blank, unswerving eyes which stare out of the helmet slits on early Greek vases. His vision is terrifying in its sobriety, cold as the winter sun." Such coldness

---

20. An early but still valuable study of Yeatsian *sprezzatura* is Arnold Stein's "Yeats: A Study in Recklessness." See also Corinna Salvadori, *Yeats and Castiglione: Poet and Courtier*.

is an essential ingredient of the Airman's final vision. Yeats's own attraction to "cold light and tumbling clouds," to "the cold and rook-delighting heaven / That seemed as though ice burned and was but the more ice," informs not only the lonely impulse of delight driving the Airman to his tumult in the clouds but also his "cold and passionate" contemplation, an excited reverie at once icily measured and burningly reckless. The same paradoxical mixture of cold lucidity and wild gaiety is to be found throughout the *Iliad*. For as Steiner also points out—again implicitly affirming the tragic lineage running directly from Homer through Nietzsche to Yeats—the eyes staring out of the helmet slits also burn with Yeatsian tragic joy, the all-appraising Zarathustrian vision of the Chinese sages who, in what may be Yeats's most Nietzschean poem, stare down on "all the tragic scene" with "ancient glittering eyes" that are "gay."[21]

The dread-transfiguring gaiety of "Lapis Lazuli" (which takes its opening "hysterical women" from Nietzsche as well) marks the pinnacle of Yeats's debt to the Homer he read in the light of the curious astringent joy of Nietzsche—an accurate guide since joy in the ineradicable energy of life confronting death is quintessentially Homeric. "Pure energy of being pervades the *Iliad* like the surge of the wine-dark sea," wrote Steiner, "and Homer rejoices in it."

> Homer had not sung
> Had he not found it certain beyond dreams
> That out of life's own self-delight had sprung
> The abounding glittering jet.
>   (VP 417)

So Yeats declared in "Ancestral Houses"—despite this fierce Homeric-Nietzschean affirmation of life's own self-delight, an elegiac dirge sung in 1922 over the Anglo-Irish aristocratic tradition symbolized by Coole Park, the ancestral house of Gregory: the property, since descent was through the male line, not of Augusta but of Robert, who had abandoned the estate to follow *his* impulse of self-delight. "Ancestral Houses" is the opening poem in Yeats's embittered sequence *Meditations in Time of Civil War*. The civil war was that internecine struggle preceded by the Anglo-Irish war, indelibly marked by the murderous Black and Tan reprisals that drove Yeats to address his bitter poem to Gregory's ghost. As one of the "cheated dead," and a knight of the air in contrast to the cowardly butchers now murdering his defenseless tenants, Gregory is still to be admired. But while the poem "brings the entire heroic code into question, points out its disastrous reper-

---

21. Steiner, *Homer*, alludes to "The Gyres" and "Lapis Lazuli." My own allusions in this paragraph are to Yeats's "The Cold Heaven" and "The Fisherman." Zarathustra's mountain laughter ("On Reading and Writing," 1.7) is repeated as the epigraph to part 3 of *Thus Spoke Zarathustra*.

cussions, and still enhances Gregory's stature," it might be argued that "Reprisals," in which "Gregory has been disinterred only to be more devastatingly buried,"[22] at least hints at a revision of the judgment the speaker was permitted to pass upon himself in the Airman soliloquy.

IV. Ulysses Redivivus

Any final judgment passed upon the Airman must be pronounced in the context provided by his closest ancestors, the Romantic solitaries who share his glory and his solipsism. The most obvious—and most anthologized, if not the most crucial—is Tennyson's Ulysses, hero of a dramatic monologue that raises the same critical question raised by the Airman poems and the Gregory elegy: to what extent is the overt celebration of the hero undermined by reservations, covert or (at least in Tennyson's case) unconscious? The Gregory poems and "Ulysses" share a similar genesis, each having been written in a consciously literary heroic tradition and in response to the death of a gifted young man close to the author. While Robert Gregory hardly occupied the position in his elegist's life that Arthur Hallam did in Tennyson's, Yeats, writing in the days following the news of Gregory's death, may have felt something of Tennyson's bleak "sense of loss and that all had gone by, but that still life must be fought out to the end." That is close to the tonality of the Gregory elegy, the interesting reversal being that the survivor's "fight" occurs in the "secret" part of the elegy, while in Tennyson's overtly bracing poem the undersong is the elegiac "sense of loss." There is a chiastic relationship, too, with the Airman poem. In "Ulysses," a young man masks his youth in a dramatic monologue of resolute and heroic old age; in "An Irish Airman," an older poet masks his age in a monologue of resolute and heroic youth. Both poems seem talismans against death and despair, with the Airman poem, like the equivocally dauntless and elegiac "Ulysses," a dramatized lyric expressing the poet's own need to go on, even in the face of life envisioned as a waste of breath.

The poet who created the epic hero in the first place "knows and proclaims," as Steiner says, "that there is that in man which loves war, which is less afraid of the terrors of combat than of the long boredom of the hearth." Driven to tumult by an impulse of "delight," the Airman thinks life without "battle joy" so much wasted breath. Tennyson's aging and "idle" Ulysses—nostalgic for the glorious days when he drank "delight of battle with my peers / Far on the ringing plains of windy Troy," and no man to burn damp fagots—opens his monologue about to leave his "still hearth" in quest of death as the last adventure. Like the Airman, he is an isolated quester who, cut off from family and countrymen (they "know not me"), is driven by an impulse urging him toward death, life without action being similarly reduced to a waste of breath:

22. The first phrase is from Harris (Coole Park and Ballylee, 118), the second from Sacks (English Elegy, 301).

How dull it is to pause, to make an end,
To rust unburnished, not to shine in use!
As though to breathe were life.

Noting the "heartfelt scorn" of Ulysses' dismissal of "mere survival,"
Harold Bloom has argued that Ulysses' own heroic rhetoric "defends
against meaningless or mere repetition, against the reduction of life to the
metonymy of breath." Such a defense is needed; as Bloom himself had
observed a year earlier: "It is not the worst part of us, necessarily, that
wants to answer back: 'To breathe is also to live.' But we are not Sublime
questers."[23] Of course, as Bloom knows, the remorseless egocentricity of
Romantic questers tends to receive internal criticism. The Wanderer in the
parent quest-text, Wordsworth's *Excursion*, explicitly warns against the
limitless desires of the Solitary, and Shelley's Wordsworthian Narrator in
Alastor, the most influential of quest-poems, implicitly disciplines and qualifies the absolutist yearnings of the Visionary. What those poets do consciously, Tennyson does subconsciously—at least he does not seem fully
aware of what has seemed evident to much subsequent criticism: the human
cost of his hero's setting out on a harebrained final quest with "no clearly
foreseen objective," unconstrained by "any conventional scruples of duty
either to his family or to the people he rules," his engagement in a selfish
and willful line of conduct that "cannot be justified in any but the most
individualistic terms."[24]

"As though to breathe were life" epitomizes Ulysses' contempt for all
those who, in a related Yeatsian phrase, "breathe on the world with timid
breath" (VP 266)—in Ulysses' case, his "aged wife" tending a "still hearth"
and his prudent son, who will subdue a "savage race" to "the useful and the
good." Telemachus "works his work, I mine." That is the condescending
judgment of the relentless quester whose own purpose is to "sail beyond the
sunset, and the baths / Of all the western stars, until I die." Such is the
purpose of the Airman, who, with no clearly foreseen object but his own
death, sails off into the wild blue yonder, leaving behind—if for the moment we crudely equate the Irish Airman with Robert Gregory—mother,
wife, children, and a savage race of tenants whom he had attempted in vain
to anglicize by teaching them cricket.[25]

But of course we ought *not* to crudely equate Airman and model. "An
Irish Airman Foresees His Death" remains, intrinsically, a notably "balanced" performance—as is "Ulysses." The internal balance of Tennyson's
monologue—heroic and elegiac, its hero's voice at once vigorous and sepul-
chral, the hero himself celebrated and yet open to criticism—is not so much
attributable to its personal genesis as to its divided literary sources. They

23. Bloom, *Poetry and Repression*, 158, and *A Map of Misreading*, 157.
24. E. D. H. Johnson, *The Alien Vision of Victorian Poetry*, 41.
25. For the cricket lessons, see Torchiana, *Yeats and Georgian Ireland*, 66.

include Homer and, more directly, ambivalent Dante, for whom the Greek enemy of Rome's Trojan founder is noble but a false counselor. The native heritage of Tennyson's Ulysses can be traced, however, to the Romantic questers: to Shelley's Visionary, a noble soul oblivious to human sympathy; to Manfred, with whom Ulysses shares restlessness (his "I cannot rest" is lifted from *Manfred*) and a penchant for defiant language borrowed from Milton's Satan; and to Keats's Endymion, another ruler who turns from societal duties to fulfill a celestial vision. The Airman—who abandons countrymen identified in "Reprisals" as "your tenants," now being murdered—would seem to be of this egocentric company. Of his monologue one might ask, as Auden did of Tennyson's, "What is [it] but a covert . . . refusal to be a responsible and useful person and a glorification of the heroical dandy?"[26]

While we may detect in the Gregory cluster covert hints of Auden's attitude, his is the judgment of a sophisticated modernist, not of the modern poet, equally sophisticated in his own way, who was most enthralled by the heroic code of this Ulysses and his Romantic forebears. However "balanced" the monologues of Airman and Ulysses, however balanced, *as* poems, *The Excursion* and *Alastor*, what matters to the quest theme is, precisely, the exclusively individualistic, limitless drive of their solitaries. Their faults are obvious. Under its enchanting, heroic rhetoric, Tennyson's poem tells of a man abandoning his faithful wife, his conscientious son "centered in the sphere / Of common duties," and his own responsibilities to the people under his rule. As he intentionally or unintentionally reveals himself in his heroic but self-centered and indifferent monologue, Yeats's Airman seems another of Auden's escapist heroical dandies, a charge that might be substantiated by noting that his heroic impulse may be tacitly qualified by the ambiguities of Yeats's prose Appreciation of Gregory and by "Reprisals." Whether the Airman in "real life," surrendering to "mere excitement" and "escape," failed in what his mother called his "duty to stay here" or in what Yeats praised as her own Nietzschean or Castiglionian "sense of feudal responsibility," is an issue as covert in the Gregory poems as it is overt, for us if not for Tennyson, in "Ulysses." But the issue, however valid, is not quintessential; though qualified, admiration of the heroes remains unmistakable.

This is even truer of Yeats's than of Tennyson's monologue. Again, it is a question of tone. Tennyson gives his hero a semi-mystical Romantic motivation: to follow the light of the untraveled world that "gleams" through the arch of experience, its margin fading "for ever and for ever when I move." But this (its three lines take, as Matthew Arnold said, longer than a whole book of the *Iliad*)[27] is far from the "impulse" of "delight" that "drove" the Airman to his "tumult" in the clouds. The sharp vigor and

26. Auden's remark is cited by J. B. Steane, *Tennyson*, 53–54.
27. Arnold, *On Translating Homer* (1861), iii.

passionate intensity of the Airman's language have, even with the waste-of-breath lines, a Homeric-Nietzschean *brio* quite alien to the Tennysonian life-weariness that, conflicting with the idiom of the heroic quest, makes "Ulysses" the great and complex poem it is. "Ulysses" is finally less an adventure than a disguised elegy for Hallam and for the elegist himself. The speaker is Greek in his laconic conviction that "death closes all" but nebulously Tennysonian in his belief that "*Something* ere the end, / *Some* work of noble note, *may* yet be done"—a "something," "some," and "may" considerably cloudier than the Airman's "somewhere," referring to the place where he *knows* he shall meet his fate.

But, really, Ulysses knows too—just as Shelley's Visionary does when he embarks in his boat. What is certain for all of them, Airman included, is that the ship to be boarded is the Ship of Death. "The vessel puffs her sail," Ulysses notes, ready to embark: "There *gloom* the *dark* broad seas." The boat boarded by Shelley's Visionary in the passage that impressed itself permanently on Yeats's imagination takes him to a narrow vale filled with "great trees" and characterized by the same gloomy darkness: "his sepulchre. More dark / And dark the shades accumulate . . . , evening gloom / Now deepening the dark shades" (*Alastor*, 430–31, 485–86). Yeats's "The Tower"—a poem resembling "Ulysses" in its merging of elegy and assertion, of an old man's memory and a death of his own making—ends by echoing *Alastor* as well. A "swan" fixes his eye upon a "fading gleam," while bodily "decreptitude" and that worse evil, "the death of friends," gradually

Seem but the clouds of the sky
When the horizon fades;
Or a bird's sleepy cry
Among the deepening shades.
  (VP 416)

Coming at the end of the passage on Anglo-Irish heroes who gave though free to refuse, the "clouds" recall those among which Robert Gregory had met his death; the "fading gleam" and fading "horizon" echo Ulysses' arch of experience through which "*Gleams* that untravelled world, whose *margin fades.*" Here as elsewhere (the Coole Park poems, "Nineteen Hundred and Nineteen," the pastoral elegy for Gregory), the swan is Shelleyan, as are the final "deepening shades," as the gloom of Yeats's own evening descends, "deepening the dark shades" that accumulated around Shelley's Visionary at the end of the quest the youthful Yeats had dreamed of emulating and which, in effect, his relatively youthful Airman *did* emulate, urged by an "impulse" to "meet lone death."

V. "Alastor" *Redivivus*

I am quoting *Alastor*, from the climax of the passage that most haunted Yeats in the work that perhaps more than any other shaped his poetry and thought.[28] Together with its preface, *Alastor*—and this passage in particular—illuminates the whole Gregory cluster. "The Wild Swans at Coole," written in 1917 but retrospectively part of the cluster, is overtly indebted to the Visionary's description of the swan; and the central iconic stanza of the Gregory elegy, which ostensibly asserts that life as a brief exciting flare is preferable to a tedious longevity—"Some burn damp faggots, others may consume / The entire combustible world in one small room / As though dried straw"—recalls *Alastor*, both in the Shelleyan image of the self-consuming flame and in the contrast between two possible modes of living and dying.

According to Shelley's preface to *Alastor*, a youth of adventurous genius is led forth by an imagination "inflamed and purified." But since it leads him to a "self-centered seclusion . . . avenged by the furies of an irresistible passion pursuing him to speedy ruin," the inflamed imagination is also "that Power which strikes the luminaries of this world with sudden darkness and extinction":

> the good die first,
> And those whose hearts are dry as summer dust
> Burn to the socket!

This, the epigraph to *Alastor*, is already ironically Wordsworthian since Shelley is applying to the aging turncoat his own words—from lines 500–502 of the first book of *The Excursion*, *Alastor*'s main source. It becomes doubly ironic when applied to the "flare"-stanza of the Gregory elegy. For the burner of damp fagots there is Yeats himself, encountered in the elegy's opening stanza tending an unpromising "fire of turf in th'ancient tower," his heart burning slowly and coldly to the socket rather than going up, in incendiary speedy ruin, in the self-consuming flare of the youthful hero.

In terms of Shelley's preface, the burner of damp fagots would be one of those "meaner spirits" whom imagination "dooms to a slow and poisonous decay," to a destiny "abject and inglorious." At the deepest level, Yeats was aware that he was no more bereft of imaginative power than Robert Gregory was a Shelleyan luminary; nevertheless, in what is both a dramatic pose and an expression of honest fear, it is as an abject and inglorious Wordsworthian survivor, withering into a premature dotage, that Yeats presents himself in the elegy and its surrounding lyrics. In the poem immediately following "An Irish Airman," Yeats employs a Greek mythological reference allying him both with Wordsworth's "old Triton" and with that most abject of "posthumous" survivors, Keats's "gray-haired Saturn, quiet as a stone" in a fallen pastoral where "a stream went voiceless by": immobile Yeats is left to "grow old among dreams, / A weather-worn, marble triton

28. For the influence of *Alastor* on Yeats, see Bloom, *Yeats*, 10–13; Bornstein, *Yeats and Shelley*, 29–66; and Adele M. Dalsimer, "My Chief of Men: Yeats's Juvenilia and Shelley's *Alastor*." George Mills Harper, who has transcribed Yeats's Automatic Script, informs me that "one of the controls in an unpublished notebook of *Vision* materials is named Alastor."

/ Among the streams" of the estate of Robert Gregory.[29] Meanwhile, the slain hero, self-consumed in "burning youth," has gone up in the exciting flare, having—as Yeats said (E&I 239) of Synge's *Deirdre*, a play for which Gregory designed and painted the stage sets—"ascended into that tragic ecstasy which is the best that art—perhaps that life—can give" (with the "perhaps" being a characteristic and important caveat).

For readers of the 1919 edition of *The Wild Swans at Coole*, the birdlike aviator would also seem to have ascended into the heavens with the swans that, in the titular poem preceding the Gregory elegy, "suddenly mount" before poor pedestrian Yeats, shuffling among the littering leaves, has completed his count—a numbering that is really the unmistakably Wordsworthian arithmetic of the aging process:

> The nineteenth autumn has come upon me
> Since I first made my count;
> . . . .
> All's changed since I, hearing at twilight,
> The first time on this shore,
> The bell-beat of their wings above my head,
> Trod with a lighter tread.

This echoes and bleakly reverses the Wordsworth who, having returned to the Wye valley after "five summers, with the length / Of five long winters," retains hope for the future,

> Though *changed*, no doubt, from what I was *when first*
> I came among these hills, when like a roe
> *I bounded* o'er the mountains, by the sides
> Of the deep rivers, and the lonely streams.
>   (lines 66–69)

Yeats's only hope for the future, one recalling the conclusion of "Tintern Abbey" and the generous final passing of the baton of joy in Coleridge's Dejection Ode, is that the eyes of *others* will be delighted when the swans have flown from him.[30]

But the deepest source of "The Wild Swans at Coole" remains *Alastor*, both in the obvious echoing of the Visionary's description of the swan and in Yeats's tacit acknowledgment that of the two options posed by Shelley's epigraph he was withering into the second, his sore heart dry as dust and slowly burning to the socket. Yet that too is ultimately Wordsworthian, given the source of the epigraph. Indeed, when in 1915 Yeats accomplished his self-assigned task of reading *The Excursion*, he must have felt a shock of

---

29. Keats, *Hyperion* 1.4, 11. Wordsworth, the sonnet "The world is too much with us."
30. "Dejection: An Ode," the final line; "Tintern Abbey," lines 66–69.

recognition encountering Wordsworth's Solitary: the parent, he would have belatedly discovered, of the Romantic solitaries who most haunted his youthful imagination. Paramount among these was the lonely quester of *Alastor*, above all in the critical passage in which he prepares to embark on his journey to death. That passage is the deep source of "An Irish Airman Foresees His Death"—appropriately, since the Airman is best understood as a minor figure in the Romantic quest tradition, the heir, specifically, of the Visionary of *Alastor*, preceded by Wordsworth's Solitary and followed by Byron's Manfred and Promethean Byron himself, as well as by such Victorian questers as Tennyson's Ulysses and Browning's Childe Roland.

As a boy Yeats played "at being a sage, a magician or a poet. I had many idols, and as I climbed along the narrow ledge I was now Manfred on his glacier, and now Prince Athanase with his solitary lamp, but I soon chose Alastor for my chief of men" (Au 64). Wanting, like Byron at the outset of *Don Juan*, a poetic hero based on an actual figure, Yeats chose Wilde, then Parnell, then Robert Gregory, "Our Sidney and our perfect man," for his Anglo-Irish chief of men (he would later settle on Swift). It is not surprising that Gregory and Shelley's Visionary coincide, a relationship reflected in the volumes in which they are featured players.

As Yeats accurately noted, Shelley's "transformation," the "discovery of his true self . . . came at the moment when he first created a passionate image which made him forgetful of himself," passing from "the litigious rhetoric of *Queen Mab* to the lonely reveries of *Alastor*" (V-B 67). In the *Alastor* volume, as in the Airman's soliloquy and the other Gregory poems in *The Wild Swans at Coole*, we are given something far indeed from *Queen Mab*: a stark image of man as solitary and alienated (a "lonely and sea-girt isle") and, as E. R. Wasserman adds, the thematic "dream of escape from chance and the world's vicissitudes," the "possibility that there is meaning in death rather than in the world of life."[31] In pursuit of a more-than-mortal ideal, the hero of *Alastor* was, for Yeats, *facile princeps* among the Romantic questers, solitaries driven by a self-destructive desire that, by virtue of its very infinitude, can have no attainable object in the natural world. They are, nevertheless, compelled to seek—necessarily, afar. Shelley's Visionary early "left / His cold fireside and alienated home" (75–76), and, after his dream-vision, spends the rest of his short life pursuing his epipsychic Maiden. Byron's incestuous variation is Astarte, the epipsyche of solitary Manfred, who pursues her even beyond the grave. As we have seen, Tennyson's Ulysses is an alien from his "still hearth" and among his own people; like Browning's Childe Roland, who is too alienated to have a home, he seeks a knowledge indistinguishable from death. The same fate is sought by the Airman, who has left Kiltartan Cross far behind and beneath him. In the case of all these problematic heroes, the very nature of their quest accelerates their departure not only from home but also from this world.

31. Wasserman, *Shelley: A Critical Reading*, 6, 5.

As a boy, Yeats cherished "Alastor" (by which he, like many others, always meant both the poem and its nameless hero) as one of the "great symbols of passion and of mood."[32] Ebremar, a character in *Mosada*—one of Yeats's early, Spenserian-Shelleyan quest dramas—imagines himself sailing "afar" in a "shallop" with his young Moorish love (VP 702), echoing the passage in which Shelley's Visionary, embarking in a "shallop," fuses his ecstatic love-quest with a longing for death, a fusion for which Yeats praised his precursor (E&I 57) and which dominates his own early quest poems: the dramas *The Seeker*, *The Island of Statues*, *Mosada*, the narrative *Wanderings of Oisin*, *The Shadowy Waters*, and that beautiful miniaturization of *Alastor*, "The Song of Wandering Aengus." He himself yearned to emulate the Shelleyan Visionary in nothing so much as "maybe at last to disappear from everybody's sight as he disappeared drifting in a boat" (Au 64; E&I 80). In the Airman poem, Eros has been displaced by Thanatos—death, or the flirting with it as both fate and mate, providing the life-intensifying ecstasy Robert Gregory could not find, as Shaw said, "through art or love." The Airman disappears in a plane rather than a shallop, but he was urged to embark by an "impulse," as was Shelley's hero.

The passage of *Alastor* (lines 272–307) that haunted Yeats early and late begins and ends with this daemonic urge. Echoing Milton, whose Christ is led into the wilderness "by some strong motion" (*Paradise Regained* 1.290), Shelley's Narrator tells us that a "strong impulse urged" the Visionary to the "lone" seashore. As he approaches, a swan rises, "and with strong wings / Scaling the upward sky, bent its bright course / High over the immeasurable main." Pursuing its flight with a longing eye, the alienated wanderer contrasts his lot to that of the swan, who has a "home / Where thy sweet mate will twine her downy neck / With thine, and welcome thy return with eyes / Bright in the lustre of their own fond joy." Precisely a century later, these wild swans reappear, "Unwearied still, lover by lover," paddling in the cold but "companionable" streams or "climb[ing] the air" over the Gregory estate at Coole. Unlike autumnal Yeats, whose "heart is sore" and whose "tread" is made heavier from having looked on those brilliant creatures, "Their hearts have not grown old; / Passion or conquest, wander where they will, / Attend upon them still" (VP 323).

At first this is reminiscent less of Shelley or of Wordsworth than of Keats, whose empathetic "heart aches" at the "happiness" of the Nightingale, another immortal bird "not born for death," whom no hungry "generations tread . . . down" as they do the poet. But the Shelleyan Visionary is also sore at heart, and for similar reasons. Though of vaster spirit and even more attuned to beauty than the swan, he is left to "linger" here, "wasting these

---

32. "Nationalism and Literature," cited by Bornstein (*Yeats and Shelley*, 30). Yeats was not alone in conflating the *daemon*, or *alastor*, with the nameless Visionary, "the Poet." According to Shelley's friend Thomas Love Peacock, "many have supposed Alastor to be the name of the hero." It was Peacock who "proposed the title, referring to the Greek Ἀλάστωρ, an evil spirit of solitude." Peacock, *Memoirs of Shelley*, 55–56.

surpassing powers," feeling, as Keats did, the allurement of death as the possible "dark gate" (*Alastor*, 211) to union with his vision. At this critical point his wandering gaze catches that boat Yeats dreamed of sailing off in, "a little shallop floating near the shore." Shelley's Visionary feels a "restless impulse" resembling the "rouzing motions" felt by Milton's Samson when, like the Airman, he experiences "presage in the mind" that "This day will be remarkable in my life / By some great act or of my days the last."[33] The climactic lines in *Alastor*—"A restless impulse urged him to embark / And meet lone death on the drear ocean's waste"—register, *mutatis mutandis*, in the Irish Airman's crucial affirmation.

Shelley's precise language, though rearranged, is still recognizable. The epithet "lone" has been transferred from "death" to "impulse," to produce the "lonely impulse" that is at once the glory and the vulnerable principle of Yeats's poem. Nine lines later, the Shelleyan Visionary "took his *lonely seat*" in the boat, reflecting Shelley's own principal source, book 4 of *The Excursion*:

> To friendship let him turn
> For succour; but perhaps he *sits alone*
> On stormy waters, tossed in a *little boat*
> That holds but him, and can contain no more!
> (4.1085–88)

These proudly impatient yet anguished lines of the Solitary provided the crucial image of *Alastor* and affected as well another passage of Shelley that fascinated Yeats, who also played at being "Prince Athanase with his solitary lamp." Wed to "Wisdom," Prince Athanase "*sate / Apart from men*, as in a *lonely* tower, / Pitying the *tumult* of their dark estate."[34] The Airman, whose "lonely" impulse drives him apart from men, does not pity their dark estate. Instead, perhaps indulging what Shelley's Cythna condemned as "the dark idolatry of self," the Airman is himself plunged into his solitary but fatal "*tumult* in the clouds."

But we are not finished with the two lines from *Alastor*. Shelley's verb "meet" reappears in the Airman's opening line: "I know that I shall meet my fate." What Shelley's Visionary is to "meet" is identical to the Airman's fate: "lone death," a word Yeats saves for last. Shelley's own last word, "waste," is shifted to the Airman's final evaluation of his past and future life—which, declared a "waste" of breath, resembles the life of the Visionary, that "weary waste of hours" burdened and blasted by "the woe / That

33. *Samson Agonistes*, 1381–83, 1387–89.
34. These lines from Shelley's "Prince Athanase" are of course echoed in Robartes's description of Yeats choosing Thoor Ballylee to live in because "of the candlelight / From the far tower where Milton's Platonist / Sat late, or Shelley's visionary prince" (VP 373; cf. E&I 522). Cythna, quoted two sentences later in this paragraph, is, to quote Yeats, "the girl in *The Revolt of Islam*" (Au 64).

wasted him" (245, 268–69). The indispensable word, "impulse," is retained, with Shelley's "urged" replaced by "drove," perhaps echoing the
verb in Shelley's definitive and self-prophetic version of his Visionary's
"little boat" mysteriously "driven" (363): "my spirit's bark is driven / Far
from the shore, far from the trembling throng / Whose sails were never to
the tempest given."[35]

From the Shelleyan perspective, Yeats's Airman gives himself to the
tumult, driven by a solitary impulse far from the throng of "public" men
and cheering "crowds." Though Shelley's Visionary seeks with "wan eyes"
for "the joy, the exultation" that "have fled," he too "eagerly pursues" with
"eager soul" his own vision, urged on, not by what the Wordsworthian
Narrator calls the "purest ministers" of Nature (which the Visionary finds
inadequate and from which he is alienated), but by that "strong impulse" of
"solitude" that, like Coleridge's midnight frost, "performed its [own] min-
istry" (196–205, 311, 414–17, 698). This is the daemonic urge allied to the
avenging "Spirit of Solitude," the *alastor* that provided Shelley (thanks to
Peacock) with his title. More drawn than his precursor to the ghostly solitude of the *antithetical* quest, Yeats, who creatively confused Visionary and
daemon, gives us, in his Irish Airman, an "Alastor" *redivivus*.

Still, tension remains. In *Alastor*, sharply discriminated perspectives are
overtly dramatized by having the elegiac biography of the hero narrated by
a speaker with his own fictive identity, with Visionary and Narrator representing Shelley's own "polarized impulses" (Wasserman, *Shelley*, 11).
Yeats's polarized impulses, *almost* muted in the Airman poem, are implicit
in the questions we are compelled to pose: Is the Airman motivated by
aspiration or nihilism, delight or despair? Is he self-activating or passively
determined—a man in ardent pursuit of his vision, or driven by it to a fated
death? Either/Or must yield, as in *Alastor*, to Both/And. Shelley's Visionary is led to death by an "insatiate hope" that, wakened by "doubt," "stung
/ His brain even like despair" (220–22)! No less than *Alastor*, or the Gregory
elegy for that matter, the Airman poem is delicately "balanced" on the
tension between opposing perspectives. Wasserman has in fact described
Alastor's dialectic or balancing dramaturgy as "Yeatsian."

> Poet-Narrator and Poet-Visionary discipline each other like the Yeatsian self and
> anti-self to prevent deception and to load each position with risks. For if the Vision-
> ary represents Shelley's yearning for the ideal Self, the Narrator is the contrary,
> mundane half of the skeptical Shelleyan self. . . . whatever is advanced in the poem is
> also withdrawn or gravely qualified.
> (*Shelley*, 34)

It would be more accurate, historically, to call the Yeatsian dialectic
"Shelleyan" since Yeats's concepts of self and anti-self, *primary* and *antitheti-*

---

35. "Adonais," lines 488–90.

cal, objective and subjective, though sharpened and intensified by the reading of Nietzsche, surely have their ultimate origin in the preface to *Alastor* and in *Alastor* itself, the work that virtually initiated Yeats's canon—as it had (with *Pauline*) Browning's. In turn, Shelley's own dialectical self-division derives from Wordsworth's self-admonition, put in the mouth of *The Excursion*'s "venerable Sage," the Wanderer, who, "Nor rapt, nor craving, but in settled peace," warns the *antithetical* Solitary about an "intense / And over-constant yearning . . . to realize the vision," "passion" leading to "ecstasy" based on "limitless desires": "There—there lies / The excess, by which the balance is destroyed" (*The Excursion*, book 4, "Despondency Corrected," 239, 174–85).

For Yeats, Wordsworth's Wanderer was the traditional "sage": "when I say the sage I think of something Asiatic, and of something that belongs to modern Europe—the pedlar in *The Excursion*." When, conversely, "I speak of the romantic movement I think more of Manfred, more of Shelley's Prometheus . . . than of . . . the fakir-like pedlar in *The Excursion*" (Ex 295, E&I 405). But while Yeats temperamentally joins Byron and Shelley in rejecting the *primary* wisdom of the Wordsworthian sage, he remains, supposedly like his Airman, aware of what the Wanderer calls an excess-preventing "balance." The soul is alternately turned, according to the Day/Night diagram in the Nietzsche anthology, toward either the quest for "knowledge" or the affirmation of "life." "All men with subjective natures," Yeats wrote shortly before his own death, "move towards a possible ecstasy, all with objective natures towards a possible wisdom" (L 917). Yeats's own extensive reading, especially after 1925, testifies to his appreciation of what Wordsworth calls in the Immortality Ode "years that bring the philosophic mind." Though considerably less sanguine than Wordsworth overtly was about the "abundant recompense" of "after years, / When these wild ecstasies shall be matured into a sober pleasure" ("Tintern Abbey," 88, 137–39), Yeats nevertheless subtly qualifies his own overt commitment to *antithetical* ecstasy with the balancing virtue of *primary* wisdom. Much the same balancing act takes place in the preface to *Alastor*, which reveals, as Bloom says, Shelley's "characteristic division between head and heart, at once intellectually disapproving but emotionally sympathizing with his poet-hero's solipsism."[36]

The peculiar tension agitating the Gregory cluster stems from a covertly Shelleyan division between intellectual disapproval of, and emotional empathy with, the *antithetical* quest of the hero. We have seen how the preface to *Alastor* illuminates the tension in the elegy, with its contrast between ecstatics who, like Robert Gregory, consume the entire combustible world, themselves included, in a spectacular flare and those who, like Yeats himself, survive to burn their damp fagots, mundanely, skeptically, and perhaps wisely. Even in the brief compass of the Airman poem, Yeats bril-

36. Bloom, *Yeats*, 14.

liantly distills the Wordsworthian dialectic dramatized in the perspectival ambiguities of *Alastor*. The Airman is driven by a lonely impulse of delight that thrills Yeats as it does the reader. Such reservations as the poet may have about the hero's ecstatic but solipsistic and self-destructive impulse are "balanced," to use the pivotal word Yeats gives the Airman, by attributing to him a kind of *primary* wisdom in which "all" is "brought . . . to mind." The intended effect may be to correct what Wordsworth's *primary* Wanderer, admonishing the *antithetical* Solitary, calls destructive passions leading along the line of limitless desires to ecstasy, the excess by which "the *balance* is destroyed." Yeats restores the balance, not by rejecting the passionate impulse or by correcting *his* Solitary's despondency, but by emphasizing *both*: the impulse is delightful and limitless, but past and future remain "a waste of breath."

Yeats's attitude was further complicated by his awareness of two facts about the actual Robert Gregory. First, Gregory was not really a Wordsworthian or Shelleyan Solitary, having enlisted for an anything but "lonely," *antithetical* reason: "out of friendship" (Ex 309 and draft of Airman poem). Second, by indulging in what was nevertheless an impulse, Gregory was not only self-destructive but had also inadvertently contributed to a cause whose victory was to bring speedy ruin to his own people, whom he had abandoned in the pursuit of a private vision, and to Coole itself, the sale of which, nine years later, was made inevitable by his death. Yet, finally, if the Airman's impulsive quest is both culpable and a failure, it can hardly be otherwise with *antithetical* questers, who "must fail in the natural world, and whose only victories are in the realm of an integral vision."[37] The hero, Yeats insists, "makes his mask . . . in defeat" (Myth 337).

VI. The Byronic Airman

Lord Byron is at once the most titanic and problematic of the Romantic heroes who make their masks in defeat, and the most compelling Byronic mask may still be that of the hero who so profoundly impressed Goethe, Nietzsche, and Yeats. For once critical of his countryman and master, Nietzsche declared in *Ecce Home*: "I have no word, only a glance, for those who dare to pronounce the word 'Faust' in the presence of Manfred."[38] But just as Manfred is a Faust *redivivus*, so the Airman is a Manfred *redivivus*, sharing the aristocratic autonomy and life-weariness reminiscent of the Shelleyan Visionary's most immediate and "romantic" heir. Though unfailingly courteous, Manfred is a solitary whose spirit from youth onward "walked *not* with the souls of men, / *Nor* looked upon the earth with human eyes; / The thirst of their ambition was *not mine*, / The aim of their existence was *not* mine." The litany of negative exclusions allies him with the

37. Ibid., 18.
38. *Ecce Homo* "Why I Am So Clever" 4.

lofty Airman, neither of them having "sympathy with *breathing* flesh." As an admirer of Coriolanus, Yeats would have been as impressed as Nietzsche was with this aristocrat who "disdained to mingle with / A herd . . . , / The lion is alone, and so am I" (*Manfred* 2.2.505–7; 3.1.121–23).

As the Airman has his lonely Shelleyan impulse urging him toward death, Manfred has his, and Byron was probably echoing the same passage in the then just-published *Alastor*. Alone on the narrow ledge of the glacier, in the Byronic posture of dangerous balance in which the young Yeats imagined him, Manfred is moved by a suicidal urge to leap. He feels "the impulse" but holds back: it is his "fatality to live." Yet his life, a "barrenness of spirit," is, like the Airman's, an Ecclesiastean waste of breath, before and after. His days and nights are "Endless, and all alike," a "future like the past" (1.2.20–24, 26–27; 2.1.53; 2.4.131). There can be no new thing under the sun for a hero whose opening speech had synopsized Ecclesiastes ("sorrow" and "knowledge" are one; powers, passions, and "the wisdom of the world" all "avail not") and who later cites the sad wisdom of Ecclesiastes that "Knowledge is not happiness."[39]

On the brink of death, Manfred, like the Visionary, contrasts himself to a bird, not a Shelleyan swan but an eagle. A "winged and cloud-cleaving minister," it is superior to his mixed essence, "Half dust, half deity, alike unfit / To sink or soar." About to soar *and* sink, poised to spring from his glacier into the "clouds" that "rise curling fast beneath me," Manfred is restrained by an old "Chamois Hunter," an admonitory figure resembling Wordsworth's Leech Gatherer and Wanderer as well as their heir, Shelley's Wordsworthian Narrator in *Alastor*. Saved for the moment, the "fatal and fated" hero does, of course, meet that fate in the final act. The one "covenant" in Ecclesiastes is "thou shalt die the death" and there is "a time to die" (3:2). That time has come for Manfred, as it will for the Airman, solitaries who—in the words of both Nietzsche's Zarathustra and Yeats—"know the time to die." "I knew, and know my hour is come," Manfred declares with the calmness of the Airman, adding the unsurprising news, "I'll die as I have lived—alone."[40]

It was Manfred's lofty solitude, will power, and uncompromising sense of autonomy that made him romantically attractive to both Yeats and Nietzsche as boys. "To Byron's Manfred I must be profoundly related," said Nietzsche in *Ecce Homo*: "all these abysses I found in myself; at the age of thirteen I was ripe for this work." Most significant to both poet and philosopher was Manfred's *antithetical* refusal to yield to the "religious"—to either the well-meaning Abbot who would save, or the Demons that would claim, his soul. It was in this latter capacity, as a fearlessly autonomous hero

---

39. *Manfred* 1.1.10–24. Keats, who elsewhere cites Manfred's Ecclesiastean equation, rewords it in the "Ode to a Nightingale," where "but to think is to be full of sorrow." Manfred's "sorrow is knowledge" is also quoted by Nietzsche (*Human, All Too Human*, 109).

40. *Manfred* 1.2.30, 40–41, 85–86; 3.4.88–90.

who "controls spirits," that Manfred was baptized by the young Nietzsche as an *Übermensch,* the first appearance of that fateful term in his writing.[41]

Like Byron and his Manfred, Nietzsche and his *Übermensch,* and Yeats and his *antithetical* "Self" in "Dialogue," the Airman seems to pass a Last Judgment on his own soul, his clairvoyance transforming fate into a personal destiny. In this sense, "An Irish Airman Foresees His Death" is allied with Byron's two major poems of self-judgment and foreseeing: the ode on Prometheus, the Greek Farseer or Forethinker, and the final lyric, in which Byron, fighting in a personally Promethean resistance to tyranny in Greece, foresaw his own death.

Since tyrannical "Fate" is "deaf," and Prometheus does not "tell" the sky-god Zeus of his eventual defeat ("The fate [Prometheus] didst so well foresee"), *we* are his auditors and the heirs of his "mighty lesson":

Thou art a symbol and a sign
　　To mortals of their fate and force;
Like thee, Man is in part divine,
　　A troubled stream from a pure source;
And Man in portions can foresee
His own funereal destiny;
His wretchedness, and his resistance,
And his sad unallied existence:
To which his Spirit may oppose
Itself—and equal to all woes,
　　And a firm will, and a deep sense,
Which even in torture can descry
　　Its own concentred recompense,
Triumphant where it dares defy,
And making Death a Victory.

The "mighty lesson" was inherited by the Demogorgon of Shelley, who condenses Byron's ode in the final stanza of *Prometheus Unbound,* by Tennyson's Ulysses, weakened by time "and fate," but, like Milton's Satan, "strong in will / To strive . . . and not to yield," and by Browning's Childe Roland, who snatches triumph from the jaws of defeat at "the end *descried.*" It is also inherited by Yeats's existential Airman, who foresees his death yet makes it a victory. In "portions" ("I know that I shall meet my fate / *Somewhere*") he too "can foresee / His own funereal destiny," and he too is a

---

41. *Ecce Homo* "Why I Am So Clever" 4; *Musarianausgabe* 1.38. Nietzsche was probably echoing Goethe's use of the word *Übermenschen* in *Faust,* a precursor of *Manfred,* but inferior to it in the youthful Nietzsche's estimation. In an 1862 letter to his sister, Nietzsche claims that his "favorite English poet," Byron, provided the major incentive for his study of English. Later, *Manfred,* "which I almost venerated as a boy," seemed to Nietzsche "madly formless." On the relationship, see David S. Thatcher, "Nietzsche and Byron," and Ralph S. Fraser, "Nietzsche, Byron, and the Classical Tradition," in *Studies in Nietzsche and the Classical Tradition,* ed. James C. O'Flaherty et al., 190–98.

creature of "fate and force," though the latter (the "impulse") is a force doubly paradoxical. An impulse of "delight," it is nevertheless "lonely" and so confirms his "unallied existence." At the same time, it is the Spirit opposed to that "sad" existence—though not by resisting, but by exultantly embracing, the foreseen fate. Unsponsored and free, the Airman goes down to darkness on extended wings.

Unlike that of Prometheus, whose *ultimate* "fate . . . so well foresee[n]" involves literal victory over tyrannical Zeus, the victory of mortals is symbolic. The hero, at least the Yeatsian hero, makes his mask in defeat, his destruction in what Keats called the external world of circumstances preparing for his triumph in the internal world of the antithetical self. The tragically joyful impulse of delight allows "this death" not only to "balance . . . this life" but also to triumph over its waste. The final giving up of breath assimilates the "waste of breath" and so asserts a "firm will," a will to power providing, not the religious "large recompense" of "Lycidas" nor the philosophic "abundant recompense" of "Tintern Abbey," but the autonomous Spirit's "*own concentred* recompense." Thus, this waste of breath, "this life [Byron agreed with Solomon, the purported author of Ecclesiastes] not worth a potato,"[42] can be transformed by the indomitable *antithetical* Spirit, capable in its ghostly solitude of "making Death a Victory."

Byron, who gave up his breath at Missolonghi, also inherited Prometheus's "mighty lesson," making his own death a triumph. Marking "My Thirty-Sixth Year," the year in which he, like Robert Gregory, was to die a soldier's death, Byron employed a triply Promethean image—the funeral "*fire* that on my *bosom preys* / Is *lone* as some volcanic isle"—from which to draw one last "Promethean spark" (*Manfred* 1.1.155). Momentarily resuming the "lesser" role of poet he thought he had abandoned for action, he completed a poem he correctly judged "better than what I usually write."[43] Effectively shifting to the distanced third-person after apostrophizing himself as "unworthy manhood," and covering precisely the ground covered in the Airman's bringing all to mind and judging as a waste "the years to come" on the basis of "the years behind," Byron asks and answers the inevitable question:

If thou regret'st thy youth, *Why live?*
    The land of honourable death
Is here:—up to the field, and give
    Away thy breath!

Byron's summing up, with its Ecclesiastean sense of wasted youth and more waste to come, parallels the Airman's calm balancing of life and death.

---

42. *Don Juan* 7.3.
43. The famous account is given in Count Pietro Gamba's 1825 *Narrative of Lord Byron's Last Journey to Greece.*

Also balancing "death" with life in the rhyming metonymic "breath," Byron's cold-eyed equanimity ("Seek out—less often sought than found— / A soldier's grave, for thee the best; / Then look around, and choose thy ground, / And take thy rest") resembles the equipoise with which the Irish Airman, a century later, freely chose to meet *his* fate by going off as an aristocratic volunteer to die in a foreign war. The Airman, Byron, and Yeats himself (though he died old and in his bed) all obey the ultimate balancing injunction:

Cast a cold eye
On life, on death.[44]

VII. Swordsman or Saint?

Byron stubbornly clung to his autonomy—in his epitaph-poem, in "Prometheus," and at the moment of his own death (he considered suing for divine mercy but remained adamant: "Come, come, no weakness! let's be a man to the last"). "Making Death a Victory," the denouement of "Prometheus," echoes Paul's rewording of Isaiah and Hosea: "Death is swallowed up in victory. O death where is thy victory."[45] But whereas in Paul "God . . . gives us the victory through our lord Jesus Christ," in Byron the autonomous Spirit provides the victory as "its own concentred recompense."

The ode also insists, "Man is in part divine, / A troubled stream from a pure source." As with the Visionary's apostrophe to the "stream! / Whose source is inaccessibly profound" (*Alastor*, 502–3; E&I 80), Yeats would have recognized the allusion to Plotinus, whose divine One is the pure "source" of the Neoplatonic emanative fountain. There may also be an allusion to Plotinus in the most haunting word Yeats put in the mouth of his Irish Airman: "lonely." Years later, in his poignant poem "For Anne Gregory," Yeats tells the slain hero's daughter, "*only God*, my dear, / Could love you for yourself *alone*, / And not your yellow hair." Though Yeats may be alluding to the Hebrew Bible (1 Samuel 16:7), the "old religious man" he cites as authority is the *primary* aspect of Yeats himself, his "text" about God alone being able to love the self alone doubtless the *Enneads* of Plotinus, which ends with the "flight of the alone to the Alone" or, as Yeats tended to best remember it from the conclusion of his friend Lionel Johnson's "The Dark Angel":

Lonely unto the Lone I go,
Divine to the Divinity.

---

44. Yeats's epitaph, which appears both on his gravestone and as the concluding lines of "Under Ben Bulben," ends with the aristocratic impulse transmitted: "Horseman, pass by!" Byron's poem, entered in his diary under the heading "On this day I complete my thirty-sixth year," was published posthumously, in 1825.

45. 1 Corinthians 15:54–55 (the passage cited in the next sentence is verse 57); cf. Isaiah 25:8 and Hosea 13:14.

Plotinus's climactic image informs Crazy Jane's return to the Plotinian One: "A lonely ghost the ghost is / That to God shall come."[46] Have Plotinus and the spiritual anything to do with the "lonely impulse of delight" that drove the Airman to his fatal "tumult in the clouds"? If the poem is a true dramatic monologue, the only possible auditor would be God. Is the Airman therefore like Yeats's Hamlet, another soul lingering on the storm-beaten threshold of sanctity? Most will find it curious to consider so. Yet the Airman resembles Tennyson's Ulysses, and Ulysses, Robert Langbaum suggests, is deliberately seeking death by undertaking "a mystical journey."[47]

But if Yeats is echoing the Plotinian flight of the alone to the Alone in the final flight of the Airman, he is, again, echoing in order to alter. In "Dialogue," Self, rejecting Soul's orthodox view that "only the dead can be forgiven," assumes, blasphemously or audaciously, what Milton condemns as Satan's false gift to fallen Adam and Eve: the winged feeling of "Divinity within." Self is content to follow to its "source"—not the Plotinian, but the *inner* self-determined source—"Every event in action or in thought; / Measure the lot; forgive myself the lot!" Though he ends in Blakean-Nietzschean joy, at this point the measuring Self is close to the Airman's "I balanced all, brought all to mind"—in fact, Yeats originally wrote, "I *measured* all." Like Self, the Airman is, in effect, assuming the role of God—not only doom-weighing Zeus but also the God of the Hebrew Bible, who weighs, numbers, balances. Those are the functions represented in the cryptic three words—*Mene, Tekel, Upharsin*—the moving finger writes in Daniel. The message is that the king, whose days and kingdom are "numbered," has been "weighed in the balances, and . . . found wanting" (Daniel 5:24-27).

The Assessor, of course, is God. It is all very well for the Airman, who dismisses both the nation he fights and the nation he guards, to resemble the Lord of Isaiah, to whom "all nations" are as "a drop of a bucket," "counted" as "less than nothing, and vanity," "as the small dust of the balance." But when he claims "*I* balanced *all*," the Airman usurps the evaluating role of God, who, according to Isaiah, has "measured," "meted out," "weighed," everything in a "balance" (40:12–15). Finding this life a waste of breath, the Airman is accounting the things of this world "as nothing; and . . . less than nothing" (Isaiah 40:17). But that is God's judgment to make, not man's, especially when the dismissal includes one's own life. "God shall bring every work into judgment," according to the pious conclusion tacked on to Ecclesiastes (12:14); but what reverberates in the somber judgment the Air-

---

46. "Crazy Jane and Jack the Journeyman." For Plotinus, see above, Chapter 5.

47. Langbaum, *The Poetry of Experience: The Dramatic Dialogue in Modern Literary Tradition*, 90. The Airman does not seem to prepare; he acts on "impulse," *spontaneously*. But that word itself etymologically brackets independence (*spontaneus*) and binding (*spons, spondere*), a submission to the *daemon* involving unmediated contact with divine presence.

man himself passes on this life, this death, is the darker voice of the Preacher: all is *hebel*, "breath of breaths."

In weighing his deeds and finding them waste of breath, the Airman endorses the dismissive vision of Ecclesiastes; in going to "meet [his] fate / Somewhere," he nods toward the God of Ecclesiastes, that inscrutable determiner of man's fate; but when he usurps God's role by bringing his deeds to *self*-judgment, he performs—if not quite the Nietzschean act of self-redemption performed by the lot-measuring Self in "Dialogue"—a purely autonomous judgment. In effect, the lonely Airman in his cockpit, refusing to the end to abide by any values but those projected by the self, becomes a deus *in* machina. Even the self-oblivion he seeks is a self-affirmation since, paradoxically, self-destruction is the ultimate validation of autonomy. With that we are back to *Manfred*, a text even more appealing to the boyish Yeats than Ecclesiastes, and with Manfred back to Byron and to the whole of the self-destructive visionary company.

In that case, even if the impulse that drives the Airman *is* "spiritual," it is less saintly than daemonic, perhaps even *demonic*. For the nobility of the self-judging Romantic questers is tainted—or enhanced—by alignment with Milton's rebellious angel, in whose "party" Blake notoriously placed Milton himself. Claiming "our puissance is our own," Satan rallied his associates to a solipsistic banner asserting the will to power and denying belatedness:

We know no time when we were not as now;
Know none before us, self-begot, self-rais'd
By our own quick'ning power.
   (*Paradise Lost* 5.861, 856–58)

In terms of Yeats, Satan's language casts *antithetical* light, not on the self-"begotten" flames of "Byzantium," but on the experience, at the end of "Stream and Sun at Glendalough," of being "Self-born, born anew"; on the "self-delighting, / Self-appeasing" soul of "A Prayer for My Daughter"; and, especially, on the self-forgiving victor of "A Dialogue of Self and Soul."

Byron's Manfred is more overtly "of the Devil's party." He, like Tennyson's Ulysses, emulates Satan's "unconquerable will, / . . . / And courage never to submit or yield" (*Paradise Lost* 1.106, 108). Defiantly autonomous to the end, Manfred dies his own death, with its own recompense:

The mind which is immortal makes itself
Requital for its good or evil thoughts,—
Is its own origin of ill and end
And its own place and time.

Following this echo of Milton's Satan, who is "not to be chang'd by Place or Time," since "The mind is its own place, and in itself / Can make a Heav'n of Hell, a Hell of Heav'n," Manfred, "Half dust, half deity," concludes that the mind's

> innate sense
> When stripp'd of this mortality, derives
> No colour from the fleeting things without,
> But is absorb'd in sufferance or in joy
> Born from the knowledge of its own desert.[48]

Little wonder Manfred qualified as first recipient of the honorific term *Übermensch*, for Nietzsche's sovereign man too determines his "*own* worth," has "a solitude within him . . . inaccessible to praise or blame, his *own* justice that is beyond appeal." "In the end," said Yeats,

> The creative energy of men depends upon their believing that they have, *within themselves*, something immortal and imperishable, and that all else is but as an image in a looking glass. So long as that belief is not a formal thing, a man will create out of a joyful energy, seeking little for any external test of an impulse that may be sacred.
> (Ex 151)

The emphasis has been shifted to *aesthetically* creative energy, and the declaration hedged by the usual Yeatsian caveats ("*believing* that . . . so *long as* . . . seeking *little* for . . . that *may* be sacred"). But this is the *antithetical* impulse, its near-solipsism validated by *Alastor's* Poet-Visionary, by Manfred, and by Nietzsche—with its "joyful energy" and secularly "sacred" nature the contribution of Nietzsche above all.

To debate whether the Airman's lonely impulse of delight is a "joyful energy" *authentically* "creative" would bring us back to the ambiguities already stressed in the Gregory elegy; to debate whether the Airman's "impulse," or, more centrally, the "impulse" Yeats is speaking of in the prose passage just cited, is or is not "sacred" would bring us, by a commodious vicus of recirculation, back to Thoor Ballylee and environs—not to the "almost finished" literal scene of the Gregory elegy but to the symbolic setting for the crucial *agon* at the heart of Yeats's life and work: the debate between Self and Soul. That dialogue ends with a blessed and blessing Self content to live it all again and yet again in a Nietzschean Eternal Recurrence—fast and yet free, singing in chains, his impulse perhaps "sacred," certainly "creative." Enough. It will suffice if the lonely and heroic Airman, foreseeing his fate stoically and yet with a strange delight, is (to quote the Gregory elegy) but "a portion" of Yeats's "mind and life." That is true even

---

48. *Manfred* 3.4.129–36; cf. similar claims at 1.1.152 and 3.1.73. *Paradise Lost* 1.254–55.

if it is the portion his "boyish intellect approved," for the boy in this case walked the ledge with Manfred and chose the Visionary of *Alastor* for his chief of men.

* * *

There are deaths more moving and of greater symbolic weight than the Irish Airman's, even than that of Byron's Manfred or Yeats's Shelleyan chief of men. There is, for example, the death of Hegel's "paragon among women," Antigone, a self-destructive solitary who also acts on an inner "impulse," maintaining her autonomy at the cost of her life rather than accede to the conventional code, the external law, others would impose on her.

Yeats chose to celebrate Sophocles' heroine as the embodiment of this daemonic impulse. What Yeats calls "that great glory" by which men and women are "driven wild" is presented by the Sophoclean chorus as an irrational and destructive "frenzy at the heart"—the power of Eros, which threatens civilization and order. The daemonic drive feared by the timid Chorus is championed by reckless Yeats, who "translates" the Eros chorus in such a way as to go beyond his earlier qualified affirmation of the politicized erotic drive that "maddened" Cathleen ni Houlihan's own self-sacrificing heroes: "What if excess of love / Bewildered them till they died? / I write it out in a verse" (VP 394).

But to the verse he wrote based on, and swerving from, the Sophoclean choral ode, Yeats added the Chorus's anapestic coda, filled with grief for the daughter of Oedipus. As a result, his own poem concludes with a poignance far more resonant than the preceding invocation of world-overcoming apocalyptic violence. "From 'The Antigone'" ends with three elegiac lines offering prayer and tears for "Oedipus' child" (the poem's title in manuscript), yet insistent, too, on the Yeatsian sine qua non: song. There can be no Nietzschean laughter in the face of this descent into "the loveless dust," but the indispensable affirmation-within-constraint is repeated from the final chant of Self in "Dialogue": "Sing I must."

This seemingly minor poem interacts not only with Sophocles and with Yeats's personal myth of Oedipus, the father of Antigone, but also with other driven women, Maud Gonne and Con Markiewicz. As the coda to *A Woman Young and Old*, it also plays a pivotal role in the matched "Young and Old" sequences that conclude Yeats's two major volumes, *The Tower* and *The Winding Stair*. For these and other reasons that will become apparent, I choose to conclude with this particular instance of Yeatsian interaction with tradition, one that leaves the poet, though the music is heartbroken, still singing in his chains.

V

CODA

9

FAITHFUL IN HIS FASHION:
YEATS AND THE EROS CHORUS FROM SOPHOCLES' *ANTIGONE*

The last kiss is given to the void.
—Yeats, 1929 letter to Sturge Moore

And I am in despair that time may bring
Approved patterns of women or of men
But not that selfsame excellence again.
—Yeats, "The Municipal Gallery Revisited".

We have been exploring instances of intertextuality, especially cases in which Yeats took the text of a predecessor as a point of departure—and then departed from that. Yeatsian interactions with tradition, both literary and philosophic, demonstrate, first, that the thankful receiver bears a plentiful harvest and, second, that gratitude does not rule out—indeed, that it demands—innovation, the exercise of what Eliot called the individual talent. It was Ezra Pound, a friend of both Eliot and Yeats, who asserted the Modernist imperative: "make it new." As we have seen, Yeats's chosen method of renovating tradition was to revise, often to reverse, what he inherited. In "Among School Children," employing the myth of the origin of sexual love as sardonically explained by Aristophanes in the *Symposium*, Yeats felt compelled to "alter Plato's parable." In his "translation" of the Eros chorus of the *Antigone*, a translation he used as the eleventh and concluding poem of his sequence *A Woman Young and Old*, Yeats performs a more dramatic alteration of a Classical statement on the nature of love. David R. Clark, who has meticulously traced the evolution of this poem through Yeats's manuscripts, notes Yeats's introduction of "a very un-Sophoclean note": Yeats's chorus, unlike that of Sophocles and all his translators, is not only acknowledging love's power but also "cheering love on."[1] True; though I would describe the alteration as not so much of Sophocles as of the limited and timid Chorus of the play.

---

1. "Sing I Must": The Manuscripts of "From the 'Antigone,'" in Clark's *Yeats at Songs and Choruses*, 211–42 (224). Of course, Yeats could only approach Sophocles through the medium

This final Chapter, or coda, examining both the published poem and its working manuscripts, tries to show precisely why and how Yeats deploys "From 'The Antigone'" as the coda to *A Woman Young and Old*, itself the coda to *The Winding Stair and Other Poems* (1933). And there are wheels within wheels. Words of Sophocles shaped not only the elegiac poem concluding *The Winding Stair* but the volume-opening elegy as well: "In Memory of Eva Gore-Booth and Con Markiewicz." This connection, in turn, illuminates Yeats's attitudes toward two other women. The first is his femme fatale and destructive Helen, Maud Gonne, as ardent a political revolutionary as Constance Markiewicz and even more extravagantly beautiful. The second is the poet's own daughter, Anne. She is the central figure of the poem in which her protective father prays that she will find serenity and civility in love, that she will develop neither the capacity for hatred nor the destructive, and self-destructive, beauty of Maud; she is also the biographical model for the serene but enamored and defiant young girl of "Father and Child," the first poem of *A Woman Young and Old*.

Thus Yeats's translation from Sophocles establishes rondure both with the opening lyric in his concentrically structured sequence and with the opening poem of the volume as a whole. It also brings the *Woman Young and Old* sequence into balance with *The Tower*'s concluding sequence, *A Man Young and Old*, which ends with another translation of a Sophoclean choral ode, this one from *Oedipus at Colonus* (VP 459). Seemingly slight as it is, then, "From 'The Antigone'" performs a number of pivotal functions in what are certainly Yeats's two finest collections—the "masculine" *Tower* and the "feminine" *Winding Stair*—and arguably two of the strongest and most tightly organized volumes of poetry ever published in English.

The translation's very centrality emphasizes the importance of Yeats's "alteration" of his source. If "works of art are," as Yeats believed, "always begotten by previous works of art" (E&I 352), "From 'The Antigone'" demonstrates a characteristic Yeatsian combination in this begetting process: an uncanny ability to penetrate through accumulated scholarly dust to the vital center of a work and the confidence and skill to re-create it, shattering it if need be to remold it nearer to the heart's desire. The process is one of inheritance and transformation, of what Pound meant by making it new, which for both poets meant returning to the spirit if not the letter of the original. Fittingly, it was to Pound, that most notorious of creative transla-

---

of translation. Though he occasionally pretended to it, he had no more knowledge of Greek than of Hebrew, both of them languages he had "forgotten." (Yeats's "I have forgotten my Hebrew" has long been a source of merriment; in 1933 he referred casually to having "forgotten" his Greek: see his note entitled "Plain Man's *Oedipus*" in the *New York Times*, 15 January 1933.) In "translating" Sophocles, Yeats depended primarily on the rendering and notes of Richard C. Jebb—with some help from cribs, the French translations of Paul Masqueray, and his friends. These included Lady Gregory, who was attuned to the plain man's ear, and Oliver St. John Gogarty, whom Yeats had earlier asked to chant passages of *Oedipus the King* in Greek so that he could capture in English at least some of the assonances of the original. Clark has shown that Yeats also knew Lewis Campbell's translation of *Antigone*.

tors, that Yeats submitted this poem, with what beneficial results we shall see.

But where, for a translator, does creative freedom end and distorting license begin? Yeats's creative interactions are too complex to be reduced to mere distortion under the mixed metaphoric rubrics of whatever was grist for the mill of a man with too many bees in his own bonnet to know or care what was really going on in the work of those he used. The concept of deliberate creative misreading—Bloom's theory of misprision and *clinamen* or swerve from the precursor—brings us much closer to Yeats's revisionary way with a text. But it is more than that too, especially in the case of Sophocles. Of all the world's literature, Yeats believed, "the Greek drama alone achieved perfection."[2] And the compelling figure was Sophocles. For more than twenty years the Irish poet was haunted by the idea of translating the Oedipus plays for the Abbey Theatre audience, a dream fulfilled when his *Sophocles' King Oedipus* and *Sophocles' Oedipus at Colonus* were completed and staged in, respectively, December 1926 and September 1927; that is, during his composition of *A Woman Young and Old*. These Sophoclean tragedies were for Yeats documents of religious as well as literary significance. Thus, while it is largely true that—as Francis Stuart once put it— "like many great artists Yeats was only really interested in, or absorbed by, what could, in often strange and oblique ways, stimulate and inspire him,"[3] the sacred texts of Sophocles were not treated by Yeats as materials to be twisted till they suited his own, often "strange and oblique," purposes. I make these prefatory remarks because those familiar with the Greek original will find Yeats's version of the choral ode from the *Antigone* a violation both of the letter and of the spirit. I hope to show not only that Yeats was perfectly aware of what he was doing, but also that his fidelity, going beyond the limited perspective of the Chorus, was to Sophocles and to his magnificent heroine. He was faithful, in his fashion.

I

It has been said of the Sophoclean Chorus familiar to us from the surviving plays that it "preserves the amenities first, and more fundamental values (if at all) later."[4] This is certainly true of the Chorus in the *Antigone*, an all-male group of Theban Elders naturally disposed to law and order. Until persuaded otherwise by Tiresias, these aristocratic valetudinarians perceive the king as essentially in the right. They have pious misgivings about the original edict forbidding the burial of Polyneices, but despite Antigone's gibe that they would approve her action "were not their lips sealed by fear"

2. Yeats made this remark, not long before his death, to Dorothy Wellesley, adding "It has never been done since; it may be thousands of years before we achieve that perfection again." Dorothy Wellesley, *Far Have I Travelled*, 169–70.
3. Francis Stuart, in Francis MacManus, ed., *The Yeats We Knew*, 35. Stuart, a distinguished Irish novelist, was for a while, as the husband of Iseult Gonne, the son-in-law of Maud.
4. Cedrick H. Whitman, *Sophocles: A Study of Heroic Humanism*, 263, n. 18.

(504),[5] they actually condemn her lawbreaking, which they feel was prompted by "folly" and "frenzy at the heart," a Fury-like infatuated impulse (603). Even after the horrible sentence of living entombment has been pronounced upon her, though they grant that her action was "reverent" and worthy of reverence and she herself pitiable, they still support the prerogatives of authority, and—sounding like the Chorus in *Ajax* (1118–19: "You may be right, but your tone is objectionable")—irrelevantly and obtusely conclude: "Thy self-willed temper hath wrought thy ruin" (872–75). To which Antigone responds by lamenting her solitary lot, "unwept, unfriended" (876). It was to stress precisely this isolation that Sophocles broke tradition. Had the Chorus consisted of sympathetic women (as it normally does in Greek tragedy when the protagonist is a woman), Antigone's isolation would have been less striking—less terrible and less splendid.[6]

Of the Chorus's six odes in the play, Yeats chose the fourth (stasimon III) and, very significantly, its anapestic coda. None of the choral odes in the *Antigone* is mere interlude or curtain-piece. The short stasimon III and the anapests pivot between two crucial episodes: the argument between Creon and Haemon and the lyric *kommos* between Antigone and the Chorus. The unspoken, undebatable heart of the dialectic between father and son is of course Haemon's love for Antigone, who is doomed to immurement at the end of this angry exchange. And the Antigone brought in under guard as the Chorus concludes its song appears in a new light: she is not the colossally heroic individual who defies a tyrannical edict in the name of the unwritten law, and not the martyr fearlessly advancing to a death she almost yearns for, but a young woman who must descend to a living entombment and who now speaks in open anguish of the nuptial love and children she will never have. Sophocles has already established Antigone as a paragon to admire; now he gives us a woman for whom we, like Haemon, would be prepared to die.

Looking before and after, the Eros ode focuses our attention on this unspoken but ever-present love between Haemon and Antigone—its power to set son against father and king; to move even the iron-willed Antigone; and (finally) to drive Haemon to the frenzy in which he will later embrace the corpse of Antigone and himself commit suicide, his body enfolding hers. This double death completes the recurrent imagery of Eros and Thanatos and is, despite the consequent working out of Creon's tragedy, the true climax of the play.

Though it is a fulcrum in this imagistic and dramatic structure, stasimon III alone (excluding, for the moment, the anapests) ironically stresses, along with unconquerable love, the terrible isolation of Antigone. An ode on the power of erotic love reminds us that, like the woman of "Chosen," the

---

5. All line references are to the enumeration in the Greek text; the translation is that of Jebb, *The Tragedies of Sophocles*.

6. It is for this reason, too, that no one, not even Ismene, the one surviving member of her family, can share the deed of Antigone.

central poem of *A Woman Young and Old*, Antigone chose her own tragic fate—not the romantic love chosen by Yeats's woman, but love of family and of the divine laws. It is because she is, in the words of a relevant Yeats poem, "high and solitary and most stern" (VP 257) that Sophocles forbids us the consolation of a single scene between his heroine and her young lover, restricting Antigone to one poignant reference to "Haemon, beloved."[7] Antigone's isolation is further stressed by the irony implicit in the ode itself. The Chorus understands that Haemon was swayed to paternal disobedience and patriotic disloyalty by the irresistible deity of Love. But, although the pathos of Antigone's fate is deepened by the Chorus's palliation of Haemon's misdeed, the ode is less a celebration than a terrified acknowledgment of Love's power:

Love, unconquered in the fight, Love, who makest havoc of wealth, who keepest thy vigil on the soft cheek of a maiden; thou roamest over the sea, and among the homes of dwellers in the wilds; no immortal can escape thee, nor any among men whose life is for a day; and he to whom thou hast come is mad.

The just themselves have their minds warped by thee to wrong, for their ruin; 'tis thou that hast stirred up this present strife of kinsmen; victorious is the love-kindling light from the eyes of the fair bride; it is a power enthroned in sway beside the eternal laws; for there the goddess Aphrodite is working her unconquerable will.
 (781-99)

Maintaining an Apollonian decorum, the Sophoclean Chorus sings of an irresistible enemy of gods and men, a twister of just minds, the cause of such quarrels as this between the king and love-maddened Haemon. Though these men of reason and (as Antigone pointedly notes) "of wealth" (780) recognize Love's "power," they envisage it as a madness that causes mind to swerve to its own destruction. As E. R. Dodds observes in *The Greeks and the Irrational*, we should not dismiss this image of Eros or Aphrodite as mere "personification." Behind it lies the "old Homeric feeling" that these irrational drives "are not within man's conscious control; they are endowed with a life and energy of their own, and so can force a man, as it were from the outside, into conduct foreign to him."[8] In this ode, Eros is neither diffused nor defused. No Freudian personifications, Eros and Aphrodite retain their divine power and their hostile relationship to civilization—to "masculine" intellect and order; to what Freud provocatively advocated in the thirties as the future "dictatorship of reason."[9]

7. Though the Laurentian MS assigns this line to Ismene, Creon's reference in the next line to "*thy* marriage," as well as the intimacy of the reference to Haemon, strongly suggest that the line is Antigone's. Most modern scholars follow Jebb in so assigning it. See Jebb, *Tragedies*, 110: 572n.
  8. *The Greeks and the Irrational*, 41. On Eros and Aphrodite, see Plato, *Symposium* 180E.
  9. See Freud's *New Introductory Lectures* and his letters to Einstein in the thirties. In *Civilization and Its Discontents*, Freud describes "eternal Eros" as a barrier *against* destructive aggression; but the seeming contradiction is easily explained. In depicting the evolution of civilization as a

II

We are dealing, in short, with the daemonic—a numinous realm that fascinated Yeats. Love may be a dreaded wreaker of havoc for the Sophoclean Chorus; but the first two movements of Yeats's poem, corresponding to the Greek strophe and antistrophe, constitute one long invocation to Love to unleash that daemonic fury. The trepidation of the discreet Greek Chorus— pillars of the community to a man—is replaced by what amounts to a Dionysian battlecry to overcome the Apollonian "order":

Overcome—O bitter sweetness,
Inhabitant of the soft cheek of a girl—
The rich man and his affairs,
The fat flocks and the fields' fatness,
Mariners, rough harvesters;
Overcome gods upon Parnassus;

Overcome the Empyrean; hurl
Heaven and Earth out of their places,
That in the same calamity
Brother and brother, friend and friend,
Family and family,
City and city may contend,
By that great glory driven wild.
    (VP 540)

Yeats's first draft had begun, "Celebrate *love*, bitter sweetness." Stressing the integration of *A Woman Young and Old*, and expecting us to recall

---

"battle of giants" between "Eros and Death, between the instinct of life and the instinct of destruction," Freud was referring not to erotic love but to the diffused eroticism that links the members of society into a community: "Eros, builder of cities," as Auden calls the god in his elegy for Freud. Indeed, since this cultural unification necessarily rests on a self-effacing submission or attachment to moral or political authority, and on massive renunciation of direct satisfaction of the unsublimated instincts, the Greek Eros and civilization are (Freud notes) more often enemies than allies. Though initially tolerated, even idealized, sexual love increasingly "comes into opposition to the interests of civilization," while in turn, "civilization threatens love with substantial restrictions." For love—in which two's company and three's a crowd—is inherently socially subversive. Further, society needs the sexuality spent between lovers in private passion "so as to diffuse it over the other members of the society and compose from it the ties of friendship and community that constitute the social nexus." See *Civilization and Its Discontents* (Freud, *Works*, 21:122, 103), and Richard Wollheim, *Sigmund Freud*, 265.

In the *Antigone*, Creon—a tyrant under a Periclean mask—repeatedly presses the claims of the unified state; but his concept substitutes servitude for the individual bonds of love and friendship needed to compose a true unity. The Chorus of reverend citizens upholds the laws that bind the state together and that would, if broken by an individual, ruin both the law's transgressor and his city. Law and order must be kept, otherwise mere anarchy is loosed upon the world. Whatever their human sympathy for Antigone, the Chorus is stunned and disapproving when, at the conclusion of its ode about "wonderful" man, with its climactic repudiation of lawbreakers, she is brought in under guard, revealed as the lawbreaker.

"love's bitter-sweet" from the earlier "Greek" poem in the sequence ("Her Vision in the Wood"), Yeats, with a calculated reticence worthy of Sophocles, later deleted direct reference to "love." By retaining only the echoing phrase in apposition, he makes love all the more present by its verbal absence (as in Sophocles' handling of the love between Antigone and Haemon) and also avoids its overt deification. A similar effect is achieved in the poem's final phrase, "loveless dust."

Whereas the power fearfully acknowledged by the Greek Chorus was divine and unconquerable, this "bitter sweetness" is profoundly human. The power whose range and destructive capacities were boundless, unrestricted by water or wilderness in the original, is here contained, domesticated, "gentled": it is, *from the outset*, the "inhabitant of the soft cheek of a girl." It had not always been so. From the first draft through all its typescripts, this had been the eighth line, completing the second of the *a b a b* quatrains. Fortunately for the poem, Yeats showed it to Ezra Pound during his visit to Rapallo in February 1928. Pound made the eighth line the second, replaced the original "and into" with "that in" in line 9, and deleted a now unnecessary "that" at the beginning of line 10. Yeats always respected though he did not always accept the critical judgments of Pound; in this instance the corrections were gratefully, and rightly, received—even at the cost of destroying the rhyme scheme, no small consideration for Yeats.[10] It may have been, in part, Pound's help on the Antigone poem that led Yeats to address to him the preface to the 1937 edition of *A Vision*, "A Packet for Ezra Pound," in which he proclaims as a "new divinity" the father of Antigone, Oedipus (V-B 27).

In addition to being placed later in the draft versions of the poem, this crucial line was initially very differently conceived. Yeats first described Love as a "horrible, unconquerable / Inhabitant of the soft cheek of a girl." This was faithful to the thought of the Chorus, for whom Love is an invincible warrior who strikes from ambush (his concealed stronghold in the soft cheek of a maiden). By accepting Pound's alteration, Yeats returned to the sequential order of the ode, but, by juxtaposing "bitter sweetness," "inhabitant," and "soft cheek of a girl," he transformed Love from an insidious, ever-watchful warrior ready to pounce on his unsuspecting victims into a power made poignantly vulnerable by its fragile human habitation.

A soft cheek is perishable flesh subject to time. The word *inhabitant* may in fact have been suggested by "this beggarly *habiliment*," Yeats's garment-image for the flesh of the withered lovers who meet "face to face" in "Meeting," the immediately preceding poem in *A Woman Young and Old*. Though Antigone is, like Wordsworth's Lucy, ironically destined never to feel the touch of earthly years, that of course only increases the pathos of the

---

10. As David Clark notes, Yeats did not accept some of Pound's punctuation changes (*Songs and Choruses*, 240–41).

line that Yeats (with Pound's help) made the fulcrum and emotional center of his poem.

While playing fast and loose with the attitude of the Chorus, Yeats has kept a deeper faith—with Sophocles' vision of Antigone, and of course with his own vision of the daemonic power of love and of conflict, particularly that between what he called the "spiritual" and "natural" or material orders. Singing in defense of reason and civilization, the Chorus in stasimon III champions mind, besieged by Love and the destructive madness it brings. The war in Yeats's version is between these spiritual and material orders, with Love the champion recklessly invoked to "overcome" everything. Yeats seems to have conflated the details of stasimon III with the *tone* of the first and last choral odes of the *Antigone*, exultant dance-songs invoking Dionysus.[11] He did so, I suspect, under the auspices of the modern prophet of Dionysus, Nietzsche, whose central imperative, as Yeats well knew, was "Overcome."[12]

Nietzschean warriors of the spirit armed with Blakean swords of mental fight may be at hand, but it is Sato's sword that is unsheathed in "From 'The Antigone,'" and what we hear is Yeats's own reckless cry for "conflict, more conflict."[13] In the first movement, the "affairs" of the rich man are not sexual but the burgherly transactions, the fumbling in a greasy till, of that bourgeois world that is too much with us, getting and spending. Though Sophocles, unlike the Chorus, stresses Creon's cash-nexus mentality, the antithesis here is, of course, deeply Yeatsian. His expansion on the Chorus's reference to "men whose life is for a day" takes the form of a contrast between dreams of money and repose on the one hand, and the rhapsodic fealty of the poet on the other. In revising his original opening— "Celebrate love, bitter sweetness; / Rich men dream of their affairs, / Flock's fatness, & fields' fatness; / Of night's repose the harvesters"—Yeats deleted the whole idea of dreaming and intensified the antithesis between the tragic singer of love and the merchants and their muscled laborers: Love is to overcome *them*—and much else besides.[14]

The rich, fat, rough world of the opening lines is that "pragmatical,

11. It is from the last song of the Chorus (1115–54) that Yeats's detail about "gods on Parnassus" seems to be taken. In this dance-song filled with nymph-brandished torches blowing in the night wind, the protector of the city, Dionysus, is invoked to come "down from Parnassus."

12. See above, Chapters 3 and 4, on Nietzschean self-overcoming. Nietzsche's "phase" (12 in Yeats's lunar scheme in *A Vision*, with Nietzsche its sole occupant) is "before all else the phase of the hero, of the man who overcomes himself, and so no longer needs . . . the submission of others . . . to prove his victory" (V-B 126–27).

13. Asked by foreign visitors for a "message to India," Yeats "strode swiftly across the room, took up Sato's sword (given him by a Japanese admirer, Junzo Sato) and unsheathed it dramatically and shouted 'Conflict, more conflict.'" See Joseph Hone, *W. B. Yeats, 1865–1939*, 459. Was he recalling Krishna's unexpected conclusion in his dialogue with Arjuna in the "Divine Song" of the *Bhagavad-Gita*: "therefore fight on!"?

14. The "rough harvesters" were originally "wild." Not only was that too honorific a Yeatsian adjective, it would have conflicted with "By that great glory driven *wild*."

preposterous pig of a world" (VP 481) whose apocalyptic destruction by mind or perfect love this last Romantic had sung in poems like "Blood and the Moon" and "Solomon and the Witch." Yet, as Sheba admits in the latter, "the world stays." The complacent materialist world, thoroughly masculine, seems impervious to a power that, however "unconquerable," is weakened by its fragile incarnation. Yet the "strong" man has often been brought down by that power. That ageless theme sometimes stresses the sinister destructive power of the femme fatale. Here, the destructive violence of "that great glory" is apotheosized, a female equivalent of the "feathered glory" of the swan-god in Yeats's "Leda and the Swan." This power Yeats desperately invokes, longing for it not only to overturn the material world but to reach beyond—to the gods on Parnassus, to the entire cosmos.

The sudden toppling of tyrannical Jupiter in Shelley's *Prometheus Unbound* here seems fused with that Nietzschean "transvaluation of all values" in which, Yeats notes, "the whole turns bottom upwards" (Ex 433). Yeats's "antistrophe" projects a dialectical reversal with, characteristically, no peaceful resolution. Heaven and earth are to be hurled out of their places, calamity and contention fiercely embraced. "By that great glory driven wild" seems, in part, the hair-raising joy, the *rhathymia*, of the Greeks in battle; in part, the destructive rage of an Achilles in the face of mutability itself.[15] Even more, it is the destructive potential of "terrible beauty"; and Yeats has, I think, two particular terrible beauties in mind: Con Markiewicz and Maud Gonne. The evidence is the imagery of the choral ode itself and of the lines immediately preceding and following it in the Jebb translation; demonstration requires, however, excursus.

III

The imagery of the Eros Chorus is instructive. The "love-kindling light" shining in the eyes of a beautiful woman is a triumphant fire-arrow—an incendiary, unconquerable power; a stirrer-up of strife; a destroyer of men, their minds, and their possessions. For the Greeks as for Yeats, the archetypal embodiment of the terrible beauty of the femme fatale is of course Helen. In the punning epithets on her name recalled by Ezra Pound in Cantos II and VII, she is called by Aeschylus helénaus, hélandros, heléptolis—destroyer of ships, destroyer of men, destroyer of cities. It is of this choral ode from the *Agamemnon* that Yeats—who, in the central lyric of *A Man Young and Old*, had referred to that woman "who had brought great Hector down / And put all Troy to wreck"—seems to be thinking in what

15. In the *Genealogy of Morals* (1.11), Nietzsche translates Pericles' *rhathymia* as "hair-raising cheerfulness and profound joy in all destruction." T. R. Whitaker has compared the "Dionysian" rage of certain Yeatsian speakers to what Rachel Bespaloff has seen in Achilles, a Dionysian "passion for destruction growing out of a hatred for the destructibility of all things." This observation from her 1947 study *On the Iliad* (105) is cited by Whitaker in *Swan and Shadow*, 228.

is, in his case, *hope* that "City and city may contend / By that great glory driven wild." As the phrase "driven wild" strongly suggests, he is thinking here, as in the *Man Young and Old* poem, of his own Helen, Maud Gonne.

The joyful contemplation of destruction that, by Yeats's own admission, became a prominent element in his thought around the turn of the century was more than fin-de-siècle apocalyptism. As his unpublished novel *The Speckled Bird* suggests, Yeats's roseate visions of apocalypse turned violent after his rejection by Maud Gonne.[16] The impossibility of possessing her brought a daemonic rage to end all things, transferred the destructive fury of Maud to the hitherto timid "Willie" himself, by that great glory driven wild. The echo in "From 'The Antigone'" of the impact on Yeats of his conjuring up of the living presence of Maud Gonne in "Among School Children" ("and thereupon my heart is *driven wild*") is more than a case of poet recalling a phrase he had used a year earlier. The whole invocation to Love to "hurl" Heaven and Earth out of their places so that in the same calamity brothers, friends, families, and cities would be set in murderous contention surely calls up the destructive revolutionary energies of that modern Helen who filled Yeats's days with the misery of unrequited love and who would have taught to ignorant men

> most violent ways,
> Or *hurled* the little streets upon the great,
> Had they but courage equal to desire.
> ("No Second Troy")

In a description that starts off being more applicable to Antigone than to either Maud or Helen, Yeats asks his readers (and himself):

> What could have made her peaceful with a mind
> That nobleness made simple as a fire,
> With beauty like a tightened bow, a kind
> That is not natural in an age like this,
> Being high and solitary and most stern?
> Why, what could she have done, being what she is?
> Was there another Troy for her to burn?

In "No Second Troy," Yeats moves from denied but obvious accusation to justification of his heroine; the Troy-less present is to be blamed for not being, as Richard Ellmann once remarked, "heroically inflammable." The Greek Chorus, on the other hand, remains commonsensical and accusatory.

---

16. The rejection of Michael Hearne by Margaret Henderson (that is, of Yeats by Maud) is followed by an apocalyptic vision of "armed figures gathering to overturn the present order of the world"—less a genuine visionary experience than the violent offshoot of erotic frustration, warriors in the lineaments of ungratified desire. *The Speckled Bird by W. B. Yeats*, ed. William H. O'Donnell, 1:82.

The clear implication of *its* fire-image is that the "light" shining in a woman's eyes "kindles" Love that, in turn, by goading men to strife, sets fires of hatred burning—even between father and son. A similar contrast informs that "soft cheek" image, employed by the Chorus as a covert place of soldierly "vigil," by Yeats as an image of fragility. The combination of "masculine" strength and "female" fragility is of course relevant to the two sides of Antigone; but the similarly paradoxical image cluster associated with Maud Gonne may also be invoked: "sternness amid charm" (VP 259); apocalyptic violence folded even within the petals of a rose (VP 169–70); "half-lion, half-child" (VP 260); a mysterious creature through whose shining eye a "sterner," supernatural eye looked "on this foul world in its decline and fall" (VP 619), and yet (as he adds in this poem, "A Bronze Head"), "yet a most gentle woman." No wonder British journalists felt that that "mysterious eye," as Yeats recounted with mingled fascination and dread, "contained the shadow of battles yet to come" (Mem 60).

That ambivalence—so reminiscent of Euripides' "so terrible, and yet most gentle" Dionysus—is crucial. Yeats's fascination with his Helen's capacity for violence was tempered by his simultaneous dread, disapproval, sense of waste and misdirected energy—above all, perhaps, by his protective love, the care of a father for his daughter, his "child":

And thereupon my heart is driven wild:
She stands before me as a living child.
    ("Among School Children")

Seeing the "wildness in her" and the "vision of terror" her soul must live through, he "had grown wild / And wandered murmuring everywhere, 'My child, my child'" ("A Bronze Head"). Inevitably, in his "Prayer for My Daughter," it is the self-destructiveness of "the loveliest woman born" that epitomizes the fate antithetical to that he wishes for his own child. That child, his daughter, Anne, is, as we shall see, a presence in "From 'The Antigone'"; and just as Maud Gonne broods over "A Prayer for My Daughter," so she is present here also.

In Yeats's translation ambivalence is left with the temporizing Greek Chorus. "From 'The Antigone'" has none of the Chorus's reservations—indeed, none of Yeats's own—about unleashed violence. Because Love is so vulnerable in its mortal sanctuary, Yeats can cry out all the more desperately for its universal triumph. Precisely this mood is caught in the elegy for Eva Gore-Booth and Con Markiewicz; but establishing the context for that poem's deeper connection to Sophocles' *Antigone* and to the Eros ode requires a glance at some of Yeats's earlier poems on Irish revolutionaries.

In those poems the "madness" of Eros is repeatedly associated with revolutionary fervor. In a contrast similar to that in "From 'The Antigone,'" "September 1913" pits against the world of common sense, materialist money-grubbing, and shivering prayer the heroism of Romantic Ireland, now thought to be "dead and gone" and "in the grave." Yeats there refers to "all that *delirium* of the brave" and compares the dead heroes' patriotism to erotic frenzy: could they come again, "You'd cry, 'Some woman's yellow hair / Has *maddened* every mother's son.'" In "Easter 1916"—an ambivalent choral celebration of the event that proved the rumors of Romantic Ireland's death to be premature—Yeats asks a final unanswerable question: "And what if *excess of love* / *Bewildered* them till they died?"

The first of the revolutionaries alluded to in "Easter 1916" and the one given most space is Con Markiewicz. I have already suggested that the moving elegy for Con and her sister, the poem that opens *The Winding Stair*, shares a common source with the concluding poem, "From 'The Antigone.'" If I am right, Yeats's reading of Sophocles, having provided the basis for a minor poem, also helped to shape a major one.

Immediately prior to the choral ode on which Yeats based the Antigone poem, Creon cries out that nothing shall "save these two girls from their doom" (769). He is reminded that Ismene has not been part of her sister's rebellion; Antigone, however, is to be immured in a sepulcher where she shall "learn, at last though late, that it is lost labour to revere the dead" (773–80). It is hard not to think of Yeats's recollection of the "*Two girls* in silk kimonos, / Both beautiful, one a gazelle" (VP 475), the now-dead Gore-Booth sisters. The second movement of their elegy begins, "Dear shadows, now you know it all." In the drafts this was even closer to Creon's pronouncement about the entombed Antigone learning at last, though late, about lost labor. Yeats began, "Instructed now beyond the grave," canceled this, and wrote:

Learn dear shadows in the *grave*
That such as ye should never fight
With a common wrong or right.

The second line was quickly changed to the final version, "All the *folly* of a fight"—which might remind us of the reception of Antigone by the Chorus when she is first led onstage, under guard:

O hapless, and child of hapless sire,—of Oedipus!
What means this? Thou brought a prisoner?—thou,
disloyal to the King's laws, and taken in *folly*?
    (376–83)

(It was from this anapestic coda to a choral ode that Yeats probably borrowed the phrase "Oedipus' child" for his own coda.) A female prisoner and lawbreaker taken in folly: Yeats would have had difficulty *not* thinking of Con, arrested by the British, condemned to death, imprisoned, pardoned, yet still caught up in what Yeats, recalling Nietzsche, called the ephemeral babble of politics, never to "learn" it was all "folly" until she was a shadow in the grave.

But the elegy does not end with the speaker still echoing Creon and the Chorus of the *Antigone*. Having declared, "The innocent and the beautiful / Have no enemy but time," the conservative, aristocratic Yeatsian speaker, echoing Ben Jonson ("Meddle with your match . . . That so the time doe catch") invokes those dear ghosts directly:

Arise and bid me strike a match
And strike another till time catch;
Should the conflagration climb,
Run till all the sages know.
We the great gazebo built,
They convicted us of guilt;
Bid me strike a match and blow.

The drafts show that Yeats initially conceived of the ghosts themselves striking the apocalyptic match ("Dear ghosts return and strike a match"), and one draft sustains the contrast between Yeats and the sisters: "*I* the great Gazebo built / *They* brought home to me the guilt." Caught up in emotion, Yeats had moved too far—from severe, Creon-like judgment, through lofty, Chorus-like kindness, to the familiar guilt of the politically uncommitted artist fabricating pleasure domes in a world of revolutionary activism. In the final version, he "finds a broader frame of reference that encompasses their political life and his artistic one." Now, in what is, as Helen Vendler has said, the "triumph" of the poem, it is "*we*" who are equally "convicted of mortal guilt by the sages who see the corruption of all earthly work." The ghostly sages

watch the poet-turned-incendiary as they watched the girls-turned-revolutionaries; they watch the gazebo-folly ignited as they watched the Post Office occupied. In the last fight, Con and Eva are the commanders and Yeats their inexperienced lieutenant, waiting for his moment of initiation—"Bid me strike a match and blow." If this is not Yeats's most authentic stance . . . , it is still a wrenched tribute to the power of the Irish activists in his memory, that to join them in thought he is willing to conceive of himself as putting the torch to all their common endeavor.[17]

This movement and final stance parallel the apostrophe in "From 'The Antigone.'" Love's bitter sweetness is to "overcome" men and gods in an apocalyptic upheaval, an ecstasy of destruction. If the parallels between the

---

17. Helen Vendler, "Four Elegies." On the elegy and the two sisters, see also Ian Fletcher "Yeats and Lissadell," in *W. B. Yeats, 1865–1965: Centenary Essays on the Art of W. B. Yeats*, ed. D. E. S. Maxwell and S. B. Bushrui, 62–78.

two poems seem more than coincidental, it is because they are *not* coincidental. The elegy for Eva and Con was written within six days of the elegy for Oedipus's child; begun, in fact, on the reverse of the sheet on which Yeats wrote the first draft of "From 'The Antigone.'"[18] Though he had only Yeats's 1906 play *Deirdre* in mind, David Clark was uncannily accurate when he wrote of "From 'The Antigone,'" "It is never safe to forget that, even though they may not appear, Yeats may have Irish instances [of the power of love] in mind" (*Songs and Choruses*, 220).

IV

These connections, of general genetic interest, illuminate the tone of the first two movements of "From 'The Antigone,'" movements corresponding to the Greek strophe and antistrophe. But another of Yeats's familiar "and yets" is still to come—a movement that, in this case, corresponds to the Greek anapests.

At this point in Sophocles' play, Antigone is brought in from the palace under guard. The entrance is marked, as usual in the Greek, by the shift to anapests, so we know these lines of the Chorus are spoken in her presence:

> But now I also am carried beyond the bounds of loyalty,
> and can no more keep back the streaming tears,
> when I see Antigone thus passing
> to the bridal chamber where all are laid to rest.
>   (800–805)

The attitude of the Chorus to Antigone has been ambivalent throughout; it temporizes, remaining in general humanly sympathetic but ideologically disapproving—the Yeats, as it were, of much of the Gore-Booth elegy. Its attitude in this ode has been one of fear and trembling regarding the outside force that causes the just man to *swerve* toward ruin (791). But in the anapestic coda, in an image also taken from the driving of racehorses, the Chorus admits that it, like Haemon, is, if not quite *"driven wild"* as in Yeats's version, at least carried beyond the bounds, outside the track,[19] both of choral impartiality and of loyalty to lawful institutions and to the ruler as, in its limited way, the Chorus perceives these things. The self-application of the horse-swerving metaphor suggests that the Chorus is moved not only by pity but also by a less intense form of that Love that drives Haemon and (in its most glorious form) Antigone herself. As in the Gore-Booth elegy, the movement is from judgment to kindness to empathy. In that poem

18. The first draft of "From 'The Antigone'" is dated by Yeats "Sept. 15"; the first draft of the Gore-Booth elegy is also dated in his hand: "Sept. 21."

19. The Greek οεϱοηαι refers to the oblique jerking aside of horses, making them swerve out of their courses.

Yeats catches precisely the poignant division of emotion expressed by the Greek Chorus—as he does in the final lines of "From 'The Antigone'":

Pray I will, and sing I must
And yet I weep—Oedipus' child
Descends into the loveless dust.

Yeats, who rarely breaks up his own lines to weep, follows Sophocles here. An earlier attempt, revealing physical empathy with the soft-cheeked girl, read: "Though I have sung, cry men must, / My cheeks are wet." That is, though as *Chorus* I *sing*, as *man* I must *weep*. This adheres to the Greek original in the giving way to human emotion, the breaking of choral decorum by empathizing with the lawbreaking heroine, and so going "beyond the bounds."

Antigone's descent out of the fruitful light—"looking my last on the sunlight that is for me no more"—may have reminded Yeats of his favorite elegiac lines, Nashe's "Brightness falls from the air, / Queens have died young and fair, / Dust hath closed Helen's eye." In the Yeats poem, we have a coalescence of "dusts." The dust Antigone placed on the corpse of her brother, that which closed Helen's eye, and the proleptic dust of Antigone herself, who is to die young and fair, mingles with the dust we all are and shall become.[20]

This is even more desolate than the Chorus's sight of Antigone passing to the bridal chamber where all are laid to rest. The descent of Oedipus's "child" into the "loveless" dust goes beyond the Marvellian reminder ("The grave's a fine and private place, / But none, I think, do there embrace") to synopsize the barrenness of Antigone's final lament just before she is led away:

No bridal bed, no bridal song hath been mine, no joy of marriage, no portion in the nurture of children; but thus, forlorn of friends, unhappy one, I go living to the vaults of death . . . the last daughter of the house of your kings.[21]

Yeats's loveless dust makes explicit the sympathetic, yet painful irony of the Chorus's word, *thalamon,* which appears often, as Yeats would know from Jebb's note, in "epitaphs on the unmarried."[22]

20. These lines from Thomas Nashe's "Litany in Time of Plague" were frequently cited by Yeats. The line of *Antigone* quoted (806–7) follows immediately after the Chorus's Anapests (800–805).

21. Lines 917–20, 914 (though Ismene survives, Antigone is right to think of herself as the last of her race). In Swinburne's *Erechtheus*, the maiden Chthonia, about to die, says to the Chorus of Athenian elders: "I, a spouseless bride and crownless but with garlands of the dead, / From the fruitless light turn silent to my dark unchilded bed."

22. Jebb, *Tragedies*, 149, note on lines 803–4. A famous example of the use of this word in the Greek Anthology is in an epitaph by Sappho.

But while the dominant tone is one of elegiac grief, the speaker, echoing Lear's beautiful words of consolation to *his* Antigone, Cordelia (*King Lear* 5.2.8–19), prays and sings in addition to weeping. It would have been a violation of his sense of Sophocles' vision, and of his own, for Yeats to have dismissed *all* hope of resurrection from that dust. Though published over the signature of other men, the following manifesto, written by Yeats in 1924, was a personal credo: "No man can create, as did Shakespeare, Homer, Sophocles, who does not believe, with all his blood and nerve, that man's soul is immortal. . . . We . . . call back the soul to its ancient sovereignty, and declare that it can do whatever it please, being made, as antiquity affirmed, from the imperishable substance of the stars."[23]

In his version of Sophocles, Yeats felt he had struck through the mask of mere scholarship to call back this ancient belief. In discussing what he called his "plain man's *Oedipus*" in 1933, he made his lack of classical scholarship a virtue:

Being an ignorant man, I may not have gone to Greece through a Latin mist. Greek literature, like old Irish literature, was founded upon belief, not like Latin literature upon documents. No man has ever prayed to or dreaded one of Virgil's nymphs, but when Oedipus at Colonus went into the Wood of the Furies he felt the same creeping in his flesh that an Irish countryman feels in certain haunted woods in Galway and in Sligo.

(*New York Times*, 15 January 1933)

Yeats's remark, on this same occasion, that he saw Ireland as sharing in the "old historical religion" of ancient Greece recalls his own experience, as recounted in a letter of December 1926 to Olivia Shakespear. During the rehearsals of his version of *Oedipus the King*, he had "but one overwhelming emotion, a sense as of the actual presence in a terrible sacrament of the god. But I have got that always, though never before so strongly, from Greek Drama" (L 705).

There is neither terrible sacrament nor joyful exaltation at the end of *A Woman Young and Old*; the tone is rather like that of Donne's "Nocturnall Upon S. Lucies Day" or of Wordsworth's "Elegiac Stanzas": a feeling that it is not *quite* without hope that we suffer and mourn. It was not the great transfiguration at the end of *Oedipus at Colonus*, but rather the muted transfiguration of the *Antigone*, overlaid with grief and loss, that Yeats wanted, and got, by ending *A Woman Young and Old* with his translation of a choral ode from that play. The sequence ends with descent into the dust; yet there is the whole image pattern of the preceding sequence to consider. The woman of "Chosen" (poem VI) had referred to the lover's "subterranean

23. *To-Morrow* 1 (August 1924). This editorial was signed by two of the new review's editors, Francis Stuart ("H. Stuart") and Cecil Salkeld. But both Mrs. Yeats (Ellmann, *Yeats: The Man and the Masks*, 245–47) and Stuart have confirmed Yeats's authorship. The final sentence is close to the passage of Plotinus cited by Yeats in his 1928 note to "The Tower."

rest" upon her body. In the next poem—"Parting," which evolved from the same drafts and which also echoes the combined imagery of love and death, nuptials and the tomb, found in *Romeo and Juliet*—the woman offered to love's play her "dark declivities." To end his sequence, Yeats chose the archetypal heroine doomed to depart this world "without marriage-song" (876), to be nuptially embraced only in the subterranean tomb.

Throughout the *Antigone*, as later in *Romeo and Juliet* and *A Woman Young and Old*, sexual joy and the tomb are closely interwoven—sarcastically by Creon (648–54), sympathetically by the Chorus in the anapests to the Eros ode, poignantly by Antigone herself (806–16, 981–94, 916–20). This imagery culminates in the speech of the Messenger, who reports that the lovers have been found in their posthumous bridal chamber, "corpse enfolding corpse," Haemon having won his "nuptial rites" only in the House of Death (1204–41). In his study of the contribution of this particular image-pattern to the play's overall tragic structure, Robert F. Goheen tentatively concludes,

In some measure the messengered union of Haimon with Antigone is a terminally symbolic action which gives to the lines of action they each chose in a divisive and frustrating situation some of the understanding and affirmation which can come from accomplished goal. Some sort of life after death is definitely asserted as a religious [fact or hypothesis] for the play. . . . But, while we are offered recognition of these matters, it is not a simple, unclouded recognition, and we should be wrong to read into the play a final glorious transfiguration for Haimon and Antigone. . . . When the nuptial imagery, even including the eschatological hypotheses of the play, is viewed in the total context and together with the emphases provided by the action, the "promise" of spiritual union provided by the linked deaths of Antigone and Haimon is a faint, heavily over-shadowed promise, under a heavy feeling of waste. The major impact provided by their deaths is tragic destruction rather than guaranteed bliss. But it is just in this building of severe tension between different realms of essential life that the fused imagery of marriage and death has its fullest bearing within the play.[24]

The statement would also serve as a description of the precarious balance and movement from a state of "depressed awareness" to one of "depressed transcendence" that, as M. L. Rosenthal has observed, characterizes so many lyrics of the past two centuries, and that certainly characterizes *A Woman Young and Old*. Against the final emphasis on descent into the loveless dust, which seems to exclude any promise of union, must be balanced the ecstatic hope of spiritual-erotic posthumous union sung in the two preceding poems, particularly in IX, "A Last Confession": "There's not a bird of day that dare / Extinguish that delight." But how does one reconcile the ending of "From 'The Antigone'" with inextinguishable de-

---

24. *The Imagery of Sophocles'* Antigone: *A Study of Poetic Image and Structure*, 40–41.

light? Perhaps that light in the "dust" lies dead; perhaps, on the other hand, the recognition of a tragically unchangeable reality and the poignant music of the final lines themselves—"Pray I will and sing I must, / And yet I weep—Oedipus' child / Descends into the loveless dust"—create just those momentary balancings Rosenthal describes as "hold[ing] off absolute loss of morale, if only through the purity with which a negative recognition is evoked and sustained."[25] If, as David Clark has said, the first thirteen lines of "From 'The Antigone'" are "splendid rhetoric," it is "the last three lines which lift the poem into greatness," balancing the "celebrations of the god's power" with "the sorrow for human suffering" (*Songs and Choruses*, 226).

V

To fully appreciate the precarious balance involved in this bittersweet descent, the reader has to bear in mind the triple context of the poem: its source in Sophocles' Oedipus cycle; its climactic position as *A Woman Young and Old*'s valediction and coda; and its relationship to the first poem of the sequence, "Father and Child."

What matters most, perhaps, is who Antigone is—in her own right and as the child of Oedipus. Writing three days after the Abbey opening of his own version of *Oedipus at Colonus* (12 September 1927; the first draft of the Antigone poem was written on 15 September), Yeats would have been particularly conscious that the "loveless dust" into which Antigone descends was that "earth riven by love" into which her father had descended before her in an apotheosis to which Yeats alludes in "A Packet for Ezra Pound" and in *On the Boiler* (V-B 27; Ex 449). Antigone herself, who passes "still living" into her bridal tomb, cherishes "good hope" that her coming will be welcome to her father, mother, and brother (891ff.). This Oedipal reunion of father and child is powerfully muted but perhaps not *utterly* obliterated by Yeats's word *dust*. Balancing the hope of reunion after death with the cruel reality of death itself, continuity with terminus, hope with loss, the archetype with the unique individual, Yeats is necessarily torn at the end of *A Woman Young and Old*—praying, singing, weeping.

Yeats knew that the descent of that father and daughter constituted a chthonic rite. Oedipus, who "sank down body and soul into the earth," is embraced by Yeats as "altogether separate from Plato's Athens and all that talk of the Good and the One, . . . all that cabinet of perfection." He is Yeats's *antithetical* counterweight to Christ, who, "crucified standing up, went into the abstract sky soul and body" (V-B 27–28).

Her father's daughter, Antigone descends to what is repeatedly referred to in the play as a *thalamon*, a hollowed-out marriage chamber; indeed, it is a dark declivity if, as Jebb surmises, the narrow passage leading to the chamber of the type of tomb in which Antigone would have been confined

---

25. *Sailing into the Unknown: Yeats, Pound, and Eliot*, 167–68.

"sloped downwards" from the entrance (lines 822–23, 850, 920, 1069; Jebb, *Tragedies*, 215). In addition to the parallel of Haemon and Antigone with Romeo and Juliet, the star-crossed lovers alluded to in poem VII, "Parting," there is a connection with the symbolic paradigm of *A Woman Young and Old*—the "Sun's passage under the earth" and his "sojourn" in the subterranean "bed of love" that is both womb and tomb. "It was in Blake at times the symbol of the grave," Yeats said in concluding the typescript note he once thought of appending to the sequence.[26] His note recalls the vaginal gate into and out of this world, imagery Blake derived from one of Yeats's own favorite sources, Porphyry's essay on the Cave of the Nymphs in Homer.

Though "only one book touching on Freudian principles was in his library, and that one a gift from a reader," Yeats *was* interested in Freud.[27] Nevertheless, the poet of winding stair and tower, "sex and the dead" (the only two subjects "worthy of a serious mind"), had little to learn about the psychoanalytical implications of the arched cavern or *fornix*. His woman in this arched and concentric sequence sees the mysteries of birth and death as intimately related. The fertile matrix of both, whence we came and whither we are going, is archetypally the same place. As the woman of poem V ("Consolation") said: "Where the crime's committed / The crime can be forgot"—here, sexually; in death, as a genitalized return to the primordial womb. Yeats would have appreciated Norman O. Brown's reference to Antigone in *Love's Body*:

The woman penetrated is a labyrinth. You emerge into another world inside the woman. The penis is the bridge; the passage to another world is coitus; the other world is a womb-cave. Cave man still drags cave woman to his cave; all coitus is fornication (*fornix*, an underground arched vault). And the cave in which coitus takes place is the grave; a chthonic fertility rite; Antigone buried alive, together with her ancestors, her bridal chamber the tomb. Death is coitus and coitus is death. Death is genitalized as a return to the womb, incestuous coitus.[28]

The tension at the heart of *A Woman Young and Old* pits this chthonic womb-tomb archetype against that of the Neoplatonists' circuitous journey of the soul. The father-daughter relationship is part of this pattern as well— and a particularly intimate part when we consider the rondural linkage of the final poem of *A Woman Young and Old* with the first. Yeats was working on the sequence at the same time that he was "translating" Sophocles' Oedipus plays. In fact, it was in 1929, the year the sequence was published,

26. The phrase, later canceled, is quoted by Jon Stallworthy, *Between the Lines: Yeats's Poetry in the Making*, 139.
27. Thomas Parkinson, "The Modernity of Yeats." Nevertheless, I am informed by George Mills Harper that "there is much evidence in the Automatic Script that Yeats and George had read and were much interested in Freud."
28. *Love's Body*, 48.

that he announced that the definitive edition of *A Vision* would proclaim Oedipus as his personal "new divinity." We may safely assume some connection in his mind between Antigone and his own daughter, Anne, the biographical model for the young girl of "Father and Child." Indeed, the original title of "From 'The Antigone'"—"Oedipus' Child," which, as David Clark says, "makes us take the attitude of a father" (*Songs and Choruses*, 221)—emphasized its connection with "Father and Child."

But the connections are more than titular. Just as Antigone defied the tyrannical ban of Creon, so the reply of the girl in "Father and Child" indicates that she will not be bound by the conventional "ban / Of all good men and women." As Western literature's most celebrated ban-breaker, Antigone is the archetypal model for such young women and, at the far end of the sequence, the perfect choice to end *A Woman Young and Old*. We expect to find Antigone championed by a writer like Virginia Woolf—for whom Sophocles' heroine was a symbolic presence from the outset of her career, with Creon rightly emblematic of weak yet oppressive male society. It is a pleasant surprise to encounter a similar response in W. B. Yeats. That Antigone should be sung, prayed, and wept for by Yeats—whose conservative "Prayer" for his own daughter would have her a quiet-loving, amiable Ismene, the well-married lady of a great house, rather than an opinionated Antigone—represents a triumph of the empathetic imagination; it endorses his claim in a 1936 letter to Dorothy Wellesley: "I can make a woman express herself. . . . I have looked out of her eyes. I have shared her desire" (LDW 108).

That empathy was present in "Father and Child," which in its first draft (beginning "It is but waste of breath to say") was written too much from the perspective of an anxious, scolding parent—understandable enough since the germ of the poem was an actual incident involving the poet's own daughter. In the second and final draft, however, Yeats accomplished the pivotal shift to the perspective of "she," the dramatic perspective that would govern the emerging sequence as a whole—even the final poem, since the cyclical structure of *A Woman Young and Old* as well as the links between these two ban-defying young women bring Anne and Antigone face to face.[29] To the limited extent that Yeats himself is to be associated with the Father of the opening poem and, more generally, with a "patriarchal" social order, the choice of Antigone indicates something of the self-liberation Yeats experienced by submitting himself imaginatively and dramatically to the perspective of such female personae as the Woman Young and Old and Crazy Jane.

In the opening poem of *A Woman Young and Old*, the Father—patriarchal tyranny and the Oedipus complex incarnate—tries to keep his child submissive, cowed by society's bans, dependent on him:

---

29. The drafts of the poem are discussed by Parkinson (*W. B. Yeats: The Later Poetry*, 64–65), who also cites the March 1926 diary entry from which the poem germinated.

She hears me strike the board and say
That she is under ban
Of all good men and women,
Being mentioned with a man
That has the worst of all bad names;
And thereupon replies
That his hair is beautiful,
Cold as the March wind his eyes.

"Father and Child" reverses both Herbert's "The Collar" and Plotinus's famous image of father and daughter as metaphor for the Divine One and the rebellious soul. In an act of self-overcoming, transcending his own fatherly scolding of his daughter, the poet also, in this opening poem, dramatically objectified a precocious remark actually made by young Anne; in the sequence's concluding poem, he repossesses and makes personal a choral threnody from the tragedy of Oedipus's daughter. Antigone descends into the loveless dust; Anne (in the form of the girl of the opening poem) awakens to the possibilities of love. By the end of the sequence, Yeats's patriarchal voice has disappeared; so, in fact, has that of the Woman Young and Old. Both are resolved into the Yeatsian choral voice celebrating the defiant Antigone and the bittersweet power—and fragility—of human love.

VI

The sequence brought to conclusion by "From 'The Antigone'" had been tracing a paradigmatic but anonymous career from youth to age. The Sophoclean translation alters that chronological pattern and, simultaneously, distances the sequence *and* makes it more poignant and personal. In fact, the shift away from the nameless "Woman" to the legendary but *specific* Antigone may reflect Yeats's despairing recognition—as he was to put it in his elegiac lines on Augusta Gregory in "The Municipal Gallery Revisited"— that "approved *patterns* of women or of men" can never be satisfactory substitutes for irreplaceable *individuals*.

This simultaneous distancing and personalizing is less paradoxical than it sounds. The choral coda provides an archetypal rounding of the sequence and a mythic resonance and distancing; it also conveys something of the death-marriage symbolism of Sophocles' play and so sustains and extends the similar imagery of the sequence it brings to conclusion. At the same time, however, charged as it is with the anguish of a specific *young* woman *forced* to descend, Yeats's "loveless dust" (which forces *us* to linger over the fullness of love in the very stressing of its loss) is an almost unbearably painful image. Had Yeats ended the sequence chronologically this poignance would have been lost. We might have been left with Yeats's Woman Old going to her grave empty, having fully expressed herself in that Blakean-

Yeatsian process of "embodiment" in which every impulse of the imagination, every desire of the lineaments, is fulfilled and then cast off. The aged
Crazy Jane, for example, *anticipates* being "a lonely ghost" precisely because
she will come to God having fully unwound, through passionate experience, the skein of love.

Without the mediation of the *Antigone*, without this *particular* young
woman who was both "Oedipus' child" and a girl whose bridal chamber
was her tomb, *A Woman Young and Old* might have ended, if not op-
timistically, on a note of near-complacency. As it is, it ends, like Antigone
herself, under protest. Yeats must have chosen this conclusion because of a
vision that is finally and essentially tragic. He desperately wants the note of
supernatural hope expressed in poem IX, "A Last Confession," and, less
rhapsodically and with considerably diminished certitude, in poem X,
"Meeting." But he is hardly the poet to deny the reality of loss. Whatever
transfigurative resonance is added by the chorus from the *Antigone*, it seems
more than balanced by the sense of tragic waste embodied in the death of
Antigone.

Like that of the Chorus in the play, Yeats's voice breaks at the end. With
the stunning shift between his versions of the ode and of the anapests—even
more dramatic than the shift in tone of the Sophoclean Chorus—the apocalyptic cry for more conflict is absorbed in the related, still protesting, but far
deeper cry of helpless anguish in the face of death. We may, through the
power of Eros, be "driven wild," but we end *choosing* to pray and *compelled*
to sing,[30] with the final tribute one of "wild tears" (VP 334):

Pray I will and sing I must,
And yet I weep—Oedipus' child
Descends into the loveless dust.

*   *   *

"Many ingenious lovely things are gone": thus Yeats began, elegiacally,
the greatest of his historical poems, one in which individual suffering is not
permitted to be absorbed in some aloof contemplation of the gyres. The
final stanza of the opening movement of this poem, "Nineteen Hundred
and Nineteen," asks the question that epitomizes human grief and glory, a
question Yeats could only answer, like Sophocles before him, with another
question:

---

30. David Clark makes two fine points about this final song and prayer. "Sing I Must": "To
sing is not merely an obligation. There is no choice. Love will reign and the song will be
sung." This is "the cry of Yeats the poet even more than it is the cry of the Chorus." The
prayer is more problematic. To whom is it directed and for what, exactly? Clark notes, in a
perceptive parenthesis: "It is typical of Yeats that prayer should be a concrete reality, while the
God prayed to is left unknown." *Songs and Choruses,* 228–29.

But is there any comfort to be found?
Man is in love and loves what vanishes,
What more is there to say?

We have been talking about the validation of the uniquely individual despite recurrent or traditional patterns, despite even the Eternal Recurrence of Nietzsche, whose role in the shaping and reinforcing of Yeats's tragic vision was not limited to exultant witnessing of the cyclical repetition of all things. Given this context, it is appropriate that the most poignant lines in "Nineteen Hundred and Nineteen," a poem once entitled "The Things That Come Again," should embody, not Nietzsche's and Yeats's antihistorical doctrine of Eternal Recurrence, but (as Erich Heller has said) "the closest equivalent in English" to Nietzsche's beautiful and untranslatable *Rosengeruch des Unwiederbringlichen*: the scent of what cannot be brought back, the vanishing rosebreath of the irretrievable.[31]

Amid the pathos of mutability, in which Antigone only precedes us in descending into the loveless dust, perhaps the only "comfort to be found" takes the form of what Wallace Stevens, another poet influenced by Nietzsche, has called "A Postcard from the Volcano." That modest means of communication nevertheless asserts, "posthumously," that the human "spirit storming in blank walls"—now the "shuttered mansion-house" of life—left behind, even in extinction, a memorial,

>   left what still is
> The look of things, left what we felt
> At what we saw.
> . . . .
> We knew for long the mansion's look
> And what we said of it became
> A part of what it is. . . .

Storming in blank walls, singing in the chains that hold us green and dying, we give utterance, make images that testify to our having been. Nietzsche's song, the one he sang on the train returning him to Basel after his complete mental breakdown in Turin in January 1889, is interpreted by Walter Berger, in Malraux's *The Walnut Trees of the Altenburg*, as a "sublime" revelation as "strong" as life itself, proof that "the greatest mystery is not that we have been flung at random between the profusion of matter and of the stars, but that within this prison we can draw from ourselves images powerful enough to deny our nothingness."[32] The last kiss may be given to

31. Heller, *The Artist's Journey into the Interior*, 196.
32. Malraux, *Les Noyers de l'Altenburg*, 99. The song was Nietzsche's poem "Venice." In the novel, Walter assists Franz Overbeck in bringing Nietzsche back to Basel (96–97).

the void, and we must all descend into the loveless dust; but Yeats, within this mortal prison and singing in chains, drew from himself and from his traditions more than his share of "images powerful enough to deny our nothingness."

That his images were powerful Yeats had no doubt, and he was insistent that their power was inseparable from their roots:

Those masterful images because complete
Grew in pure mind, but out of what began?

Like ourselves, our images are flung "*between* the profusion of matter and of the stars." The most complete of Yeats's masterful images are those that, like "Attis' image" in "Vacillation," hang between and reconcile such antinomies as male and female, time and eternity. To be complete, the crucial images must be composite: tower and winding stair, sword and flowering silk, and—perhaps Yeats's *most* "complete" composite image—the "great-rooted blossomer," its foliage flowering into the heavens, its roots deep in the earth. In exploring Yeats's own roots in tradition, I have stressed his deviations from them, this poet's relationship with the past being too complex to qualify as one of "radical innocence." In the poem in which that radical, rooted innocence is celebrated, Yeats prays for the daughter who reenters his poetry, covertly, in "Father and Child." The implicit connection between these two poems may serve as a final illustration of my root-and-blossom theme.

Yeats's "Prayer for My Daughter" takes as one of its two organizing icons (the other is the Horn of Plenty) the Romantic image of the tree—here, however, less indebted to those organicist Romantics who stressed dynamic process than to "haughtier-headed Burke that proved the state a tree," "unconquerable" and persisting through "century after century" (VP 481). However understandable given the historical storm (the "mere anarchy . . . loosed upon the world" in the poem immediately preceding), Yeats's conservative Burkean prayer may place inordinate emphasis on stability:

O may she live like some green laurel
Rooted in one dear perpetual place.

The "spreading laurel tree" emerges as the poem's emblem for "custom," that inherited and decorously cultivated sense of tradition in which "innocence and beauty" are "born" and bred. Like Burke, Yeats exalts an aristocratic order in which "all's accustomed, ceremonious"—a discipline diametrically opposed to that *laisser aller* Nietzsche found indistinguishable from mere anarchy. But Yeats knows too that the organic must change or die. The "roots" of tradition itself wither if, as Nietzsche warned the antiquarian venerators of custom, they are "no longer animated and inspired by the fresh life of the present." With that need to rejuvenate in mind, I conclude by suggesting that Yeats is in effect altering the "rootedness" of his own "Prayer" for his daughter when, in "Father and Child," he not only anticipates but also celebrates, however covertly and proleptically, his daughter's rebellion against established authority.

"Father and Child" derives from an actual domestic incident recorded in Yeats's 1926 diary: "George has just told me that yesterday she said to Anne: 'I don't like so and so,' so and so being a little boy of Anne's age, 'He is a very nasty child.' Anne replied 'Yes but he has such lovely hair and his eyes are as cold as a March wind.'" Though Anne was only seven at the time, Yeats saw at once the poetic potential in her "Yeatsian" ("Yes but") elevation of the aesthetic over the merely ethical: "I should put that into verse for it is the cry of every woman who loves a blackguard."[33]

In the poem, Yeats's paternal disapproval is "fathered" onto the unattractive even tyrannical speaker, leaving the girl free to break from Yeats's own cherished "ceremony" and "custom" by embracing Nietzsche's "fresh life of the present." The "haystack- and roof-levelling wind, / Bred on the Atlantic" can no longer "be stayed," as it was in "Prayer"; this turbulent wind, from which his daughter even as an infant in the cradle was only "half-hid," sweeps into "Father and Child" in the form of the dangerous but exciting young man, his hair beautiful, "Cold as the March wind his eyes."

As in the elegy for Eva and Con, and as in Yeats's reanimating alteration of Sophocles' Eros Chorus, judgment is replaced by empathy with a "ban"-breaking heroine. But while Yeats can be folded in a single party with Con and Eva only when they are "dear shadows," and the Oedipal reunion of father and child in the *Antigone* can take place only in the grave, it is achieved in "Father and Child" *here*, in life—through the empathetic *poet's* rather than the disapproving *parent's* response to that liberating March wind heralding spring and summer. "O what a bursting out there was / And what a blossoming," cries the lover of "Summer and Spring," seated (in the matching sequence, *A Man Young and Old*) "under that very tree" he learns he must share with a rival. In "Father and Child," which is not only an anecdote for fathers but also a parable of the Romantic interaction between tradition and revolution, the parent who would keep his daughter "rooted in one dear perpetual place" yields to the poet who responds to her vital bursting out and blossoming.

The girl's aesthetic-erotic reply, its language barely altered from Anne's as recorded in Yeats's diary, animates the poem. It also transforms its literary and philosophic "roots": Herbert's "The Collar" (see above, Chapter 5) and Plotinus's image of the soul as a daughter who "takes up with another love, a mortal, leaves her father and falls. But one day coming to hate her shame, she puts away the evil of earth, once more seeks the father,

---

33. Quoted by Parkinson, *The Later Poetry*, 64–65.

and finds her peace" (*Enneads* 6.9.9). But of course, in "Father and Child,"
the girl's life-affirming fall from paternal grace and implicit initiation into
love's bitter mystery are identical with Yeats's *antithetical* rebellion against
these very traditions: the Christian bondage submitted to by Herbert and
Plotinian Neoplatonism, both of which denigrate "fallen" life on earth and
summon the rebellious "generated" soul to return to the divine Father as
source of all. It is a position double-minded Yeats notionally accepts but
emotionally dissents from, even defies—another "Yes but. . . ." Poetically
distanced and dramatically advanced to the age of puberty, the "Anne" of
"Father and Child" proves herself, as Antigone had, her father's daughter.
Identified with the "rooted" tree of "Prayer," she here expresses a bursting
out and blossoming analogous to the triumphant transformations of inherited tradition by that "great-rooted blossomer," William Butler Yeats himself.

WORKS CITED

A. Yeats's Writings

References to Yeats's frequently cited works are abbreviated and included parenthetically in the text. For those citations, see Abbreviations, p. xi. The Yeats Archives, Center for Contemporary Arts and Letters, State University of New York, Stony Brook, is the source for all unpublished Yeats material cited, except where otherwise indicated.

Other Writings by Yeats (in alphabetical order)

"Editorial." In *To-Morrow* 1 (1 August 1924).

"Friends of My Youth." Undelivered 1910 lecture. Edited by Joseph Ronsley as "Yeats's Lecture Notes for 'Friends of My Youth.'" In *Yeats and the Theatre*, edited by Robert O'Driscoll and Lorna Reynolds. Toronto: Macmillan of Canada; Niagara Falls, N.Y.: Maclean-Hunter Press, 1975.

Is the Order of R.R. & A.C. to remain a Magical Order? Privately printed pamphlet, 1901. Reprinted as an appendix in George Mills Harper, *Yeats's Golden Dawn*. London: Macmillan, 1974.

On the Boiler. Dublin: Cuala Press, 1938.

Introduction to *Oxford Book of Modern Verse*, ed. Yeats. Oxford: Clarendon Press, 1936.

"Preface" to Oliver St. John Gogarty, *Wild Apples*. Dublin: Cuala Press, 1930.

The Speckled Bird by W. B. Yeats. 2 vols. Edited by William H. O'Donnell. Dublin: Dolmen Press, 1974.

W. B. Yeats: Interviews and Recollections. 2 vols. Edited by E. H. Mikhail. London: Macmillan; New York: Harper & Row, 1977.

B. Nietzsche's Writings

Except for references to the Thomas Common anthology of Nietzsche annotated by Yeats (see below, *Nietzsche as Critic, Philosopher, Poet and Prophet*), all numbers in my citations refer not to pages but to aphorisms or sections, which are the same in all editions of Nietzsche, regardless of language. For the reader's convenience, and in the interests of accuracy and stylistic felicity, I have cited the best modern translations—except where indicated, those of Walter Kaufmann, either in *The Portable Nietzsche* (New York: Viking, 1954) or in the series published by Vintage Books. As indicated, however, I have also consulted the volumes of Nietzsche included in Yeats's library, maintained by Anne Yeats, the poet's daughter, at "Avalon," her home in Dalkey, Ireland. Though Yeats's copies of the books sent to him in September 1902 by John Quinn (*Thus Spoke Zarathustra, On the Genealogy of Morals*, and

311

The Case of Wagner) have been lost, his library does contain selected volumes in both early editions of Nietzsche in English:

The Complete Works of Friedrich Nietzsche. 18 vols. Edited by Oscar Levy. Edinburgh and London: T. N. Foulis, 1909–1911.
The Works of Friedrich Nietzsche. Edited by Alexander Tille. London: T. Fisher Unwin, 1899–1903.

The library also contains a collection entitled *Nietzsche in Outline and Aphorism*, edited by O. R. Orage (Edinburgh and London: T. N. Foulis, 1907). The collection famous because of Yeats's annotations, originally lent to him by John Quinn, is now housed in the Special Collections Department of the library at Northwestern University (item T.R. 193 N 67n.); this is *Nietzsche as Critic, Philosopher, Poet and Prophet: Choice Selections from His Works*, compiled by Thomas Common (London: Grant Richards, 1901). For untranslated work, two editions have been cited:

Werke und Briefe: Historisch-Kritische Gesamtausgabe. 9 vols. Edited under the supervision of the "Stiftung Nietzsche-Archiv." Munich: Beck, 1933–1942.
Gesammelte Werke, Musarionausgabe. 23 vols. Munich: Musarion Verlag, 1920–1929.

Individual Nietzsche works cited are given in alphabetical order. I also include the German title, date of initial publication, and cross references to the translations in Yeats's library:

The Antichrist. [*Der Antichrist*, published in 1895, after Nietzsche had become insane.] In *The Portable Nietzsche*, 565–656. For 62, marked by Yeats, I have used the Thomas Common translation, in vol. 3 of the Tille edition (1899).
Beyond Good and Evil. [*Jenseits von Gut und Böse*, 1886.] New York: Vintage, 1966.
The Birth of Tragedy. [*Die Geburt der Tragödie*, 1872.] New York: Vintage, 1967. Yeats's was the William Haussmann translation in the Levy edition; originally vol. 1 (1909).
The Case of Wagner. [*Der Fall Wagner*, published in 1895, after Nietzsche had become insane.] New York: Vintage, 1966.
The Dawn. [*Die Morgenröte*, 1881.] *Daybreak*, translated by R. J. Hollingdale. Cambridge: Cambridge University Press, 1982. In Chapter 2, I cite the J. M. Kennedy translation, *The Dawn of Day*, in the Levy edition; Yeats's library also contains the Johanna Volz translation, vol. 4 in the Tille edition.
The Gay Science. [*Die Fröhliche Wissenschaft*, 1882.] New York: Vintage, 1974.
On the Genealogy of Morals. [*Zur Genealogie der Moral*, 1887.] New York: Vintage, 1967. Yeats's was the William Haussmann-John Gray translation, vol. 1 in the Tille edition (1899); he also annotated heavily the Common translation in *Nietzsche as Critic, Philosopher, Poet and Prophet*.
On the Uses and Disadvantages of History for Life. [*Vom Nutzen und Nachteil der Historie für das Leben*, 1874.] The second in Nietzsche's four *Untimely Meditations*. Translated by R. J. Hollingdale. Cambridge: Cambridge University Press, 1983. Yeats's edition, vols. 4 and 5 of the Levy set, was entitled *Thoughts Out of Season*, translated by Adrian Collins.
Nietzsche contra Wagner. [Published in 1895, after Nietzsche had become insane.] In *The Portable Nietzsche*, 661–83. Yeats's translation, by Common, was part of vol. 3 of the Tille edition.
Philosophy in the Tragic Age of the Greeks. ["Philosophie im tragischen Zeitalter der

Griechen," early unpublished essay.] Translated by Marianne Cowan. Chicago: Gateway, 1962.

Thus Spoke Zarathustra. [*Also Sprach Zarathustra*, 1883–1885.] In *The Portable Nietzsche*, 103–439; also issued separately (New York: Viking, 1966). Yeats was introduced to the work in the Alexander Tille translation (1896).

Twilight of the Idols. [*Die Götzen-Dämmerung*, 1889.] In *The Portable Nietzsche*, 463–563. Vol. 3 of the Tille edition contains Thomas Common's translation.

The Wanderer and His Shadow. [*Der Wanderer und sein Schatten*, 1880.] In vol. 9 of the Musarion edition of the *Gesammelte Werke*.

The Will to Power. [*Der Wille zur Macht*, a selection from Nietzsche's notebooks, chosen and published by his sister, 1901, 1904, and, in a cumulative edition, 1906.] Translated by Walter Kaufmann and R. J. Hollingdale. New York: Random House, 1967. Volumes 14 and 15 of the Levy edition contain a translation by Anthony M. Ludovico.

C. Books and Articles Cited

Abrams, M. H. *The Correspondent Breeze: Essays on English Romanticism*. New York: Norton, 1984.

———. "Kant and the Theology of Art." *Notre Dame English Journal* 13 (1981):75–106.

———. *Natural Supernaturalism: Tradition and Revolution in Romantic Literature*. New York: Norton, 1971.

Adams, Hazard. *Blake and Yeats: The Contrary Vision*. Ithaca: Cornell University Press, 1955.

———. *Philosophy of the Literary Symbolic*. Tallahassee: University Presses of Florida, 1983.

Albright, Daniel. *The Myth Against Myth: A Study of Yeats's Imagination in Old Age*. London: Oxford University Press, 1972.

Allen, James L. "Yeats's Use of the Serious Pun." *Southern Quarterly* 1 (1963):153–66.

Allt, Peter. "W. B. Yeats." *Theology* 42 (1941):81–99.

———. "Yeats, Religion, and History." *Sewanee Review* 60 (1952):622–58.

Archibald, Douglas. *Yeats*. Syracuse: Syracuse University Press, 1983.

Arnold, Matthew. *On Translating Homer*. London: J. Murray, 1905.

———. *Poems by Matthew Arnold*. 3 vols. London and New York: Macmillan, 1895.

———. *Unpublished Letters of Matthew Arnold*. Edited by Arnold Whitridge. New Haven: Yale University Press, 1925.

Auden, W. H. "Yeats as an Example." *Kenyon Review* 10 (1948). Reprinted in *The Permanence of Yeats*, edited by James Hall and Martin Steinmann. New York: Macmillan, Collier, 1961 [1950].

Bacon, Sir Francis. *Works*. Edited by J. Spedding, R. L. Ellis, and D. D. Heath. 15 vols. St. Clair Shores, Mich.: Scholarly Press, 1976 [1858–1874].

Balzac, Honoré de. *Comédie Humaine*. Temple Edition. 40 vols. Edited by George Saintsbury. New York: Macmillan, 1901. Vol. 19: *The Jealousies of a Country Town*, translated by Ellen Marriage. Vol. 34: *Séraphita*, translated by Clara Bell. (Yeats's set)

Barrett, William. "Determinism and Novelty." In *Determinism and Freedom in the Age of Modern Science*, edited by Sidney Hook. New York: Macmillan, 1970.

Berkeley, George. *Berkeley's Commonplace Book*. Edited by G. A. Johnston. London: Faber & Faber, 1930.

————. *The Works of George Berkeley*. 2 vols. Dublin: John Exshaw, 1784.

Bhartrihari. *The Satakas or Wise Sayings of Bhartrihari*. Translated by J. M. Kennedy. London: T. Werner Laurie, 1913.

Blackmur, R. P. *Form and Value in Modern Poetry*. Garden City: Doubleday/Anchor, 1957.

Blake, William. *The Complete Poetry and Prose of William Blake*. Edited by David V. Erdman, commentary by Harold Bloom. Berkeley and Los Angeles: University of California Press; Garden City: Doubleday/Anchor, 1965.

————. *Songs of Innocence and of Experience*. Introduction and commentary by Sir Geoffrey Keynes. London: Rupert Hart-Davis, in association with The Trianon Press, 1967.

Bloom, Harold. *The Anxiety of Influence: A Theory of Poetry*. New York: Oxford University Press, 1973.

————. *A Map of Misreading*. New York: Oxford University Press, 1975.

————. *Poetry and Repression: Revisionism from Blake to Stevens*. New Haven and London: Yale University Press, 1976.

————. *Yeats*. London, Oxford, New York: Oxford University Press, 1970.

Bloom, Harold, et al., eds. *Oxford Anthology of English Literature*. Vol. 2. New York, London, Toronto: Oxford University Press, 1973.

Bly, Robert. *News of the Universe*. San Francisco: Sierra Club Books, 1980.

Bohlmann, Otto. *Yeats and Nietzsche: An Exploration of Major Nietzschean Echoes in the Writings of William Butler Yeats*. Totowa, N.J.: Barnes & Noble, 1982.

Bordo, Susan. *The Flight to Objectivity: Essays on Cartesianism and Culture*. Albany: State University of New York Press, 1987.

Bornstein, George. *Transformations of Romanticism in Yeats, Eliot, and Stevens*. Chicago: University of Chicago Press, 1976.

————. *Yeats and Shelley*. Chicago: University of Chicago Press, 1970.

Bové, Paul A. "Cleanth Brooks and Modern Irony: A Kierkegaardian Critique." *Boundary 2* 4 (1976):727–59.

Bradford, Curtis. *Yeats at Work*. Carbondale and Edwardsville: Southern Illinois University Press, 1965.

Brombert, Victor. *The Romantic Prison: The French Tradition*. Princeton: Princeton University Press, 1978.

Brooks, Cleanth. *The Hidden God*. New Haven: Yale University Press, 1963.

————. *Modern Poetry and the Tradition*. Chapel Hill: University of North Carolina Press, 1939.

————. *The Well Wrought Urn: Studies in the Structure of Poetry*. New York: Reynal and Hitchcock, 1947.

Brown, Norman O. *Love's Body*. New York: Vintage, 1966.

Burke, Edmund. *Letters on a Regicide Peace* and *Reflections on the Revolution in France*. In *The Works of the Right Honourable Edmund Burke*, 8 vols. Bohn's Standard Library. London: George Bell, 1877–1883. (Yeats's set)

Bush, Douglas. *Science and English Poetry: A Historical Sketch, 1590–1950*. New York: Oxford University Press, 1950.

Butterfield, Herbert. *The Origins of Modern Science, 1300–1800*. New York: Free Press, 1964.

Byron, Lord. *The Selected Poetry of Lord Byron*. Edited by Leslie A. Marchand. New York: Modern Library, 1967.

Campbell, C. A. *Selfhood and Godhood*. New York: Macmillan, 1957.

Campbell, Joseph. *The Hero with a Thousand Faces.* 2d ed. Princeton: Princeton University Press, Bollingen Series, 1968 [1948].

Cardozo, Nancy. *Lucky Eyes and a High Heart: The Life of Maud Gonne.* Indianapolis and New York: Bobbs-Merrill, 1978.

Carne-Ross, D. S. *Pindar.* New Haven: Yale University Press, 1985.

Clark, David R. *Yeats at Songs and Choruses.* Amherst: The University of Massachusetts Press, 1983.

Clarke, Austin. "Poet and Artist." *The Arrow* ["W. B. Yeats Commemoration Number"] (Summer 1939):8–9.

Cobban, Alfred. *Edmund Burke and the Revolt Against the Eighteenth Century.* London: Macmillan, 1929.

Cohane, J. J. "Cowley and Yeats." *Times Literary Supplement* 56 (10 May 1957):289.

Coleridge, Samuel Taylor. *Biographia Literaria.* Edited by James Engell and W. Jackson Bate. Princeton: Princeton University Press, Bollingen Series, 1984. This is a one-volume paperback of the two-volume edition published in 1983 as vol. 7 of *The Collected Works of Samuel Taylor Coleridge,* 16 vols., general editor, Kathleen Coburn. Princeton: Princeton University Press, Bollingen Series; London: Routledge & Kegan Paul, 1969- .

————. *Collected Letters of Samuel Taylor Coleridge.* 6 vols. Edited by Earl Leslie Griggs. Oxford: Clarendon Press, 1956–1971.

————. *The Complete Poetical Works of Samuel Taylor Coleridge.* 2 vols. Edited by E. H. Coleridge. Oxford: Clarendon Press, 1912.

————. *The Friend.* 2 vols. Edited by Barbara Rooke. In the Bollingen *Collected Works,* vol. 4 (1969).

————. *The Notebooks of Samuel Taylor Coleridge.* Edited by Kathleen Coburn. New York: Pantheon-Bollingen, 1957- .

Cowell, Raymond. *W. B. Yeats.* New York: Arco, 1969.

Cox, Roger. "On Wordsworth's Immortality Ode." *Explicator* 19 (March 1961): item 34.

Crane, R. S. "Notes on the Organization of Locke's *Essay.*" In Crane's *The Idea of the Humanities and Other Essays Critical and Historical,* 2 vols. Chicago: University of Chicago Press, 1967.

Culler, Jonathan. "Issues in Contemporary Critical Debate." In *American Criticism in the Poststructuralist Age,* edited by Ira Konigsberg. Ann Arbor: University of Michigan Press, 1981.

Cullingford, Elizabeth. *Yeats, Ireland and Fascism.* New York: New York University Press, 1981.

Dalsimer, Adele M. "'My Chief of Men': Yeats's Juvenilia and Shelley's *Alastor.*" *Éire-Ireland* 8 (1973):71–90.

Dangerfield, George. *The Damnable Question: One Hundred and Twenty Years of Anglo-Irish Conflict.* Boston and Toronto: Little, Brown, 1976.

Davie, Donald. "Yeats, Berkeley, and Romanticism" (1955). Reprinted in *English Literature and British Philosophy,* edited by S. P. Rosenbaum. Chicago: University of Chicago Press, 1971.

de Beauvoir, Simone. *The Second Sex.* New York: Knopf, 1957.

de la Varenne, Maton. *Histoire particulière des événements . . . de juin, de juillet, d'août et de septembre 1792.* Paris: Périsse et Compere, 1806.

Derrida, Jacques. "The Ends of Man." In *The Structuralist Controversy,* edited by Richard Macksey and Richard Donato. Baltimore: The Johns Hopkins University Press, 1972.

Diggory, Terence. *Yeats and American Poetry: The Tradition of the Self.* Princeton: Princeton University Press, 1983.

Dodds, E. R. *The Greeks and the Irrational.* Berkeley and Los Angeles: University of California Press, 1971.

Donne, John. *John Donne: The Sermons.* 10 vols. Edited by G. R. Potter and E. M. Simpson. Berkeley: University of California Press, 1953–1962.

―――. *The Poems of John Donne.* 2 vols. Edited by Herbert J. C. Grierson. London: Oxford University Press, 1912.

Donoghue, Denis. "The Hard Case of Yeats." *New York Review of Books* 24 (26 May 1977):3–6.

―――. *William Butler Yeats.* New York: Viking, 1971.

Donoghue, Denis, and J. R. Mulryne, eds. *An Honoured Guest: New Essays on W. B. Yeats.* New York: St. Martin's Press, 1965.

Dryden, John. *The Poetry of John Dryden.* 4 vols. Edited by James Kinsley. Oxford: Clarendon Press, 1958.

Easlea, Brian. *Witch-Hunting: Magic and the New Philosophy.* Atlantic Highlands, N.J.: Humanities Press, 1980.

Ehrenpreis, Irvin. *Acts of Implication: Suggestions and Covert Meaning in the Works of Dryden, Swift, Pope, and Austen.* Berkeley, Los Angeles, and London: University of California Press, 1980.

Eichner, Hans. "The Rise of Modern Science and the Genesis of Romanticism." *PMLA* 97 (1982):8–30.

Eliot, T. S. "A Foreign Mind" [review of Yeats's *The Cutting of an Agate*]. *Athenaeum,* 4 July 1919.

―――. *Selected Prose of T. S. Eliot.* Edited by Frank Kermode. New York: Harcourt, Brace, Jovanovich / Farrar, Strauss, Giroux, 1975.

―――. *The Use of Poetry and the Use of Criticism.* London: Faber & Faber, 1950 [1933].

Ellmann, Richard. *Eminent Domain: Yeats Among Wilde, Joyce, Eliot, and Auden.* New York: Oxford University Press, 1967.

―――. *The Identity of Yeats.* 2d ed. New York: Oxford University Press, 1964.

―――. *Yeats: The Man and the Masks.* New York: Macmillan, 1948.

Ellmann, Richard, and Charles Feidelson, eds. *The Modern Tradition.* New York: Oxford University Press, 1965.

Erdman, David V. *Blake: Prophet Against Empire.* 3d ed. Princeton: Princeton University Press, 1977 [1954].

Eunapius. *Vita Maximi.* Excerpted in *Select Passages Illustrating Neoplatonism,* edited by E. R. Dodds. London: Society for Promoting Christian Knowledge, 1923.

Evans, Walter. "From Wordsworth's *The Prelude* to Yeats's 'The Second Coming.'" *Yeats-Eliot Review* 6 (1979):31–37.

Finneran, Richard J. "W. B. Yeats." In *Anglo-Irish Literature: A Review of Research,* edited by Finneran. New York: Modern Language Association, 1976.

―――. "W. B. Yeats." In *Recent Research on Anglo-Irish Writers,* edited by Finneran. New York: Modern Language Association, 1983.

Finneran, Richard J., ed. *W. B. Yeats, The Poems: A New Edition.* New York: Macmillan, 1983.

FitzGerald, Mary. "The Writing of *The Words upon the Window-pane.*" *Colby Library Quarterly* 17 (1981):61–73.

Fletcher, Ian. "Yeats and Lissadell." In *W. B. Yeats, 1865-1965: Centenary Essays on the Art of W. B. Yeats*, edited by D. E. S. Maxwell and S. B. Bushrui. Ibadan, Nigeria: Ibadan University Press, 1965.

Foster, John Burt, Jr. *Heirs to Dionysus: A Nietzschean Current in Literary Modernism.* Princeton: Princeton University Press, 1981.

Fraser, G. S. *Vision and Rhetoric: Studies in Modern Poetry.* London: Faber & Faber, 1959.

Fraser, Ralph S. "Nietzsche, Byron and the Classical Tradition." In *Studies in Nietzsche and the Classical Tradition*, edited by James C. O'Flaherty et al. Chapel Hill: University of North Carolina Press, 1976.

Freud, Sigmund. *Standard Edition of the Complete Psychological Works of Sigmund Freud.* 23 vols. Edited by James Strachey et al. New York: Macmillan, 1964- .

Friedman, Norman. "Permanence and Change: What Happens in Yeats's 'Dialogue of Self and Soul.'" *Yeats-Eliot Review* 5 (1978):21–30.

Frost, Robert. *The Poetry of Robert Frost*, edited by Edward Connery Lathem. New York: Holt, Rinehart, Winston, 1979.

Frye, Northrop. *Fearful Symmetry: A Study of William Blake.* Boston: Beacon Press, 1962 [1947].

———. "The Road to Excess" (1963). In *Romanticism and Consciousness: Essays in Criticism*, edited by Harold Bloom. New York: Norton, 1970.

———. *Spiritus Mundi: Essays on Literature, Myth and Society.* Bloomington and London: Indiana University Press, 1976.

———. *The Stubborn Structure: Essays on Criticism and Society.* Ithaca: Cornell University Press, 1970.

Gadamer, Hans-Georg. *Truth and Method.* New York: Seabury Press, 1975.

Gardner, Helen. *The Composition of "Four Quartets."* New York: Oxford University Press, 1978.

Gibbs, A. M. "The 'Rough Beasts' of Yeats and Shakespeare." *Notes & Queries* 17 (February 1970):48–49.

Goheen, Robert F. *The Imagery of Sophocles' Antigone: A Study of Poetic Image and Structure.* Princeton: Princeton University Press, 1951.

Gordon, D. S., and Ian Fletcher. *W. B. Yeats: Images of a Poet.* Manchester: University of Manchester, 1961.

Gregory, Lady Augusta. *Lady Gregory's Journals, 1916–1930.* Edited by Lennox Robinson. London: Macmillan, 1947.

———. *Seventy Years.* New York: Macmillan, 1976.

———. *Sir Hugh Lane: His Life and Legacy.* Gerrards Cross: Smythe, 1973 [1921].

———. *Visions and Beliefs in the West of Ireland.* 2 vols. New York: Putnam, 1920 [1914].

Grierson, Herbert J. C. "Preface" to V. K. Narayana Menon, *The Development of W. B. Yeats.* Edinburgh: Oliver & Boyd, 1942.

Gross, Harvey. *The Contrived Corridor: History and Fatality in Modern Literature.* Ann Arbor: University of Michigan Press, 1972.

Grünbaum, Adolf. "Freewill and the Laws of Human Behavior." *American Philosophical Quarterly* 8 (1971):299–317.

Haar, Michael. "Nietzsche and Metaphysical Language." *Man and World* 4 (1971). Reprinted in *Nietzsche: A Collection of Critical Essays*, edited by Robert Soloman. Garden City: Doubleday/Anchor, 1973.

Hall, James, and Martin Steinmann, eds. *The Permanence of Yeats.* New York: Macmillan, Collier, 1961 [1950].

Hardy, Thomas. *Collected Poems*. Edited by James Gibson. New York: Macmillan, 1976.

Harper, George Mills. "The Authors Are in Eternity." Lecture delivered in 1982 at Le Moyne College, Syracuse, N.Y.

_____. "The Creator as Destroyer: Nietzschean Morality in Yeats's *Where There Is Nothing*." *Colby Library Quarterly* 15 (1979):114–25.

_____. *The Making of Yeats's "A Vision": A Study of the Automatic Script*. 2 vols. Carbondale: Southern Illinois University Press, 1987.

_____. "'A Subject for Study': Miracle at Mirebeau." In *Yeats and the Occult*, edited by Harper. Toronto: Macmillan of Canada, 1975.

_____. *Yeats's Golden Dawn*. London: Macmillan, 1974.

Harris, Daniel. *Yeats: Coole Park and Ballylee*. Baltimore: The Johns Hopkins University Press, 1974.

Hartman, Geoffrey. *Beyond Formalism*. New York: Yale University Press, 1970.

_____. *Criticism in the Wilderness: The Study of Literature Today*. New Haven: Yale University Press, 1980.

_____. "Romanticism and Anti-self-consciousness." In *Romanticism: Points of View*, edited by Robert F. Gleckner and Gerald E. Enscoe. Detroit: Wayne State University Press, 1975.

_____. "Toward Literary History." In *In Search of Literary Theory*, edited by Morton W. Bloomfield. Ithaca: Cornell University Press, 1972.

Hazlitt, William. *The Spirit of the Age*. In *The Complete Works of William Hazlitt*, 21 vols. London and Toronto: Dent, 1930–1934.

Hegel, G. W. F. *The Logic of Hegel*. Translated by W. Wallace. Oxford and Fairlawn, N.J., 1892.

_____. *The Phenomenology of Mind*. Translated by J. B. Baillie. New York: Harper Torchbook, 1967.

Heidegger, Martin. *Being and Time*. New York: Harper and Row, 1962 [1927].

Heller, Erich. *The Artist's Journey into the Interior*. New York: Random House, 1965.

_____. *The Disinherited Mind: Essays in Modern German Literature and Thought*. Expanded ed. New York and London: Harcourt, Brace, Jovanovich, 1975.

Henn, T. R. *The Lonely Tower: Studies in the Poetry of W. B. Yeats*. 2d ed. New York: Barnes & Noble, 1965 [1950].

Hillman, James. *The Myth of Analysis*. New York: Harper and Row, 1972.

Hollander, John. *The Figure of Echo: A Mode of Allusion in Milton and After*. Berkeley: University of California Press, 1981.

Holroyd, Michael, ed. *The Best of Hugh Kingsmill*. London: Victor Gollancz, 1970.

Homer. *The Iliad of Homer*. Translated by Richmond Lattimore. Chicago and London: University of Chicago Press, 1951.

Hone, Joseph. *W. B. Yeats, 1865–1939*. 2d ed. New York: St. Martin's Press, 1962 [1942].

Hueffer, Ford Madox [later Ford Madox Ford]. "The Poet's Eye. III." *New Freewoman* 1 (15 September 1913):126–27.

Hume, David. *The Philosophy of David Hume*. Edited by V. C. Chappell. New York: Modern Library, 1963.

Ingarden, Roman. *The Literary Work of Art*. Translated by George G. Grabowicz. Evanston: Northwestern University Press, 1974 [1931].

Iser, Wolfgang. *The Act of Reading: A Theory of Aesthetic Response*. Baltimore: The Johns Hopkins University Press, 1980.

Jacobs, Edward C. "Yeats and the Artistic Epiphany." *Discourse* 12 (1969):292–305.

Jeffares, A. Norman. *A Commentary on the Collected Poems of W. B. Yeats.* Stanford: Stanford University Press, 1968.

———. *W. B. Yeats, Man and Poet.* 2d ed. New York: Barnes & Noble, 1966 [1949].

Jochum, K. P. S. *W. B. Yeats: A Classified Bibliography of Criticism.* Urbana, Chicago, London: University of Illinois Press, 1978.

Johnson, E. D. H. *The Alien Vision of Victorian Poetry.* Princeton: Princeton University Press, 1952.

Kant, Immanuel. *Kant's Critical Philosophy for English Readers.* 3d ed. Translated by J. P. Mahaffy and J. H. Bernard. London: Macmillan, 1915. Vol. 2, containing Kant's synopsis of the first *Critique* (the *Prolegomena*), is in Yeats's library.

Kaufmann, Walter. *Nietzsche: Philosopher, Psychologist, Antichrist.* 4th ed. Princeton: Princeton University Press, 1974.

Keane, Patrick J. "The Human Entrails and the Starry Heavens: Some Instances of Visual Patterns for Yeats's Mingling of Heaven and Earth." *Bulletin of Research in the Humanities* 84 (1981):366–91.

———. "On Truth and Lie in Nietzsche." *Salmagundi* 29 (1975):67–94.

———. "Revolutions French and Russian: Burke, Wordsworth, and the Genesis of Yeats's 'The Second Coming.'" *Bulletin of Research in the Humanities* 82 (1979):18–52.

———. "Time's Ruins and the Mansions of Eternity." *Bulletin of Research in the Humanities* 86 (1983):33–66.

Keane, Patrick J., ed. *William Butler Yeats: A Collection of Criticism.* New York: McGraw-Hill, 1973.

Keats, John. *Letters of John Keats.* 2 vols. Edited by Hyder Rollins. Cambridge: Harvard University Press, 1958.

———. *The Poems of John Keats.* Edited by Jack Stillinger. Cambridge: The Belknap Press of Harvard University Press, 1978.

Kenner, Hugh. "The Sacred Book of the Arts." In Kenner's *Gnomon.* New York: Ivan Obolenski, 1958.

———. "Unpurged Images." *Hudson Review* 8 (1956):607–17.

Kermode, Frank. *Romantic Image.* New York: Vintage, 1964 [1957].

———. Review article. *London Review of Books* (5 June 1986):9–11.

Kirk, Russell. *The Conservative Mind.* 3d ed. Chicago: Henry Regnery, 1960.

Langbaum, Robert. *The Mysteries of Identity: A Theme in Modern Literature.* New York: Oxford University Press, 1977.

———. *The Poetry of Experience: The Dramatic Monologue in Modern Literary Tradition.* New York: Random House, 1957.

Lenin, Vladamir I. *Collected Works.* Vol. 19. New York: International Publishers, 1942.

Lerner, Laurence. "W. B. Yeats: Poet and Crank." *Proceedings of the British Academy* 49 (1963):49–67. Also issued as a pamphlet. London: Oxford University Press, 1964.

Lovejoy, Arthur. *Essays in the History of Ideas.* Baltimore: The Johns Hopkins University Press, 1948.

Lowes, John Livingston. *The Road to Xanadu: A Study in the Ways of the Imagination.* Boston: Houghton Mifflin, 1927.

Löwith, Karl. *Meaning in History.* Chicago: University of Chicago Press, 1949.

McAlindon, T. "Yeats and the English Renaissance." *PMLA* 82 (1967):147–69.

McFarland, Thomas. *Originality and Imagination*. Baltimore and London: The Johns Hopkins University Press, 1985.

MacLeish, Archibald. "Public Speech and Private Speech in Poetry." A 1938 *Yale Review* article read by Yeats. Reprinted in MacLeish's *Time to Speak*. Boston: Houghton Mifflin, 1940.

MacManus, Francis, ed. *The Yeats We Knew*. Cork: Mercier Press, 1965.

McNiece, Gerald. *Shelley and the Revolutionary Idea*. Cambridge: Harvard University Press, 1969.

Macrobius. *Commentary on the Dream of Scipio*. Translated by W. H. Stahl. New York: Columbia University Press, 1952.

Malraux, André. *Les Noyers de l'Altenburg*. Paris: Gallimard, 1948 [1943].

Mann, Thomas. *Reflections of a Non-Political Man*. New York: Frederick Ungar, 1983.

Martin, Graham. "The Wild Swans at Coole." In *An Honoured Guest: New Essays on W. B. Yeats*, edited by Denis Donoghue and J. R. Mulryne. New York: St. Martin's Press, 1965.

Marvell, Andrew. *The Poems and Letters of Andrew Marvell*. 2 vols. Edited by H. M. Margoliouth. Oxford: Clarendon Press, 1927.

Marx, Karl. "Theses on Feuerbach" and "Towards a Critique of Hegel's Philosophy of the Right." In *The Marx-Engels Reader*. 2d ed. Edited by Robert C. Tucker. New York and London: Norton, 1978.

Melchiori, Giorgio. *The Whole Mystery of Art: Pattern into Poetry in the Work of W. B. Yeats*. New York: Macmillan, 1961.

Merchant, Carolyn. *The Death of Nature*. San Francisco: Harper and Row, 1980.

Mill, John Stuart. "On Nature." In *Collected Works of John Stuart Mill*. 27 projected vols. General editors F. E. L. Priestlley and John Robson. London: Routledge & Kegan Paul; Toronto: University of Toronto Press, 1963- .

Miller, Dickenson [under the pseudonym R. E. Hobart]. "Free Well as Involving Determinism and Inconceivable without It." *Mind* 43 (1934):1–27.

Miller, J. Hillis. *Poets of Reality: Six Twentieth-Century Writers*. Cambridge: Harvard University Press, 1965.

Milton, John. *John Milton: Complete Poems and Major Prose*. New York: 1957.

Miner, Earl. *Dryden's Poetry*. Bloomington and London: Indiana University Press, 1967.

Molesworth, Charles. *The Fierce Embrace: A Study of Contemporary American Poetry*. Columbia and London: University of Missouri Press, 1979.

Moore, Richard. "The Balancer: Yeats and His Supernatural System." *Yale Review* 72 (1983):385–98.

Moore, Virginia. *The Unicorn: William Butler Yeats's Search for Reality*. New York: Macmillan, 1954.

Murphy, William. *Prodigal Father: The Life of John Butler Yeats, 1839–1922*. Ithaca: Cornell University Press, 1978.

Murry, John Middleton. "Mr. Yeats' Swan Song." In Murry's *Aspects of Literature*. New York: Knopf, 1920.

Neumann, Erich. *The Great Mother: An Analysis of the Archetype*. Princeton: Princeton University Press, Bollingen Series, 1963.

Nolte, Ernst. *Three Faces of Fascism*. Translated by Leila Vennewitz. New York: Mentor, 1969.

Olney, James. *The Rhizome and the Flower: The Perennial Philosophy—Yeats and Jung*. Berkeley, Los Angeles, London: University of California Press, 1980.

————. "W. B. Yeats's Daimonic Memory." *Sewanee Review* 85 (1977):583–603.

O'Shea, Edward. *A Descriptive Catalog of W. B. Yeats's Library*. New York and London: Garland, 1985.

Palmer, A. H. *Samuel Palmer: A Memoir*. London, 1882.

Palmer, A. H., ed. *The Life and Letters of Samuel Palmer*. London, 1892.

Parkinson, Thomas. "The Modernity of Yeats." *Southern Review* 5 (1969):922–23.

————. *W. B. Yeats: The Later Poetry*. Berkeley and Los Angeles: University of California Press, 1966.

Pater, Walter. *The Renaissance: Studies in Art and Poetry*. London: Macmillan, 1913.

Peacock, Thomas Love. *Memoirs of Shelley*. London: Frowde, 1909.

Perloff, Marjorie. "The Consolation Theme in Yeats's 'In Memory of Major Robert Gregory.'" *Modern Language Quarterly* 17 (1966):302–21.

Plato. *The Dialogues of Plato*. 2 vols. Translated by B. Jowett. New York: Random House, 1937 [1892].

Plotinus. *Plotinus [The Enneads]*. 6 vols. Translated by Stephen MacKenna. London: P. L. Warner for the Medici Society, 1917–1930.

Pope, Alexander. *The Twickenham Edition of the Poems of Alexander Pope*. 11 vols. General editor John Butt. London, 1939–1967.

Porphyry. *De antro nympharum*. Translated by Thomas Taylor. In *Thomas Taylor the Platonist: Selected Writings*. Edited by Kathleen Raine and George Mills Harper. Princeton: Princeton University Press, Bollingen Series, 1969.

Pound, Ezra. *The Letters of Ezra Pound, 1907–1941*. Edited by D. D. Paige. New York: Harcourt Brace, 1950.

Pritchard, William. "The Uses of Yeats's Poetry." In *W. B. Yeats: A Critical Anthology*, edited by Pritchard. Baltimore: Penguin, 1972.

————. "W. B. Yeats: Theatrical Nobility." In Pritchard's *Lives of the Modern Poets*. New York: Oxford University Press, 1980.

Quint, David. *Origin and Originality in Renaissance Literature: Versions of the Source*. New Haven: Yale University Press, 1983.

Raine, Kathleen. "Hades Wrapped in Cloud." In *Yeats and the Occult*, edited by George Mills Harper. Toronto: Macmillan of Canada, 1975.

————. *Yeats, the Tarot and the Golden Dawn*. Dublin: Dolmen Press, 1972.

Rajan, Balachandra. *W. B. Yeats: A Critical Introduction*. London: Hutchinson, 1965.

Regardie, Israel. *The Golden Dawn*. 2 vols. Chicago: Aries Press, 1937.

Reid, B. L. *W. B. Yeats: The Lyric of Tragedy*. Norman: University of Oklahoma Press, 1961.

Romilly, Sir Samuel. *Memoirs* (1940). Quoted in Asa Briggs, *The Age of Improvement 1783–1867*. London: David McKay, 1960.

Rosenbaum, S. P. "'Among School Children,' Stanza V." *Explicator* 23 (October 1964):item 14.

Rosenberg, Harold. *The Tradition of the New*. New York: Horizon Press, 1959.

Rosenthal, M. L. *Sailing into the Unknown: Yeats, Pound, and Eliot*. New York: Oxford University Press, 1978.

Rosenthal, M. L., and Sally Gall. *The Modern Poetic Sequence: The Genius of Modern Poetry*. New York: Oxford University Press, 1983.

Ruskin, John. *Modern Painters*. In Ruskin, *Works, Library Edition*, edited by E. T. Cook and Alexander Wedderburn. London: George Allen, 1903–1913.

Sacks, Peter. *The English Elegy: Studies in the Genre from Spenser to Yeats*. Baltimore and London: The Johns Hopkins University Press, 1985.

Salvadori, Corrina. *Yeats and Castiglione: Poet and Courtier*. New York: Barnes & Noble, 1965.

Saul, George Brandon. "In . . . Luminous wind." In *The Dolmen Press Centenary Edition*, edited by Liam Miller. Dublin: The Dolmen Press, 1965–1968.

———. *Prolegomena to the Study of Yeats's Poems*. Philadelphia: University of Pennsylvania Press, 1957.

Savage, D. S. *The Personal Principle*. London: Routledge, 1944.

Schleiermacher, Friedrich. *On Religion: Speeches to Its Cultured Despisers*. Translated by John Oman. New York: Harper Torchbook, 1958.

Schorer, Mark. *William Blake: The Politics of Vision*. New York: Vintage, 1959.

Schutte, Ofelia. *Beyond Nihilism: Nietzsche without Masks*. Chicago: University of Chicago Press, 1984.

Searle, John. *Minds, Brains and Science*. Cambridge: Harvard University Press, 1984.

Shelley, Percy Bysshe. *The Complete Poetical Works of Percy Bysshe Shelley*. Edited by Thomas Hutchinson. London: Oxford University Press, 1905.

———. *The Letters of Percy Bysshe Shelley*. 2 vols. Edited by F. L. Jones. Oxford: Clarendon Press, 1964.

Skelton, Robin. "The First Printing of W. B. Yeats's 'What Then?'" *Irish Book* 2 (1963):129–30.

Smythe, Colin, ed. *Robert Gregory 1881–1918*. Gerrards Cross: Smythe, 1981.

Snukal, Ronald. *High Talk: The Philosophical Poetry of W. B. Yeats*. Cambridge: Cambridge University Press, 1973.

Soll, Ivan. "Reflections on Recurrence." In *Nietzsche: A Collection of Critical Essays*, edited by Robert Solomon. Garden City: Doubleday/Anchor, 1973.

Solomon, Robert, ed. *Nietzsche: A Collection of Critical Essays*. Garden City: Doubleday/Anchor, 1973.

Sophocles. *The Tragedies of Sophocles*. Translated by Sir Richard Jebb. Cambridge: Cambridge University Press, 1912.

Spencer, Theodore. *Selected Essays*. Edited by Alan Purves. New Brunswick: Rutgers University Press, 1966.

Spenser, Edmund. *The Poetical Works of Edmund Spenser*. Edited by J. C. Smith and Ernest de Selincourt. London: Oxford University Press, 1912.

Stallworthy, Jon. *Between the Lines: Yeats's Poetry in the Making*. Oxford: Clarendon Press, 1963.

———. *Vision and Revision in Yeats's Last Poems*. Oxford: Clarendon Press, 1969.

Stauffer, Donald. *The Golden Nightingale: Essays on Some Principles of Poetry in the Lyrics of William Butler Yeats*. New York: Macmillan, 1949.

Steane, J. B. *Tennyson*. New York: Arco, 1969.

Stein, Arnold. "Yeats: A Study in Recklessness." *Sewanee Review* 57 (1949):603–26.

Steiner, George. Introduction to *Homer: Twentieth Century Views*. Englewood Cliffs, N.J.: Prentice-Hall, 1962.

Stern, Karl. *The Flight from Woman*. New York: Noonday, 1964.

Stock, A. G. *W. B. Yeats: His Poetry and Thought*. Cambridge: Cambridge University Press, 1973.

Tate, Allen. "Yeats's Romanticism: Notes and Suggestions." *Southern Review* 7 (1941–1942). Reprinted in *The Permanence of Yeats*, edited by James Hall and Martin Steinmann. New York: Macmillan, Collier, 1961 [1950].

Taylor, Richard, ed. *Frank Pearce Sturm: His Life, Letters, and Collected Works*. Urbana: University of Illinois Press, 1969.

Taylor, Thomas. *Thomas Taylor the Platonist: Selected Writings*. Edited by Kathleen

Raine and George Mills Harper. Princeton: Princeton University Press, Bollingen Series, 1969.

Thatcher, David S. "Nietzsche and Byron." *Nietzsche Studien* 3 (1974):130–51.

———. *Nietzsche in England 1890–1914: The Growth of a Reputation.* Toronto: University of Toronto Press, 1970.

Tindall, William York. *W. B. Yeats.* New York: Columbia University Press, 1966.

Torchiana, Donald. *W. B. Yeats and Georgian Ireland.* Evanston: Northwestern University Press, 1966.

Tracy, Robert. "Energy, Ecstasy, Elegy: Yeats and the Death of Robert Gregory." *Éire-Ireland* 19 (1984):26–47.

Unger, Leonard. *Eliot's Compound Ghost: Influence and Confluence.* University Park: Pennsylvania State University Press, 1982.

Unterecker, John. *A Reader's Guide to William Butler Yeats.* New York: Noonday, 1959.

Ure, Peter. "The Hero on the World Tree: Yeats's Plays." *English* 15 (1965):169–72.

———. *Towards a Mythology: Studies in the Poetry of W. B. Yeats.* Liverpool: University Press of Liverpool; London: Hodder and Stoughton, 1946.

———. *W. B. Yeats.* New York: Grove Press, 1964.

Vaihinger, Hans. *The Philosophy of "As If."* 2d ed. London: Routledge & Kegan Paul, 1935.

Vendler, Helen. "Four Elegies." In *Yeats, Sligo, and Ireland: Essays to Mark the 21st Yeats International Summer School,* edited by A. Norman Jeffares. Totowa, N.J.: Barnes & Noble, 1980.

———. *Wallace Stevens: Words Chosen Out of Desire.* Knoxville: University of Tennessee Press, 1984.

———. *Yeats's* Vision *and the Later Plays.* Cambridge: Harvard University Press, 1963.

Viëtor, Karl. *Goethe the Thinker.* Cambridge: Harvard University Press, 1950.

von Hügel, Baron. *The Mystical Element in Religion.* London, 1908.

Walter, Gerard. *Les Massacres de septembre.* Paris: Payot, 1932.

Wasserman, Earl R. *Shelley: A Critical Reading.* Baltimore and London: The Johns Hopkins University Press, 1971.

Wellesley, Lady Dorothy. *Far Have I Travelled.* London: James Barrie, 1952.

Whitaker, Thomas R. *Swan and Shadow: Yeats's Dialogue with History.* Chapel Hill: University of North Carolina Press, 1964.

Whitehead, Alfred North. *Science and the Modern World.* New York: Free Press, 1953 [1925].

Whitman, Cedric H. *Sophocles: A Study of Heroic Humanism.* Cambridge: Harvard University Press, 1966.

Wilson, F. A. C. *W. B. Yeats and Tradition.* New York: Macmillan, 1958.

———. *Yeats's Iconography.* London: Victor Gollancz, 1970.

Wimsatt, W. K. *The Day of the Leopards: Essays in Defense of Poems.* New Haven: Yale University Press, 1976.

Winters, Ivor. *The Poetry of W. B. Yeats.* Denver: Allen Swallow, 1960.

Witt, Marion. "The Making of an Elegy: Yeats's 'In Memory of Major Robert Gregory.'" *Modern Philology* 48 (1950):112–21.

Wollheim, Richard. *Sigmund Freud.* New York: Viking, 1971.

Yeats, John Butler. *J. B. Yeats: Letters to His Son W. B. Yeats and Others, 1869–1922.* Edited by Joseph Hone. New York: Dutton, 1946.

INDEX

Abrams, M. H.: *Natural Supernaturalism* and Romantic tradition, xvi, xvii, 15–16, 113, 175*n*; on Coleridge, 53*n*; on "A Dialogue of Self and Soul," 150*n*; on Kant, 161*n*; on Blake, 180
AE. *See* Russell, George
Allt, Peter: and Yeats's resistance to Christianity, 21, 115*n*; on Yeats and the supernatural, 114–15
Amor Fati, 19, 160, 160*n*, 181, 183, 186
Anglo-Irish tradition: and Yeats, xviii, 40, 81, 81*n*, 195, 261, 269. *See also* Berkeley; Burke; Gregory (Lady Augusta and Robert); Swift
Antithetical-primary distinction in Yeats, xiv, xvii, xviii, xix, 17, 18, 19, 104, 110, 112–17, 122, 126, 135, 140–41, 146, 148, 149, 154–55, 157, 164, 170, 174, 177, 179, 188, 191, 192, 202–3, 227, 245, 272–75, 281, 302, 310
Auden, W. H.: "In Memory of W. B. Yeats," 15, 201; on Yeats's occultism, 60, 112; on Tennyson's "Ulysses," 265
Augustine, St.: *Confessions*, 115; and excremental vision, 123; and predestination, 150, 162, 165, 175

Balzac, Honoré de: and Yeats, 4*n*, 88; praised by Yeats, 88, 97; identified by Yeats with Nietzsche, 89*n*, 175; paired by Yeats with Dante, 96; *Séraphita*, 142, 152, 164, 175
Bembo, Pietro. *See* Castiglione: his *Courtier*
Berkeley, George: as Yeats's Anglo-Irish champion, xviii, 42–47 *passim*, 63; on autonomy, 258
Bhartrihari: and "What Then?," 29, 30*n*, 35
Blake, William: and Yeats's "great-rooted blossomer," xiii, xvi; as precursor of Yeats, xiv, xviii-xix, 4*n*, 7, 8, 17, 73, 82, 84, 86, 97, 105; allied by Yeats with Nietzsche, xiv, 31, 150–51, 165, 169, 173, 187; on the "thankful receiver" bearing "a plentiful harvest," xiv, 7, 173; opposed to "Bacon, Newton, Locke," xviii-xix, 13, 41, 41*n*, 47–49, 53, 54, 55, 60, 62, 230; Northrop Frye on, xx, 76*n*; *all* favorite word of, 7, 118, 236; on generalization, 16; and "The Second Coming," 17, 73, 76, 98–100, 135; on "contraries," 35, 105, 152; and perspectivism, 39; and "divinity within," 44, 149, 172; Ellis-Yeats edition of, 47, 128; distorted or swerved from by Yeats, 48, 62, 105; and the "female will," 50; and the "idiot reasoner," 56; in Yeats's "An Acre of Grass," 62, 66, 69; parodies Burke, 79; critical of Wordsworth, 86–87; and "infant joy," 123, 150–51, 173, 187; and "A Last Confession," 128; opposed to cyclicism, 137, 170, 177, 180–82; and "A Dialogue of Self and Soul," 169–73; and "organized innocence," 175; "Prolific and Devourer," 181; disciples Palmer and Calvert, 195, 204, 223, 230; on Milton, 280; and Porphyry, 303; mentioned, 14, 44, 52, 53, 55, 66, 75–76, 80*n*, 87, 123, 125–26, 149, 164, 171–73, 180, 219, 305
—Works: "And did those feet?," 48, 61; *Book of Thel*, 24–25; *Europe: A Prophecy*, 56, 99*n*, 120; *The Four Zoas*, 76*n*; *The Gates of Paradise*, 124; *Jerusalem*, 48, 49, 55, 56*n*, 76*n*; *The Marriage of Heaven and Hell*, xiv, 7, 31, 35, 39, 44, 55, 105, 175; "The Mental Traveller," 39, 181; *Milton*, 56, 120; "Mock on, Mock on, Voltaire, Rousseau," 60–61; *Visions of the Daughters of Albion*, 55, 56*n*, 59, 146, 151, 171–73; *Vision of the Last Judgment*, 124, 144
Bloom, Harold: influence-theory, xvii-xviii, 6, 7, 15–16, 85; on "Tintern Abbey," 88*n*, 229*n*; on "The Second Coming," 100–101; attacks Yeats on determinism, 173*n*, 179, 179*n*, 180–82, 189*n*; on Gregory elegy, 200, 216, 231, 242; on Tennyson's "Ulysses," 264; on Shelley's *Alastor*, 267*n*, 273
Body-Soul debate tradition, 24, 34–36, 113–15, 124, 141–53 *passim*
Bolshevik terrorism: and "The Second Coming," 17, 64, 75–79, 101, 103. *See also* French Revolution
Browning, Robert: "Childe Roland," 171, 256, 256*n*, 260, 269, 276; "Andrea del Sarto," 192; "My Last Duchess," 221; "Pauline," 273
Burke, Edmund: and Anglo-Irish heritage, xviii, 4*n*, 63, 72, 76–80, 89, 97; champion of organic conservatism and anti-Jacobinism, xviii, 76; and "The Second Coming," 17, 64, 76–84, 89, 94, 254; Wordsworth and Coleridge eventually agree with, 92; on the "Sublime," 102; in "Blood and the Moon," 308
—Works: *Reflections on the Revolution in France*, 64, 77–84, 94; *Letters on a Regicide Peace*, 84*n*
Bush, Douglas: on Romantics and Newton, 41*n*; on "Fragments," 48
Byron, Lord: dialectic of aspiration and disillu-